HOUGHTON MIFFLIN
Spelling and Vocabulary
Words for Readers and Writers

Shane Templeton
Senior Author

Donald R. Bear
Author

Brenda Sabey
Consultant

Sylvia Linan-Thompson
Consultant

 HOUGHTON MIFFLIN   BOSTON

Acknowledgments

Select definitions and etymologies in the Spelling Dictionary are adapted and reprinted by permission from the following Houghton Mifflin Company publications:

Copyright © 2003 THE AMERICAN HERITAGE CHILDREN'S DICTIONARY

Copyright © 2003 THE AMERICAN HERITAGE STUDENT DICTIONARY

Copyright © 2000 THE AMERICAN HERITAGE DICTIONARY OF THE ENGLISH LANGUAGE, Fourth Edition

Copyright © 2003 THE AMERICAN HERITAGE DICTIONARY OF IDIOMS

Printed in the U.S.A.

ISBN: 0-618-49196-1

18 19 20 21-0877-16 15 14

4500500452

Contents

Cycle 1

Unit 1

Short Vowels   18
- **Think and Sort**
- **Spelling-Meaning Connection**
- **Word Structure:** Word Families
- **Dictionary:** Guide Words
- **Proofreading and Writing**
  Journal Entry
- **Test Format Practice**
- **Real-World Vocabulary**
  Science: Forces That Shape the Earth

Unit 2

Long *a* and Long *e*   24
- **Think and Sort**
- **Spelling-Meaning Connection**
- **Vocabulary:** Analogies
- **Thesaurus:** Synonyms
- **Proofreading and Writing**
  Tall Tale
- **Test Format Practice**
- **Real-World Vocabulary**
  Social Studies: Maps and Globes

Unit 3

Long *i* and Long *o*   30
- **Think and Sort**
- **Spelling-Meaning Connection**
- **Word Structure:** The Word Root *pos* or *pose*
- **Dictionary:** Definitions
- **Proofreading and Writing**
  Advertisement
- **Test Format Practice**
- **Real-World Vocabulary**
  Life Skills: Cooking

Unit 4

Vowel Sounds: /o͞o/, /yo͞o/   36
- **Think and Sort**
- **Spelling-Meaning Connection**
- **Vocabulary:** Words Often Confused
- **Dictionary**
  Spelling Table
- **Proofreading and Writing**
  Travel Guide
- **Test Format Practice**
- **Real-World Vocabulary**
  Math: Probability

Learning to Spell

1 **Look** at the word.
- What are the letters in the word?
- What does the word mean?
- Does it have more than one meaning?

fountain

2 **Say** the word.
- What are the consonant sounds?
- What are the vowel sounds?

3 **Think** about the word.
- How is each sound spelled?
- Do you see any familiar spelling patterns?
- Do you see any suffixes, prefixes, or other word parts?

4 **Write** the word.
- Think about the sounds and the letters.
- Form the letters correctly.

5 **Check** the spelling of the word.
- Does it match the spelling on your word list?
- Do you need to write the word again?

Learning Vocabulary

1 Look at the word.

- Do suffixes, prefixes, or other word parts give clues to the meaning?
- Do you know a related word that can help you think about what the new word means?

2 Study the context of the word.

- Do other words or phrases around the word hint at the word's meaning?

3 Check the dictionary.

- Check the pronunciation of the word. Practice it.
- Study the definition and the sample sentence.
- Reread the context to see how the word fits in.

4 Create a word-study notebook.

- Write the definition of each word and your own sample sentence.
- Make webs of related vocabulary words.
- Use your notebook when you write.

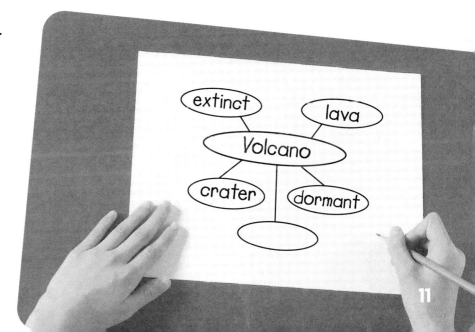

Sorting Words

What Is a Word Sort?

In a word sort, you sort words into groups. Word sorts help you learn to spell, to think about words, and to read other words. Each unit in this book begins with a word sort.

You can sort words by

- **sound** (such as long *a* or short *a*)
- **spelling pattern** (such as *ai* or *ay* for long *a*)
- **syllable pattern** (such as VCCV or VCV)
- **word structure** (such as prefixes or suffixes)
- **word meaning** (such as "types of clothing")
- **other features**

Making a Word Sort

You can make your own word sorts, using Spelling Words from one or more units. Here's how.

1 **Read the words.**

2 **Think of sorting categories.**

- Write them as column heads on a sheet of paper.
- Include an *Other* column for words that don't fit your categories.

3 **Write each word under the correct heading.**

4 **Add your own words to the sort.**

mis-	un-	Other
mislead	unable	united
mislaid	unwise	
	unknown	

Sorting with a Partner

Write your sorting categories and your Spelling Words on separate cards or slips of paper.

1 **Share a sort.**

- Trade category and word cards with a partner, and sort.

2 **Challenge each other.**

- Exchange word cards.

- Figure out each other's categories, and sort.

3 **Go on a word hunt.**

- Choose one or more sorting categories.
- Look for words that fit each category.

Your Word-Study Notebook

As you sort words, add to your word-study notebook.

- Expand on sorts you have begun, or make up new ones.

- Collect tricky words, such as *freight*, or words you confuse, such as *chose* and *choose*.

- Collect interesting vocabulary words, such as words about baseball, animals, checkers, or bodies of water.

Thinking and Writing

When you write, use new **vocabulary** words and correct **spelling**. Here is how vocabulary and spelling fit into the steps of the **writing process**.

prewrite → draft → revise → proofread → publish

① Prewrite

- Jot down exact words as you brainstorm ideas and plan your work. You can use them when you draft.
- Look in your word-study notebook to find interesting words.

② Draft

- Don't worry about spelling now. Let your ideas flow.
- If an interesting word pops into your mind, write it. You can change it later if it does not really fit.

③ Revise

- Replace unclear or uninteresting words with exact ones.
- Use a thesaurus to find just the right word.
- Check the dictionary if you are unsure of a word's definition.

④ Proofread

- Check each word. Correct any spelling mistakes.

- If you can't remember how to spell a word, use the strategies below.

⑤ Publish —Share Your Writing!

- Your new vocabulary words will interest your readers.

- Your correct spelling will make your writing easy to read.

Spelling Strategies

- Say the word. Do the sounds suggest the spelling?

- Picture the word in your mind. Does it match the spelling you used?

- Think of the parts of the word. Is each part spelled correctly?

- Look up the word in a dictionary.

Using a Computer Spell Checker

Use your spell checker wisely.

What It Can Do

- It highlights many types of spelling mistakes.

- It finds some errors in capitalization.

What It Can't Do

- It can't find words that should be joined.
  air plane

- It can't find incorrect homophones.
  Let's climb that peek!

- It won't catch a misspelled word that is the correct spelling of a different word.
  I will past a photo on my collage.

Weekly Spelling Tests

1 **Before the test,**

practice the words with a friend or a family member.

2 **At test time,**

get a clean sheet of paper and a pencil or a pen.

3 **Pay attention**

as your teacher reads a word and uses it in a sentence. Write only after listening to the whole sentence.

4 **Write the word.**

Carefully form each letter so it is easy to read.

5 **When it is time to correct the test,**

listen closely as your teacher spells each word. Check each letter. Circle any mistakes.

6 **Look at each corrected word.**

Then close your eyes and spell the word to yourself.

7 **Write the correct spelling.**

Rewrite each word you misspelled.

Spelling Test
1. sign
2. groan
3. dough
4. throan   thrown
5. strike
6. mighty
7. compos   compose

Standardized Tests

1 **Make sure you understand the test format.**

- Ask for help if you need it.

2 **For each question.**

- Rule out answers that you know are wrong. Then mark the right answer.
- Guess only if you have to.

3 **On a spelling test**

- Recall spelling patterns that you have learned.
- Think about the spelling of prefixes, suffixes, and other word parts.

4 **On a vocabulary test**

- Look for context clues in phrases or sentences.
- Try to find meaning hints in word parts such as prefixes.

**Watch for test-taking tips in this book.
You will find them on the pages
with practice tests.**

PART **1** Spelling (and) Phonics

/ă/ Sound

1. _____
2. _____
3. _____

/ĕ/ Sound

4. _____
5. _____
6. _____
7. _____
8. _____

/ĭ/ Sound

9. _____
10. _____
11. _____
12. _____

/ŏ/ Sound

13. _____
14. _____
15. _____
16. _____

/ŭ/ Sound

17. _____
18. _____
19. _____
20. _____

Read the Spelling Words and sentences.

Basic

1.	breath	*breath*	Hold your **breath** under the water.
2.	closet	*closet*	The coats are in the **closet**.
3.	blister	*blister*	The hiker got a **blister** on his foot.
4.	crush	*crush*	Step on the box to **crush** it.
5.	direct	*direct*	Can you **direct** me to the bus stop?
6.	promise	*promise*	I **promise** to do my homework.
7.	grasp	*grasp*	You must **grasp** the rail tightly.
8.	fund	*fund*	I am putting money in our travel **fund**.
⚠ 9.	hymn	*hymn*	Beth sang a **hymn** at church.
⚠ 10.	shovel	*shovel*	Dig the hole with this **shovel**.
11.	demand	*demand*	Babies may cry to **demand** food.
12.	frantic	*frantic*	The mother was **frantic** with worry.
13.	swift	*swift*	The rabbit made a **swift** escape.
14.	feather	*feather*	A bird's **feather** fell from the sky.
15.	comic	*comic*	Is that **comic** strip funny?
16.	bundle	*bundle*	Gus tied the sticks in a **bundle**.
17.	solid	*solid*	The pond has frozen **solid**.
18.	weather	*weather*	The **weather** today is rainy.
19.	energy	*energy*	Living things use the sun's **energy**.
20.	stingy	*stingy*	A **stingy** person does not like to share.

Review	23. track	**Challenge**	28. summit
21. bunch	24. pleasant	26. instruct	29. massive
22. district	25. odd	27. distress	30. physical

Think and Sort

Short vowel sounds are usually spelled with a single letter followed by a consonant sound. This is called the short vowel pattern.

/ă/ gr**a**sp /ĕ/ **e**nergy /ĭ/ sw**i**ft /ŏ/ c**o**mic /ŭ/ b**u**ndle

The short vowel sound /ĕ/ may also be spelled *ea* as in w**ea**ther.

⚠ How is the short vowel sound spelled in each Memory Word?

Write each Basic Word under the vowel sound in its *stressed* syllable.

Word Analysis/Phonics

Write the Basic Word that begins with each consonant cluster.

21. gr   **22.** sw   **23.** cl   **24.** cr

Vocabulary: Definitions

Write the Basic or Review Word that fits each meaning.

25. money set aside for a special purpose

26. very excited or anxious

27. humorous or amusing

28. a path for runners

29. part of an area set aside for a purpose

Challenge Words

Write the Challenge Word that completes each sentence. Use your Spelling Dictionary.

30. I need some _____ exercise.

31. Do you want to climb to the _____ of that mountain?

32. Several _____ boulders blocked the highway.

33. I will _____ you in how to use that program.

34. A climber in _____ may need to be rescued.

Spelling-Meaning Connection

35–36. Take a *breath*. Then *breathe* out. The words *breath* and *breathe* are related in spelling and meaning. Write both words. Underline the two letters in each word that are the same but that spell different vowel sounds.

breath
breathe

At Home With a family member, take turns thinking of clues for Spelling Words and spelling the words.

Word Analysis
21. _____
22. _____
23. _____
24. _____

Definitions
25. _____
26. _____
27. _____
28. _____
29. _____

Challenge Words
30. _____
31. _____
32. _____
33. _____
34. _____

Spelling-Meaning
35. _____
36. _____

Word Structure

1. _____
2. _____
3. _____
4. _____
5. _____
6. _____

Word Structure: Word Families

A **word family** is a base word and all its forms. It includes words made by adding endings and other word parts to the base word.

Example: demand   demanded   undemanding

Practice Complete each sentence with a word from the box. Use your Spelling Dictionary.

direct	direction	redirected
director	directly	directory

1. The library is _____ opposite the school.
2. The _____ of a movie plans each scene.
3. In which _____ should we walk?
4. Look up the number in the telephone _____.
5. The tunnel flooded, so traffic was _____.
6. Try to make your point in a clear, _____ way.

Dictionary

7. _____
8. _____
9. _____
10. _____
11. _____
12. _____
13. _____
14. _____

Dictionary: Guide Words

Two **guide words** are at the top of each dictionary page. They show the first and last entry words alphabetized on that page.

guide words
↓

closet | crush
clos•et (klŏz´ ĭt) *n., pl.* **closets** A small room in which clothes or household supplies can be kept.

Practice 7–14. Write eight words from the list below that you would expect to find on the dictionary page with the guide words *breath* and *bundle*. List them in alphabetical order.

breakfast   brush   building   brother   burst
brittle   breezy   buffalo   breed   bucket

Proofread a Journal Entry

Spelling, Capitalization, and End Marks Use proofreading marks to correct **ten** misspelled Basic or Review Words and **four** mistakes in capitalization and end marks in this journal entry.

Example: Did you bundle up for the cold ~~weathur~~ *weather* ?

> **April 1**
>
> What was my day like. I'll tell you, and I won't be stingey with details. I awoke to find snow on the ground. Outside I could see my breath. I began to shovel snow from the walkway. Under the snow there was sollid ice. As I worked, I developed a blistur on my thumb. "I want winter to end right now!" I yelled.
>
> Suddenly, something od happened. the sun began to shine with great enurjy. The ice began to melt. A mild breeze felt as soft and light as a fether? The air held the promiss of spring. The rest of the day was plesant, too. What caused the swift change in the wether? who cares? I am just glad that my demend was met.

Proofreading Marks

¶	Indent
∧	Add
⊙	Add a period
℘	Delete
≡	Capital letter
/	Small letter

Basic
breath
closet
blister
crush
direct
promise
grasp
fund
hymn
shovel
demand
frantic
swift
feather
comic
bundle
solid
weather
energy
stingy

Review
bunch
district
track
pleasant
odd

Challenge
instruct
distress
summit
massive
physical

Write a Journal Entry

prewrite → draft → revise → proofread → publish

Write a journal entry about a time when the weather affected you or your plans.

- Tell about a single **event or experience**. Include **details** about the setting.
- Use some Spelling Words and at least one question.
- Proofread your work for **spelling, capitalization,** and **end marks.**

Power Proofreading
www.eduplace.com/kids/sv/

Test Tip Read the directions carefully.

Example:

Ⓐ Ⓑ ● Ⓓ

Directions For numbers 1 through 8, choose the word that is spelled correctly and best completes the sentence.

Example: Children who live in this _____ attend Emerson School.

  A disstrict
  B districk
  C district
  D distrect

Answer Sheet

1. Ⓐ Ⓑ Ⓒ Ⓓ

2. Ⓕ Ⓖ Ⓗ Ⓙ

3. Ⓐ Ⓑ Ⓒ Ⓓ

4. Ⓕ Ⓖ Ⓗ Ⓙ

5. Ⓐ Ⓑ Ⓒ Ⓓ

6. Ⓕ Ⓖ Ⓗ Ⓙ

7. Ⓐ Ⓑ Ⓒ Ⓓ

8. Ⓕ Ⓖ Ⓗ Ⓙ

More Practice
Now write each correctly spelled word on a sheet of paper.

Spelling Games
www.eduplace.com/kids/sv/
Review for your test.

1. Dad needs the _____ to dig a hole.
  A shovle
  B shuvel
  C shovel
  D shovul

2. It was hard to learn this _____.
  F hymn
  G himm
  H hym
  J hymm

3. Sophie is a _____ and friendly girl.
  A plesent
  B plesant
  C pleasent
  D pleasant

4. Please hang your jacket in the _____.
  F closit
  G closet
  H clossit
  J clozit

5. Mr. Valdez will _____ the actors in the play.
  A derict
  B derect
  C direct
  D durect

6. Mom bought a _____ of bananas at the store.
  F bunnch
  G bunch
  H bunsch
  J bunsh

7. This cake is as light as a _____.
  A fehther
  B feathur
  C fether
  D feather

8. Tie the newspapers in a _____.
  F bundle
  G bundel
  H bunndle
  J buntle

Real-World Vocabulary

Science: Forces That Shape the Earth

All the words in the box relate to our solid earth. Look up these words in your Spelling Dictionary. Then write the words to complete this sign at a national park.

COYOTE CANYON PARK

The beautiful canyons, mountains, and other ____(1)____ in Coyote Canyon Park were created by powerful forces above and below the ____(2)____ of the earth. Some of the features were formed through ____(3)____ forces, which build up land masses. Coyote Peak, for instance, was created by a series of ____(4)____ eruptions. Lava welled up from deep within the earth and gradually formed the mountain you see before you.

Other natural features in the park were caused by ____(5)____ forces, which break down rocks and soil. These natural forces include wind, water, and huge ice masses called ____(6)____. All three forces cause ____(7)____, the washing away of rock and soil. Coyote Canyon was carved out by the flowing waters of the Blue Jay River. Forming the canyon was a long, slow ____(8)____ that may have taken over four million years!

eWord Game
www.eduplace.com/kids/sv/

Spelling Word Link
solid

surface
constructive
destructive
erosion
volcanic
glaciers
landforms
process

1. _____
2. _____
3. _____
4. _____
5. _____
6. _____
7. _____
8. _____

Try This CHALLENGE

Quiz Questions Write four quiz questions on a separate piece of paper, about how nature changes the face of the earth. Use at least one word from the box in each question. Then trade papers with a partner and take each other's quiz.

PART 1 Spelling and Phonics

Read the Spelling Words and sentences.

Basic

1.	awake	*awake*	I am too tired to stay **awake**.
2.	feast	*feast*	We ate the Thanksgiving **feast**.
3.	stray	*stray*	That **stray** cat needs a good home.
4.	greet	*greet*	Do you **greet** your friends with hugs?
5.	praise	*praise*	We **praise** our dog when he obeys.
6.	disease	*disease*	Chicken pox is a **disease**.
7.	repeat	*repeat*	Would you **repeat** what you just said?
8.	display	*display*	The store window has a new **display**.
9.	scale	*scale*	Use the big **scale** to weigh the melon.
ⓘ 10.	thief	*thief*	The **thief** took my purse!
11.	ashamed	*ashamed*	Do not be **ashamed** to cry.
12.	sleeve	*sleeve*	There's a hole in the **sleeve** of my jacket.
13.	waist	*waist*	This belt should fit around your **waist**.
14.	beneath	*beneath*	It was cool **beneath** the tree's branches.
15.	sheepish	*sheepish*	Ali's **sheepish** grin hid his confusion.
16.	release	*release*	May I **release** the bird from its cage?
17.	remain	*remain*	Will you leave or **remain** here?
18.	sway	*sway*	Trees **sway** when a strong wind blows.
19.	brain	*brain*	The skull protects the **brain**.
ⓘ 20.	niece	*niece*	My **niece** Fran is my brother's daughter.

Review		**Challenge**	
21. stale	23. freedom	26. terrain	28. betray
22. afraid	24. eager	27. succeed	29. motivate
	25. explain		30. upheaval

Think and Sort

The /ā/ sound is often spelled *a*-consonant-*e* as in *scale*, or with two letters, as in *praise* and *display*. The /ē/ sound is usually spelled *ea* as in f**ea**st, or *ee* as in gr**ee**t.

ⓘ How is /ē/ spelled in the Memory Words?

Write each Basic Word under the vowel sound in its *stressed* syllable.

/ā/ Sound

1. _____
2. _____
3. _____
4. _____
5. _____
6. _____
7. _____
8. _____
9. _____
10. _____

/ē/ Sound

11. _____
12. _____
13. _____
14. _____
15. _____
16. _____
17. _____
18. _____
19. _____
20. _____

Word Analysis/Phonics

Write the Basic Word that rhymes with each word below.

21. leave   **22.** priest   **23.** nail   **24.** taste

Vocabulary: Classifying

Write the Basic or Review Word that belongs in each group.

25. moldy, rotten, _____

26. grandparent, cousin, _____

27. heart, lungs, _____

28. liberty, independence, _____

29. sickness, infection, _____

Challenge Words

Write the Challenge Word that fits each definition. Use your Spelling Dictionary.

30. to reach a goal

31. the surface features of an area of land

32. to aid an enemy

33. a sudden upset or big change

34. to move to action

Spelling-Meaning Connection

35–36. *Praiseworthy* is made up of two words—*praise* and *worthy*. A *praiseworthy* deed is *worthy* of *praise*. Write *praiseworthy*. Then write the first word part of this compound.

praise + worthy = praiseworthy

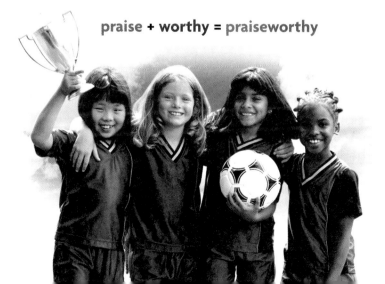

Word Analysis

21. _____

22. _____

23. _____

24. _____

Classifying

25. _____

26. _____

27. _____

28. _____

29. _____

Challenge Words

30. _____

31. _____

32. _____

33. _____

34. _____

Spelling-Meaning

35. _____

36. _____

At Home   Conduct a word hunt with a family member. Look for words with the /ā/ or the /ē/ sound in a story or a newspaper article.

Vocabulary

1. _____
2. _____
3. _____
4. _____
5. _____
6. _____
7. _____
8. _____

Vocabulary: Analogies

An **analogy** compares word pairs that are related in some way. **Antonyms,** words with opposite meanings, are compared in one type.

Example: *Rough* is to *smooth* as *sharp* is to *blunt*.

Practice Write the word from the box that best completes each analogy. Use your Spelling Dictionary.

sheepish	purchase	shrink	moody
withhold	cramped	retreat	unearth

1. *Broad* is to *narrow* as *spacious* is to _____.
2. *Borrow* is to *lend* as _____ is to *sell*.
3. *Sensible* is to *foolish* as *proud* is to _____.
4. *Bury* is to _____ as *conceal* is to *reveal*.
5. *Cheerful* is to _____ as *willing* is to *stubborn*.
6. *Lose* is to *gain* as _____ is to *expand*.
7. *Advance* is to _____ as *arrive* is to *depart*.
8. *Accept* is to *reject* as *give* is to _____.

Thesaurus

9. _____
10. _____
11. _____
12. _____
13. _____
14. _____

Thesaurus: Synonyms

A **thesaurus** is a reference source with synonyms. Use a thesaurus to choose precise and lively words.

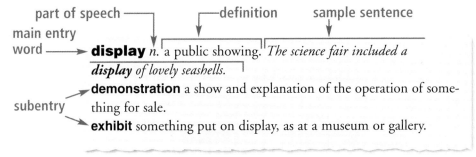

display *n.* a public showing. *The science fair included a display of lovely seashells.*

demonstration a show and explanation of the operation of something for sale.

exhibit something put on display, as at a museum or gallery.

Practice Read pages 258–259 to learn how to use your Thesaurus. Then write the two subentries given in your Thesaurus for each of these words.

9–10. mixture   **11–12.** join   **13–14.** order

✎ Proofread a Tall Tale

Spelling, Capitalization, and End Marks Use proofreading marks to correct **ten** misspelled Basic or Review Words and **four** mistakes in capitalization and end marks in this tall tale.

Example: the corn began to swaye in the wind.

Farmer Hoedown and the Drought

A stubborn cloud hung over Corn Valley, refusing to releese her rain. Farmer Hoedown went to grete that strey cloud every morning. "howdy, pretty lady," he said, but she was not eeger to accept praise. He tried to explane why Corn Valley needed her rain. "Stop being so selfish Share some water!" he scolded, but she was not ashaimed of herself. "I'm afrayed things can't remane as they are," said Farmer Hoedown at last. He stood beneeth the cloud and reached up with his sharp hoe. it helped that Farmer Hoedown was tall. Why, his wayst was as high as a silo! He gave that cloud a jab. At once, rain soaked the thirsty land below. "Soon we'll have a corn feast!" exclaimed Farmer Hoedown. Well, they did, and what a display of treats it was

Proofreading Marks

¶ Indent
∧ Add
⊙ Add a period
⌐ Delete
≡ Capital letter
/ Small letter

Basic
awake
feast
stray
greet
praise
disease
repeat
display
scale
thief
ashamed
sleeve
waist
beneath
sheepish
release
remain
sway
brain
niece

Review
stale
afraid
freedom
eager
explain

Challenge
terrain
succeed
betray
motivate
upheaval

✎ Write a Tall Tale

prewrite ➔ draft ➔ revise ➔ proofread ➔ publish

Write a tall tale, a fantastic story about an impossible event.

- Think of a **heroic main character** with amazing abilities. Create a **problem** for this character to solve.
- Use some Spelling Words and at least one exclamatory sentence.
- Proofread your work for **spelling, capitalization,** and **end marks.**

Power Proofreading
www.eduplace.com/kids/sv/

PART 4 Spelling Test Practice

✓ **Test Tip** Be sure to fill in the whole circle.

Test Format Practice

Directions Find the phrase containing an underlined word that is <u>not</u> spelled correctly. If all the underlined words are spelled correctly, mark "All correct."

Example: **A** <u>fredom</u> of speech
B light as a <u>feather</u>
C a <u>swift</u> runner
D rainy <u>weather</u>
E All correct

Example:

● Ⓑ Ⓒ Ⓓ Ⓔ

Answer Sheet

1. Ⓐ Ⓑ Ⓒ Ⓓ Ⓔ

2. Ⓕ Ⓖ Ⓗ Ⓙ Ⓚ

3. Ⓐ Ⓑ Ⓒ Ⓓ Ⓔ

4. Ⓕ Ⓖ Ⓗ Ⓙ Ⓚ

5. Ⓐ Ⓑ Ⓒ Ⓓ Ⓔ

6. Ⓕ Ⓖ Ⓗ Ⓙ Ⓚ

1. **A** <u>awak</u> or asleep
B a <u>sleeve</u> with a cuff
C <u>ashamed</u> of a mistake
D to catch a <u>disease</u>
E All correct

2. **F** to <u>release</u> your grip
G to <u>repete</u> the question
H to <u>remain</u> at home
J to <u>greet</u> a friend
K All correct

3. **A** a <u>brain</u> for thinking
B <u>praise</u> for good work
C to <u>swaiy</u> back and forth
D around the <u>waist</u>
E All correct

4. **F** <u>niece</u> and nephew
G <u>stale</u> crackers
H to <u>explain</u> the answer
J a <u>sheepish</u> grin
K All correct

5. **A** a <u>scale</u> on a fish
B <u>afraid</u> of spiders
C a holiday <u>feast</u>
D a <u>displey</u> of artwork
E All correct

6. **F** <u>eager</u> to join in
G <u>beneath</u> the table
H a jewel <u>theif</u>
J to <u>stray</u> from the path
K All correct

More Practice
Now write all the misspelled words correctly on a separate sheet of paper.

Spelling Games
www.eduplace.com/kids/sv/
Review for your test.

28 Unit 2

Real-World Vocabulary

Social Studies: Maps and Globes

All the words in the box relate to maps. Look up these words in your Spelling Dictionary. Write the words to complete this diagram.

A ___(1)___ makes maps of the earth. This globe shows the imaginary lines mapmakers use to help people find and describe locations.

Lines that run north-south around the earth and meet at the North and South Poles are called ___(2)___. They show ___(3)___, or east-west position.

The lines that run east-west around the earth are called ___(6)___. They indicate ___(7)___, or north-south position.

The ___(4)___ is an imaginary line around the middle of the earth. It divides the earth into two ___(5)___.

The ___(8)___ shows the directions north, south, east, and west on a map.

1. _____
2. _____
3. _____
4. _____
5. _____
6. _____
7. _____
8. _____

eWord Game
www.eduplace.com/kids/sv/

Try This CHALLENGE

True or False? Write *true* if the sentence is true. Write *false* if the sentence is false.

9. The equator is a line of longitude.

10. The Northern Hemisphere is the northern half of the world.

11. The lines of latitude are also known as parallels.

12. The lines of latitude come together at the North and South Poles.

9. _____
10. _____
11. _____
12. _____

PART 1 Spelling and Phonics

Read the Spelling Words and sentences.

Basic

1.	sign	*sign*	The **sign** shows the name of my street.
2.	groan	*groan*	Please don't **groan** at this silly joke!
3.	reply	*reply*	Please **reply** to the letter soon.
4.	thrown	*thrown*	Ted has **thrown** the ball to Rick.
5.	strike	*strike*	Never **strike** a puppy with your hand.
6.	mighty	*mighty*	Our **mighty** soccer team won again!
7.	stroll	*stroll*	We can **stroll** along this garden path.
8.	compose	*compose*	Does the singer also **compose** songs?
9.	dough	*dough*	The **dough** is ready to be baked.
10.	height	*height*	The plant is two feet in **height**.
11.	excite	*excite*	A win by this team will **excite** the fans.
12.	apply	*apply*	Are you going to **apply** for that job?
13.	slight	*slight*	Even a **slight** crack can weaken a pole.
14.	define	*define*	Can you **define** this word?
15.	odor	*odor*	What a strong **odor** a skunk gives off!
16.	spider	*spider*	A **spider** spins a web to catch insects.
17.	control	*control*	Pull on the line to **control** the kite.
18.	silent	*silent*	The empty room was dark and **silent**.
19.	brighten	*brighten*	Yellow paint will **brighten** this wall.
20.	approach	*approach*	Never **approach** a wild animal.

Review		Challenge	
21. sigh	23. shown	26. require	28. defy
22. twice	24. tonight	27. reproach	29. plight
	25. remote		30. opponent

Think and Sort

The /ī/ sound and the /ō/ sound may be spelled with the vowel-consonant-*e* pattern or with patterns of one or more letters.

/ī/ str**i**ke, sp**i**der, repl**y**, m**igh**ty   /ō/ comp**o**se, str**o**ll, gr**oa**n, thr**ow**n

! What four letters spell /ī/ or /ō/ in the Memory Words?

Write each Basic Word under the vowel sound in its *stressed* syllable. Underline the letters that make each vowel sound.

/ī/ Sound

1. _____
2. _____
3. _____
4. _____
5. _____
6. _____
7. _____
8. _____
9. _____
10. _____
11. _____
12. _____

/ō/ Sound

13. _____
14. _____
15. _____
16. _____
17. _____
18. _____
19. _____
20. _____

Word Analysis/Phonics

21–25. Write the five Basic Words that begin with the *gr*, *br*, *thr*, or *str* consonant cluster.

Vocabulary: Analogies

Write the Basic or Review Word that best completes each analogy.

26. *Alert* is to *sleepy* as _____ is to *powerless*.

27. *Irritate* is to *please* as *bore* is to _____.

28. *Soiled* is to *clean* as *noisy* is to _____.

29. *Recent* is to *ancient* as *nearby* is to _____.

Challenge Words

Write Challenge Words to complete the paragraph. Use your Spelling Dictionary.

Winning this game will ___(30)___ teamwork! Just remember that we are better prepared than our ___(31)___. I ___(32)___ anyone to say otherwise! When the Sharks meet us, they'll wonder how they ever got in such a terrible ___(33)___. Their fans will ___(34)___ them for daring to challenge us, the greatest kickball team on the planet!

Spelling-Meaning Connection

35–36. How can you remember how to spell the vowel sound in the second syllable of *composition*? Think of the /ō/ sound in the related words *compose* and *composure*. Write *compose* and *composition*. Underline the letters that both words share.

Word Analysis
21. _____
22. _____
23. _____
24. _____
25. _____

Analogies
26. _____
27. _____
28. _____
29. _____

Challenge Words
30. _____
31. _____
32. _____
33. _____
34. _____

Spelling-Meaning
35. _____
36. _____

composure

compose

composition

At Home — Make word crosses with a family member. Write one Spelling Word across a page. Take turns writing Spelling Words that cross the words you write.

31

Word Structure

1. _____
2. _____
3. _____
4. _____
5. _____
6. _____
7. _____
8. _____

Word Structure: The Word Root *pos* or *pose*

A **word root** is a word part that has meaning but usually cannot stand alone. The word root *pos* or *pose* means "to put or place."

Practice Each word in the box contains the word root *pos*. Write a word to match each definition. Use your Spelling Dictionary.

compose	proposal	expose	transpose
impose	preposition	oppose	disposal

1. an offer or a plan that is put forth
2. to place in a different, changed order
3. to speak or fight against
4. the act of getting rid of something
5. to place out in the open
6. to put together or make
7. to take unfair advantage
8. a word that shows the relationship between a noun or pronoun and another word in a sentence

Dictionary

9. _____
10. _____
11. _____
12. _____
13. _____
14. _____

Dictionary: Definitions

A dictionary entry may include several numbered definitions.

ap•ply (ə plī´) *v.* **applied, applying, applies 1.** To put on, upon, or to: *I should apply some hair gel before I leave.* **2.** To put into action: *Apply the rocket's thrusters now.* **3.** To devote (oneself or one's efforts) to something: *You must apply yourself to your homework.*

Practice Write *1, 2,* or *3* to show which definition of *apply* is used in each sentence.

9. He needs to apply all his efforts to passing the test.
10. The doctor will apply a bandage to the wound.
11. To stop the car, apply the brakes.
12. Apply the throttle to increase your speed.
13. We can win today if we apply ourselves in practice.
14. Should I apply a new coat of paint to the chair?

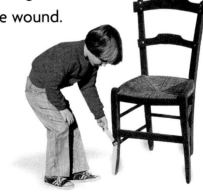

✏ Proofread an Advertisement

Spelling and Proper Nouns Use proofreading marks to correct **ten** misspelled Basic or Review Words and **four** mistakes in capitalizing proper nouns in this advertisement.

Example: My friend jenna will ~~grone~~ *groan* if she loses at bowling.

Bowl for the Fun of It!

What will you do tonit? Don't just punch the remote controle for your television. Come see Pete and lily at Bowl World and applie your talents to an activity that will excite you and your family!

Picture yourself bowling in our clean, modern lanes. You stand at your full hight. You grip the ball and make your approch. You release the ball with a slite twist of the wrist. The ball heads for the pins. Wow! That's your fifth strik of the game! That's mitey fine!

We are just a short stroll from downtown pineville, on benton street. Look for the sighn with the lighted bowling pins. Those ten pins breighten the entire block!

Proofreading Marks

¶ Indent
∧ Add
⊙ Add a period
ᕂ Delete
≡ Capital letter
/ Small letter

Basic
sign
groan
reply
thrown
strike
mighty
stroll
compose
dough
height
excite
apply
slight
define
odor
spider
control
silent
brighten
approach

Review
sigh
twice
shown
tonight
remote

Challenge
require
reproach
defy
plight
opponent

✏ Write an Advertisement

prewrite → draft → revise → proofread → publish

Write an advertisement for a place where you go for fun.

- Describe **the place** and explain **why people should go there.**
- Use some Spelling Words and some proper nouns.
- Proofread your work for **spelling** and **capitalization.**

Power Proofreading
www.eduplace.com/kids/sv/

> **Test Tip** Read every answer choice before deciding on
> an answer.

Test Format Practice

Directions Read each group of sentences. Decide if one of the underlined words is spelled wrong or if there is *No mistake*. Fill in the space for the answer you have chosen.

Example: A One <u>sleeve</u> has a rip.
B Please <u>remain</u> quiet.
C Words of <u>praise</u> sound sweet.
D No mistake

Example:

Ⓐ Ⓑ Ⓒ ⬤

Answer Sheet

1. Ⓐ Ⓑ Ⓒ Ⓓ
2. Ⓕ Ⓖ Ⓗ Ⓙ
3. Ⓐ Ⓑ Ⓒ Ⓓ
4. Ⓕ Ⓖ Ⓗ Ⓙ
5. Ⓐ Ⓑ Ⓒ Ⓓ
6. Ⓕ Ⓖ Ⓗ Ⓙ
7. Ⓐ Ⓑ Ⓒ Ⓓ
8. Ⓕ Ⓖ Ⓗ Ⓙ

1. A What a <u>mighty</u> storm!
B Should we walk fast or <u>stroll</u>?
C Please <u>replye</u> to my request.
D No mistake

2. F Cut shapes from cookie <u>dogh</u>.
G I have a <u>slight</u> cold.
H We are having chicken <u>tonight</u>.
J No mistake

3. A Please <u>control</u> the dog.
B Dictionaries <u>defign</u> words.
C The <u>sign</u> said For Sale.
D No mistake

4. F A <u>spyder</u> is not an insect.
G They landed on a <u>remote</u> island.
H Visitors <u>excite</u> the younger dogs.
J No mistake

5. A The rider was <u>thrown</u> from the horse.
B Garlic has a strong <u>owder</u>.
C Pitchers try to <u>strike</u> out batters.
D No mistake

6. F Would you <u>repeat</u> your name?
G Richard broke his <u>promise</u>.
H I gave a <u>sye</u> of relief.
J No mistake

7. A Tom is <u>afraid</u> of bears.
B The baby is <u>awake</u>.
C Please knock <u>twise</u>.
D No mistake

8. F Eve has <u>shoan</u> me her report.
G The music was <u>pleasant</u>.
H Throw away the <u>stale</u> bread.
J No mistake

More Practice

Now write all the misspelled words correctly on a separate sheet of paper.

Spelling Games
www.eduplace.com/kids/sv/
Review for your test.

Real-World Vocabulary

Life Skills: Cooking

All the words in the box relate to making pie dough. Look up these words in your Spelling Dictionary. Then write the words to complete this recipe.

Spelling Word Link
dough

- utensil
- liquid
- sift
- preheat
- pastry
- ginger
- spatula
- whole grain

HOW TO MAKE FLAKY PIE DOUGH

First, _____(1)_____ 1½ cups flour and ½ teaspoon salt together into a large bowl. White flour is best because _____(2)_____ flour may make the crust tough. Tip: Add a dash of cinnamon or _____(3)_____ to give the crust more flavor. Cut ½ cup butter into the dry mix with a knife, _____(4)_____, or other kitchen _____(5)_____. Add 3 tablespoons water or milk. (Remember, when making pie or any other type of _____(6)_____, either _____(7)_____ must be ice cold.) Next, mix the dough until it begins to stick together. Then chill it for 30 minutes for easy rolling. While the dough is chilling, make the pie filling and _____(8)_____ the oven so that it will be ready to bake the pie.

1. _____
2. _____
3. _____
4. _____
5. _____
6. _____
7. _____
8. _____

eWord Game
www.eduplace.com/kids/sv/

Try This CHALLENGE

Word Riddles Write the word that answers each riddle.

9. I am used to scrape the sides of a bowl.
10. A cook does this to get the oven hot before baking.
11. I am something you can pour.
12. This is what you do to flour to make it fluffy.

9. _____
10. _____
11. _____
12. _____

PART 1 Spelling and Phonics

Read the Spelling Words and sentences.

Basic

1.	glue	glue	Use **glue** to repair the broken plate.
2.	flute	flute	Matt is learning to play the **flute**.
3.	youth	youth	Our street was a farm in Papa's **youth**.
4.	accuse	accuse	Never **accuse** someone falsely.
5.	bruise	bruise	Ice reduces the swelling of a **bruise**.
6.	stew	stew	Put meat and carrots in the **stew**.
7.	choose	choose	You may **choose** the apple or the pear.
8.	loose	loose	That handle is **loose** and may fall off.
⚠ 9.	lose	lose	Kate may **lose** her hat in the wind.
⚠ 10.	view	view	Climb a hill for a good **view** of the city.
11.	confuse	confuse	Run-on sentences can **confuse** readers.
12.	cruise	cruise	The family took a **cruise** to the islands.
13.	jewel	jewel	The ruby is my favorite **jewel**.
14.	dilute	dilute	Please **dilute** the juice by adding water.
15.	route	route	The best **route** to town is West Road.
16.	cartoon	cartoon	What makes a **cartoon** funny?
17.	avenue	avenue	Traffic was noisy on the **avenue**.
18.	include	include	Will you **include** me in your plans?
19.	assume	assume	I **assume** you will pass the test.
20.	souvenir	souvenir	This cup is a **souvenir** from my trip.

Review	23. refuse	**Challenge**	28. intrude
21. fruit	24. argue	26. conclude	29. subdue
22. group	25. foolish	27. pursuit	30. presume

Think and Sort

The /ōō/ and the /yōō/ sounds may be spelled with the
u-consonant-*e* pattern or with two letters. A consonant sound
usually follows the patterns *oo*, *ui*, and *ou*.

/ōō/ or /yōō/ acc**use**, l**oo**se, st**ew**, gl**ue**, y**ou**th, br**ui**se

⚠ How are the vowel sounds spelled in the Memory Words?

Write each Basic Word under /ōō/ or /yōō/. Write *youth* under /ōō/.

/ōō/ Sound

1. _____
2. _____
3. _____
4. _____
5. _____
6. _____
7. _____
8. _____
9. _____
10. _____
11. _____
12. _____
13. _____
14. _____
15. _____
16. _____
17. _____

/yōō/ Sound

18. _____
19. _____
20. _____

Word Analysis/Phonics

21–26. Write the six Basic Words that end with the /z/ sound spelled *s*.

Vocabulary: Making Inferences

Write the Basic or Review Word that fits each clue.

27. More than two people are needed to form this.

28. A cook needs a pot to make this.

29. Berries and melons are examples of this.

Challenge Words

Write the Challenge Word that fits each meaning. Use your Spelling Dictionary.

30. to enter without being invited

31. to bring to an end

32. the act of chasing

33. to bring under control

34. to suppose to be true

Spelling-Meaning Connection

35–36. The vowel sounds in *youth* and *youthful* are different from the vowel sound in *young*, but the three words are connected in spelling and meaning. Write *youth* and *young*. Underline the two letters that spell the vowel sound in each word.

y**ou**th

y**ou**thful

y**ou**ng

Word Analysis

21. _____

22. _____

23. _____

24. _____

25. _____

26. _____

Making Inferences

27. _____

28. _____

29. _____

Challenge Words

30. _____

31. _____

32. _____

33. _____

34. _____

Spelling-Meaning

35. _____

36. _____

At Home With a family member, take turns printing the first and last letters of a Spelling Word, with blanks in between. The other person finishes the word.

Vocabulary

1. _____
2. _____
3. _____
4. _____
5. _____
6. _____
7. _____
8. _____

Vocabulary: Words Often Confused

Some words are often misspelled because they look and sound similar to other words. Each word below has a different meaning, spelling, and pronunciation.

Practice Complete each sentence with a word from the box. Use your Spelling Dictionary.

loose	raise	sit	lie
lose	rise	set	lay

1. The sun will _____ at six tomorrow morning.
2. Will the team win, or will it _____?
3. Please _____ on the chair.
4. Jin has a _____ tooth.
5. It is so restful to _____ in a hammock.
6. Just _____ your head on the pillow, and relax.
7. If you have a question, _____ your hand.
8. Please _____ the chairs near the table.

Dictionary

9. _____
10. _____
11. _____
12. _____
13. _____
14. _____
15. _____
16. _____

Dictionary: Spelling Table

The **Spelling Table** lists different spellings for vowel and consonant sounds. Use the Spelling Table to find a word in a dictionary when you are not sure how the word is spelled.

Sounds	Spellings	Sample Words
/yo͞o/	eau, ew, iew, u, ue	beauty, few, view, fuse, fuel, cue

Practice Say each pronunciation below. Listen for the vowel sound. Use the Spelling Table on pages 281–282 to write the spellings for the vowel sound. Then find the word in your Spelling Dictionary. Write it correctly.

9–10. /goun/   **13–14.** /brēf/

11–12. /flo͞ot/   **15–16.** /spŭnj/

PART 3 Spelling and Writing

Proofread a Travel Guide

Spelling and Possessive Nouns Use proofreading marks to correct **ten** misspelled Basic or Review Words and **two** apostrophes missing from singular possessive nouns in this travel guide.

Example: We must not ~~loose~~ *lose* the directions to the woman's house.

Proofreading Marks

¶ Indent
∧ Add
⊙ Add a period
ℒ Delete
≡ Capital letter
/ Small letter

MOOSEWAY *(population 1,200)*

Mooseway is a little juel tucked away in the woods. Some visitors confuse this lively town with the sleepy fishing village of Mooseport, which is far to the east. Just assoum you are on the correct roote if you pass through Glenview. Mooseway's main avenew has many charming restaurants. Many folks choose Edgar's Eatery, famous for the chefs tasty stews. Be sure to drive up to Pine Point to buy a soovernier and see a grand vue of the valley. You would be fulish to rifuse a chance to crooze on beautiful Blue Lake. No one will argyue with you if you say that a visit to Mooseway can make a busy persons cares vanish.

Basic
glue
flute
youth
accuse
bruise
stew
choose
loose
lose
view
confuse
cruise
jewel
dilute
route
cartoon
avenue
include
assume
souvenir

Review
fruit
group
refuse
argue
foolish

Challenge
conclude
pursuit
intrude
subdue
presume

Write a Travel Guide

prewrite → draft → revise → proofread → publish

Write a short travel guide for a place you know or would like to visit.

- Include **details** about activities and sites.
- Use some Spelling Words and singular possessive nouns.
- Proofread your work for **spelling** and for the correct use of **apostrophes.**

Power Proofreading
www.eduplace.com/kids/sv/

Test Tip Avoid making stray marks on your paper.

Test Format Practice

Example:

Ⓐ Ⓑ ● Ⓓ Ⓔ

Answer Sheet

1. Ⓐ Ⓑ Ⓒ Ⓓ Ⓔ
2. Ⓙ Ⓚ Ⓛ Ⓜ Ⓝ
3. Ⓐ Ⓑ Ⓒ Ⓓ Ⓔ
4. Ⓙ Ⓚ Ⓛ Ⓜ Ⓝ
5. Ⓐ Ⓑ Ⓒ Ⓓ Ⓔ
6. Ⓙ Ⓚ Ⓛ Ⓜ Ⓝ
7. Ⓐ Ⓑ Ⓒ Ⓓ Ⓔ
8. Ⓙ Ⓚ Ⓛ Ⓜ Ⓝ

Directions This test will show how well you can spell.

- Many of the questions in this test have spelling mistakes. Some do not have any mistakes at all.
- Look for mistakes in spelling.
- If there is a mistake, fill in the answer space on your answer sheet that has the same letter as the **line** with the mistake.
- If there is no mistake, fill in the last answer space.

Example:
  A demand
  B feather
  C yuth
  D release
  E *(No mistakes)*

1. **A** jewel
  B stew
  C avenue
  D group
  E *(No mistakes)*

2. **J** confuse
  K floute
  L compose
  M foolish
  N *(No mistakes)*

3. **A** cruise
  B choose
  C suvenir
  D bruise
  E *(No mistakes)*

4. **J** gloo
  K route
  L view
  M comic
  N *(No mistakes)*

5. **A** argue
  B beneath
  C incloode
  D niece
  E *(No mistakes)*

6. **J** fruit
  K height
  L apply
  M dilewt
  N *(No mistakes)*

7. **A** hymn
  B cartoun
  C assume
  D lose
  E *(No mistakes)*

8. **J** loose
  K shown
  L refews
  M accuse
  N *(No mistakes)*

More Practice

Now write all the misspelled words correctly on a separate sheet of paper.

Spelling Games
www.eduplace.com/kids/sv/
Review for your test.

Real-World Vocabulary

Math: Probability

All the words in the box relate to probability. Look up these words in your Spelling Dictionary. Then write the words to complete this paragraph from a math lesson.

Figuring Probability

Imagine you have a cube with sides numbered 1 to 6. It would be _____(1)_____ for you to roll a 7 with that cube. How _____(2)_____ is it that you would roll a 3? You can show the probability of rolling a 3 by writing a fraction. On the top, put the number 1, because only one side of the cube has a 3 on it. On the bottom, write a 6, because there are six possible _____(3)_____: you could roll 1, 2, 3, 4, 5, or 6. So, the probability of rolling 3 is one in six ($\frac{1}{6}$). You can write this as the _____(4)_____ 1:6, or 1 to 6. You can show this as a _____(5)_____: there is a 16.67 percent chance that you will roll a 3. What if you had the _____(6)_____ of choosing a second number besides 3? What would be the _____(7)_____ of rolling one of those two numbers? You may learn how to solve this problem when you study _____(8)_____.

eWord Game
www.eduplace.com/kids/sv/

Spelling Word Link
choose

algebra
impossible
likelihood
option
outcomes
percentage
probable
ratio

1. _____
2. _____
3. _____
4. _____
5. _____
6. _____
7. _____
8. _____

CHALLENGE

Questions and Answers Write the word from the box that answers each question.

9. Which word means the same as *choice*?

10. Is it probable or impossible that you would roll an 8 on a 6-sided cube?

11. What is another word for the probability of an event?

12. What looks somewhat like a fraction written left to right?

9. _____
10. _____
11. _____
12 _____

PART 1 Spelling and Phonics

/ou/ Sound

1. _____
2. _____
3. _____
4. _____
5. _____

/ô/ Sound

6. _____
7. _____
8. _____
9. _____
10. _____
11. _____
12. _____
13. _____
14. _____

/oi/ Sound

15. _____
16. _____
17. _____
18. _____
19. _____
20. _____

Read the Spelling Words and sentences.

Basic

1. ounce — *ounce* — One eighth of a cup is an **ounce**.
2. sprawl — *sprawl* — My dog likes to **sprawl** on the rug.
3. launch — *launch* — When did the rocket **launch** take place?
4. loyal — *loyal* — The fans remained **loyal** to their team.
5. avoid — *avoid* — Is there a way to **avoid** catching a cold?
6. falter — *falter* — Do not **falter** on the path to your goal.
7. moist — *moist* — Cover the cake to keep it **moist**.
8. haunt — *haunt* — The gym is Will's favorite **haunt**.
9. scowl — *scowl* — It is better to smile than to **scowl**.
10. naughty — *naughty* — It is **naughty** to tease the cat.
11. destroy — *destroy* — Big waves can **destroy** a sand castle.
12. saucer — *saucer* — The kitten drinks milk from a **saucer**.
13. pounce — *pounce* — Will the cat **pounce** on the toy mouse?
14. poison — *poison* — Rattlesnakes have **poison** in their fangs.
15. August — *August* — Summer's last full month is **August**.
16. auction — *auction* — I bid on an old desk at the **auction**.
17. royal — *royal* — The **royal** family lives in a palace.
18. coward — *coward* — Even a **coward** may act bravely at times.
19. awkward — *awkward* — At first I felt **awkward** on skates.
20. announce — *announce* — The judge will **announce** the winner.

Review
21. cause
22. faucet
23. tower
24. false
25. amount

Challenge
26. poise
27. loiter
28. exhaust
29. assault
30. alternate

Think and Sort

The /ou/, /ô/, and /oi/ sounds are often spelled with two letters. The letter *a* sometimes spells /ô/ before the consonant *l*. The *ou*, *au*, and *oi* patterns are usually followed by a consonant sound.

/ou/ **ou**nce, c**ow**ard   /ô/ la**u**nch, spr**aw**l, f**a**lter   /oi/ l**oy**al, m**oi**st

How is /ô/ spelled in the Memory Word?

Write each Basic Word under the vowel sound in its *stressed* syllable.

Word Analysis/Phonics

21–24. Write the four Basic Words in which the letter *c* has the /s/ sound.

Vocabulary: Analogies

Write the Basic or Review Word that best completes each analogy.

25. *Write* is to *erase* as *build* is to _____ .

26. *Foolish* is to *wise* as _____ is to *true*.

27. *Graceful* is to _____ as *swift* is to *sluggish*.

28. *Basic* is to *luxurious* as *common* is to _____ .

29. *Medicine* is to _____ as *health* is to *illness*.

Challenge Words

Write the Challenge Word that best completes each phrase. Use your Spelling Dictionary.

30. to _____ at the snack shop with nothing to do

31. spoke with confidence and _____

32. led the _____ on the fort

33. to _____ turns with a partner

34. long, difficult tasks that _____ workers

Spelling-Meaning Connection

35–36. The words *moist*, *moisten*, and *moisture* are related in spelling and meaning. Write the words *moist* and *moisten*. Underline the consonant that is pronounced in *moist* but silent in *moisten*.

Word Analysis

21. _____

22. _____

23. _____

24. _____

Analogies

25. _____

26. _____

27. _____

28. _____

29. _____

Challenge Words

30. _____

31. _____

32. _____

33. _____

34. _____

Spelling-Meaning

35. _____

36. _____

At Home With a family member, write each Spelling Word on a small piece of paper. Work together to arrange the words in alphabetical order.

43

Vocabulary

1. _____
2. _____
3. _____
4. _____
5. _____
6. _____
7. _____
8. _____

Vocabulary: Words for Facial Expressions

Practice Write the word from the box that matches each description. Use your Spelling Dictionary.

scowl	glare	grimace	pout
squint	sneer	smirk	beam

1. to contort the face, showing pain or disgust
2. to wrinkle the brow and lower the eyebrows in anger
3. to curl up one corner of the upper lip to show scorn
4. to stare angrily at someone
5. to push out the lips to show disappointment
6. to smile in a smug, self-satisfied way
7. to look with eyes narrowed, as in bright sunlight
8. to grin with great happiness

Dictionary

9. _____
10. _____
11. _____
12. _____
13. _____
14. _____

Dictionary: Pronunciation Key

The pronunciation in a dictionary entry tells you how the word should be said. The **pronunciation key** helps you understand the symbols in the pronunciation.

Pronunciation
false (fôls)

Pronunciation Key
ô paw
oi oil
ou out

Practice 9–14. Write the correct spelling for each dictionary pronunciation. Use the Pronunciation Key on page 285 of your Spelling Dictionary.

9. (hônt) hunt, haunt
10. (tou´ ər) tour, tower
11. (loi´ əl) loyal, laurel
12. (vôlt) volt, vault
13. (oi´ stər) ouster, oyster
14. (kloud) clawed, cloud

Proofread an Advice Column

Spelling and Possessive Nouns Use proofreading marks to correct **ten** misspelled Basic or Review Words and **two** apostrophes missing from plural possessive nouns in this letter in an advice column.

Example: We avoid the ~~poisen~~ *poison* ivy near the campers' tents.

Dear Henry Helpful,

I will be vacationing with my family in Awgust.
I plan to swim in the lake, sprall on the dock,
lounch a rowboat, and have a great time. Unfortunately,
a problem has come up. My mom and dad said I could
invite my bcst friend. I was all set to announce my choice,
but then I remembered: I have TWO best friends! No
amont of begging will change my parents minds. They say
there is room for only one friend, but I am loiyal to both
friends. I could avoyed the problem by not inviting anyone.
Does that make me a cowerd? I don't think so. I just
don't want to hurt my two friends feelings or cawse the
friendships to faulter. What do you advise? I don't want
this awkward decision to huant me!

Unable to Decide

Proofreading Marks

- ¶ Indent
- ∧ Add
- ⊙ Add a period
- ⌐ Delete
- ≡ Capital letter
- / Small letter

Basic
ounce
sprawl
launch
loyal
avoid
falter
moist
haunt
scowl
naughty
destroy
saucer
pounce
poison
August
auction
royal
coward
awkward
announce

Review
cause
faucet
tower
false
amount

Challenge
poise
loiter
exhaust
assault
alternate

Write an Advice Column

prewrite ⟶ draft ⟶ revise ⟶ proofread ⟶ publish

Write a response from Henry Helpful that suggests a solution.

- Begin your letter with the greeting *Dear Unable to Decide.*
- Use some Spelling Words and plural possessive nouns.
- Proofread your work for **spelling** and for the correct use of **apostrophes.**

Power Proofreading
www.eduplace.com/kids/sv/

✓ **Test Tip** Answer the easiest questions first.

Test Format Practice

Directions Read the sentences in each group. Decide if one of the underlined words has a spelling mistake or if there is *No mistake*. Fill in the space for your answer choice.

Example: **A** We heard the music of the <u>flute</u>.
  B Visit us in <u>August</u>.
  C The sailors will <u>lawnch</u> the ship.
  D No mistake

Example:

Ⓐ Ⓑ ● Ⓓ

Answer Sheet

1. Ⓐ Ⓑ Ⓒ Ⓓ

2. Ⓕ Ⓖ Ⓗ Ⓙ

3. Ⓐ Ⓑ Ⓒ Ⓓ

4. Ⓕ Ⓖ Ⓗ Ⓙ

5. Ⓐ Ⓑ Ⓒ Ⓓ

6. Ⓕ Ⓖ Ⓗ Ⓙ

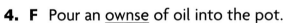

1. A The lion is ready to <u>pounce</u>.
  B Who can fix the dripping <u>fawcet</u>?
  C The <u>royal</u> family lives in a castle.
  D No mistake

2. F He grew weak and began to <u>falter</u>.
  G The queen tried to <u>poison</u> Snow White.
  H We bought a used couch at an <u>ouction</u>.
  J No mistake

3. A Please <u>repeat</u> your name.
  B That <u>nauty</u> puppy is full of mischief.
  C Is the answer true or <u>false</u>?
  D No mistake

4. F Pour an <u>ownse</u> of oil into the pot.
  G Anger made her <u>scowl</u>.
  H No one knows the <u>cause</u> of the fire.
  J No mistake

5. A A stone <u>touwer</u> stood on the hill.
  B When will you <u>announce</u> the news?
  C Sunbathers <u>sprawl</u> on the beach.
  D No mistake

6. F I took an <u>awkward</u> step and stumbled.
  G Put the cup in its matching <u>sawser</u>.
  H How can we <u>avoid</u> the danger?
  J No mistake

More Practice

Now write all the misspelled words correctly on a separate sheet of paper.

Spelling Games
www.eduplace.com/kids/sv/
Review for your test.

Real-World Vocabulary

Social Studies: Voyage of Discovery

All the words in the box relate to exploring the world through sailing. Look up these words in your Spelling Dictionary. Then write the words to complete this travel diary.

Spelling Word Link
launch

destination
expedition
exploration
harbor
mast
navigation
rigging
sailor

September 1, 1542

I haven't had much time to write. The work of a _____(1) fills nearly every hour of the day. Since this is my first great _____(2), I have much to learn. I'm getting better at reading maps, however. Each day that I help the captain chart our course, my _____(3) skills improve. I'm also able to climb up the ropes of the _____(4) like the more experienced men. Even when I'm near the top of the tallest _____(5), I don't get dizzy anymore.

Our _____(6) of Alta California is going well. Yesterday we discovered a fine natural _____(7), where we dropped anchor for the night. I'm enjoying my time at sea, but I will be happy once we reach our final _____(8) and can turn toward home.

1. _____
2. _____
3. _____
4. _____
5. _____
6. _____
7. _____
8. _____

eWord Game
www.eduplace.com/kids/sv/

Try This

CHALLENGE

Quick Sketch On a separate sheet of paper, draw a sketch of a sailing ship in port. Show some sailors. Label a <u>sailor</u>, the <u>mast</u>, the ship's <u>rigging</u>, and the <u>harbor</u>.

Spelling Review

Unit 1

1. _____
2. _____
3. _____
4. _____
5. _____
6. _____
7. _____
8. _____
9. _____
10. _____

Unit 2

11. _____
12. _____
13. _____
14. _____
15. _____
16. _____
17. _____
18. _____
19. _____
20. _____

Unit 1		Short Vowels		pages 18–23
grasp	breath	blister	! hymn	! shovel
stingy	energy	feather	comic	frantic

Spelling Strategy Remember that a short vowel sound is usually spelled by a single vowel and followed by a consonant sound.

/ă/→ *a*   /ĕ/→ *e, ea*   /ĭ/→ *i*   /ŏ/→ *o*   /ŭ/→ *u*

Context Sentences Write the word that completes each sentence.

1. You can see your _____ in the cold air.
2. The sun gives off light and thermal _____.
3. Can a tight sneaker cause a _____?
4. The child played with a pail and _____.
5. The minister asked the choir to sing a _____.
6. That _____ came from a parrot.

Analogies Write the word that best completes each analogy.

7. *Sensible* is to *foolish* as *calm* is to _____.
8. *Generous* is to _____ as *kind* is to *mean*.
9. *Playful* is to *stern* as _____ is to *serious*.
10. *Drop* is to _____ as *dump* is to *scoop*.

Unit 2		Long *a* and Long *e*		pages 24–29
stray	praise	scale	disease	! thief
ashamed	sleeve	waist	beneath	! niece

Spelling Strategy

/ā/→ *a*-consonant-*e, ai, ay*   /ē/→ *ea, ee*

Word Clues Write the word that fits each clue.

11. a lost animal
12. opposite of *proud*
13. someone who steals
14. a synonym for *under*
15. a tool for weighing
16. a brother's daughter
17. "Great job!", for example
18. arm covering
19. mumps or flu
20. bend here to touch your toes

Unit 3 — Long *i* and Long *o* — pages 30–35

reply	thrown	compose	⚠ dough	⚠ height
spider	control	brighten	excite	define

Spelling Strategy

/ī/→ *i*-consonant-*e, igh, i*   /ō/→ *o*-consonant-*e, o, oa, ow*

Classifying Write the word that belongs in each group.

21. length, width, _____
22. insect, tick, _____
23. darken, whiten, _____
24. limit, prevent, _____
25. batter, frosting, _____
26. thrill, fascinate, _____
27. write, create, _____
28. describe, label, _____
29. respond, answer, _____
30. pitched, tossed, _____

Unit 4 — Vowel Sounds: /o͞o/, /yo͞o/ — pages 36–41

youth	choose	bruise	⚠ lose	⚠ view
avenue	dilute	cartoon	jewel	souvenir

Spelling Strategy

/o͞o/ and /yo͞o/→ *u*-consonant-*e, oo, ue, ew, ui, ou*

Context Paragraph Write the words that complete this paragraph.

Grandma asked me to ___(31)___ a hiking trail, so I picked Hoover Hill. Grandma hiked up the trail as fast as a ___(32)___ half her age. I began to ___(33)___ sight of her. I scrambled to keep up, fell, and got a ___(34)___ on my knee. Still, the ___(35)___ from the top was worth the climb. Far below Grandma and me, Loon Lake glittered like a ___(36)___.

Definitions Write the word that fits each meaning.

37. an item kept as a reminder of an event
38. to make weaker or less pure
39. a wide street
40. a drawing of a humorous situation

Unit 3

21. _____
22. _____
23. _____
24. _____
25. _____
26. _____
27. _____
28. _____
29. _____
30. _____

Unit 4

31. _____
32. _____
33. _____
34. _____
35. _____
36. _____
37. _____
38. _____
39. _____
40. _____

Spelling Review

Unit 5	Vowel Sounds: /ou/, /ô/, /oi/			pages 42–47
ounce	falter	scowl	moist	❗ naughty
poison	destroy	awkward	announce	auction

Spelling Strategy

/ou/→ **ou, ow**   /ô/→ **aw, au, a** before **l**   /oi/→ **oi, oy**

Analogies Write the word that best completes each analogy.

41. *Friend* is to *enemy* as *grin* is to _____.

42. *Dry* is to _____ as *chilly* is to *warm*.

43. *Polite* is to *rude* as *graceful* is to _____.

44. *Harmful* is to *helpful* as _____ is to *obedient*.

Classifying Write the word that belongs in each group.

45. smash, break, _____

46. recite, declare, _____

47. ton, pound, _____

48. stumble, pause, _____

49. trade, sale, _____

50. danger, deadly, _____

Challenge Words		Units 1–5		pages 18–47
massive	subdue	require	opponent	succeed
assault	loiter	summit	pursuit	terrain

Context Sentences Write the word that completes each sentence.

51. If you score more points than your _____, you win.

52. The _____ of happiness is a basic human right.

53. Did you _____ in reaching your goal?

54. It is against school rules to sit or _____ on the stairs.

55. We climbed to the _____ of the mountain.

56. Constant noise is an _____ on the ears.

57. Police officers tried to _____ the rowdy mob.

58. It is easier to cycle on flat _____ than on hills.

59. People _____ food, clothing, and shelter.

60. How did the pyramid builders move such _____ stones?

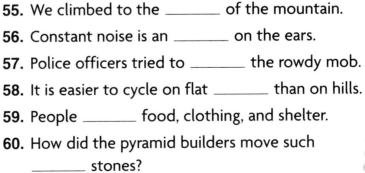

Unit 5

41. _____
42. _____
43. _____
44. _____
45. _____
46. _____
47. _____
48. _____
49. _____
50. _____

Challenge Words

51. _____
52. _____
53. _____
54. _____
55. _____
56. _____
57. _____
58. _____
59. _____
60. _____

50 Unit 6

Spelling and Writing

Proofread a Description

Spelling and Grammar Mixed Review Use proofreading marks to correct this description. There are **eight** misspelled Basic Words from the last five units. There are **three** incorrect or missing end marks, and **one** error in a possessive noun.

Example: What a ~~freindly~~ *friendly* dog Clancy is!

	Proofreading Marks
¶	Indent
∧	Add
⊙	Add a period
✄	Delete
≡	Capital letter
/	Small letter

Kangaroo

Our family found Kangaroo on our doorstep one Augus

day two years ago. He was a skinny stray kitten then. How it

disturbed us to hear his cries of hunger? We put out a sawcer

of milk and some sollid food. After gobbling up everything, he

dashed indoors, taking a straight roote to the closit. There he

hid for hours.

Eventually he came out to grete us with loud meows. He

made a mighety leap right into my mothers lap! Does it surprise

you that we named him Kangaroo.

Today, Kangaroo is a playful bundle of energy who loves to

leap and pounse. He will relax with me, purring

with pleasure as I stroke his velvety silver fur I

am truly happy that Kangaroo's home is with us.

KITTEN

Write a Description

prewrite → draft → revise → proofread → publish

Write a description of a pet, a person, or a place you like very much.

- Use some Spelling Words from Units 1 through 5 in your description.
- Proofread your work for **spelling, end marks,** and correct use of **possessive nouns.**

Tips
- Choose a topic that you can describe clearly.
- Brainstorm details that appeal to two or more senses.
- Organize the details so that readers can "see" your subject.

Power Proofreading

Spelling Test Practice

Test Tip Read all the answer choices carefully. Eliminate the choices that contain spelling mistakes.

Test Format Practice

Directions For numbers 1 through 8, choose the word that is spelled correctly and best completes the sentence.

Example: Coughing can spread germs that cause _____.

   A desease

   B diseese

   C disseze

   D disease

Example:

Ⓐ Ⓑ Ⓒ ●

Answer Sheet

1. Ⓐ Ⓑ Ⓒ Ⓓ

2. Ⓕ Ⓖ Ⓗ Ⓙ

3. Ⓐ Ⓑ Ⓒ Ⓓ

4. Ⓕ Ⓖ Ⓗ Ⓙ

5. Ⓐ Ⓑ Ⓒ Ⓓ

6. Ⓕ Ⓖ Ⓗ Ⓙ

7. Ⓐ Ⓑ Ⓒ Ⓓ

8. Ⓕ Ⓖ Ⓗ Ⓙ

More Practice

Now write each correctly spelled word on a sheet of paper.

Spelling Games

www.eduplace.com/kids/sv/
Review for your test.

1. The family gathered for the holiday _____.

   A feast

   B feazt

   C feest

   D fiest

2. Thank you for being such a _____ friend.

   F loyle

   G loil

   H loyel

   J loyal

3. Dark clouds are a _____ of rain.

   A sine

   B sien

   C sign

   D sighn

4. If you make a _____, you must keep it.

   F promise

   G prommis

   H promiss

   J promisse

5. Did you tighten the _____ lid?

   A lous

   B loose

   C lose

   D luce

6. Where shall I put this _____ of laundry?

   F bundel

   G bundal

   H boundle

   J bundle

7. There is a _____ in the basement.

   A spieder

   B spyder

   C spider

   D spiter

8. Don't _____ that the clouds will bring rain.

   F asume

   G assume

   H asoon

   J asoume

Test Tip Read the directions carefully.

Directions Read the sentence with the missing word and the question relating to that word. Then choose the word that best answers the question.

Test Format Practice

Example: Make sure to _____ some beautiful ripe lemons.

Which of these words would indicate that the lemons are being stacked on a store shelf?

    A crush   **C** display

    B demand   **D** grasp

Example:

Ⓐ Ⓑ ● Ⓓ

Answer Sheet

1. Ⓐ Ⓑ Ⓒ Ⓓ

2. Ⓕ Ⓖ Ⓗ Ⓙ

3. Ⓐ Ⓑ Ⓒ Ⓓ

4. Ⓕ Ⓖ Ⓗ Ⓙ

---

1. Everyone noticed Bo's _____ expression.

Which of these words would indicate that Bo felt embarrassed?

    A eager   **C** pleasant

    B comic   **D** sheepish

2. We need to _____ the juice.

Which of these words would indicate that the juice needs water added?

    F avoid   **H** include

    G dilute   **J** choose

3. The crowd made a loud _____ when the final score was announced.

Which of these words would indicate that the crowd was very disappointed?

    A sigh   **C** groan

    B breath   **D** reply

4. "Please do not _____ me," Christie said.

Which of these words would indicate that Christie was afraid of being blamed?

    F confuse   **H** refuse

    G accuse   **J** choose

PART 1 Spelling and Phonics

Read the Spelling Words and sentences.

Basic

1.	glory	*glory*	The winner will bring **glory** to her school.
2.	aware	*aware*	Are you **aware** of how late it is?
3.	carton	*carton*	Pack the books in a **carton**.
4.	adore	*adore*	My sisters **adore** our cute new puppy.
5.	aboard	*aboard*	"All **aboard**!" called the train conductor.
6.	dairy	*dairy*	How often are cows milked at a **dairy**?
7.	bore	*bore*	It is hard to finish books that **bore** me.
8.	pardon	*pardon*	I beg your **pardon,** but I must disagree.
9.	warn	*warn*	Who will **warn** visitors of the danger?
10.	vary	*vary*	The flower colors **vary** from red to pink.
11.	barely	*barely*	I can **barely** see my hands in the dark.
12.	torch	*torch*	A runner led the way with a lit **torch**.
13.	barge	*barge*	A **barge** carried goods down the river.
14.	soar	*soar*	The kite will really **soar** in this breeze.
15.	beware	*beware*	Please **beware** of thorns on the roses.
16.	absorb	*absorb*	Sponges **absorb** water.
17.	armor	*armor*	Body **armor** protected knights of old.
18.	stairway	*stairway*	A **stairway** leads to the second floor.
19.	perform	*perform*	When will we **perform** our play?
20.	former	*former*	The **former** dancer is now a teacher.

Review		Challenge	
21. board	23. sharp	26. discard	28. orchestra
22. repair	24. square	27. forfeit	29. gracious
	25. compare		30. hoard

Think and Sort

Each word has one of these vowel + /r/ sounds.

/ôr/ gl**ory**, s**oar**, b**ore**   /âr/ aw**are**, d**airy**   /är/ c**ar**ton

⚠ How are the /ôr/ and the /âr/ sounds spelled in the Memory Words?

Write each Basic Word under the correct heading.

/ôr/ Sounds

1. _____
2. _____
3. _____
4. _____
5. _____
6. _____
7. _____
8. _____
9. _____
10. _____

/âr/ Sounds

11. _____
12. _____
13. _____
14. _____
15. _____
16. _____

/är/ Sounds

17. _____
18. _____
19. _____
20. _____

Word Analysis/Phonics

21–24. Write the four Basic Words that have a final /ē/ sound.

Vocabulary: Classifying

Write the Basic or Review Word that belongs in each group.

25. flashlight, lamp, _____

26. rectangle, circle, _____

27. ladder, escalator, _____

28. boat, raft, _____

29. fly, glide, _____

Challenge Words

Write Challenge Words to complete this paragraph. Use your Spelling Dictionary.

Look at my __(30)__ of free passes to the symphony! These will admit me to concerts performed by our __(31)__ all season long. I must be careful not to __(32)__ any of the passes when I clean my room. I do not want to __(33)__ even one chance to hear such wonderful music. I am going to be __(34)__ and generous and invite all my friends to be my guests at the concerts.

Spelling-Meaning Connection

35–36. How can you remember how to spell the vowel sound in the first syllable of *adore* and the related word *adorable*? Think of the /ă/ sound in the first syllable of *adoration*. Write *adore* and *adoration*. Underline the letter in *adoration* that helps you spell the first sound in *adore*.

Word Analysis

21. _____

22. _____

23. _____

24. _____

Classifying

25. _____

26. _____

27. _____

28. _____

29. _____

Challenge Words

30. _____

31. _____

32. _____

33. _____

34. _____

Spelling-Meaning

35. _____

36. _____

adore

adoration

adorable

At Home Make word crosses with a family member. Write one Spelling Word across a page. Take turns writing other Spelling Words that cross the words you write.

55

Vocabulary

1. _____
2. _____
3. _____
4. _____
5. _____
6. _____
7. _____
8. _____

Vocabulary: Analogies

Remember that an analogy compares related word pairs. **Synonyms,** words with similar meanings, are compared in one type of analogy.

Example: *Dark* is to *dim* as *hidden* is to *concealed.*

Practice Write the word from the box that best completes each analogy. Use your Spelling Dictionary.

carton	meander	bough	motto
fury	regal	hurl	illusion

1. *Proud* is to *haughty* as *royal* is to _____.
2. *Stem* is to *stalk* as *limb* is to _____.
3. *Shove* is to *push* as *wander* is to _____.
4. *Goal* is to *purpose* as *fantasy* is to _____.
5. *Kindness* is to *goodness* as *rage* is to _____.
6. *Gift* is to *present* as *box* is to _____ .
7. *Run* is to *dash* as *throw* is to _____.
8. *Guidance* is to *advice* as *saying* is to _____.

Dictionary

9. _____
10. _____
11. _____
12. _____
13. _____
14. _____
15. _____
16. _____

Dictionary: Stressed Syllables

A **syllable** is a word part that has one vowel sound. In a word with two or more syllables, one syllable is said more strongly, or with more stress. The dictionary pronunciation for a word shows which syllable is stressed, with bold type and an accent mark.

stressed syllable ⬐ ⬐ accent mark

a•dore (ə **dôr´**) *v.*

Practice Look at each word and its pronunciation. Write each word in syllables. Draw a line between the syllables. Then underline the stressed syllable.

9. perform (pər **fôrm´**)
10. aboard (ə **bôrd´**)
11. pardon (**pär´** dn)
12. former (**fôr´** mər)
13. absorb (əb **sôrb´**)
14. repair (rĭ **pâr´**)
15. aware (ə **wâr´**)
16. compare (kəm **pâr´**)

Proofread a Magazine Article

Spelling and Grammar Use proofreading marks to correct **ten** misspelled Basic or Review Words and **two** usage errors with the verbs *be* and *have* in this humorous article from a nature magazine.

Example: Pardonne us, but we has to deliver an urgent message.
(Pardon) *(have)*

Proofreading Marks

¶ Indent
∧ Add
⊙ Add a period
✐ Delete
≡ Capital letter
/ Small letter

The Nine-banded Armadillo

This message are for all insects in the southern United States: Be awhere that the nine-banded armadillo is on the prowl! This animal has been known to barge into anthills and other insect homes. Three worms and a snail bairly escaped from it last week! Reports on the creature's size varry, but we would compair it to a large rodent. It have a long snout, bony plates that serve as body armer, and sharpe claws to dig and repair burrows. We warne all bugs to parform their chores with caution. With the nine-banded armadillo around, life will not be a boare.
Bugs bewair!

Basic
glory
aware
carton
adore
aboard
dairy
bore
pardon
warn
vary
barely
torch
barge
soar
beware
absorb
armor
stairway
perform
former

Review
board
repair
sharp
square
compare

Challenge
discard
forfeit
orchestra
gracious
hoard

Write a Magazine Article

prewrite → draft → revise → proofread → publish

Write an article about your favorite animal.

- Describe your animal. Include details about its **habitat** and **characteristics**.
- Use some Spelling Words and forms of the verbs *be* and *have*.
- Proofread your work for **spelling** and correct **verb forms**.

Power Proofreading
www.eduplace.com/kids/sv/

Test Tip Skip questions that seem hard at first and go back to them later.

Test Format Practice

Directions Find the phrase containing an underlined word that is not spelled correctly. If all the underlined words are spelled correctly, mark "All correct."

Example: **A** to climb a <u>staireway</u>
B to <u>beware</u> of danger
C to <u>control</u> a car
D sticky <u>glue</u>
E All correct

Example:

● Ⓑ Ⓒ Ⓓ Ⓔ

Answer Sheet

1. Ⓐ Ⓑ Ⓒ Ⓓ Ⓔ

2. Ⓕ Ⓖ Ⓗ Ⓙ Ⓚ

3. Ⓐ Ⓑ Ⓒ Ⓓ Ⓔ

4. Ⓕ Ⓖ Ⓗ Ⓙ Ⓚ

5. Ⓐ Ⓑ Ⓒ Ⓓ Ⓔ

6. Ⓕ Ⓖ Ⓗ Ⓙ Ⓚ

7. Ⓐ Ⓑ Ⓒ Ⓓ Ⓔ

8. Ⓕ Ⓖ Ⓗ Ⓙ Ⓚ

More Practice

Now write all the misspelled words correctly on a separate sheet of paper.

Spelling Games
www.eduplace.com/kids/sv/
Review for your test.

---

1. **A** a loaded <u>barge</u>
   B a <u>square</u> or a circle
   C to <u>absorbe</u> knowledge
   D to <u>vary</u> the routine
   E All correct

2. **F** to <u>lose</u> the game
   G the greatest <u>glorry</u>
   H to spread <u>disease</u>
   J from a great <u>height</u>
   K All correct

3. **A** a flaming <u>torch</u>
   B an empty <u>carton</u>
   C to <u>compare</u> and contrast
   D to <u>bore</u> with a dull speech
   E All correct

4. **F** to beg your <u>pardon</u>
   G hawks that <u>soar</u>
   H <u>aware</u> of the risk
   J <u>dairee</u> foods
   K All correct

5. **A** <u>sharp</u> as a tack
   B <u>barely</u> used
   C <u>abord</u> the train
   D a knight's <u>armor</u>
   E All correct

6. **F** a quick <u>reply</u>
   G to <u>warn</u> of danger
   H to <u>repare</u> the damage
   J beef <u>stew</u>
   K All correct

7. **A** to <u>adore</u> a pet
   B a wooden <u>bord</u>
   C to <u>perform</u> the job
   D <u>awkward</u> movements
   E All correct

8. **F** cold <u>weather</u>
   G to <u>remain</u> at home
   H a <u>former</u> best friend
   J wide <u>awake</u>
   K All correct

Real-World Vocabulary

Drama: A Play Performance

All the words in the box relate to the performance of a play. Look up these words in your Spelling Dictionary. Then write the words to complete this play review.

School Play Is Big Hit!

Last Friday the drama club gave a wonderful performance of *Willy Wonka and the Chocolate Factory*. This popular story has mystery and suspense, but it's a comedy, not a ___(1)___. It took students and parents many weeks to build the set and sew the ___(2)___. The actors needed hours of ___(3)___ to learn their ___(4)___. Mr. Woo, the ___(5)___ of the play, had to show the actors how to move properly on stage. Fortunately, everyone's hard work paid off. The story grabbed the audience's attention right away and built to an exciting ___(6)___ near the end. Afterward, the audience gave Mr. Woo and the actors a standing ___(7)___ for their fine performance. My only complaint was that there should have been another ___(8)___ so the audience could stretch their legs. Two hours is too long to sit on a metal chair!

Spelling Word Link
perform

intermission
director
ovation
dialogue
costumes
rehearsal
tragedy
climax

1. _____
2. _____
3. _____
4. _____
5. _____
6. _____
7. _____
8. _____

eWord Game
www.eduplace.com/kids/sv/

Try This
CHALLENGE

Category Clue Write a word from the box that fits each category.

9. Words About Clothing

10. Types of Speech

11. Ways to Show Appreciation

12. Jobs in Theater

9. _____

10. _____

11. _____

12. _____

PART 1 Spelling and Phonics

Read the Spelling Words and sentences.

Basic

1. earth	earth	Plant the seeds in the **earth**.
2. peer	peer	Did you **peer** through the telescope?
3. twirl	twirl	Pat will **twirl** her baton in the parade.
4. burnt	burnt	Scrape the crumbs off the **burnt** toast.
5. smear	smear	There is a greasy **smear** on the glass.
6. further	further	This class will **further** our knowledge.
7. appear	appear	How bright the stars **appear** tonight!
8. worthwhile	worthwhile	Ty gives money to **worthwhile** causes.
9. nerve	nerve	It takes **nerve** and skill to climb a cliff.
10. pier	pier	Nola dived off the **pier** into the water.
11. squirm	squirm	A worm will **squirm** if you pick it up.
12. weary	weary	The **weary** travelers fell asleep.
13. alert	alert	When crossing a road, be **alert** for cars.
14. murmur	murmur	Listen to the **murmur** of the breeze.
15. sturdy	sturdy	These big books need **sturdy** shelves.
16. reverse	reverse	Put the car in **reverse** to back up.
17. worship	worship	A church is a place used for **worship**.
18. career	career	Ed wants a **career** in medicine.
19. research	research	Sam did **research** to find the answers.
20. volunteer	volunteer	Did you **volunteer** to make dinner?

Review
21. early
22. world
23. rear
24. current
25. cheer

Challenge
26. yearn
27. engineer
28. interpret
29. dreary
30. external

Think and Sort

Each word has one of these vowel + /r/ sounds.

/ûr/ tw**ir**l, f**ur**ther, **ear**th, w**or**thwhile   /îr/ p**eer**, sm**ear**

What is the spelling of the /îr/ sounds in the Memory Word?

Write each Basic Word under the correct heading.

/ûr/ Sounds
1.
2.
3.
4.
5.
6.
7.
8.
9.
10.
11.
12.
13.

/îr/ Sounds
14.
15.
16.
17.
18.
19.
20.

Word Analysis/Phonics

Write the Basic Word that includes each consonant cluster or sound below.

21. sh   **22.** squ   **23.** ch

Vocabulary: Making Inferences

Write the Basic or Review Word that fits each clue.

24. This is more than just a job.
25. This sends signals inside a body.
26. This is like a whisper.
27. Reports that are up-to-date are this.
28. This could describe dawn.
29. This is built out from the shore.

Challenge Words

Write the Challenge Word that fits each meaning. Use your Spelling Dictionary.

30. boring and dull
31. on the outside of something
32. to explain or translate

33. to wish for deeply
34. a person who uses science to design or build things

Spelling-Meaning Connection

35–36. A *worthwhile* activity is worth doing, unlike a *worthless* activity. These words are related in meaning and spelling. Write the compound word *worthwhile*. Then write the first word in it.

Word Analysis
21. _____
22. _____
23. _____

Making Inferences
24. _____
25. _____
26. _____
27. _____
28. _____
29. _____

Challenge Words
30. _____
31. _____
32. _____
33. _____
34. _____

Spelling-Meaning
35. _____
36. _____

worth
worthless
worthwhile

At Home With a family member, take turns writing the first three letters of a Spelling Word. The other person finishes the word.

Word Structure

1. _____
2. _____
3. _____
4. _____
5. _____
6. _____
7. _____
8. _____

Word Structure: The Word Root *vers* or *vert*

Latin, the language of ancient Rome, is the source of the word root *vers* or *vert*. The root means "to turn or turn around."

Practice Complete each sentence with a word from the box. Use your Spelling Dictionary.

reverse	avert	divert	versatile
anniversary	revert	adversity	version

1. Music can _____ us because it turns us away from our cares.
2. Turn an old story into a new one by writing another _____.
3. Turn around to _____ your direction.
4. This _____ piece of furniture can be used as a chair, a table, or a bed.
5. It is easy to _____ to bad habits, so try not to turn back to them.
6. The driver turned away in time to _____ the accident.
7. The farmers faced _____ during the flood.
8. Each year Mr. and Mrs. Fisher have a party to celebrate their wedding _____.

Dictionary

9. _____
10. _____
11. _____
12. _____
13. _____
14. _____
15. _____
16. _____

Dictionary: Parts of Speech

A dictionary entry includes every part of speech for the entry word. The parts of speech are abbreviated.

n. noun	*adj.* adjective	*prep.* preposition
v. verb	*adv.* adverb	*pron.* pronoun

smear (smîr) *v.* **smeared, smearing** To cover or spread with a sticky or greasy substance. — *n., pl.* **smears 1.** A stain or blotch. **2.** A substance or preparation placed on a slide for microscopic study.

Practice Write the parts of speech given in your Spelling Dictionary for each word. Write them in the order they appear. Do not abbreviate.

9–10. murmur   **11–13.** volunteer   **14–16.** alert

Proofread a Mystery Story

Spelling and Subject-Verb Agreement Use proofreading marks to correct **ten** misspelled Basic or Review Words and **two** errors in subject-verb agreement in this part of a mystery story.

Example: Ana and Vin ~~does~~ *do* careful ~~reserch~~ *research* to find clues.

— *Chapter 1*—

Junior detective Ana Ramos and her friend Vin leave the empty cabin by the reer door. As they walk, Ana notices footprints in the erth that apear to have been made by high heels. She and Vin bends to peir at the marks.

"Why in the wold would anyone hike in high heels?" Vin asks. Ana begins to twurl her braid. Doing this makes her more alirt. Ana hopes to have a career as a detective. For now, she is happy to vollunteer her services.

Ana walks farther and quickly spot two more clues. She finds a stick with a bernt tip and a smeere of something white. "A woman in dressy clothes has been toasting marshmallows," she murmurs. "That's very odd."

Proofreading Marks
¶	Indent
∧	Add
⊙	Add a period
⌿	Delete
≡	Capital letter
/	Small letter

Basic
earth
peer
twirl
burnt
smear
further
appear
worthwhile
nerve
pier
squirm
weary
alert
murmur
sturdy
reverse
worship
career
research
volunteer

Review
early
world
rear
current
cheer

Challenge
yearn
engineer
interpret
dreary
external

Write a Mystery Story

prewrite → draft → revise → proofread → publish

Write the first part of a mystery story.

• Introduce a **detective**, and describe what **mysterious thing** the detective finds.

• Use some Spelling Words.

• Proofread your work for **spelling** and **subject-verb agreement**.

Power Proofreading
www.eduplace.com/kids/sv/

PART 4 Spelling Test Practice

Test Tip Avoid making stray marks on your paper.

Test Format Practice

Example:

Ⓐ Ⓑ ● Ⓓ

Answer Sheet

1. Ⓐ Ⓑ Ⓒ Ⓓ
2. Ⓕ Ⓖ Ⓗ Ⓙ
3. Ⓐ Ⓑ Ⓒ Ⓓ
4. Ⓕ Ⓖ Ⓗ Ⓙ
5. Ⓐ Ⓑ Ⓒ Ⓓ
6. Ⓕ Ⓖ Ⓗ Ⓙ

More Practice

Now write all the misspelled words correctly on a separate sheet of paper.

Spelling Games
www.eduplace.com/kids/sv/
Review for your test.

Directions Read each group of sentences. Decide if one of the underlined words is spelled wrong or if there is *No mistake*. Fill in the space for the answer you have chosen.

Example: **A** I smell <u>burnt</u> toast.
B Some birds <u>soar</u> high.
C They sailed around the <u>wurld</u>.
D No mistake

1. **A** Did you <u>peer</u> into the cave?
B People often fish from the <u>pier</u>.
C The log bridge was <u>sturdey</u>.
D No mistake

2. **F** Hard work made them <u>wery</u>.
G It takes <u>nerve</u> to walk a tightrope.
H Andy will <u>volunteer</u> to help.
J No mistake

3. **A** The <u>current</u> in the river is strong.
B Start your <u>research</u> at the library.
C Reading is a <u>worthwhile</u> activity.
D No mistake

4. **F** I like to <u>smear</u> jam on bread.
G Paul and Lin <u>chear</u> for their team.
H How <u>early</u> do you wake up?
J No mistake

5. **A** Children sometimes <u>squirm</u> in their seats.
B A <u>murmur</u> may be hard to hear.
C Write your name on the <u>reverce</u> side.
D No mistake

6. **F** The mine tunneled into the <u>earth</u>.
G The <u>rear</u> seat is roomy.
H They spoke out to <u>futher</u> their cause.
J No mistake

Real-World Vocabulary

Science: The Human Body

All the words in the box have to do with the human body. Look up these words in your Spelling Dictionary. Then write the words to complete this diagram.

Spelling Word Link

nerve

- muscle
- abdomen
- cartilage
- ligaments
- organs
- skeleton
- intestines
- esophagus

The Human Body

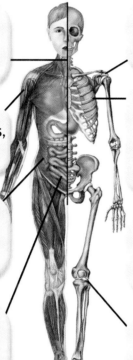

The ___(1)___ is a tube connecting the throat and the stomach.

When a ___(2)___ contracts, it causes bones to move.

The ___(3)___ extends from the chest down to the top of the legs.

The ___(4)___ are where food goes after it leaves the stomach.

The ___(5)___ is made up of all the bones in the body.

The ribs protect two of the body's most vital ___(6)___, the heart and the lungs.

Tough white ___(7)___ is attached to the surface of bones near joints.

The ___(8)___ connect bones to other bones.

1. _____
2. _____
3. _____
4. _____
5. _____
6. _____
7. _____
8. _____

eWord Game
www.eduplace.com/kids/sv/

Try This

CHALLENGE

Clue Match Write a word from the box to match each clue.

9. They do jobs such as digest food and pump blood.

10. It's the structure that supports your body.

11. Food slides down this when you swallow it.

12. You use this to move your bones.

9. _____
10. _____
11. _____
12. _____

Read the Spelling Words and sentences.

Basic

1. steel	*steel*	The new bridge is made of **steel**.
2. steal	*steal*	What jewelry did the thief **steal**?
3. aloud	*aloud*	We heard José read his poem **aloud**.
4. allowed	*allowed*	Bike riding is **allowed** on park roads.
5. pore	*pore*	Detectives **pore** over every clue.
6. pour	*pour*	May I **pour** the batter into the pan?
7. lesson	*lesson*	This **lesson** is on homophones.
8. lessen	*lessen*	It seemed the gale would never **lessen**.
9. who's	*who's*	Please see **who's** at the door.
10. whose	*whose*	I wonder **whose** hat was left behind.
11. manor	*manor*	A castle was part of a lord's **manor**.
12. manner	*manner*	I hope the doctor has a kindly **manner**.
13. pedal	*pedal*	Place that foot on the bike's left **pedal**.
14. peddle	*peddle*	My friends **peddle** fruit to make money.
15. berry	*berry*	Pick a **berry** only if it is ripe.
16. bury	*bury*	I like to **bury** my feet in the sand.
17. hanger	*hanger*	Is there a coat **hanger** in the closet?
18. hangar	*hangar*	The new plane was stored in a **hangar**.
19. overdo	*overdo*	You will ache if you **overdo** an exercise.
20. overdue	*overdue*	Please return the **overdue** library book.

Review	23. vain		**Challenge**	28. site
21. wait	24. vane		26. canvass	29. sight
22. weight	25. vein		27. canvas	30. cite

Think and Sort

Homophones are words that sound alike but have different spellings and meanings.

(pôr) p**ore** "to read or study with great care and attention"
(pôr) p**our** "to cause to flow or stream, as from a container"

Write the Basic Word pairs under the correct heading.

One-Syllable Homophones

1. _____

2. _____

3. _____

4. _____

5. _____

6. _____

Two-Syllable Homophones

7. _____

8. _____

9. _____

10. _____

11. _____

12. _____

13. _____

14. _____

15. _____

16. _____

17. _____

18. _____

Homophones with *over-*

19. _____

20. _____

Word Analysis/Phonics

21–24. Write the four Basic Words that have two syllables and end with the /ər/ sounds.

Vocabulary: Analogies

Write the Basic or Review Word that best completes each analogy.

25. *Brighten* is to *enliven* as _____ is to *weaken*.

26. *Honest* is to *trustworthy* as _____ is to *arrogant*.

27. *Closed* is to *open* as *forbidden* is to _____.

28. *Glance* is to *peek* as _____ is to *examine*.

29. *Heaviness* is to _____ as *distance* is to *length*.

Challenge Words

Write the Challenge Word that fits each clue. Use your Spelling Dictionary.

30. what an artist paints on

31. the sense that eyes provide

32. to specify a source used in research

33. to gather votes or opinions

34. a place for a particular activity

Spelling-Meaning Connection

35–36. Creatures that *steal* use *stealth*, a quiet way of moving. The words *steal* and *stealth* are related in spelling and meaning. Write both words. Then underline the two letters in each word that are the same but that spell different vowel sounds.

Word Analysis

21. _____

22. _____

23. _____

24. _____

Analogies

25. _____

26. _____

27. _____

28. _____

29. _____

Challenge Words

30. _____

31. _____

32. _____

33. _____

34. _____

Spelling-Meaning

35. _____

36. _____

steal
stealth

At Home — With a family member, take turns using a homophone in a sentence. The other person writes the correct homophone.

67

Word Structure

1. _____
2. _____
3. _____
4. _____
5. _____
6. _____

Word Structure: The Word Root *ped*

The ancient language of Latin is the source of the word root *ped*. *Ped* can mean "foot."

Practice Write the word from the box that matches each meaning. Use your Spelling Dictionary.

pedal	biped	pedestrian
pedometer	quadruped	pedestal

1. someone who travels on foot
2. a lever controlled by the foot
3. an animal with four feet
4. a device that counts footsteps
5. a two-footed creature
6. the base, or foot, of a statue

Dictionary

7. _____
8. _____
9. _____
10. _____
11. _____
12. _____
13. _____
14. _____
15. _____

Dictionary: Homophones

A dictionary entry should tell you whether a word has a homophone.

ped•dle (pĕd′ l) *v.* **ped•dled, ped•dling, ped•dles 1.** To travel about selling (goods): *We peddle magazines to raise money for our team.*
◆ *These sound alike:* **peddle, pedal** (lever).

Practice Write the homophone for each word in items 7–9. Then use all six homophones to complete sentences 10–15. Use your Spelling Dictionary.

7. bore   **8.** peer   **9.** waist

10. You may _____ food if you take more than you need.
11. Movies with too much talking _____ me.
12. The _____ of these jeans is too loose.
13. I used a flashlight to _____ into the darkened room.
14. A huge wild _____ tore up many plants.
15. Rita fishes from this _____ every Saturday.

✎ Proofread a Fable

Spelling and Irregular Verbs Use proofreading marks to correct **ten** misspelled Basic or Review Words and **two** mistakes in the past tense of irregular verbs in this fable.

Example: Squirrel ~~growed~~ *grew* the fruit in a skillful ~~manor⊙~~ *manner*.

Proofreading Marks

¶	Indent
∧	Add
⊙	Add a period
⌐	Delete
≡	Capital letter
/	Small letter

Squirrel and the Juice

One warm day, Squirrel made bery juice to peddal from a wagon. "I think I'll pore myself a cup as I wate for customers," Squirrel said. The sun beat down. Squirrel, who's thirst grew stronger by the second, allowed himself another cup, and then another. "Whose to know if I take a little more?" he asked alowd. A steal cage would not have kept Squirrel from that pitcher of juice! Time flied by. Finally Squirrel's first customers arrived. Of course, the pitcher had growed lighter in weight. As a matter of fact, it contained no more juice to steal or to sell! "I suppose there's a lessen to be learned," Squirrel decided. "When you do something for yourself, don't overdue it!"

Basic
steel
steal
aloud
allowed
pore
pour
lesson
lessen
who's
whose
manor
manner
pedal
peddle
berry
bury
hanger
hangar
overdo
overdue

Review
wait
weight
vain
vane
vein

Challenge
canvass
canvas
site
sight
cite

✎ Write a Fable

prewrite → draft → revise → proofread → publish

Write a fable, a story with a moral.

- Create an **animal character.** Tell what the character **does** and **learns.**
- Use some Spelling Words and past tense forms of the verbs *fly*, *grow*, or *know*.
- Proofread your work for **spelling** and for the correct use of **irregular verb forms.**

Power Proofreading

> **Test Tip** Watch the time. Don't spend too much time on one question.

Directions Find the phrase containing an underlined word that is <u>not</u> spelled correctly. If all the underlined words are spelled correctly, mark "All correct."

Example: A rooms of the <u>manor</u>
B two-hour <u>wait</u>
C a <u>steel</u> trap
D to <u>peddle</u> goods
E All correct

Example:

Ⓐ Ⓑ Ⓒ Ⓓ ●

Answer Sheet

1. Ⓐ Ⓑ Ⓒ Ⓓ Ⓔ
2. Ⓕ Ⓖ Ⓗ Ⓙ Ⓚ
3. Ⓐ Ⓑ Ⓒ Ⓓ Ⓔ
4. Ⓕ Ⓖ Ⓗ Ⓙ Ⓚ
5. Ⓐ Ⓑ Ⓒ Ⓓ Ⓔ
6. Ⓕ Ⓖ Ⓗ Ⓙ Ⓚ
7. Ⓐ Ⓑ Ⓒ Ⓓ Ⓔ
8. Ⓕ Ⓖ Ⓗ Ⓙ Ⓚ

More Practice

Now write all the misspelled words correctly on a separate sheet of paper.

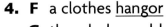

Spelling Games
www.eduplace.com/kids/sv/
Review for your test.

1. A to <u>lessen</u> the burden
   B an <u>overdo</u> train
   C <u>allowed</u> and encouraged
   D a purple <u>berry</u>
   E All correct

2. F an airport <u>hangar</u>
   G a helpful <u>manner</u>
   H a bicycle <u>pedal</u>
   J to <u>pore</u> the juice
   K All correct

3. A to <u>steal</u> a base
   B to try in <u>vain</u>
   C to <u>burry</u> treasure
   D to say <u>aloud</u>
   E All correct

4. F a clothes <u>hangor</u>
   G the whole <u>world</u>
   H an electric <u>current</u>
   J a painted <u>board</u>
   K All correct

5. A height and <u>weight</u>
   B a weather <u>vain</u>
   C <u>whose</u> hat
   D to <u>pore</u> over your notes
   E All correct

6. F birds that <u>soar</u> high
   G to <u>bore</u> with a long story
   H to <u>adore</u> a kitten
   J to fish from the <u>pier</u>
   K All correct

7. A <u>who's</u> there
   B blood in a <u>vane</u>
   C a <u>lesson</u> to learn
   D to <u>peer</u> through the glass
   E All correct

8. F an <u>overdew</u> book
   G to <u>vary</u> your diet
   H to <u>warn</u> of danger
   J to <u>appear</u> happy
   K All correct

Real-World Vocabulary

Social Studies: The Law

All the words in the box relate to the law. Look them up in your Spelling Dictionary. Then write the words to complete this newspaper article.

Spelling Word Link
allowed

attorney
citation
courtroom
guilty
illegal
innocent
jury
ordinance

Dog Owner Breaks Leash Law

FAIRVIEW, Aug. 9 — Spectators packed a City Hall ____(1)____ yesterday to hear the case against resident David Boxer. He was charged with ignoring the city ____(2)____ that requires dog owners to keep their dogs on a leash in public.

Ms. Airedale, the ____(3)____ defending Mr. Boxer, said that her client was ____(4)____ of the charges because he didn't know about the city's leash law. The city's lawyer argued that Mr. Boxer had received his first

official ____(5)____ a year ago. After that, he knew it was ____(6)____ for his dog to be off-leash on city streets. Nonetheless, he continued to let the animal run free, and he received six more tickets for doing so.

After conferring, the members of the ____(7)____ found Mr. Boxer ____(8)____ of the charges. Now he will have to pay the full amount of all his fines, plus additional fees and penalties.

eWord Game
www.eduplace.com/kids/sv/

1. _____
2. _____
3. _____
4. _____
5. _____
6. _____
7. _____
8. _____

Try This
CHALLENGE

Yes or No? Write *yes* if the underlined word is used correctly. Write *no* if it is not.

9. The <u>ordinance</u> the woman received was for littering.

10. The <u>jury</u> defended the man charged with theft.

11. Everyone in the <u>courtroom</u> stood up when the judge entered.

12. The city has a <u>citation</u> against littering.

9. _____
10. _____
11. _____
12. _____

Read the Spelling Words and sentences.

Basic

1. wildlife	*wildlife*	Deer and ducks are common **wildlife**.
2. uproar	*uproar*	Pam's angry speech caused an **uproar**.
3. home run	*home run*	What a long **home run** the batter hit!
4. headache	*headache*	Dana had a cold and a **headache**.
5. top-secret	*top-secret*	Do not reveal the **top-secret** plan.
6. teammate	*teammate*	Our new **teammate** will help us win.
7. wheelchair	*wheelchair*	A ramp was built for the **wheelchair**.
8. light bulb	*light bulb*	The lamp needs a new **light bulb**.
9. well-known	*well-known*	The **well-known** author writes daily.
10. throughout	*throughout*	We worked hard **throughout** the day.
11. lifeguard	*lifeguard*	A **lifeguard** watched the swimmers.
12. barefoot	*barefoot*	Take off your socks to walk **barefoot**.
13. part-time	*part-time*	Neil has a **part-time** job after school.
14. warehouse	*warehouse*	The boxes are stored in a **warehouse**.
15. overboard	*overboard*	No one on deck fell **overboard**.
16. post office	*post office*	Mail the package at the **post office**.
17. outspoken	*outspoken*	He is an **outspoken** movie critic.
18. up-to-date	*up-to-date*	How **up-to-date** is your computer?
19. awestruck	*awestruck*	We were **awestruck** by the waterfall.
20. newscast	*newscast*	View the **newscast** for today's news.

Review		Challenge	
21. goodbye	23. forever	26. motorcycle	28. quick-witted
22. all right	24. twenty-two	27. overseas	29. stomachache
	25. somebody		30. bulletin board

Think and Sort

A **compound word** is made up of two or more smaller words. The smaller words may be written as one word, connected with a hyphen or hyphens, or written as separate words.

up + roar = **uproar**   part + time = **part-time**

light + bulb = **lightbulb**

Write each Basic Word under the heading that tells how the compound word is written.

One Word

1. _____
2. _____
3. _____
4. _____
5. _____
6. _____
7. _____
8. _____
9. _____
10. _____
11. _____
12. _____
13. _____

With a Hyphen

14. _____
15. _____
16. _____
17. _____

Separate Words

18. _____
19. _____
20. _____

Word Analysis/Phonics

21–23. Write the three Basic Words that include the same vowel +
/r/ sounds as in *square*.

Vocabulary: Synonyms

Write the Basic or Review Word that is a synonym for each
underlined word.

24. Is <u>anyone</u> there?

25. The protesters created a noisy <u>commotion</u>.

26. The movie critic gave her <u>frank</u> opinion.

27. We gathered to hear the <u>current</u> election results.

28. I craned my neck to see the <u>famous</u> actor.

29. The patient felt <u>fine</u> after the operation.

Challenge Words

Write the Challenge Word that best completes each group of words.
Use your Spelling Dictionary.

30. flew _____ on business

31. a _____ from overeating

32. a _____ detective

33. messages on a _____

34. a speedy, powerful _____

Spelling-Meaning Connection

35–36. *Wild* animals are *wildlife*, and they may live in the *wilderness*.
The words *wild*, *wildlife*, and *wilderness* are related in
meaning and spelling. Write the compound word *wildlife*.
Then write the first word in it.

wild
wildlife
wilderness

Word Analysis

21. _____

22. _____

23. _____

Synonyms

24. _____

25. _____

26. _____

27. _____

28. _____

29. _____

Challenge Words

30. _____

31. _____

32. _____

33. _____

34. _____

Spelling-Meaning

35. _____

36. _____

At Home With a family member,
take turns writing four
Spelling Words on pieces of
paper. Cut each into the
smaller words that make it
up. Mix them up. The other
person joins the smaller
words to form compound
words.

Vocabulary

1. _____
   _____
2. _____
   _____
3. _____
   _____
4. _____
   _____
5. _____
6. _____
   _____
7. _____
8. _____
   _____

Thesaurus

9. _____
10. _____
11. _____
12. _____

Vocabulary: Idioms with *over*

An **idiom** is an expression with a meaning different from the meaning of each separate word.

Example: The exam is *over with*! (*Over with* means "finished.")

Practice Replace the underlined word or words in each sentence with an idiom from the box. Use your Spelling Dictionary.

go overboard	cry over spilled milk	go over
over the top	once-over	over my head
over and above	over and over	

1. The child listened to the story <u>many times</u>.
2. The book was <u>too hard for me to understand</u>.
3. You may shop, but don't <u>do too much</u>.
4. Try not to <u>regret a mistake that can't be fixed</u>.
5. I will give your report a <u>quick review</u>.
6. Those costs are <u>in addition to</u> the price of the car.
7. Let's <u>review</u> the chapter together before the test.
8. The decorating in that apartment is <u>much too fancy</u>.

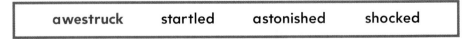

Thesaurus: Exact Words for *surprised*

Why is *awestruck* a better word than *surprised* in this sentence?
Brian was <u>awestruck</u> when he saw the Lincoln Memorial.

Awestruck is better because it describes the way Brian was surprised. A thesaurus will help you find exact synonyms.

Practice Read the entry for *surprised* in your Thesaurus. Then write the synonym from the box that best describes each person.

awestruck	startled	astonished	shocked

9. someone who finds out that a friend revealed a secret
10. a tourist seeing the Grand Canyon for the first time
11. children awakened at night by a loud clap of thunder
12. a woman who gasps when a parrot repeats her words

Proofread a Sports Column

Spelling and Contractions Use proofreading marks to correct **ten** misspelled Basic or Review Words and **two** errors in contractions in this sports column.

Example: The pitching was ~~alright~~ *all right*, but it ~~was't~~ *wasn't* great.

Proofreading Marks

¶	Indent
∧	Add
⊙	Add a period
⋅	Delete
≡	Capital letter
/	Small letter

One for the Record Books

by Ron Cleveland

Glenwood's baseball team set a record yesterday that may stand for ever! In a game against Pickwick, Grady Jackson hit a home-run in the second inning with the bases loaded. His teamate Mandy Wilson, a part-time player this year, belted another grand slam in the third inning. The fans could'nt believe their eyes. In the fourth inning, with the bases full again, the awestruck crowd waved goodby to another Jackson rocket. Jackson didn't stop there. He hit another in the eighth! He seemed to have a top-secrete plan for smacking grand slams throought the game. Glenwood's hitting, a well-known strength, was a big headace for Pickwick! The final score was twentytwo to five. The evening news-cast showed the final uprore. This game wont soon be forgotten!

Write a Sports Column

prewrite → draft → revise → proofread → publish

Write a sports column about a real or an imaginary game.

- Tell **who** played and **what** happened in the game.
- Use some Spelling Words and contractions with *not*.
- Proofread your work for **spelling** and **contractions**.

Basic
wildlife
uproar
home run
headache
top-secret
teammate
wheelchair
light bulb
well-known
throughout
lifeguard
barefoot
part-time
warehouse
overboard
post office
outspoken
up-to-date
awestruck
newscast

Review
goodbye
all right
forever
twenty-two
somebody

Challenge
motorcycle
overseas
quick-witted
stomachache
bulletin board

Power Proofreading
www.eduplace.com/kids/sv/

Test Tip Change an answer only if you are sure your first choice was wrong.

Test Format Practice

Directions Choose the word that is spelled correctly and best completes the sentence.

Example: Emma went on a _____ errand.

    A top secret
    B topsecret
    C top-secret
    D top-seecrit

Example:

Ⓐ Ⓑ ● Ⓓ

Answer Sheet

1. Ⓐ Ⓑ Ⓒ Ⓓ
2. Ⓕ Ⓖ Ⓗ Ⓙ
3. Ⓐ Ⓑ Ⓒ Ⓓ
4. Ⓕ Ⓖ Ⓗ Ⓙ
5. Ⓐ Ⓑ Ⓒ Ⓓ
6. Ⓕ Ⓖ Ⓗ Ⓙ
7. Ⓐ Ⓑ Ⓒ Ⓓ
8. Ⓕ Ⓖ Ⓗ Ⓙ

1. Mr. Wing runs _____ miles a week.
    A twenty too
    B twenty-two
    C twenty-too
    D twentytwo

2. Ashley works as a _____ each summer.
    F life gard
    G lifeguard
    H life-guard
    J lifegard

3. We need a _____ for this lamp.
    A lightbulb
    B lite bulb
    C lite-bulb
    D light bulb

4. Scott is looking for a _____ job.
    F partime
    G parttime
    H part-time
    J part time

5. That noise gives me a _____.
    A headdache
    B head-ache
    C headache
    D hedache

6. I bought stamps at the _____.
    F post office
    G post-office
    H posttoffice
    J postoffice

7. Our club does many _____ activities.
    A worthwhile
    B worthwile
    C wurth-wile
    D wurth-while

8. Olga was _____ at the acrobats' performance.
    F awstruck
    G aw-struck
    H awe struck
    J awestruck

More Practice
Now write each correctly spelled word on a sheet of paper.

Spelling Games
www.eduplace.com/kids/sv/
Review for your test.

Real-World Vocabulary

Life Skills: A Job Hunt

All the words in the box relate to getting a job. Look up these words in your Spelling Dictionary. Then write the words to complete the list of job-hunting tips.

Spelling Word Link
part-time

want ads
benefits
employment
experience
interview
training
schedule
wages

Tips for Job Hunting

These tips will help you find fun and rewarding part-time _____(1).

- Look in the _____(2) of your local paper for jobs baby-sitting, mowing lawns, watering gardens, or walking dogs.

- Get permission from your parents first. Then contact the person who placed the ad and describe your job skills and your past work _____(3).

- Ask how much time the job takes, and discuss the work _____(4) you would prefer, such as after school or on weekends.

- If you are new to this kind of work, ask if there is any special _____(5) you will need.

- If the person invites you for an _____(6), be sure to arrive on time.

- Find out what your pay, or _____(7), will be. Also ask if there are any extra _____(8), such as milk and cookies when the job is done.

1. _____
2. _____
3. _____
4. _____
5. _____
6. _____
7. _____
8. _____

eWord Game
www.eduplace.com/kids/sv/

Try This CHALLENGE

Write four questions you might ask about a job. Use the words *experience*, *training*, *wages*, and *schedule*. Use a separate sheet of paper.

77

PART 1 Spelling and Phonics

Read the Spelling Words and sentences.

Basic

1. cellar	*cellar*	These stairs lead down to the **cellar**.
2. flavor	*flavor*	Do you like the **flavor** of vanilla?
3. molar	*molar*	A **molar** is one of your back teeth.
4. chapter	*chapter*	Have you read the next **chapter**?
5. mayor	*mayor*	A **mayor** governs a city.
6. anger	*anger*	The actor raised his voice in **anger**.
7. senator	*senator*	Did the **senator** vote for the bill?
8. passenger	*passenger*	Each **passenger** has a train ticket.
9. major	*major*	What is a **major** product of our state?
10. popular	*popular*	Soccer is a **popular** sport everywhere.
11. tractor	*tractor*	Lee drives a **tractor** to plow the fields.
12. thunder	*thunder*	If you hear **thunder**, look for lightning.
13. pillar	*pillar*	Each corner of the roof sat on a **pillar**.
14. messenger	*messenger*	A **messenger** delivered the package.
15. calendar	*calendar*	Mark the date on your **calendar**.
16. quarter	*quarter*	A **quarter** is one-fourth of a dollar.
17. lunar	*lunar*	A moon map shows **lunar** valleys.
18. proper	*proper*	Oliver is always polite and **proper**.
19. elevator	*elevator*	Ride the **elevator** to the tenth floor.
20. bitter	*bitter*	This salad has a nasty, **bitter** taste.

Review	23. doctor	**Challenge**	28. tremor
21. collar	24. enter	26. stellar	29. circular
22. honor	25. answer	27. clamor	30. adviser

Think and Sort

Each word ends with the schwa + /r/ sounds. The **schwa sound,** shown as /ə/, is a weak vowel sound in an unstressed syllable. The /ər/ sounds at the end of a word may be spelled *er*, *or*, or *ar*.

/ər/ ang**er**, flav**or**, mol**ar**

Write each Basic Word under its spelling of /ər/.

er Pattern

1. _____
2. _____
3. _____
4. _____
5. _____
6. _____
7. _____
8. _____

or Pattern

9. _____
10. _____
11. _____
12. _____
13. _____
14. _____

ar Pattern

15. _____
16. _____
17. _____
18. _____
19. _____
20. _____

Proofread a Script

Spelling and Contractions Use proofreading marks to correct **eight** misspelled Basic or Review Words and **two** mistakes with contractions in this part of a script.

Example: They've put out a new ~~flaver~~ *flavor* of toothpaste.

GAIL: Welcome, Dr. Dennis. It's an honor to have you as our guest.
I'm Gail. This is where we enter the auditorium.

DR. DENNIS: Thank you, Gail. *(Looks puzzled)* I wonder why
every passenger in the elevater was staring at me.

GAIL: Well, docter, youve got to admit that you *are* holding
something strange. It looks like an enormous tooth, but it
has eyes and a mouth.

DR. DENNIS: *(Brightly)* Oh, I see you have'nt met Toothie yet.
I always bring this molor with me when I give talks about
the propper care of teeth and gums.

GAIL: You and Toothie will both be populer. We've been reading
about dental care in a chaptar of our health
book. We're ready with lots of questions.

DR. DENNIS: I'll try to anser them. And I promise
not to *brush* over any majer topic!

Write a Script

prewrite → draft → revise → proofread → publish

Write a script for a short skit with two characters.

- Create a brief conversation between the characters. Include some stage directions.
- Use some Spelling Words and some contractions with *have*.
- Proofread your work for **spelling** and **contractions.**

Power Proofreading
www.eduplace.com/kids/sv/

Basic
cellar
flavor
molar
chapter
mayor
anger
senator
passenger
major
popular
tractor
thunder
pillar
messenger
calendar
quarter
lunar
proper
elevator
bitter

Review
collar
honor
doctor
enter
answer

Challenge
stellar
clamor
tremor
circular
adviser

✔ **Test Tip** Read the directions carefully.

Test Format Practice

Directions Read the sentences in each group. Decide if one of the underlined words has a spelling mistake or if there is *No mistake*. Fill in the space for your answer choice.

Example:
A The dentist checked the <u>molar</u>.
B Does the house have a storm <u>celler</u>?
C We heard a large clap of <u>thunder</u>.
D No mistake

Example:

Ⓐ ● Ⓒ Ⓓ

Answer Sheet

1. Ⓐ Ⓑ Ⓒ Ⓓ
2. Ⓕ Ⓖ Ⓗ Ⓙ
3. Ⓐ Ⓑ Ⓒ Ⓓ
4. Ⓕ Ⓖ Ⓗ Ⓙ
5. Ⓐ Ⓑ Ⓒ Ⓓ
6. Ⓕ Ⓖ Ⓗ Ⓙ

1. A The farmer drove the <u>tractor</u>.
 B The state <u>senater</u> gave a speech.
 C One <u>quarter</u> is worth twenty-five cents.
 D No mistake

2. F I like the <u>flavor</u> of strawberries.
 G A highway is a <u>major</u> route.
 H I'll mark the date in my <u>calender</u>.
 J No mistake

3. A Every <u>passenger</u> needs a seat belt.
 B A <u>messenger</u> arrived with a package.
 C The <u>pillar</u> was made of stone.
 D No mistake

4. F The food tasted <u>bitter</u>.
 G Why is that movie so <u>popular</u>?
 H City voters elected a <u>mayer</u>.
 J No mistake

5. A When did the first <u>luner</u> spacecraft land?
 B The dog has a leash and a <u>collar</u>.
 C Which students are on the <u>honor</u> roll?
 D No mistake

6. F Please wear <u>proper</u> clothes to the party.
 G The toddler stamped his foot in <u>angar</u>.
 H Did the <u>doctor</u> give you a flu shot?
 J No mistake

More Practice

Now write all the misspelled words correctly on a separate sheet of paper.

Spelling Games
www.eduplace.com/kids/sv/
Review for your test.

Real-World Vocabulary

Art: Architecture and Design

All the words in the box have to do with describing homes. Look up these words in your Spelling Dictionary. Then write the words to complete this advertisement.

Spelling Word Link

cellar

design
real estate
fixtures
interior
pantry
architect
dimensions
exterior

Gracious Home for Sale — $199,000

This beautiful home, designed by well-known ___(1)___ June Morgan, is a superb piece of ___(2)___ for the money. The brick-and-wood ___(3)___ of the house needs a little work, but the inside is in excellent condition. As you walk through the rooms, you'll see that the entire ___(4)___ has a fresh coat of paint. You'll also appreciate the large ___(5)___ of the rooms. The living room alone is 20 feet by 25 feet, and there are enough shelves in the ___(6)___ to store anything you may need. Perhaps the most charming room is the dining room, with its elegant wallpaper ___(7)___. The light ___(8)___ on the ceiling are also lovely. They date back to 1935.

1. _____
2. _____
3. _____
4. _____
5. _____
6. _____
7. _____
8. _____

eWord Game
www.eduplace.com/kids/sv/

Try This CHALLENGE

Draw a quick cutaway sketch of a house. Label the *exterior*, the *interior*, the *pantry*, and two *fixtures*. Use a separate sheet of paper.

UNIT 12
Review:
Units 7–11

Unit 7

1. _____
2. _____
3. _____
4. _____
5. _____
6. _____
7. _____
8. _____
9. _____
10. _____

Unit 8

11. _____
12. _____
13. _____
14. _____
15. _____
16. _____
17. _____
18. _____
19. _____
20. _____

Unit 7		Vowel + /r/ Sounds		pages 54–59
aware	aboard	bore	⚠ warn	⚠ vary
torch	absorb	stairway	barge	perform

Spelling Strategy

/ôr/ → **or, oar, ore**   /âr/ → **are, air**   /är/ → **ar**

Context Sentences Write the word that completes each sentence.

1. When can I go _____ the ocean liner?
2. The Statue of Liberty holds a _____ in her right hand.
3. A narrow _____ led up to the tower.
4. A _____ carrying coal arrived at the port.
5. Soil will _____ the rain.

Analogies Write the word that best completes each analogy.

6. *Speak* is to *recite* as *act* is to _____.
7. *Change* is to _____ as *choose* is to *select*.
8. *Clarify* is to *confuse* as *interest* is to _____.
9. *Halt* is to *stop* as _____ is to *caution*.
10. *Awake* is to *asleep* as _____ is to *ignorant*.

Unit 8		More Vowel + /r/ Sounds		pages 60–65
twirl	worthwhile	peer	appear	⚠ pier
research	murmur	reverse	career	sturdy

Spelling Strategy

/ûr/ → **ir, ur, er, ear, or**   /îr/ → **eer, ear**

Word Clues Write the word that fits each clue.

11. to become visible
12. a walkway over water
13. a person's profession
14. valuable to do
15. a soft sound
16. what a spinning top does
17. a way to find facts
18. to look closely
19. strong and solid
20. to go the opposite way

Unit 9 — Homophones — pages 66–71

aloud	peddle	pour	berry	who's
allowed	pedal	pore	bury	whose

Spelling Strategy Remember that homophones are words that sound alike but have different spellings and meanings.

Context Paragraph Write the words that complete this paragraph.

I'm the kind of person __(21)__ always reading. Nothing makes me happier than to __(22)__ my nose in a book. I like to __(23)__ over newspaper articles. I also like to read picture books __(24)__ to little children. I wish I were __(25)__ to live at the library!

Definitions Write the word that fits each meaning.

26. to make something flow from a container
27. to travel to sell goods
28. the possessive form of *who*
29. a lever operated by a foot
30. a small fruit

Unit 10 — Compound Words — pages 72–77

uproar	headache	top-secret	light bulb	throughout
lifeguard	part-time	post office	up-to-date	awestruck

Spelling Strategy Remember that a compound word is made of two or more smaller words. A compound word may be written as one word, a hyphenated word, or separate words.

Classifying Write the word that belongs in each group.

31. sun, candle, _____
32. school, library, _____
33. current, modern, _____
34. bruise, cramp, _____
35. around, beside, _____
36. amazed, dazzled, _____
37. confusion, noise, _____
38. firefighter, nurse, _____
39. mysterious, hidden, _____
40. full-time, half-time, _____

Unit 9

21. _____
22. _____
23. _____
24. _____
25. _____
26. _____
27. _____
28. _____
29. _____
30. _____

Unit 10

31. _____
32. _____
33. _____
34. _____
35. _____
36. _____
37. _____
38. _____
39. _____
40. _____

Spelling Review

Unit 11		Final Schwa + /r/ Sounds		pages 78–83
flavor	molar	anger	senator	passenger
pillar	lunar	elevator	bitter	proper

Spelling Strategy

/ər/ → **er, or, ar**

Analogies Write the word that best completes each analogy.

41. *Doorway* is to *entrance* as _____ is to *column*.

42. *Happiness* is to _____ as *joy* is to *rage*.

43. *Tangy* is to _____ as *fragrant* is to *smelly*.

44. *Courteous* is to *polite* as *appropriate*
is to _____.

45. *Pilot* is to *aviator* as *rider* is to _____.

Word Clues Write the word that fits each clue.

46. a lawmaker

47. of the moon

48. goes from floor to floor

49. what chews food

50. added to food by spices

Unit 11

41. _____

42. _____

43. _____

44. _____

45. _____

46. _____

47. _____

48. _____

49. _____

50. _____

Challenge Words		Units 7–11		pages 54–83
stellar	motorcycle	site	cite	stomachache
tremor	external	gracious	interpret	discard

Context Sentences Write the word that completes each sentence.

51. A _____ has two wheels and an engine.

52. The _____ we felt was a small earthquake.

53. Be sure to _____ your sources in your report.

54. This skin cream is for _____ use only.

55. Where can we _____ old tires?

56. The astronomers studied the constellation for _____ events.

57. This _____ will be the location of the new school.

58. Every reader seems to _____ the poem differently.

59. The _____ host made everyone feel welcome.

60. Irene ate some unripe berries, which gave her a _____.

Challenge Words

51. _____

52. _____

53. _____

54. _____

55. _____

56. _____

57. _____

58. _____

59. _____

60. _____

Proofread a Personal Essay

Spelling and Grammar Mixed Review Use proofreading marks to correct this personal essay. Find **ten** misspelled Basic Words and **four** grammar errors from the last five units. These are **two** incorrect contractions and **two** errors in forms of the verb *be*.

Example: I *is aloud* to play my drums in the basement.
(am allowed written above "is aloud")

Proofreading Marks

¶	Indent
∧	Add
⊙	Add a period
⌐	Delete
=	Capital letter
/	Small letter

A Dream Come True

Six weeks ago, I circled a date on my calender. Every day I would stare at the date, and my heart would soor. Now that day has finally come. A majer event in my life has happened. I had my first drum lessen!

I am so happy that my teacher is Jeff Wheeler. He is a former member of a well-nown band. I do'nt mean to overdue the praise, but he may be the best drummer on erth! He's also a populer teacher, and it isn't hard to see why. His manner and voice is so kind! He showed me the proper way to grip the sticks and beat a steady pattern of quater notes. Ive begun practicing already!

My dream am to furthur my training and play with a famous band. I will stay alert for opportunities. Wouldn't it be great if my dream came true?

Write a Personal Essay

prewrite → draft → revise → proofread → publish

Write a personal essay about someone or something that is important to you.

- Use some Spelling Words from Units 7–11 in your essay.
- Proofread your work for **spelling, contractions,** and correct use of the **verb *be*.**

Tips

- Choose something you can write about with feeling.
- List some reasons for your opinion or feeling.
- Include an introduction and a conclusion.

Power Proofreading
www.eduplace.com/kids/sv/

Spelling Test Practice

Test Tip If you change an answer, erase your first answer completely.

Directions Find the phrase containing an underlined word that is <u>not</u> spelled correctly. If all the underlined words are spelled correctly, mark "All correct."

Example:
- **A** a window <u>display</u>
- **B** to sing the <u>hymn</u>
- **C** an aunt's <u>neice</u>
- **D** a <u>loyal</u> friend
- **E** All correct

Example:

Ⓐ Ⓑ ● Ⓓ Ⓔ

Answer Sheet

1. Ⓐ Ⓑ Ⓒ Ⓓ Ⓔ
2. Ⓕ Ⓖ Ⓗ Ⓙ Ⓚ
3. Ⓐ Ⓑ Ⓒ Ⓓ Ⓔ
4. Ⓕ Ⓖ Ⓗ Ⓙ Ⓚ
5. Ⓐ Ⓑ Ⓒ Ⓓ Ⓔ
6. Ⓕ Ⓖ Ⓗ Ⓙ Ⓚ
7. Ⓐ Ⓑ Ⓒ Ⓓ Ⓔ
8. Ⓕ Ⓖ Ⓗ Ⓙ Ⓚ

More Practice
Now write all the misspelled words correctly on a separate sheet of paper.

Spelling Games
www.eduplace.com/kids/sv/
Review for your test.

1.
- **A** a nightly <u>newscast</u>
- **B** to <u>direct</u> traffic
- **C** to <u>smeer</u> paint
- **D** stormy <u>weather</u>
- **E** All correct

2.
- **F** a shameful <u>coward</u>
- **G** the city <u>mayor</u>
- **H** the final <u>chapter</u>
- **J** fame and <u>glorey</u>
- **K** All correct

3.
- **A** wide <u>awake</u>
- **B** to <u>approach</u> slowly
- **C** a luxury <u>cruise</u>
- **D** <u>barefoot</u> runners
- **E** All correct

4.
- **F** to <u>perform</u> a solo
- **G** tired and <u>weery</u>
- **H** milk from the <u>dairy</u>
- **J** a <u>passenger</u> on a bus
- **K** All correct

5.
- **A** sticky <u>glue</u>
- **B** lightning and <u>thunder</u>
- **C** <u>burndt</u> logs
- **D** to wiggle and <u>squirm</u>
- **E** All correct

6.
- **F** to <u>beware</u> of danger
- **G** to fall <u>overboard</u>
- **H** a pleasant <u>stroll</u>
- **J** an airplane <u>hanger</u>
- **K** All correct

7.
- **A** to play with a <u>teamate</u>
- **B** metal <u>armor</u>
- **C** to <u>vary</u> your wardrobe
- **D** to <u>accuse</u> a thief
- **E** All correct

8.
- **F** to <u>pour</u> the lemonade
- **G** to beg someone's <u>pardon</u>
- **H** an <u>elevator</u> to the roof
- **J** <u>wheelchair</u> races
- **K** All correct

Vocabulary Test Practice

Test Tip Read every answer choice before deciding on an answer.

Directions Choose the word or group of words that means almost the same as the underlined word. Fill in the space on the answer sheet for the answer you have chosen.

Test Format Practice

Example: A <u>manor</u> is a —
    A section of a barn
    B way of acting
    C large house
    D guidebook

Example:

Ⓐ Ⓑ ● Ⓓ

Answer Sheet

1. Ⓐ Ⓑ Ⓒ Ⓓ
2. Ⓕ Ⓖ Ⓗ Ⓙ
3. Ⓐ Ⓑ Ⓒ Ⓓ
4. Ⓕ Ⓖ Ⓗ Ⓙ
5. Ⓐ Ⓑ Ⓒ Ⓓ
6. Ⓕ Ⓖ Ⓗ Ⓙ
7. Ⓐ Ⓑ Ⓒ Ⓓ
8. Ⓕ Ⓖ Ⓗ Ⓙ

1. To <u>volunteer</u> is to —
    A offer to do a job
    B dream of the future
    C be a servant
    D greet politely

2. A <u>warehouse</u> is a —
    F clothing shop
    G factory
    H storage building
    J barge full of goods

3. To <u>adore</u> is to —
    A shout
    B love
    C add to
    D confuse

4. To be <u>weary</u> is to be —
    F tired
    G angry
    H pleased
    J tall

5. To be <u>outspoken</u> is to be —
    A outdoors
    B unfair
    C heard and seen
    D blunt and frank

6. To <u>lessen</u> is to —
    F teach
    G learn
    H make smaller
    J pay close attention

7. A <u>cellar</u> is a —
    A kind of vegetable
    B part of a shirt
    C business owner
    D basement

8. To <u>release</u> is to —
    F buy
    G set free
    H look back
    J try again

PART 1 Spelling and Phonics

Read the Spelling Words and sentences.

Basic

1. bargain	*bargain*	Two apples for a nickel is a **bargain**.
2. journey	*journey*	Our **journey** takes us through a desert.
3. pattern	*pattern*	The flowered **pattern** on that shirt is lovely!
4. arrive	*arrive*	The bus should **arrive** soon.
5. object	*object*	Do you **object** to the new rules?
6. suppose	*suppose*	I **suppose** the dog is hungry again.
7. shoulder	*shoulder*	The pitcher hurt her **shoulder**.
8. permit	*permit*	Will your mom **permit** you to go camping?
9. sorrow	*sorrow*	I felt great **sorrow** when I lost my cat.
10. tunnel	*tunnel*	We drove through a long, dark **tunnel**.
11. subject	*subject*	The **subject** of my report is trains.
12. custom	*custom*	Celebrating July 4th is an American **custom**.
13. suggest	*suggest*	I **suggest** that you put on a sweater.
14. perhaps	*perhaps*	**Perhaps** we should go straight home.
15. lawyer	*lawyer*	The **lawyer** spoke quietly to the judge.
16. timber	*timber*	They sawed the tree into **timber**.
17. common	*common*	My friends and I have a lot in **common**.
18. publish	*publish*	Who will **publish** her new book?
19. burden	*burden*	That heavy backpack must be a **burden**.
20. scissors	*scissors*	Use **scissors** to cut the paper in half.

Between Double Consonants

1. _____
2. _____
3. _____
4. _____
5. _____
6. _____
7. _____
8. _____

Between Different Consonants

9. _____
10. _____
11. _____
12. _____
13. _____
14. _____
15. _____
16. _____
17. _____
18. _____
19. _____
20. _____

Review		Challenge	
21. perfect	23. narrow	26. narrate	28. attempt
22. danger	24. survive	27. mentor	29. collide
	25. valley		30. ignore

Think and Sort

Each two-syllable word has the VCCV pattern. Divide the words between the double consonants or the different consonants.

VC / CV	VC / C V
pat / tern	**bar / gain**

Write each Basic Word under the heading that shows where it is divided into syllables. Draw a line between the syllables.

Word Analysis/Phonics

Write the four Basic Words that end with a long vowel sound.

21. /ē/   **22.** /ī/   **23–24.** /ō/

Vocabulary: Classifying

Write the Basic or Review Word that belongs in each group.

25. design, arrangement, _____
26. trip, voyage, _____
27. mountain, river, _____
28. knife, clippers, _____
29. hip, knee, _____

Challenge Words

Write the Challenge Word that fits each meaning. Use your Spelling Dictionary.

30. to try to do something
31. to pay no attention to
32. to tell a story
33. to bump into something with great force
34. a wise and helpful adviser

Spelling-Meaning Connection

35–36. A good way to remember how to spell the /sh/ sound in *objection* is to think of the related word *object*. Write *objection* and *object*. Underline the letter that is the same in both but spells different consonant sounds.

Word Analysis
21. _____
22. _____
23. _____
24. _____
Classifying
25. _____
26. _____
27. _____
28. _____
29. _____
Challenge Words
30. _____
31. _____
32. _____
33. _____
34. _____
Spelling-Meaning
35. _____
36. _____

I object!

Your objection is overruled!

At Home — With a family member, take turns writing four Spelling Words on a piece of paper. Cut the syllables apart. Mix them up. The other person joins the parts to spell the words.

91

Vocabulary

1. _____
2. _____
3. _____
4. _____
5. _____
6. _____
7. _____
8. _____

Vocabulary: Analogies

You know that analogies can match synonyms and also antonyms. Another type of analogy matches a tool with its action.

Practice Write the word from the box that best completes each analogy. Use your Spelling Dictionary.

scissors	bore	squeegee	pluck
dissect	buffer	vise	pestle

1. *Wrench* is to *twist* as _____ is to *clamp*.
2. *Scythe* is to *reap* as *scalpel* is to _____.
3. *File* is to *smooth* as *tweezers* is to _____.
4. *Drill* is to _____ as *crowbar* is to *pry*.
5. *Trowel* is to *spread* as _____ is to *polish*.
6. *Mallet* is to *pound* as _____ is to *cut*.
7. *Chip* is to *chisel* as *mash* is to _____.
8. *Shovel* is to *dig* as _____ is to *wipe*.

Thesaurus

9. _____
10. _____
11. _____
12. _____
13. _____
14. _____
15. _____
16. _____

Thesaurus: Antonyms

A thesaurus lists antonyms as well as synonyms. Here are some antonyms for *sorrow*.

antonyms: joy, gladness, happiness

Practice Review pages 258–259 on how to use your Thesaurus. Then write two antonyms your Thesaurus gives for each of these words.

9–10. create **11–12.** protect **13–14.** dangerous **15–16.** funny

Proofread an Adventure Story

Spelling and Comparative Forms Use proofreading marks to correct **ten** misspelled Basic or Review Words and **two** mistakes in forms of *good* and *bad* in this part of an adventure story.

Example: It was the ~~most~~ best ~~journy~~ *journey* I've ever taken!

Some choices make perfact sense, but others can lead to dager. Our baddest choice ever was on Flint Peak. We had a permit to hike up the mountain. We should have had gooder sense and hiked right back to the valley. Instead, we entered a nerrow, dark tunel. A strong smell and a low growl greeted us. It's commen to panic at such times, and we did! As we fled, I ran into some tember. I felt a sharp pain in my sholder, but I ignored it and dove through the opening. We were lucky to servive! Purhaps I will pubblish a book about our adventure someday.

Proofreading Marks

¶	Indent
∧	Add
⊙	Add a period
⌎	Delete
≡	Capital letter
/	Small letter

Basic
bargain
journey
pattern
arrive
object
suppose
shoulder
permit
sorrow
tunnel
subject
custom
suggest
perhaps
lawyer
timber
common
publish
burden
scissors

Review
perfect
danger
narrow
survive
valley

Challenge
narrate
mentor
attempt
collide
ignore

Write an Adventure Story

prewrite → draft → revise → proofread → publish

Think of an exciting adventure, and write a brief story about it.

- Describe the events **in sequence**, and add some **exciting details.**
- Use some Spelling Words and forms of *good* and *bad*.
- Proofread for **spelling** and for correct **comparative forms**.

Power Proofreading
www.eduplace.com/kids/sv/

93

Test Tip Be sure to fill in the whole circle.

Test Format Practice

Directions Find the phrase containing an underlined word that is <u>not</u> spelled correctly. If all the underlined words are spelled correctly, mark "All correct."

Example: **A** a delicious <u>flavor</u>
B a <u>major</u> attraction
C an annoying <u>headace</u>
D a constant <u>uproar</u>
E All correct

Example:

Ⓐ Ⓑ ● Ⓓ Ⓔ

Answer Sheet

1. Ⓐ Ⓑ Ⓒ Ⓓ Ⓔ
2. Ⓙ Ⓚ Ⓛ Ⓜ Ⓝ
3. Ⓐ Ⓑ Ⓒ Ⓓ Ⓔ
4. Ⓙ Ⓚ Ⓛ Ⓜ Ⓝ
5. Ⓐ Ⓑ Ⓒ Ⓓ Ⓔ
6. Ⓙ Ⓚ Ⓛ Ⓜ Ⓝ
7. Ⓐ Ⓑ Ⓒ Ⓓ Ⓔ
8. Ⓙ Ⓚ Ⓛ Ⓜ Ⓝ

More Practice

Now write all the misspelled words correctly on a separate sheet of paper.

Spelling Games
www.eduplace.com/kids/sv/
Review for your test.

1. **A** a <u>part-time</u> worker
B a <u>bargin</u> price
C a <u>common</u> language
D loud <u>thunder</u>
E All correct

2. **J** a favorite <u>subject</u>
K a luxury <u>cruise</u>
L deep <u>sorrow</u>
M a <u>lunar</u> eclipse
N All correct

3. **A** a wire <u>hanger</u>
B a spelling <u>lesson</u>
C a long <u>journey</u>
D a <u>barefoot</u> boy
E All correct

4. **J** a brave <u>lifeguard</u>
K a stately <u>manor</u>
L an <u>outspoken</u> editor
M an ancient <u>custem</u>
N All correct

5. **A** a <u>passenger</u> zone
B a new <u>mayor</u>
C a brilliant <u>lawer</u>
D <u>proper</u> behavior
E All correct

6. **J** a nightly <u>newscast</u>
K to <u>sugest</u> a solution
L a musty <u>cellar</u>
M a <u>bitter</u> taste
N All correct

7. **A** a bicycle <u>pedal</u>
B a <u>top-secret</u> code
C the final <u>chapter</u>
D a heavy <u>burdin</u>
E All correct

8. **J** a camping <u>permet</u>
K a storm <u>alert</u>
L <u>burnt</u> toast
M a <u>steel</u> bridge
N All correct

Real-World Vocabulary

Social Studies: The Sioux Nation

All the words in the box relate to customs of the Sioux. Look up these words in your Spelling Dictionary. Then write the words to complete this history text.

Spelling Word Link
custom

myth
belief
ancestors
ceremony
culture
legends
oral
rituals

Customs of the Sioux People

Today, many Sioux are working hard to keep alive the _____(1), or way of life, of their parents and other _____(2). Through storytelling, tribal elders are passing down the _____(3) history and the language of their people. The ancient Sioux religion, or _____(4) system, centered on the Wakan Tanka, or Great Spirit. The Sioux believed that the buffalo was a gift of Wakan Tanka. In one _____(5), or story, Wakan Tanka gives healing plants to the Sioux.

To prepare for an important _____(6), such as the Sun Dance, the Sioux enter the sweat lodge to cleanse themselves. The Sioux have many special _____(7), or customs. One that is still strong in Sioux culture is listening to tribal _____(8) told by storytellers.

1. _____
2. _____
3. _____
4. _____
5. _____
6. _____
7. _____
8. _____

eWord Game
www.eduplace.com/kids/sv/

Try This CHALLENGE

Word Clues Write the word that fits each clue.

9. These are members of your family who lived many years ago.

10. This is a formal celebration, like a graduation or a marriage.

11. These are things you do the same way all the time.

12. These are stories that have been handed down through the years and may be true.

9. _____
10. _____
11. _____
12. _____

Read the Spelling Words and sentences.

Basic

1. human	*human*	Food and shelter are **human** needs.
2. exact	*exact*	You need **exact** change for the bus.
3. award	*award*	Paco received an **award** for attendance.
4. behave	*behave*	Is your puppy learning to **behave**?
5. credit	*credit*	I give her **credit** for doing the work.
6. basic	*basic*	Addition is a **basic** skill in math.
7. vivid	*vivid*	What a **vivid** sunset this is!
8. evil	*evil*	Superheroes battle **evil** characters.
9. modern	*modern*	**Modern** cars use computer technology.
10. nation	*nation*	Each **nation** has its own flag.
11. robot	*robot*	What tasks can that **robot** do?
12. panic	*panic*	Do not **panic** when the alarm sounds.
13. select	*select*	She will **select** a movie for tonight.
14. cousin	*cousin*	My **cousin** is my uncle's son.
15. item	*item*	I read a news **item** about a lazy lion.
16. police	*police*	The **police** fight crime.
17. prefer	*prefer*	Do you **prefer** vanilla or strawberry?
18. menu	*menu*	Order lunch from the **menu**.
19. novel	*novel*	I checked a new **novel** out of the library.
20. deserve	*deserve*	Did the gymnast **deserve** a gold medal?

Review
21. figure
22. total
23. model
24. equal
25. amaze

Challenge
26. autumn
27. nuisance
28. logic
29. column
30. laser

After the Consonant

1. _____
2. _____
3. _____
4. _____
5. _____
6. _____
7. _____
8. _____

Before the Consonant

9. _____
10. _____
11. _____
12. _____
13. _____
14. _____
15. _____
16. _____
17. _____
18. _____
19. _____
20. _____

Think and Sort

Divide a VCV word into syllables before or after the consonant. Pay attention to the spelling of the unstressed syllable.

VC / V
cred / it   viv / id

V / CV
hu / man   a / ward

Write each Basic Word under the heading that tells where the word is divided. Use your Spelling Dictionary to check your work.

Word Analysis/Phonics

21–23. Write the three Basic Words that have the /ā/ sound in either syllable.

Vocabulary: Synonyms

Write the Basic or Review Word that is a synonym for each underlined word. Use your Spelling Dictionary.

24. the <u>precise</u> amount

25. <u>up-to-date</u> furniture

26. to <u>astound</u> the audience

27. a first-place <u>prize</u>

28. to <u>choose</u> from a list

29. the <u>sum</u> of two numbers

Challenge Words

Write Challenge Words to complete the paragraph. Use your Spelling Dictionary.

Every ____(30)____, students groan about getting up for school. At first, the alarm clock is an unbearable ____(31)____, but slowly students begin to arise more willingly. They see the ____(32)____ in studying to gain knowledge. Each ____(33)____ of numbers becomes neater, each paragraph smoother. Now students look forward to special activities, such as using a ____(34)____ on a science field trip.

Spelling-Meaning Connection

35–36. The people of a *nation* share a *nationality* and feel *national* pride. The words *nation, nationality,* and *national* are related in spelling and meaning. Write *nationality*. Then write the Basic Word that is in it.

nation
national
nationality

Word Analysis

21. _____

22. _____

23. _____

Synonyms

24. _____

25. _____

26. _____

27. _____

28. _____

29. _____

Challenge Words

30. _____

31. _____

32. _____

33. _____

34. _____

Spelling-Meaning

35. _____

36. _____

At Home With a family member, take turns writing three Spelling Words on a piece of paper. Cut all the letters apart and mix them up. The other person joins the letters to spell the words.

97

Word Structure: The Word Root *cred*

Practice Each word in the box contains the Latin word root *cred*, meaning "believe" or "trust." Write the word that matches each definition. Use your Spelling Dictionary.

credit	credentials	incredible	creditor	credulity
credo	creditable	incredulous	credible	credence

1. documents proving a person's qualifications
2. worthy of confidence; believable
3. a statement of principles or beliefs
4. disbelieving, doubtful
5. someone to whom money is owed
6. a disposition to believe too easily
7. hard to believe; unbelievable
8. an arrangement to buy now and pay later
9. deserving of praise
10. acceptance as true; belief

Dictionary: Homographs

Homographs are words that are spelled alike but have different meanings and histories. They may also be pronounced differently. Homographs are listed separately in a dictionary.

nov•el[1] (nŏv´ əl) *adj.* Very new, unusual, or different.
nov•el[2] (nŏv´ əl) *n., pl.* **novels** A made-up story that is long enough to fill a book.

Practice Write *novel*[1], *novel*[2], *object*[1], or *object*[2] to complete each sentence. Use your Spelling Dictionary.

11. Linking owners and pets electronically is a _____ concept.
12. Do you _____ to my playing music while you're reading?
13. What a beautiful glass _____ that is on the shelf!
14. Did you read that new science fiction _____?
15. My _____ in soccer is to play well in every game.

Word Structure
1. _____
2. _____
3. _____
4. _____
5. _____
6. _____
7. _____
8. _____
9. _____
10. _____

Dictionary
11. _____
12. _____
13. _____
14. _____
15. _____

Proofread a Magazine Article

Spelling and Using *more* and *most* Use proofreading marks to correct **eight** misspelled Basic or Review Words and **two** mistakes in using *more* and *most* in this magazine article.

Example: What is the ~~more~~ important ~~aword~~ a chef can win?
(most) *(award)*

ARE CHEFS ARTISTS?

A painter is an artist who creates vivved artwork on a canvas. It may not be the more exact image of the model, but it expresses the painter's feelings. A sculptor works with a block of stone. From this baisic shape, the sculptor chisels a humen figer that can become a museum piece.

What about chefs? Do they disserv to be called artists? Would they prefer to be? I think they would. A chef must create a menew to suit every diner. The food must amaze the eye as well as the tongue. The most exotic the food is, the more beautiful it must look on the plate. Every itum must contribute to this edible work of art. As you can see, chefs are artists too!

Proofreading Marks

¶	Indent
∧	Add
⊙	Add a period
⌿	Delete
=	Capital letter
/	Small letter

Basic
human
exact
award
behave
credit
basic
vivid
evil
modern
nation
robot
panic
select
cousin
item
police
prefer
menu
novel
deserve

Review
figure
total
model
equal
amaze

Challenge
autumn
nuisance
logic
column
laser

Write a Magazine Article

prewrite → draft → revise → proofread → publish

Write a magazine article about someone you think is an artist.

- Tell **who, what,** and **why** about your artist.
- Use some Spelling Words and include the words *more* and *most*.
- Proofread for **spelling** and the correct use of *more* and *most*.

Power Proofreading
www.eduplace.com/kids/sv/

PART 4 Spelling Test Practice

Test Tip Watch the time. Don't spend too much time on one question.

Directions Read the sentences in each group. Decide if one of the underlined words has a spelling mistake or if there is *No mistake*. Fill in the space for your answer choice.

Example: **A** Our <u>natien</u> elects a president every four years.
      B Do you know the <u>exact</u> time?
      C You <u>deserve</u> a rest now.
      D No mistake

Example:

● Ⓑ Ⓒ Ⓓ

Answer Sheet

1. Ⓐ Ⓑ Ⓒ Ⓓ
2. Ⓕ Ⓖ Ⓗ Ⓙ
3. Ⓐ Ⓑ Ⓒ Ⓓ
4. Ⓕ Ⓖ Ⓗ Ⓙ
5. Ⓐ Ⓑ Ⓒ Ⓓ
6. Ⓕ Ⓖ Ⓗ Ⓙ
7. Ⓐ Ⓑ Ⓒ Ⓓ
8. Ⓕ Ⓖ Ⓗ Ⓙ

More Practice

Now write all the misspelled words correctly on a separate sheet of paper.

Spelling Games
www.eduplace.com/kids/sv/
Review for your test.

1. **A** What is your favorite kind of <u>novel</u>?
  B The <u>pollice</u> arrived five minutes later.
  C I got a fishing <u>permit</u>.
  D No mistake

2. **F** A <u>lawyer</u> took our case.
  G The news <u>item</u> mentioned the lost dog.
  H I bought a <u>modle</u> car.
  J No mistake

3. **A** The magician will <u>amaze</u> you with his tricks.
  B The restaurant changes its <u>menu</u> weekly.
  C The <u>robut</u> can rake leaves.
  D No mistake

4. **F** My <u>cuzzin</u> will visit during the summer.
  G Our <u>journey</u> was long.
  H My favorite <u>subject</u> is art.
  J No mistake

5. **A** The movie was a classic tale of good and <u>evel</u>.
  B My <u>shoulder</u> aches from carrying my books.
  C Can you <u>figure</u> this out?
  D No mistake

6. **F** Red is a <u>vivid</u> color.
  G These <u>modern</u> gadgets make life easier.
  H The <u>scissors</u> are dull.
  J No mistake

7. **A** I got extra <u>credit</u> for my work.
  B Try not to <u>panik</u> in a fire.
  C My friend and I have a lot in <u>common</u>.
  D No mistake

8. **F** The new <u>tunnel</u> is open.
  G Please <u>behave</u> yourself in the theater.
  H We believe in <u>equel</u> justice for all.
  J No mistake

Real-World Vocabulary

Science: The Balance of Nature

All the words in the box relate to how human actions affect the environment. Look up these words in your Spelling Dictionary. Write the words to complete this part of a trail guide.

Spelling Word Link
human

beneficial
consequences
detrimental
ecosystem
impact
recovery
organism
nourish

Disturbing the Balance in a Forest

The ___(1)___ of a forest is the community of living and nonliving things in it. Even minor changes can have a huge ___(2)___ on the life of the forest. A ___(3)___ change occurs when humans cut down large numbers of trees. This has immediate ___(4)___ for many living things. Trees no longer produce food for the simplest kind of ___(5)___ in the forest, bacteria. These helpful bacteria ___(6)___ the plants that are consumed by small animals, which are in turn eaten by larger animals. Planting new trees will restore the ___(7)___ bacteria and the balance of the forest, but it takes many years for this ___(8)___ to happen.

1. _____
2. _____
3. _____
4. _____
5. _____
6. _____
7. _____
8. _____

eWord Game
www.eduplace.com/kids/sv/

Try This CHALLENGE

Clue Match Write a word from the box to match each clue.

9. having a positive effect
10. having a negative effect
11. a name for a living thing
12. what you do when you give a living thing good food

9. _____
10. _____
11. _____
12. _____

VC/CCV Pattern

1. _____
2. _____
3. _____
4. _____
5. _____
6. _____
7. _____
8. _____
9. _____
10. _____
11. _____
12. _____
13. _____
14. _____
15. _____
16. _____

VCC/CV Pattern

17. _____
18. _____
19. _____
20. _____

Read the Spelling Words and sentences.

Basic

1.	conflict	*conflict*	The Civil War was a terrible **conflict**.
2.	orphan	*orphan*	A lion cub without parents is an **orphan**.
3.	instant	*instant*	Just add water to make **instant** pudding.
4.	complex	*complex*	The **complex** equation had many parts.
5.	simply	*simply*	Describe the event **simply** and clearly.
6.	burglar	*burglar*	The **burglar** stole jewelry and clothing.
7.	laundry	*laundry*	Is Monday your day to wash the **laundry**?
8.	laughter	*laughter*	The baby's **laughter** made everyone smile.
9.	employ	*employ*	The new diner will **employ** four cooks.
10.	anchor	*anchor*	The ship dropped its **anchor** in the bay.
11.	merchant	*merchant*	The **merchant** sold his goods at the fair.
12.	improve	*improve*	Did your score **improve** this time?
13.	arctic	*arctic*	Wear a warm coat in this **arctic** weather.
14.	mischief	*mischief*	What **mischief** those kittens cause!
15.	freckles	*freckles*	Brett has **freckles** on his arms.
16.	purchase	*purchase*	Did you **purchase** your suit at this shop?
17.	dolphin	*dolphin*	The **dolphin** swam up to the boat.
18.	partner	*partner*	Share the book with your **partner**.
19.	complain	*complain*	Did you **complain** about the noise?
20.	tremble	*tremble*	The leaves **tremble** in the breeze.

Review
21. hundred
22. example
23. although
24. supply
25. empty

Challenge
26. anthem
27. illustrate
28. function
29. conscience
30. apostrophe

Think and Sort

Two-syllable words with the VCCCV pattern have two consonants that spell one sound or that form a cluster. Divide a VCCCV word into syllables before or after those consonants.

VC / CCV: **dol/phin**   VCC / CV: **pa<u>r</u>t/ner**

Write each Basic Word under the correct heading. Draw a line between the syllables. Check your work in your Spelling Dictionary.

Word Analysis/Phonics

21–24. Write the four Basic Words that contain the consonant cluster *pl*.

Vocabulary: Classifying

Write the Basic or Review Word that belongs in each group.

25. giggles, chuckles, _____

26. rudder, sail, _____

27. million, thousand, _____

28. frigid, freezing, _____

29. prank, trick, _____

Challenge Words

Write the Challenge Word that fits each meaning. Use your Spelling Dictionary.

30. a person's feelings about right and wrong

31. a mark that replaces one or more letters in a word

32. a song of loyalty

33. the correct purpose or use

34. to create images that help to explain something

Spelling-Meaning Connection

35–36. Can you see the word *complex* in *complexity*? The *-ity* suffix turns the adjective *complex* into a noun. Write *complexity*. Then write the Basic Word that is related in spelling and meaning.

complex
complexity

Word Analysis

21. _____

22. _____

23. _____

24. _____

Classifying

25. _____

26. _____

27. _____

28. _____

29. _____

Challenge Words

30. _____

31. _____

32. _____

33. _____

34. _____

Spelling-Meaning

35. _____

36. _____

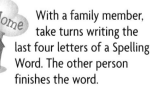

At Home With a family member, take turns writing the last four letters of a Spelling Word. The other person finishes the word.

Vocabulary

1. _____
2. _____
3. _____
4. _____
5. _____
6. _____

Vocabulary: Words About Time

Practice 1–6. Order the words in the box from least to most time expressed by each word. The sentences will give you clues to the meaning of each word. Use your Spelling Dictionary.

instant	decade	millennium
eternity	eon	fortnight

It has been an <u>eon</u> since dinosaurs walked the earth.

He can drive across the country in a <u>fortnight</u>.

We haven't seen a hurricane in more than a <u>decade</u>.

Our dog can zip across the yard in an <u>instant</u>.

<u>Eternity</u> is an infinite amount of time.

People have used paper money for more than a <u>millennium</u>.

Thesaurus

Positive

7. _____
8. _____
9. _____

Neutral

10. _____
11. _____
12. _____

Negative

13. _____
14. _____
15. _____

Thesaurus: Connotations

The feelings and associations that a word suggests are called **connotations**. They can be positive, neutral, or negative.

Practice 7–15. Look up *complain, laugh,* and *candid* in your Thesaurus. Then write each subentry below under the heading *Positive, Neutral,* or *Negative* to describe its connotation.

object	whine	protest
frank	sincere	blunt
guffaw	snicker	chuckle

Proofread a Newspaper Story

Spelling and Proper Adjectives Use proofreading marks to correct **ten** misspelled Basic or Review Words and **two** mistakes in capitalizing proper adjectives in this newspaper story.

Example: Mr. Cruz will ~~perchase~~ *purchase* a chinese vase.

Surprised Resident Foils Thief

Diego Cruz, a local merchant, helped nab a burgler Monday. Cruz, who sells asian pottery, came home from his suply firm to find a window open. He called 911. Then, allthough he did not want conflic, he went inside. An instant later a thief ran out. His hands were emty. Later, Cruz found a sack in the loundry. It held jewelry and a mexican silver dolfin. A police officer interviewed Cruz while her partener tracked down a suspect. Cruz's voice began to trembul. "He's the thief!" he said. "I know him by his frekuls!"

Proofreading Marks

¶	Indent
∧	Add
⊙	Add a period
℘	Delete
≡	Capital letter
/	Small letter

Basic
conflict
orphan
instant
complex
simply
burglar
laundry
laughter
employ
anchor
merchant
improve
arctic
mischief
freckles
purchase
dolphin
partner
complain
tremble

Review
hundred
example
although
supply
empty

Challenge
anthem
illustrate
function
conscience
apostrophe

Write a Newspaper Story

prewrite → draft → revise → proofread → publish

Write a newspaper story about an exciting event.

- Tell **who, what, where, when,** and **why** about the event.
- Use some Spelling Words and some proper adjectives.
- Proofread your work for **spelling** and **capitalization**.

Test Tip Eliminate answer choices that you know are incorrect.

Test Format Practice

Directions: Choose the word that is spelled correctly and best completes the sentence.

Example: The new movie is _____ wonderful.

    A simply
    B simbly
    C simpley
    D simpel

Example:

● Ⓑ Ⓒ Ⓓ

Answer Sheet

1. Ⓐ Ⓑ Ⓒ Ⓓ
2. Ⓕ Ⓖ Ⓗ Ⓙ
3. Ⓐ Ⓑ Ⓒ Ⓓ
4. Ⓕ Ⓖ Ⓗ Ⓙ
5. Ⓐ Ⓑ Ⓒ Ⓓ
6. Ⓕ Ⓖ Ⓗ Ⓙ

1. We bought a basket from the straw _____.
    A murchant
    B merchent
    C murechant
    D merchant

2. The cub is an _____ because its mother died.
    F orphan
    G oarfan
    H orphen
    J ophan

3. Please give me an _____ of your work.
    A exsample
    B egsample
    C example
    D exampel

4. Our smiles soon turned to _____.
    F laffter
    G laughter
    H laugher
    J laghter

5. I need to _____ a new winter coat.
    A perchase
    B purchase
    C purchess
    D perchuss

6. She wants to _____ her math grades.
    F inprove
    G improove
    H impove
    J improve

More Practice

Now write each correctly spelled word on a sheet of paper.

Spelling Games
www.eduplace.com/kids/sv/
Review for your test.

Real-World Vocabulary

Social Studies: Alaska's Arctic Region

All the words in the box have to do with life in the Arctic. Look up these words in your Spelling Dictionary. Write the words to complete this travel ad.

Spelling Word Link

arctic

caribou
climate
frigid
midnight sun
kayak
permafrost
tundra
whiteout

Visit Alaska's Arctic Region

The best time to visit Alaska is late spring through summer! Gone are the ___(1)___ winds and subzero temperatures of winter. The ___(2)___ changes drastically as the weather heats up. No storm or ___(3)___ threatens the warm days. During summer in the land of the ___(4)___, the sun shines for about twenty hours a day! Grasses and mosses sprout through the topsoil, despite the ___(5)___ below them. They bring color to the treeless ___(6)___.

Watch a herd of ___(7)___ as it heads north for summer grazing. Visit an Inuit village, or paddle a ___(8)___ along the coastline. A vacation in Alaska is one you'll never forget!

1. _____
2. _____
3. _____
4. _____
5. _____
6. _____
7. _____
8. _____

eWord Game
www.eduplace.com/kids/sv/

Try This CHALLENGE

Yes or No? Write *yes* or *no* to answer each question.

9. Does permafrost ever thaw?
10. Are caribou related to deer?
11. Is the tundra covered with trees?
12. Can you use a kayak on a highway?

9. _____
10. _____
11. _____
12. _____

Read the Spelling Words and sentences.

Basic

1. actual	*actual*	My story is based on an **actual** event.
2. cruel	*cruel*	It is **cruel** to tease an animal.
3. patriot	*patriot*	A **patriot** is loyal to his or her country.
4. diet	*diet*	Fresh fruit should be part of any **diet**.
5. museum	*museum*	Did you see the artwork at the **museum**?
6. casual	*casual*	Shorts and sandals are **casual** clothing.
7. ruin	*ruin*	Hungry deer can **ruin** a garden.
8. pioneer	*pioneer*	The first **pioneer** settled here in 1841.
9. trial	*trial*	All suspects have the right to a fair **trial**.
10. visual	*visual*	A map is a **visual** layout of a place.
11. realize	*realize*	Didn't you **realize** the test was today?
12. create	*create*	Clear the brush to **create** a bike trail.
13. riot	*riot*	The crowd stayed calm and did not **riot**.
14. genuine	*genuine*	Ben has a **genuine** buffalo-head nickel.
15. area	*area*	The park has a playground **area**.
16. annual	*annual*	Every May we hold our **annual** reunion.
17. audio	*audio*	The radio is one kind of **audio** device.
18. dial	*dial*	Take my phone and **dial** the number.
19. theater	*theater*	Is that movie playing at a **theater** now?
20. violet	*violet*	Mix red and blue paint to make **violet**.

Review
21. video
22. science
23. February
24. period
25. usual

Challenge
26. diagnose
27. media
28. appreciate
29. society
30. prior

Two Syllables

1. _____
2. _____
3. _____
4. _____
5. _____
6. _____
7. _____

Three Syllables

8. _____
9. _____
10. _____
11. _____
12. _____
13. _____
14. _____
15. _____
16. _____
17. _____
18. _____
19. _____
20. _____

Think and Sort

In the VV syllable pattern, two vowels appear together and spell two vowel sounds. To find the syllables, divide between the vowels.

V/V: **ru / in**   V/V: **tri / al**   V/V: **ar•e / a**

Write each Basic Word under the heading that tells how many syllables the word has. Draw a line between the two vowels in each VV syllable pattern. Check your work in your Spelling Dictionary.

Word Analysis/Phonics

21–26. Write the six Basic Words that have the / ī / sound in the first syllable.

Vocabulary: Analogies

Write Basic or Review Words to complete these analogies. Use your Spelling Dictionary.

27. *Make* is to _____ as *gather* is to *harvest*.

28. *Slothful* is to *energetic* as _____ is to *kindly*.

29. *Sturdy* is to *durable* as *authentic* is to _____.

Challenge Words

Write the Challenge Word that best fits each clue. Use your Spelling Dictionary.

30. a synonym for *previous*

31. forms of mass communication

32. a group with something in common

33. something a doctor does

34. to recognize the value of something

Spelling-Meaning Connection

35–36. How can you remember how to spell the /ə/ sound in the last syllable of *patriot*? Think of the /ŏ/ sound in the related word *patriotic*. Write *patriot* and *patriotic*. Then underline the vowel in *patriotic* that has a different sound in *patriot*.

patriot
patriotic

Word Analysis

21. _____

22. _____

23. _____

24. _____

25. _____

26. _____

Analogies

27. _____

28. _____

29. _____

Challenge Words

30. _____

31. _____

32. _____

33. _____

34. _____

Spelling-Meaning

35. _____

36. _____

At Home With a family member, take turns writing four Spelling Words on a piece of paper. Cut the syllables apart. Mix them up. The other person puts the parts together to spell the words.

109

Word Structure

1. _____
2. _____
3. _____
4. _____
5. _____
6. _____
7. _____
8. _____

Word Structure: The Word Root *vis/vid*

Practice All the words in the box contain the word root *vis* or *vid* ("to see"). Write the word that matches each description. Use your Spelling Dictionary.

visual	visionary	improvise	revise
supervise	videotape	television	vista

1. to direct or watch over a performance or work
2. a person who imagines future possibilities
3. device that displays images on a screen
4. a view into the distance
5. to make changes in written work
6. to invent or perform on the spot
7. material for recording visual images of live action
8. having to do with the sense of sight or a mental image

Thesaurus

9. _____
10. _____
11. _____
12. _____
13. _____
14. _____

Thesaurus: Exact Words for *create*

Why is *invent* a better word than *create* in this sentence?

Ian wants to <u>invent</u> a tree-climbing robot.

Invent tells you that the robot will be the first of its kind. A thesaurus helps you find exact words for the meaning you want.

Practice Read the entry for *create* in your Thesaurus. Then write the word from the box that best replaces *create* in each sentence.

establish	design	invent	cause	manufacture	construct

9. Thelton will <u>create</u> a layout for the new school garden.
10. It took Thomas Edison many tries to <u>create</u> a functional light bulb.
11. Regina's dogs often <u>create</u> a disturbance at night.
12. The citizens voted to <u>create</u> a new city.
13. Those factories <u>create</u> toys and games of all kinds.
14. This spider can <u>create</u> a gigantic web in a short time.

Proofread an Opinion Letter

Spelling and Demonstrative Adjectives Use proofreading marks to correct **ten** misspelled Basic or Review Words and **two** mistakes in the use of *this*, *that*, and *those* in this part of an opinion letter.

Example: My widdeo shows what is wrong with those plan.

Dear Councilman Morales:

I strongly oppose the city's plan to build a shopping center near the theather and the art museam next Febuary. This center will ruen the visual appeal of a green airea where people enjoy cazual walks. Please relize that these plan will creeate too much traffic. Instead of trees and violet flowers, the block will be filled with buildings, cement, and air pollution. There has already been an anual increase in traffic over this past five-year peroid. A shopping center will only make this problems worse.

Basic
actual
cruel
patriot
diet
museum
casual
ruin
pioneer
trial
visual
realize
create
riot
genuine
area
annual
audio
dial
theater
violet

Review
video
science
February
period
usual

Challenge
diagnose
media
appreciate
society
prior

Write an Opinion Letter

prewrite ➔ draft ➔ revise ➔ proofread ➔ publish

Write a letter to someone who can help with a special project for your community.

- **Describe** the project and give **reasons** why it is worthwhile.
- Use some Spelling Words and the adjectives *this*, *that*, and *those*.
- Proofread your work for **spelling** and the correct use of ***this, that,*** and ***those.***

Power Proofreading

Test Tip Avoid making stray marks on your paper.

Directions This test will show how well you can spell.

- Many of the questions in this test have spelling mistakes. Some do not have any mistakes at all.
- Look for mistakes in spelling.
- If there is a mistake, fill in the answer space on your answer sheet that has the same letter as the **line** with the mistake.
- If there is no mistake, fill in the last answer space.

Example:

Ⓐ ● Ⓒ Ⓓ Ⓔ

Answer Sheet

1. Ⓐ Ⓑ Ⓒ Ⓓ Ⓔ
2. Ⓙ Ⓚ Ⓛ Ⓜ Ⓝ
3. Ⓐ Ⓑ Ⓒ Ⓓ Ⓔ
4. Ⓙ Ⓚ Ⓛ Ⓜ Ⓝ
5. Ⓐ Ⓑ Ⓒ Ⓓ Ⓔ
6. Ⓙ Ⓚ Ⓛ Ⓜ Ⓝ
7. Ⓐ Ⓑ Ⓒ Ⓓ Ⓔ
8. Ⓙ Ⓚ Ⓛ Ⓜ Ⓝ

Example:
- **A** cruel
- **B** dile
- **C** journey
- **D** museum
- **E** *(No mistakes)*

1.
- **A** period
- **B** realize
- **C** riot
- **D** actuall
- **E** *(No mistakes)*

2.
- **J** area
- **K** pionear
- **L** ruin
- **M** trial
- **N** *(No mistakes)*

3.
- **A** audeo
- **B** human
- **C** equal
- **D** visual
- **E** *(No mistakes)*

4.
- **J** casual
- **K** genuine
- **L** theater
- **M** violet
- **N** *(No mistakes)*

5.
- **A** diet
- **B** annual
- **C** sience
- **D** dolphin
- **E** *(No mistakes)*

6.
- **J** mischief
- **K** vivid
- **L** vedio
- **M** modern
- **N** *(No mistakes)*

7.
- **A** complain
- **B** publish
- **C** suggest
- **D** Febuary
- **E** *(No mistakes)*

8.
- **J** usal
- **K** simply
- **L** basic
- **M** instant
- **N** *(No mistakes)*

More Practice

Now write all the misspelled words correctly on a separate sheet of paper.

Spelling Games
www.eduplace.com/kids/sv/
Review for your test.

Real-World Vocabulary

Art: The Color Wheel

All the words in the box relate to color. Look up these words in your Spelling Dictionary. Write the words to complete the diagram and the paragraph.

Spelling Word Link
violet

complementary
primary
spectrum
hues
vermilion
aquamarine
indigo
apricot

red-violet, or magenta

red

violet

red-orange, or ___(3)___

blue-violet, or ___(1)___

orange

blue

yellow-orange, or ___(4)___

blue-green, or ___(2)___

yellow

green

yellow-green, or chartreuse

This color wheel shows a ___(5)___ of twelve colors, or ___(6)___. The three ___(7)___ colors are red, yellow, and blue. All the other colors are mixtures of red, yellow, and blue. Any two colors directly across from each other on the wheel are ___(8)___ colors. They contrast sharply and make each other stand out. Any three colors next to each other on the wheel go well together.

1. _____
2. _____
3. _____
4. _____
5. _____
6. _____
7. _____
8. _____

 eWord Game
www.eduplace.com/kids/sv/

Try This CHALLENGE

Who Am I? Write the word that best answers each riddle.

9. I mean the same as *colors*.

10. I am a mixture of red and orange.

11. I am a mixture of blue and green.

12. I describe colors opposite each other on the color wheel.

9. _____
10. _____
11. _____
12. _____

113

PART 1 Spelling and Phonics

el Pattern

1. _____
2. _____
3. _____
4. _____
5. _____

al Pattern

6. _____
7. _____
8. _____
9. _____
10. _____

le Pattern

11. _____
12. _____
13. _____
14. _____
15. _____
16. _____
17. _____
18. _____

Other Pattern

19. _____
20. _____

Read the Spelling Words and sentences.

Basic

1.	central	*central*	City Hall is in the **central** part of town.
2.	whistle	*whistle*	My sisters **whistle** to call our dog.
3.	label	*label*	The **label** shows the size of the shirt.
4.	puzzle	*puzzle*	This **puzzle** has five hundred pieces.
5.	legal	*legal*	Lawyers work within the **legal** system.
6.	angle	*angle*	Bend this wire so it forms a right **angle**.
7.	normal	*normal*	What is a **normal** temperature for spring?
8.	needle	*needle*	You need a **needle** and thread to sew.
9.	angel	*angel*	The **angel** in the painting had huge wings.
ⓘ 10.	pupil	*pupil*	The **pupil** listened to the teacher.
11.	struggle	*struggle*	We won, but only after a long **struggle**.
12.	level	*level*	The skating rink was smooth and **level**.
13.	local	*local*	I walk to our **local** bakery every day.
14.	bicycle	*bicycle*	Mike rode his **bicycle** to the picnic.
15.	channel	*channel*	The boat sailed out into the **channel**.
16.	global	*global*	Many nations joined the **global** effort.
17.	stumble	*stumble*	You may **stumble** on a dark, rocky path.
18.	quarrel	*quarrel*	Stop your **quarrel** and shake hands!
19.	article	*article*	We found the lost **article** of clothing.
ⓘ 20.	fossil	*fossil*	Every dinosaur **fossil** is very old.

Review	23. special	**Challenge**	28. mineral
21. title	24. trouble	26. identical	29. colonel
22. nickel	25. simple	27. vehicle	30. artificial

Think and Sort

Each word ends with the final /l/ or /əl/ sounds. These sounds may be spelled *el*, *al*, and *le*.

lab**el**	cent**ral**	whist**le**

ⓘ How are the final /əl/ sounds spelled in the Memory Words?

Write each Basic Word under the spelling of its final /l/ or /əl/ sounds.

Word Analysis/Phonics

21. Write the Basic Word that has the /j/ sound spelled *g*.

22–23. Write the Basic Words that have the /s/ sound spelled *c*.

Vocabulary: Classifying

Write the Basic or Review Word that belongs in each category.
Use your Spelling Dictionary.

24. ancient, bone, _____

25. quarter, penny, _____

26. strait, canal, _____

27. argue, fight, _____

28. mystery, problem, _____

29. international, worldwide, _____

Challenge Words

Write Challenge Words to complete the paragraph. Use your
Spelling Dictionary.

The officer, a ___(30)___, stepped out of the limousine and onto a
lengthy carpet of ___(31)___ turf. Guards on both sides of the walkway
performed ___(32)___ salutes as the old soldier exited the ___(33)___.
The sun glinted on the thick handle of his cane, which appeared to
be carved from a green ___(34)___ such as jade.

Spelling-Meaning Connection

35–36. How can you remember how to spell the /ə/ sound in *legal*?
Think of the /ă/ sound in the related word *legality*. Write
legal and *legality*. Underline the letter that has the /ə/ sound
in one word and the /ă/ sound in the other word.

legal

legality

Word Analysis	
21.	
22.	
23.	
Classifying	
24.	
25.	
26.	
27.	
28.	
29.	
Challenge Words	
30.	
31.	
32.	
33.	
34.	
Spelling-Meaning	
35.	
36.	

At Home With a family member, take turns writing the first three letters of a Spelling Word. The other person finishes the word.

115

Word Structure

1. _____
2. _____
3. _____
4. _____
5. _____
6. _____
7. _____
8. _____

Word Structure: Word Family for *local*

The word *local* comes from the Latin word *locus*, or "place."

Practice Write the word from the box that matches each definition. Use your Spelling Dictionary.

local	dislocate	locate	allocate
localize	locals	locale	relocate

1. people from a particular place
2. the setting of a particular event
3. to find the position of something
4. to move or force out of position
5. to set aside for a purpose
6. to limit to a nearby area
7. related to a limited area
8. to move to a new place

Dictionary

9. _____

_____

10. _____

_____

11. _____

_____

12. _____

_____

13. _____

_____

14. _____

_____

Dictionary: Idioms

An **idiom** is a phrase that has a meaning different from the meaning of each separate word. To find an idiom in a dictionary, look up the entry for a main word in the idiom.

needle (nēd´ l) *n., pl.* **needles** A small, slender sewing tool made of polished steel, pointed at one end and having an eye at the other through which a length of thread is passed and held.
◇ *Idiom* **on pins and needles.** In a state of anxiety; nervous.

Practice Write the idiom from the box that best completes each sentence. Use your Spelling Dictionary.

blew the whistle	whistling in the dark	wet my whistle
my level best	on pins and needles	on the level

9. That glass of lemonade really _____.
10. We knew we couldn't win the race and were just _____.
11. An employee _____ on the dangerous working conditions.
12. I will do _____ to get to the game on time.
13. Is that story about finding buried treasure really _____?
14. While her cats were missing, Lin spent the whole time _____.

PART 3 Spelling and Writing

✏ **Proofread a Mystery Story**

Spelling and Double Negatives Use proofreading marks to correct **ten** misspelled Basic or Review Words and **two** double negatives in this part of a mystery story.

Example: I didn't have no cause to ~~quarrle~~ *quarrel* with the police.

The missing artical was a speciel statue made of nickle. The locle police said it was kept in an old shed in a box with a bicycle on the lable. This case would be simpel to solve!

Without hardly trying, I managed to stumbel upon a rundown toolshed. Was I about to solve the puzzle? The rusty old door didn't give me no troubel. I had barely begun to struggal when it flew open. In the dim light, I saw boxes stacked at every possible angal. I would have to work fast.

Proofreading Marks

¶	Indent
∧	Add
⊙	Add a period
✗	Delete
≡	Capital letter
∕	Small letter

Basic
central
whistle
label
puzzle
legal
angle
normal
needle
angel
pupil
struggle
level
local
bicycle
channel
global
stumble
quarrel
article
fossil

Review
title
nickel
special
trouble
simple

Challenge
identical
vehicle
mineral
colonel
artificial

✏ **Write a Mystery Story**

prewrite → draft → revise → proofread → publish

Write a brief mystery story about a missing object.

- Try to create a **feeling of suspense** as you describe the events.
- Use some Spelling Words.
- Proofread your work for **spelling** and **double negatives.**

Power Proofreading
www.eduplace.com/kids/sv/

117

✓ **Test Tip** Read every answer choice before deciding on an answer.

Test Format Practice

Directions For Numbers 1 through 8, find the phrase containing an underlined word that is <u>not</u> spelled correctly. If all the underlined words are spelled correctly, mark "All correct."

Example: **A** the <u>central</u> bus station
B important <u>legul</u> papers
C a friendly <u>nation</u>
D a <u>level</u> section of land
E All correct

Example:

Ⓐ ● Ⓒ Ⓓ Ⓔ

Answer Sheet

1. Ⓐ Ⓑ Ⓒ Ⓓ Ⓔ
2. Ⓕ Ⓖ Ⓗ Ⓙ Ⓚ
3. Ⓐ Ⓑ Ⓒ Ⓓ Ⓔ
4. Ⓕ Ⓖ Ⓗ Ⓙ Ⓚ
5. Ⓐ Ⓑ Ⓒ Ⓓ Ⓔ
6. Ⓕ Ⓖ Ⓗ Ⓙ Ⓚ
7. Ⓐ Ⓑ Ⓒ Ⓓ Ⓔ
8. Ⓕ Ⓖ Ⓗ Ⓙ Ⓚ

1. A a <u>pupal</u> in school
   B an <u>angel</u> food cake
   C a friendly <u>nation</u>
   D a crossword <u>puzzle</u>
   E All correct

2. F a plant <u>fossil</u>
   G a heavy <u>anchor</u>
   H the <u>local</u> time
   J <u>normel</u> school hours
   K All correct

3. A to dig a <u>channel</u>
   B to <u>tremble</u> in fear
   C to <u>titel</u> a paper
   D to <u>arrive</u> late
   E All correct

4. F a <u>globel</u> concern
   G a loud <u>quarrel</u>
   H a pair of <u>scissors</u>
   J a fierce <u>struggle</u>
   K All correct

5. A a <u>casual</u> remark
   B the eye of the <u>needil</u>
   C a narrow <u>angle</u>
   D the <u>dial</u> of a watch
   E All correct

6. F nothing in <u>common</u>
   G a newspaper <u>artical</u>
   H my mother's <u>cousin</u>
   J a good <u>bargain</u>
   K All correct

7. A a shiny <u>nickel</u>
   B a torn <u>label</u>
   C a shrill <u>whistel</u>
   D a <u>human</u> being
   E All correct

8. F to <u>employ</u> a worker
   G to feel great <u>sorrow</u>
   H to build a <u>robot</u>
   J to <u>stumbil</u> on a rock
   K All correct

More Practice
Now write all the misspelled words correctly on a separate sheet of paper.

Spelling Games
www.eduplace.com/kids/sv/
Review for your test.

Real-World Vocabulary

Math: Geometry

All the words in the box relate to angles. Look up these words in your Spelling Dictionary. Then write the words to complete the captions for this textbook page.

Spelling Word Link

angle

acute angle
hypotenuse
obtuse angle
polygons
rectangle
rhombus
right angle
triangle

Plane Figures

All the figures shown are _____(1)_____.

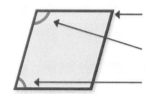

A _____(2)_____ has four equal sides.

An _____(3)_____ has a measure greater than 90°.

An _____(4)_____ has a measure less than 90°.

A _____(5)_____ has two pairs of sides with equal length, and four equal angles.

A _____(6)_____ has a measure of 90°.

A _____(7)_____ has three sides and three angles.

The longest side of a right triangle is the _____(8)_____.

1. _____
2. _____
3. _____
4. _____
5. _____
6. _____
7. _____
8. _____

eWord Game
www.eduplace.com/kids/sv/

Try This — CHALLENGE

True or False? Write *true* if the sentence is true. Write *false* if it is not.

9. An obtuse angle has a larger measure than an acute angle has.

10. A perfectly square corner is the same as a right angle.

11. A triangle can have two obtuse angles.

12. All polygons have four sides and four angles.

9. _____
10. _____
11. _____
12. _____

Spelling Review

Unit 13

1. _____
2. _____
3. _____
4. _____
5. _____
6. _____
7. _____
8. _____
9. _____
10. _____

Unit 13	VCCV Pattern			pages 90–95
journey	pattern	arrive	permit	sorrow
subject	lawyer	scissors	publish	burden

Spelling Strategy In two-syllable words with a VCCV pattern, divide the words between the two consonants.

Context Sentences Write the word that completes each sentence.

1. Don't let that heavy _____ weigh you down.
2. The explorers set off on a _____ of discovery.
3. My shirt has a _____ of stripes and dots.
4. I experienced deep _____ when my dog died.
5. We will _____ our stories in the school magazine.

Analogies Write the word that best completes each analogy.

6. *Forbid* is to _____ as *denounce* is to *praise*.
7. *Rock* is to *stone* as _____ is to *topic*.
8. *Dials* are to *knobs* as *shears* are to _____.
9. *Vanish* is to *appear* as *depart* is to _____.
10. *Writer* is to *author* as _____ is to *attorney*.

Unit 14

11. _____
12. _____
13. _____
14. _____
15. _____
16. _____
17. _____
18. _____
19. _____
20. _____

Unit 14	VCV Pattern			pages 96–101
award	behave	credit	evil	modern
robot	cousin	prefer	novel	deserve

Spelling Strategy Divide a VCV word into syllables before or after the consonant, depending on the vowel sound in the first syllable.

Word Clues Write the word that fits each clue.

11. opposite of old-fashioned
12. my dad's sister's son
13. a machine that does a job
14. to like something better
15. to act properly
16. what an author might write
17. what a superhero fights against
18. a prize
19. something that is earned
20. to be worthy of

Unit 15   VCCCV Pattern   pages 102–107

| conflict | instant | simply | laughter | anchor |
| improve | arctic | mischief | complain | tremble |

Spelling Strategy When two consonants in a VCCCV word spell one sound or form a cluster, divide the word into syllables before or after those two consonants.

Context Paragraph Write the words that complete this paragraph.

The weather was __(21)__ awful on the day of the track meet. I wondered what else could go wrong. When Lisa's dog broke free, I knew it would get into __(22)__. Sure enough, it started running on the track. The other team started to __(23)__ loudly. "Maybe the dog can __(24)__ your running times," the announcer joked. In an __(25)__, the mood of the crowd got better. What could have been a nasty __(26)__ between rivals was instead a friendly match—thanks to a runaway dog and a clever announcer!

Classifying Write the word that belongs in each group.

27. shake, quiver, _____
28. frozen, polar, _____
29. ship, port, _____
30. joke, joy, _____

Unit 16   V V Pattern   pages 108–113

| actual | cruel | casual | ruin | trial |
| realize | genuine | riot | area | annual |

Spelling Strategy When the two vowels in a VV pattern spell two vowel sounds, divide the word into syllables between the vowels.

Synonyms Write the word that has almost the same meaning as each word or phrase below.

31. real
32. relaxed
33. destroy
34. understand
35. yearly
36. region
37. exact or true
38. test run
39. wild disturbance
40. mean

Unit 15
21. _____
22. _____
23. _____
24. _____
25. _____
26. _____
27. _____
28. _____
29. _____
30. _____

Unit 16
31. _____
32. _____
33. _____
34. _____
35. _____
36. _____
37. _____
38. _____
39. _____
40. _____

121

Spelling Review

Unit 17

41. _____

42. _____

43. _____

44. _____

45. _____

46. _____

47. _____

48. _____

49. _____

50. _____

Unit 17	Final Schwa + /l/ Sounds		pages 114–119	
whistle	label	puzzle	normal	⚠ pupil
level	local	stumble	quarrel	⚠ fossil

Spelling Strategy

Final /l/ or /əl/ → **al, el, le**.

Analogies Write the word that best completes each analogy.

41. *General* is to *specific* as *global* is to _____.

42. *Regular* is to _____ as *clever* is to *bright*.

43. *Complete* is to *finish* as _____ is to *trip*.

44. *Sloping* is to _____ as *genuine* is to *artificial*.

Classifying Write the word that belongs in each group.

45. class, teacher, _____

46. argument, disagreement, _____

47. tag, sticker, _____

48. rock, remains, _____

49. riddle, mystery, _____

50. flute, recorder, _____

Challenge Words

51. _____

52. _____

53. _____

54. _____

55. _____

56. _____

57. _____

58. _____

59. _____

60. _____

Challenge Words	Units 13–17		pages 90–119	
narrate	identical	logic	appreciate	nuisance
anthem	vehicle	prior	illustrate	mentor

Definitions Write the word that fits each meaning.

51. to be grateful for

52. clear reasoning

53. to tell a story

54. a song of praise

55. a device for carrying people or equipment

56. to explain, using pictures

57. a bother

58. coming before

59. a wise and trusted adviser

60. exactly alike

Proofread a Story

Spelling and Grammar Mixed Review Use proofreading marks to correct this part of a story. There are **nine** misspelled words, **two** errors with comparative forms, and **one** incorrect proper adjective.

Example: Maya was from an ~~areea~~ *area* near Moscow, a russian city.

Proofreading Marks

¶ Indent
∧ Add
⊙ Add a period
⌐ Delete
≡ Capital letter
/ Small letter

Billy was like most kids. He had a vivvid imagination. He loved sports and animals. The difference was that Billy didn't talk. One day his parents read an artical about the Owens marine Center. Ilia, a young orfan dollfin there, was part of a pionear language program for kids. His dad took Billy to meet Ilia. It was the better thing ever for Billy! He rode his bicycal there every day. He learned to give Ilia basic hand commands. The two were genuine friends.

Maya, Ilia's humin trainer, had an idea. She said, "I sugest you say the words as you give the hand signs." Maya saw Billy's struggel. "I know it's hard," she said, "but the most you try, the easier it will get."

Write a Story

prewrite → draft → revise → proofread → publish

Write a story about a character who faces a challenge.

- Think of a **character** and a **problem or challenge** for the character.
- Use Spelling Words from Units 13–17 and comparative adjectives.
- Proofread your story for **spelling** and **grammar.**

Tips

- Introduce the character and the problem at the beginning.
- Have the character try more than one solution.
- Have the character solve the problem at the story's high point, or climax.

Power Proofreading
www.eduplace.com/kids/sv/

Spelling Test Practice

Test Tip Read the directions carefully.

Directions This test will show how well you can spell.

- Many of the questions in this test have spelling mistakes. Some do not have any mistakes at all.
- Look for mistakes in spelling.
- If there is a mistake, fill in the answer space on your answer sheet that has the same letter as the **line** with the mistake.
- If there is no mistake, fill in the last answer space.

Example:

Ⓐ Ⓑ Ⓒ ● Ⓔ

Answer Sheet

1. Ⓐ Ⓑ Ⓒ Ⓓ Ⓔ
2. Ⓙ Ⓚ Ⓛ Ⓜ Ⓝ
3. Ⓐ Ⓑ Ⓒ Ⓓ Ⓔ
4. Ⓙ Ⓚ Ⓛ Ⓜ Ⓝ
5. Ⓐ Ⓑ Ⓒ Ⓓ Ⓔ
6. Ⓙ Ⓚ Ⓛ Ⓜ Ⓝ
7. Ⓐ Ⓑ Ⓒ Ⓓ Ⓔ
8. Ⓙ Ⓚ Ⓛ Ⓜ Ⓝ

Example:
  A vivid
  B wheelchair
  C carton
  D sholder
  E *(No mistakes)*

---

1. A bargain
  B itum
  C flute
  D repeat
  E *(No mistakes)*

2. J object
  K fund
  L complix
  M strike
  N *(No mistakes)*

3. A legul
  B stew
  C launch
  D suppose
  E *(No mistakes)*

4. J burglar
  K tractor
  L former
  M violut
  N *(No mistakes)*

5. A nerve
  B royal
  C wild-life
  D bundle
  E *(No mistakes)*

6. J worship
  K alert
  L home run
  M central
  N *(No mistakes)*

7. A merchant
  B avoid
  C apply
  D bearly
  E *(No mistakes)*

8. J demand
  K tunnil
  L object
  M haunt
  N *(No mistakes)*

More Practice

Now write all the misspelled words correctly on a separate sheet of paper.

Spelling Games
www.eduplace.com/kids/sv/
Review for your test.

Vocabulary Test Practice

Test Tip If you change an answer, erase the first answer completely.

Directions Read each sentence. Use the other words in the sentence to help you decide what the underlined word means. Fill in the space on your answer sheet for your answer choice.

Example: I wonder who will <u>invent</u> the first personal rocket ship. <u>Invent</u> means —

    A direct   **C** purchase

    B deserve   **D** create

Example:

Ⓐ Ⓑ Ⓒ ●

Answer Sheet

1. Ⓐ Ⓑ Ⓒ Ⓓ
2. Ⓕ Ⓖ Ⓗ Ⓙ
3. Ⓐ Ⓑ Ⓒ Ⓓ
4. Ⓕ Ⓖ Ⓗ Ⓙ
5. Ⓐ Ⓑ Ⓒ Ⓓ

---

1. The hammer is a <u>simple</u> tool that should be included in every toolbox. <u>Simple</u> means —

    A basic   **C** odd

    B mighty   **D** complex

2. Robins are a <u>usual</u> sight in our backyard. <u>Usual</u> means —

    F part-time   **H** remote

    G common   **J** perfect

3. A <u>burglar</u> broke into the warehouse and stole a carton of new sneakers. A <u>burglar</u> is a —

    A lifeguard   **C** thief

    B robot   **D** passenger

4. That box is not <u>solid</u> enough to stand on. <u>Solid</u> means —

    F sturdy   **H** visual

    G special   **J** exact

5. A baby might <u>peer</u> at a new pet before trying to play with it. <u>Peer</u> means —

    A grasp   **C** look

    B thunder   **D** strike

Read the Spelling Words and sentences.

Basic

1.	scrubbed	*scrubbed*	I **scrubbed** the floor with a large brush.
2.	listening	*listening*	Are you **listening** to your new CD?
3.	stunned	*stunned*	How **stunned** we were when we won!
4.	knitting	*knitting*	I'm **knitting** a wool scarf for you.
5.	carpeting	*carpeting*	Our floors have wall-to-wall **carpeting**.
6.	wandered	*wandered*	We **wandered** slowly around the park.
7.	gathering	*gathering*	Start **gathering** blueberries for a pie.
8.	beginning	*beginning*	Do not miss the **beginning** of the movie.
9.	skimmed	*skimmed*	He rapidly **skimmed** the science chapter.
10.	chatting	*chatting*	I was **chatting** on the phone with Kim.
11.	shrugged	*shrugged*	She **shrugged** and said she didn't know.
12.	bothering	*bothering*	These pesky flies are **bothering** me!
13.	whipped	*whipped*	Ty **whipped** cream for a dessert topping.
14.	quizzed	*quizzed*	Our teacher **quizzed** us in math today.
15.	suffering	*suffering*	Charlotte is **suffering** from a bad cold.
16.	scanned	*scanned*	A sailor **scanned** the horizon for ships.
17.	ordered	*ordered*	We **ordered** pizza and then picked it up.
18.	totaled	*totaled*	All of our purchases today **totaled** $50.
19.	answered	*answered*	I heard the bell and **answered** the door.
20.	upsetting	*upsetting*	News of the fire was very **upsetting**.

Review
21. wandering
22. dimmed
23. stripped
24. offered
25. snapping

Challenge
26. compelling
27. deposited
28. occurred
29. threatening
30. canceled

Think and Sort

Each word has *-ed* or *-ing* added to a base word. Each base word ends with a vowel and a consonant. The consonant is doubled in one-syllable words. It is often not doubled in longer words.

stun + ed = stu**nn**ed   order + ed = order**ed**

Write each Basic Word under the heading that shows what happens to the base word when *-ed* or *-ing* is added.

Final Consonant Doubled

1. _____
2. _____
3. _____
4. _____
5. _____
6. _____
7. _____
8. _____
9. _____
10. _____
11. _____

Final Consonant Not Doubled

12. _____
13. _____
14. _____
15. _____
16. _____
17. _____
18. _____
19. _____
20. _____

Word Analysis/Phonics

21–25. Write the five Basic Words that contain the /ŭ/ sound.

Vocabulary: Classifying

Write the Basic or Review Word that belongs in each group. Use your Spelling Dictionary.

26. replied, responded, _____

28. talking, conversing, _____

27. disturbing, annoying, _____

29. roamed, rambled, _____

Challenge Words

Write the Challenge Words to complete the paragraph. Use your Spelling Dictionary.

An unusual event ___(30)___ the other day. My mother ___(31)___ an order she had put in for a handmade picture frame. She called the framer to ask him to return her check. "I'm sorry, I need a ___(32)___ reason to do that. I have started the work and have ___(33)___ your check," the framer said. The conflict was ___(34)___ to intensify, but it ended peacefully when Mother said she would pay the framer for the work he had already done.

Spelling-Meaning Connection

35–36. The words *carpeting* and *carpet* are related in spelling and meaning. Write *carpet*. Then write the Basic Word that means "material or fabric used for carpets."

carpet
carpeting

Word Analysis

21. _____

22. _____

23. _____

24. _____

25. _____

Classifying

26. _____

27. _____

28. _____

29. _____

Challenge Words

30. _____

31. _____

32. _____

33. _____

34. _____

Spelling-Meaning

35. _____

36. _____

At Home Take turns with a family member finding Spelling Words that can use the other ending, for example, an *-ed* ending for an *-ing* word or an *-ing* ending for an *-ed* word. Write the new words.

127

Vocabulary

1. _____
2. _____
3. _____
4. _____
5. _____
6. _____
7. _____
8. _____

Vocabulary: Analogies

An analogy compares word pairs in some way. One way is to show a difference of degree. Another is to link a process with its product.

Difference of Degree: *Happy* is to *overjoyed* as *angry* is to *enraged*.

Process and Product: *Painting* is to *portrait* as *baking* is to *bread*.

Practice Write the word from the box that best completes each analogy.

knitting	harvesting	mining	pleased
stunned	directing	exhausted	frigid

1. *Loud* is to *deafening* as *tired* is to _____.
2. *Nervous* is to *frantic* as _____ is to *delighted*.
3. *Sewing* is to *shirt* as _____ is to *sweater*.
4. *Cool* is to _____ as *warm* is to *torrid*.
5. *Writing* is to *book* as _____ is to *crop*.
6. *Cooking* is to *meal* as _____ is to *play*.
7. *Annoyed* is to *furious* as *surprised* is to _____.
8. *Drilling* is to *oil* as _____ is to *coal*.

Dictionary

9. _____
10. _____
11. _____
12. _____
13. _____
14. _____
15. _____
16. _____

Dictionary: Base Words and Endings

A dictionary does not include an entry for every form of a word. To find a word that ends with *-ed*, *-ing*, *-er*, or *-est*, look up the base word. Word forms follow the part of speech in the entry.

wander (wŏn´ dər) *v.* **wandered, wandering**
rough (rŭf) *adj.* **rougher, roughest**

Practice Write the base word that you would look up in the dictionary to find each word below.

9. skimmed
10. beginning
11. quieter
12. chatting
13. oddest
14. steeper
15. scrubbed
16. swiftest

Proofread a Letter

Spelling and Compound Sentences Use proofreading marks to correct **ten** misspelled Basic or Review Words and **two** mistakes in commas in compound sentences in this part of a letter.

Example: Raoul is ~~suffurring~~ *suffering* from chicken pox, but he helped too!

Proofreading Marks

¶ Indent
∧ Add
⊙ Add a period
⌐ Delete
≡ Capital letter
/ Small letter

Dear Sonya,

Guess what? We remodeled our family room! In the begining, the project was easy. While Mom and I were gatherring paint samples, Dad orderred the new flooring. Back home, we skanned our list and saw we'd forgotten a few things. Mom and I returned to the store and Dad totald the costs.

Then we got to work. We stippd the wallpaper and skrubed the glue off the walls. Listening to music made it fun. Dad ripped out the old carpetting and then we began laying the new floor. Soon we saw that the boards weren't straight. Our hopes of finishing quickly dimd, but then our neighbor oferred to help. You'll be stunned at how great the room looks now!

Write a Letter

prewrite → draft → revise → proofread → publish

Write a letter to a friend about a project you have completed.

- Tell what happened **in order.**
- Use some Spelling Words and some compound sentences.
- Proofread your work for **spelling** and for correct **comma use.**

Basic
scrubbed
listening
stunned
knitting
carpeting
wandered
gathering
beginning
skimmed
chatting
shrugged
bothering
whipped
quizzed
suffering
scanned
ordered
totaled
answered
upsetting

Review
wandering
dimmed
stripped
offered
snapping

Challenge
compelling
deposited
occurred
threatening
canceled

✔ **Test Tip** Don't spend too much time on one question.

Test Format Practice

Directions Read each group of sentences. Decide if one of the underlined words is spelled wrong or if there is *No mistake*. Fill in the space for the answer you have chosen.

Example: **A** The teacher <u>answered</u> our questions before the test.
B The <u>carpetting</u> was worn in several places.
C I <u>ordered</u> a book online.
D No mistake

Example:

Ⓐ ⬤ Ⓒ Ⓓ

Answer Sheet

1. Ⓐ Ⓑ Ⓒ Ⓓ
2. Ⓕ Ⓖ Ⓗ Ⓙ
3. Ⓐ Ⓑ Ⓒ Ⓓ
4. Ⓕ Ⓖ Ⓗ Ⓙ
5. Ⓐ Ⓑ Ⓒ Ⓓ
6. Ⓕ Ⓖ Ⓗ Ⓙ
7. Ⓐ Ⓑ Ⓒ Ⓓ
8. Ⓕ Ⓖ Ⓗ Ⓙ

---

1. **A** The family <u>gathering</u> began at noon.
   B I returned the sweater for <u>credit</u>.
   C I love <u>lisenning</u> to music.
   D No mistake

2. **F** My <u>cousin</u> enjoyed her vacation in Mexico.
   G The teacher <u>quized</u> Jan on today's lesson.
   H That fly is really <u>bothering</u> me.
   J No mistake

3. **A** Pam <u>stripped</u> the sheets off the bed.
   B Never be <u>cruel</u> to a pet.
   C Patrick Henry was a famous <u>patriot</u>.
   D No mistake

4. **F** Watch out for the <u>snaping</u> turtle!
   G The new library is in a <u>central</u> location.
   H Which <u>channel</u> shows the news at 5:00 P.M.?
   J No mistake

5. **A** I need to <u>purchase</u> a book.
   B Teri <u>wipped</u> up an omelet for lunch.
   C My brother would not <u>behave</u> last night.
   D No mistake

6. **F** Tony <u>scanned</u> the menu looking for fish.
   G I need to <u>improve</u> my math skills.
   H The dog <u>wanderred</u> off into the trees.
   J No mistake

7. **A** The farmer <u>skimed</u> the cream off the milk.
   B Sako got an <u>award</u> for bravery.
   C Our savings <u>totaled</u> $23.85.
   D No mistake

8. **F** Gran is <u>knitting</u> me a sweater for my birthday.
   G I put my new <u>model</u> airplane together.
   H The <u>museum</u> has a new dinosaur exhibit.
   J No mistake

More Practice
Now write all the misspelled words correctly on a separate sheet of paper.

Spelling Games
www.eduplace.com/kids/sv/
Review for your test.

Real-World Vocabulary

Art: Fashion

All the words in the box relate to designing and making clothes. Look up these words in your Spelling Dictionary. Then write the words to complete this magazine article.

Spelling Word Link

knitting

designer
fabric
fashion
garment
linen
stylish
trend
wardrobe

Giving an Old Material a New "Wrinkle"

Where does a ___(1)___ get ideas for ___(2)___ new ready-to-wear clothes? Inspiration may come from a particular period in history, a scene in a movie, an exotic culture, or a painting by a great master. At ___(3)___ shows in the world's design capitals, you can see the latest ___(4)___ in formal or casual clothing.

Sometimes design ideas involve using an old ___(5)___, or type of cloth, in new ways. For example, no summer ___(6)___ is complete without an outfit made of ___(7)___. This strong material comes from the fibers of the flax plant and has been used for clothing since the days of ancient Egypt. Today, it offers a crisp, cool look for summer. Anyone wearing a ___(8)___ of this material makes a timeless style statement.

1. _____
2. _____
3. _____
4. _____
5. _____
6. _____
7. _____
8. _____

eWord Game
www.eduplace.com/kids/sv/

Try This CHALLENGE

Draw a design for a piece of clothing you'd like to wear. Use a separate piece of paper. Write some sentences about what you have designed.

PART 1 Spelling and Phonics

Read the Spelling Words and sentences.

Basic

1. tiring	*tiring*	Running a marathon is very **tiring**.
2. borrowed	*borrowed*	I **borrowed** my sister's coat yesterday.
3. freezing	*freezing*	Wear mittens in **freezing** weather.
4. delivered	*delivered*	Has the mail been **delivered** yet?
5. whispered	*whispered*	Ted **whispered** the secret to Julia.
6. losing	*losing*	Is the team winning or **losing**?
7. decided	*decided*	Have you **decided** on a flavor yet?
8. amazing	*amazing*	Isn't Mt. Rushmore an **amazing** sight?
9. performing	*performing*	Tony is **performing** in the school play.
10. resulting	*resulting*	A leak is **resulting** in water damage.
11. related	*related*	I can't believe you two are **related**!
12. attending	*attending*	Is Nan **attending** tonight's concert?
13. damaged	*damaged*	Don't buy that **damaged** skateboard!
14. remarked	*remarked*	Mom **remarked** on how well we did.
15. practicing	*practicing*	The band is **practicing** for an audition.
16. supported	*supported*	Two strong beams **supported** the roof.
17. united	*united*	The town **united** to build a library.
18. expected	*expected*	Ron **expected** a good grade in math.
19. amusing	*amusing*	What an **amusing** cartoon this is!
20. repeated	*repeated*	The bulletin was **repeated** every hour.

Review		Challenge	
21. pleasing	23. traveled	26. assigned	28. operated
22. dared	24. checking	27. entertaining	29. rehearsing
	25. landed		30. donated

Think and Sort

As you know, a base word is a word to which endings can be added. If a base word ends in *e*, the *e* is dropped when an ending is added.

decide + ed = decid**ed**   lose + ing = los**ing**

deliver + ed = deliver**ed**   attend + ing = attend**ing**

Write each Basic Word under the heading that tells what happens when *-ed* or *-ing* is added.

Final *e* Dropped

1. _____
2. _____
3. _____
4. _____
5. _____
6. _____
7. _____
8. _____
9. _____
10. _____

No Spelling Change

11. _____
12. _____
13. _____
14. _____
15. _____
16. _____
17. _____
18. _____
19. _____
20. _____

Word Analysis/Phonics

21–24. Write the four Basic Words that contain the prefix *re-*.

Vocabulary: Classifying

Write the Basic or Review Word that belongs in each group. Use your Spelling Dictionary.

25. singing, acting, _____

26. inspecting, testing, _____

27. risked, challenged, _____

28. awaited, counted on, _____

29. murmured, mumbled, _____

Challenge Words

Write the Challenge Word that best fits each clue. Use your Spelling Dictionary.

30. practicing a role in a play

31. gave a special task to

32. amusing an audience

33. ran a machine such as a forklift

34. contributed money or time to a good cause

Spelling-Meaning Connection

35–36. The words *decided* and *decision* are related in spelling and meaning. A *decision* is the result of what has been *decided*. Write the words. Underline the vowel that spells a different sound in each word.

decision

decided

Word Analysis

21. _____

22. _____

23. _____

24. _____

Classifying

25. _____

26. _____

27. _____

28. _____

29. _____

Challenge Words

30. _____

31. _____

32. _____

33. _____

34. _____

Spelling-Meaning

35. _____

36. _____

At Home With a family member, write each Spelling Word on a small piece of paper. Work together to arrange the words in alphabetical order.

Word Structure

1. _____
2. _____
3. _____
4. _____
5. _____
6. _____
7. _____
8. _____
9. _____

Word Structure: Number Prefixes

The prefixes *uni-*, *bi-*, and *tri-* mean "one," "two," and "three."

unicycle = **one** wheel   **bi**cycle = **two** wheels   **tri**cycle = **three** wheels

Practice Write a word from the box to complete each sentence. Use your Spelling Dictionary.

united	bifocals	triplets
unicorn	bicentennial	triangle
unique	bilingual	triceratops

1. Our nation's _____ was celebrated in 1976.
2. My neighbor just had _____, two girls and a boy.
3. Eyeglasses with two-part lenses are _____.
4. A _____ is a figure with three sides.
5. The odd building has a _____ design.
6. The _____ is an imaginary creature with one horn.
7. The parties have _____ to speak with one voice today.
8. The _____ was a dinosaur with three horns on its head.
9. A sign with a message in English and French is _____.

Thesaurus

10. _____
11. _____
12. _____
13. _____
14. _____

Thesaurus: Exact Words for *damaged*

Practice Look up the entry for *damaged* in your Thesaurus. Then write the best word from the box to replace *damaged* in each sentence.

scratched	tattered	dented	shattered	bruised

10. The soft spot on the apple showed that it was <u>damaged</u>.
11. My shirt was <u>damaged</u> after the puppy chewed holes in it.
12. The cat's claws <u>damaged</u> the leg of the chair.
13. The result of my clumsiness was a <u>damaged</u> vase.
14. The car was <u>damaged</u> when the shopping cart hit it.

Proofread a Travel Diary

Spelling and Commas in a Series Use proofreading marks to correct **ten** misspelled Basic or Review Words and **two** mistakes in commas in a series in this travel diary.

Example: ~~related~~
I rellated a tale about a mine, a miner, and a donkey.

> We landed in Arizona and travled from the airport by bus. It deliverred us to the South Rim of the Grand Canyon. I expeckted to be impressed, but the canyon is amaizing! It seems to go on forever! You can explore it on foot or by bus horse, or mule. My brother and I desided to hike into the canyon the next morning, so we got a good night's sleep in a pleesing room. Checking our packs early the next day, we made sure we had sunscreen, hats bottles of water, and energy bars. We also borowed a map to avoid loseing our way. The hike was awesome! We saw deer, ammusing chipmunks, and lizards. The climb back up was tyring, but the hike was worth the effort!

Proofreading Marks
¶ Indent
∧ Add
⊙ Add a period
✄ Delete
≡ Capital letter
/ Small letter

Basic
tiring
borrowed
freezing
delivered
whispered
losing
decided
amazing
performing
resulting
related
attending
damaged
remarked
practicing
supported
united
expected
amusing
repeated

Review
pleasing
dared
traveled
checking
landed

Challenge
assigned
entertaining
operated
rehearsing
donated

Write a Travel Diary

prewrite → draft → revise → proofread → publish

Write a paragraph that could go in a travel diary. Tell about a trip you took to a place you had never seen before.

- Describe the **place** and tell **what happened** there.
- Use some Spelling Words and include some items in a series.
- Proofread your work for **spelling** and the correct use of **commas**.

Power Proofreading
www.eduplace.com/kids/sv/

✓ **Test Tip** Change an answer only if you are sure your first choice was wrong.

Directions This test will show how well you can spell.

- Many of the questions in this test have spelling mistakes. Some do not have any mistakes at all.
- Look for mistakes in spelling.
- If there is a mistake, fill in the answer space on your answer sheet that has the same letter as the **line** with the mistake.
- If there is no mistake, fill in the last answer space.

Example:

Ⓐ Ⓑ Ⓒ ● Ⓔ

Answer Sheet

1. Ⓐ Ⓑ Ⓒ Ⓓ Ⓔ
2. Ⓙ Ⓚ Ⓛ Ⓜ Ⓝ
3. Ⓐ Ⓑ Ⓒ Ⓓ Ⓔ
4. Ⓙ Ⓚ Ⓛ Ⓜ Ⓝ
5. Ⓐ Ⓑ Ⓒ Ⓓ Ⓔ
6. Ⓙ Ⓚ Ⓛ Ⓜ Ⓝ
7. Ⓐ Ⓑ Ⓒ Ⓓ Ⓔ
8. Ⓙ Ⓚ Ⓛ Ⓜ Ⓝ

More Practice

Now write all the misspelled words correctly on a separate sheet of paper.

Spelling Games
www.eduplace.com/kids/sv/
Review for your test.

Example: A checking
                B knitting
                C dared
                D tireing
                E *(No Mistakes)*

1. A carpeting
   B atending
   C shrugged
   D chatting
   E *(No Mistakes)*

2. J delivered
   K quizzed
   L landid
   M upsetting
   N *(No Mistakes)*

3. A suported
   B expected
   C scanned
   D remarked
   E *(No Mistakes)*

4. J united
   K whisperred
   L listening
   M dimmed
   N *(No Mistakes)*

5. A frezing
   B losing
   C wandered
   D stunned
   E *(No Mistakes)*

6. J practecing
   K decided
   L offered
   M traveled
   N *(No Mistakes)*

7. A performing
   B pleasing
   C totaled
   D damadged
   E *(No Mistakes)*

8. J whipped
   K snapping
   L amusing
   M borrowed
   N *(No Mistakes)*

Real-World Vocabulary

Science: Basic Chemistry

All the words in the box relate to physical changes in substances. Look up these words in your Spelling Dictionary. Then write the words to complete this class discussion.

Spelling Word Link
freezing

particles
density
evaporation
gaseous
condenses
matter
substance
cooling

Teacher: As you know, class, our Earth is made up of three states of ___(1)___. Who can tell me what they are?

Sako: The three states are solid, liquid, and gas.

Teacher: Good. What are the tiny bits that all matter is made of?

Tim: All matter is made up of ___(2)___, some of which are called molecules. In a solid, the molecules are packed together and don't move around much. In liquids the molecules move around more. In ___(3)___ matter the molecules are farthest apart and move fastest.

Teacher: Thank you, Tim. Now let's talk about physical changes. If you let an ice cube melt, it becomes a puddle of water. As the water turns into water vapor, the puddle dries up. That process is called ___(4)___. Suppose you boil a kettle of water. The steam that escapes is water vapor. As that vapor moves through the air, it begins ___(5)___. As it cools, it ___(6)___ back into liquid water. The property that compares the amount of matter in a ___(7)___ to the space it takes up is ___(8)___. Water is denser than water vapor.

1. _____
2. _____
3. _____
4. _____
5. _____
6. _____
7. _____
8. _____

 **eWord Game**
www.eduplace.com/kids/sv/

Try This CHALLENGE

True or False Write *true* if the sentence is true. Write *false* if it is not.

9. Molecules in gaseous matter move slowly.

10. Cooling can result in a physical change.

11. Water vapor never condenses into a liquid.

12. Evaporation takes place when water boils.

9. _____
10. _____
11. _____
12. _____

Read the Spelling Words and sentences.

Basic

1. duties	*duties*	Your **duties** include weeding the garden.
2. earlier	*earlier*	The sun rises **earlier** in June than in May.
3. loveliest	*loveliest*	Which flower do you think is the **loveliest**?
4. denied	*denied*	The judge sternly **denied** the request.
5. ferries	*ferries*	Cars get to the island via **ferries**.
6. sunnier	*sunnier*	I hope today is **sunnier** than yesterday.
7. terrified	*terrified*	The huge thunderclap **terrified** our dog.
8. abilities	*abilities*	Develop your **abilities** by practicing.
9. dirtier	*dirtier*	Uniforms get **dirtier** on rainy days.
10. scariest	*scariest*	Which monster mask is the **scariest**?
11. trophies	*trophies*	Do all winners get shiny **trophies**?
12. cozier	*cozier*	More heat will make the room **cozier**.
13. enemies	*enemies*	We were **enemies**, but now we are friends.
14. iciest	*iciest*	Avoid the **iciest** spots on the snowy road.
15. greediest	*greediest*	The **greediest** gull swiped the most food.
16. drowsier	*drowsier*	Jan felt **drowsier** after lunch than before.
17. victories	*victories*	How does your team celebrate **victories**?
18. horrified	*horrified*	Ken's bad manners **horrified** his friends.
19. memories	*memories*	I have great **memories** of last summer.
20. strategies	*strategies*	Good **strategies** help teams win games.

Review

21. easier
22. families
23. studied
24. countries
25. happiest

Challenge

26. unified
27. dictionaries
28. boundaries
29. satisfied
30. tragedies

Think and Sort

If a word ends with a consonant and *y*, change the *y* to *i* when adding -*es*, -*ed*, -*er*, or -*est*.

trophy + es = troph**ies** deny + ed = den**ied**

sunny + er = sunn**ier** greedy + est = greed**iest**

Write each Basic Word under its ending.

-es or -ed

1. _____
2. _____
3. _____
4. _____
5. _____
6. _____
7. _____
8. _____
9. _____
10. _____
11. _____

-er or -est

12. _____
13. _____
14. _____
15. _____
16. _____
17. _____
18. _____
19. _____
20. _____

Word Analysis/Phonics

21–24. Write the four Basic Words that have the /ī/ sound.

Vocabulary: Context Paragraph

Write Basic or Review Words to complete the paragraph.

My great-aunt is a person with many remarkable ___(25)___.
One of these is a knack for learning languages. She ___(26)___ Spanish
for only two years, but she is able to speak the language fluently. We
have visited many ___(27)___ together, and she always has an ___(28)___
time learning phrases than I do. I have asked her what ___(29)___ she
uses to learn so quickly. She says she just listens carefully.

Challenge Words

Write the Challenge Word that fits each meaning. Use your Spelling
Dictionary.

30. pleased

31. joined together into one

32. very unfortunate events

33. edges or borders

34. books that give information
about words

Spelling-Meaning Connection

35–36. People with *abilities* are *able* to do things. *Abilities* and *able*
are related in meaning but have different initial vowel sounds.
Write *abilities* and *able*. Underline the letter that is the same
in both words but that spells the /ə/ sound in one of the
words and in the other the /ā/ sound.

Word Analysis

21. _____

22. _____

23. _____

24. _____

Context Paragraph

25. _____

26. _____

27. _____

28. _____

29. _____

Challenge Words

30. _____

31. _____

32. _____

33. _____

34. _____

Spelling-Meaning

35. _____

36. _____

abilities
able

At Home With a family member,
look through a newspaper
or magazine article. Take turns
finding words in which the
final *y* has been changed to
i before adding *-es*, *-ed*,
-er, or *-est*.

139

Word Structure

1. _____
2. _____
3. _____
4. _____
5. _____
6. _____

Word Structure: The Word Root *terr*

The word root *terr* comes from a Latin verb that means "to frighten."

Practice Write the word from the box that means the same as the underlined words. Use your Spelling Dictionary.

terrified	terror	terrifically
terribly	terrific	terrorize

1. The band played <u>in a very great way</u> all afternoon.
2. I was <u>very frightened</u> by the thunderstorm.
3. The movie was <u>absolutely</u> boring.
4. Cartoons of monsters cause <u>feelings of great fear</u> in some children.
5. We thought the show was <u>wonderful</u>.
6. The old rooster tries to <u>badly frighten</u> our new puppies.

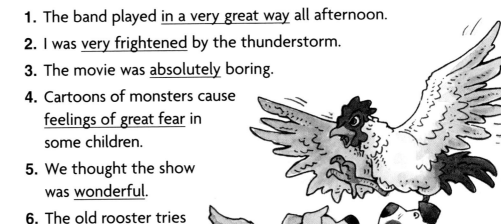

Dictionary

7. _____
8. _____
9. _____
10. _____
11. _____
12. _____
13. _____
14. _____
15. _____
16. _____

Dictionary: Endings for Adjectives

Adjectives that end in *-er* or *-est*, such as *cozier* and *coziest*, are usually listed with their base words in the dictionary.

co • zy (kō′ zē) *adj.* **cozier, coziest**

Practice Write the *-er* and *-est* forms of each word. Use your Spelling Dictionary.

7–8. early

9–10. dirty

11–12. drowsy

13–14. lovely

15–16. scary

Proofread a Human Interest Feature

Spelling and Interjections Use proofreading marks to correct **ten** misspelled Basic or Review Words and **four** mistakes in capitalizing or punctuating interjections in this newspaper feature.

Example: hurrah! The teams of my favorite ~~countrys~~ *countries* won!

A FAMILY ON THE RUN

I hear my sister's loud voice. "Hey It's time to get up!" In our family, each day starts with a workout. We rise earlier than any of the other famileys on our block. We are happyest when we are running, even on the icyest paths. brrr! Of course, running is better when it's sunniyer. Ah it's much easyr to warm up in mild weather.

Our family competes in races, too. wow! The trophees in our den carry great memores of past victoriys. Yet we don't focus only on winning, and we never use unfair strategies. We do not see opponents as enemeys, nor do we neglect our other duteys. Athletic abilities and hard work go hand in hand.

Write a Human Interest Feature

prewrite → draft → revise → proofread → publish

Write a short article about something you like to do with your family, a club, or a group.

- Describe the activity and what makes it enjoyable.
- Use some Spelling Words and some interjections.
- Proofread your work for **spelling** and correct **capitalization and punctuation of interjections**.

Proofreading Marks

¶	Indent
∧	Add
⊙	Add a period
⌐	Delete
=	Capital letter
/	Small letter

Basic
duties
earlier
loveliest
denied
ferries
sunnier
terrified
abilities
dirtier
scariest
trophies
cozier
enemies
iciest
greediest
drowsier
victories
horrified
memories
strategies

Review
easier
families
studied
countries
happiest

Challenge
unified
dictionaries
boundaries
satisfied
tragedies

Power Proofreading
www.eduplace.com/kids/sv/

Test Tip If you change an answer, erase the first answer completely.

Test Format Practice

Directions Read the sentences in each group. Decide if one of the underlined words has a spelling mistake or if there is *No mistake*. Fill in the space for your answer choice.

Example: **A** I hope tomorrow will be <u>sunnier</u> than today.
B Stan picked the <u>loveliest</u> rose.
C Stop <u>chatting</u> while I am talking.
D No mistake

Example:

Ⓐ Ⓑ Ⓒ ●

Answer Sheet

1. Ⓐ Ⓑ Ⓒ Ⓓ
2. Ⓕ Ⓖ Ⓗ Ⓙ
3. Ⓐ Ⓑ Ⓒ Ⓓ
4. Ⓕ Ⓖ Ⓗ Ⓙ
5. Ⓐ Ⓑ Ⓒ Ⓓ
6. Ⓕ Ⓖ Ⓗ Ⓙ

1. **A** The <u>ferrys</u> cross the bay all day.
B How many <u>countries</u> have you visited?
C This recipe is <u>easier</u> than that one.
D No mistake

2. **F** The washcloth is <u>dirtier</u> than the towel.
G The pelican <u>skimmed</u> the waves.
H The kitchen is <u>cozeyer</u> than the hall.
J No mistake

3. **A** Who <u>damaged</u> Mika's sculpture?
B The suspect <u>denied</u> all the charges.
C The <u>greedest</u> guest took five hot dogs.
D No mistake

4. **F** I have won two <u>trophies</u>.
G Are you really <u>terrified</u> of chickens?
H Nell has been <u>practicing</u> free throws.
J No mistake

5. **A** My purchases <u>totaled</u> four dollars even.
B Claire <u>studeyd</u> hard for her science test.
C Rex got up <u>earlier</u> than his brother did.
D No mistake

6. **F** Hans never brags about his <u>victories</u>.
G What is the <u>scareiest</u> movie you have seen?
H Anita <u>ordered</u> the puppy to sit.
J No mistake

More Practice

Now write all the misspelled words correctly on a separate sheet of paper.

Spelling Games
www.eduplace.com/kids/sv/
Review for your test.

Real-World Vocabulary

Social Studies: The Civil War

All the words in the box relate to combat during the American Civil War. Look up these words in your Spelling Dictionary. Then write the words to complete this encyclopedia article.

Spelling Word Link
victories

military
battlefield
cavalry
infantry
troops
regiments
retreat
skirmishes

The Battle of Bull Run

The armies of the North and the South faced each other in a major battle for the first time on July 21, 1861. The _____(1)_____ where the fighting occurred was near a stream called Bull Run, near Manassas, Virginia. In this battle, the _____(2)_____, or foot soldiers, had trouble telling friend from foe: on each side, the _____(3)_____, or groups of soldiers from particular places, wore different kinds of uniforms. The _____(4)_____, or horse soldiers, had the same problem. For a while, the Northerners were winning most _____(5)_____. Then a Confederate general called for Southern _____(6)_____ to join some Virginians who were fighting well. The Southerners began moving forward, forcing the Northerners to _____(7)_____. Credit for the South's victory was given to Thomas Jackson, the leader of the Virginians. In the words of another _____(8)_____ leader, Jackson stood "like a stone wall."

1. _____
2. _____
3. _____
4. _____
5. _____
6. _____
7. _____
8. _____

eWord Game
www.eduplace.com/kids/sv/

Try This CHALLENGE

Questions On a separate sheet of paper, write a question about this first battle of the Civil War, the Battle of Bull Run. Use some words from the box. Trade questions with a classmate and try to answer them.

Suffixes: -ful, -ly, -ness, -less, -ment

Read the Spelling Words and sentences.

Basic

1. lately	*lately*	Have you read a good book **lately**?
2. settlement	*settlement*	The **settlement** grew into a city.
3. watchful	*watchful*	Lions are **watchful** for signs of prey.
4. countless	*countless*	We saw **countless** stars in the sky.
5. steadily	*steadily*	We worked **steadily** all day.
6. closeness	*closeness*	The **closeness** of the fire scared us.
7. calmly	*calmly*	Did Mac speak **calmly** or nervously?
8. government	*government*	Democracy is a form of **government**.
9. agreement	*agreement*	Make an **agreement** not to argue.
10. cloudiness	*cloudiness*	The **cloudiness** reduced visibility.
11. delightful	*delightful*	The songs made the play **delightful**!
12. noisily	*noisily*	Crows cawed **noisily** in the yard.
13. tardiness	*tardiness*	Oversleeping can cause **tardiness**.
14. forgetful	*forgetful*	The **forgetful** girl left her bike out.
15. forgiveness	*forgiveness*	I am sorry and ask for **forgiveness**.
16. harmless	*harmless*	Don't fear that **harmless** snake.
17. enjoyment	*enjoyment*	I get much **enjoyment** from my pets.
18. appointment	*appointment*	Be on time for your **appointment**!
19. effortless	*effortless*	How can I make this job **effortless**?
20. plentiful	*plentiful*	The harvest was **plentiful** this year.

Think and Sort

Each word has a base word and a suffix. A suffix is a word part added to the end of a base word. A suffix adds meaning.

delight + ful = delight**ful**   count + less = count**less**

late + ly = late**ly**   agree + ment = agree**ment**

cloudy + ness = cloud**iness**

Write each Basic Word under its suffix.

-ful or -less

1. _____
2. _____
3. _____
4. _____
5. _____
6. _____
7. _____

-ly

8. _____
9. _____
10. _____
11. _____

-ment or -ness

12. _____
13. _____
14. _____
15. _____
16. _____
17. _____
18. _____
19. _____
20. _____

Review
21. clumsiness
22. movement
23. pavement
24. lonely
25. penniless

Challenge
26. suspenseful
27. merciless
28. seriousness
29. contentment
30. suspiciously

Word Analysis/Phonics

21–25. Write each Basic Word in which the final *y* of the base word was changed to *i* when the suffix was added.

Vocabulary: Analogies

Write the Basic or Review Word that best completes each analogy.

26. *Hungry* is to *starving* as *poor* is to _____.
27. *Deadly* is to _____ as *irritating* is to *soothing*.
28. *Bravely* is to *fearfully* as _____ is to *frantically*.
29. *Tasty* is to *delicious* as *appealing* is to _____.

Challenge Words

Write the Challenge Word that belongs in each group. Use your Spelling Dictionary.

30. happiness, satisfaction, _____
31. earnestness, thoughtfulness, _____
32. exciting, thrilling, _____
33. cautiously, warily, _____
34. cruel, relentless, _____

Spelling-Meaning Connection

35–36. The base word in *government* and *governor* is *govern*. You can remember the *n* in the second syllable of *government* by thinking of the related word *governor*. Write *government* and *governor*. Underline the base word in each.

govern
governor
government

21. _____
22. _____
23. _____
24. _____
25. _____

Analogies

26. _____
27. _____
28. _____
29. _____

Challenge Words

30. _____
31. _____
32. _____
33. _____
34. _____

Spelling-Meaning

35. _____
36. _____

At Home With a family member, take turns writing five Spelling Words with different suffixes on a piece of paper. Cut apart the base words and suffixes. Mix them up. Take turns putting the parts together again.

145

Word Structure

1. _____
2. _____
3. _____
4. _____
5. _____
6. _____

Word Structure: Word Family for *count*

Word parts can be added to the base word *count* to form new words.

Practice Write a word from the box to complete each sentence. Use your Spelling Dictionary.

miscount	counted	discount
counter	countless	recount

1. Please _____ the ballots to see whether the total is correct.
2. You will get a twenty percent _____ with this card.
3. Do not leave your books on the _____.
4. I have been to that park _____ times.
5. Careless clerks often _____ change.
6. Have you _____ the tickets yet?

Dictionary

7. _____
8. _____
9. _____
10. _____
11. _____
12. _____
13. _____
14. _____

Dictionary: Suffixes

Dictionaries list suffixes in alphabetical order among the entry words. To find the meaning of a word with a suffix, look up both the base word and the suffix. Combine the meanings.

-ness A suffix that forms nouns and means "condition" or "quality": *emptiness*.

Practice Look up *-ness*, *-ly*, and *-less* in your Spelling Dictionary. Then write the underlined word combined with a suffix to match each clue.

7. in a <u>strange</u> way
8. without <u>humor</u>
9. the condition of being <u>sweet</u>
10. the condition of being <u>prepared</u>
11. without <u>worth</u>
12. the condition of being <u>rowdy</u>
13. in a <u>messy</u> way
14. the quality of being <u>fuzzy</u>

Proofread a Dialogue

Spelling and Quotation Marks Use proofreading marks to correct **ten** misspelled Basic or Review Words and **four** mistakes in the use of quotation marks in this dialogue.

Example: Mrs. Wilson said, I get great ~~enjoyement~~ *enjoyment* from watching birds.

As Mrs. Wilson was clipping her shrubs, her new neighbor, Kara, approached her. "Mrs. Wilson, I have a question," Kara said. "Lateley, people in town seem wachful, as if they're worried about missing an appointement. Why?"

They're waiting for autumn, and so am I, explained Mrs. Wilson. "When it arrives, counless geese will glide across the sky," she continued. "On land, geese squabble noisily, but in the air they seem in perfect agrement. They fly steadily, and each movment appears effort-less."

How do geese maintain closenness in flight? Kara asked.

Mrs. Wilson smiled and said, "Observing migrating birds is a delightful way to pass a fall day in this little settlment. It's impossible to feel loanly during the great autumn air show!"

Write a Dialogue

prewrite → draft → revise → proofread → publish

Write a brief dialogue about an event.

- Think of a real **event.** Then imagine two **characters** who might be interested in it, and write a **conversation** between them.
- Use some Spelling Words and some synonyms for *said.*
- Proofread for **spelling** and correct use of **quotation marks.**

Power Proofreading
www.eduplace.com/kids/sv/

Proofreading Marks

¶ Indent
∧ Add
⊙ Add a period
ℐ Delete
≡ Capital letter
/ Small letter

Basic
lately
settlement
watchful
countless
steadily
closeness
calmly
government
agreement
cloudiness
delightful
noisily
tardiness
forgetful
forgiveness
harmless
enjoyment
appointment
effortless
plentiful

Review
clumsiness
movement
pavement
lonely
penniless

Challenge
suspenseful
merciless
seriousness
contentment
suspiciously

PART 4

Spelling Test Practice

Test Tip Skip questions that seem hard and go back to them later.

Test Format Practice

Directions Find the phrase containing an underlined word that is not spelled correctly. If all the underlined words are spelled correctly, mark "All correct."

Example: **A** to be tired <u>lately</u>
    B a sudden <u>movement</u>
    C a <u>harmless</u> insect
    D to feel <u>lonley</u>
    E All correct

Example:

Ⓐ Ⓑ Ⓒ ● Ⓔ

Answer Sheet

1. Ⓐ Ⓑ Ⓒ Ⓓ Ⓔ
2. Ⓕ Ⓖ Ⓗ Ⓙ Ⓚ
3. Ⓐ Ⓑ Ⓒ Ⓓ Ⓔ
4. Ⓕ Ⓖ Ⓗ Ⓙ Ⓚ
5. Ⓐ Ⓑ Ⓒ Ⓓ Ⓔ
6. Ⓕ Ⓖ Ⓗ Ⓙ Ⓚ
7. Ⓐ Ⓑ Ⓒ Ⓓ Ⓔ
8. Ⓕ Ⓖ Ⓗ Ⓙ Ⓚ

More Practice
Now write all the misspelled words correctly on a separate sheet of paper.

Spelling Games
www.eduplace.com/kids/sv/
Review for your test.

1. **A** <u>plentiful</u> food
  B a bustling <u>settlement</u>
  C <u>whipped</u> cream
  D frequent <u>tardyness</u>
  E All correct

2. **F** <u>scrubbed</u> clean
  G a <u>watchful</u> eye
  H a <u>forgettful</u> clerk
  J temporarily <u>penniless</u>
  K All correct

3. **A** hot gray <u>paveament</u>
  B <u>countless</u> snowflakes
  C skillful <u>knitting</u>
  D <u>effortless</u> grace
  E All correct

4. **F** to walk <u>steadily</u>
  G <u>chatting</u> happily
  H great <u>enjoyement</u>
  J <u>suffering</u> from a cold
  K All correct

5. **A** family <u>closeness</u>
  B occasional <u>clumsieness</u>
  C <u>related</u> to someone
  D to react <u>calmly</u>
  E All correct

6. **F** a <u>government</u> leader
  G a <u>borrowed</u> sweater
  H a fair <u>agreement</u>
  J a <u>damaged</u> bicycle
  K All correct

7. **A** increasing <u>cloudyness</u>
  B a <u>delightful</u> movie
  C the <u>scariest</u> story
  D happy <u>memories</u>
  E All correct

8. **F** to forget an <u>appointment</u>
  G to bark <u>noisily</u>
  H neighboring <u>countries</u>
  J to ask for <u>forgivness</u>
  K All correct

Real-World Vocabulary

Science: Snakes

All the words in the box relate to snakes. Look up these words in your Spelling Dictionary. Then write the words to complete these entries in a science notebook.

Spelling Word Link
harmless

antidote
burrow
constrict
fangs
poisonous
slither
venom
viper

Snake Notes

Pythons climb trees and _____ (1) along the ground. They _____ (2) their victims by wrapping around them and then squeezing.

Coral snakes _____ (3) after lizards that try to hide underground. The _____ (4) of these snakes can be deadly. Stay clear of this colorful reptile and its two nasty _____ (5)!

The copperhead, like the coral snake, is a _____ (6). That means it is a _____ (7) snake. Some hospitals keep on hand an _____ (8) that acts against a copperhead's poison. Quick treatment can save a life!

1. _____
2. _____
3. _____
4. _____
5. _____
6. _____
7. _____
8. _____

eWord Game
www.eduplace.com/kids/sv/

Try This
CHALLENGE

Questions On a separate sheet of paper, write a question about each snake described in the notebook. Use some words from the box. Trade questions with a classmate and try to answer them.

PART 1 Spelling and Phonics

Two Syllables

1. _____
2. _____
3. _____
4. _____
5. _____
6. _____
7. _____
8. _____

Three Syllables

9. _____
10. _____
11. _____
12. _____
13. _____
14. _____
15. _____
16. _____
17. _____
18. _____
19. _____
20. _____

Read the Spelling Words and sentences.

Basic

1.	salsa	*salsa*	I put hot **salsa** on my chicken taco.
2.	mattress	*mattress*	Is a soft **mattress** better to sleep on?
3.	tycoon	*tycoon*	That **tycoon** owns a bank and a hotel.
4.	burrito	*burrito*	What is in the **burrito** besides beans?
5.	bandanna	*bandanna*	Cover your hair with this **bandanna**.
6.	tomato	*tomato*	Slice a ripe red **tomato** into the salad.
7.	poncho	*poncho*	I wear a **poncho** in the rain.
8.	dungarees	*dungarees*	Sam wore **dungarees** instead of slacks.
9.	lasso	*lasso*	Use this rope to make a **lasso** to twirl.
10.	patio	*patio*	We sit on the **patio** on sunny days.
11.	siesta	*siesta*	A **siesta** after lunch restores energy.
12.	cargo	*cargo*	That boat carries a **cargo** of lumber.
13.	vanilla	*vanilla*	My favorite ice cream flavor is **vanilla**.
14.	tsunami	*tsunami*	The **tsunami** was a wave fifty feet tall!
15.	iguana	*iguana*	That big green lizard is an **iguana**.
16.	plaza	*plaza*	The town **plaza** covers one square block.
17.	caravan	*caravan*	A camel **caravan** crossed the desert.
18.	hammock	*hammock*	Dora is lying in a **hammock** outside.
19.	pajamas	*pajamas*	The toddler sleeps in blue **pajamas**.
20.	tortilla	*tortilla*	Put meat in the **tortilla** and roll it up.

Review		**Challenge**	
21. canyon	23. magazine	26. mosquito	28. alligator
22. mirror	24. rodeo	27. cathedral	29. tambourine
	25. monkey		30. sombrero

Think and Sort

English has borrowed words from many languages. Some of these words have become quite common. Others may be unfamiliar. Saying the words and breaking them into syllables can help you learn to spell them.

sal / sa   car / a / van

Write each Basic Word under the number of syllables it has.

Word Analysis/Phonics

21–25. Write the five Basic Words that have the /ē/ sound spelled *i*.

Vocabulary: Definitions

Write the Basic or Review Word that matches each definition.

26. pants made of sturdy fabric

27. a large, colorful handkerchief

28. loose-fitting garments often worn as sleepwear

29. a cloak with a hole for a head in the middle

Challenge Words

Write Challenge Words to complete the sentences. Use your Spelling Dictionary.

30. A _____ will keep the sun off your face.

31. The _____ is an instrument that makes a jangling sound.

32. Never approach an _____, even if it is small.

33. Swat that buzzing _____ before it bites you.

34. That _____ has many stained glass windows.

Spelling-Meaning Connection

The word *burro* in Spanish means "donkey." The Spanish ending *-ito* can be added to change the meaning to "little donkey": *burrito*. *Burrito* can also mean "a flour tortilla wrapped around a filling." Write *burro* and *burrito*. Underline the Spanish ending that means "little."

burro
burr_ito_

Word Analysis

21. _____

22. _____

23. _____

24. _____

25. _____

Definitions

26. _____

27. _____

28. _____

29. _____

Challenge Words

30. _____

31. _____

32. _____

33. _____

34. _____

Spelling-Meaning

35. _____

36. _____

At Home With a family member, take turns writing two Spelling Words on a piece of paper. Cut all the letters apart and mix them up. The other person puts the letters together to spell the words.

Vocabulary

1. _____
2. _____
3. _____
4. _____
5. _____
6. _____

Dictionary

7. _____

8. _____

9. _____

10. _____

11. _____

12. _____

13. _____

14. _____

Vocabulary: Clothing Words from Spanish

The English language has borrowed a number of words for types of clothing worn in Spanish-speaking countries or areas.

Example: _chinos_—pants made of heavy tan cotton

Practice Write the word from the box that matches each description. Use your Spelling Dictionary.

poncho	mantilla	sombrero
huaraches	serape	chaps

1. a woolen cloak with a head-hole and open sides
2. leather sandals with flat soles
3. heavy trouser fronts worn by cowboys
4. a large straw hat with a round, upcurled brim
5. a cloak with a hole for a head in its center
6. a lace scarf worn over the head

Dictionary: Word Histories

Every word has its own history. When a word's history is shown in a dictionary, it is usually the last part of an entry. Read the word history of _poncho_.

♦ American Spanish, from Spanish, cape, perhaps variant of _pocho_, faded, discolored.

Practice Find the origins of each of these words in your Spelling Dictionary. List the language or languages each came from.

7. tycoon   9. dungarees   11. caravan   13. hammock

8. tomato   10. patio   12. tsunami   14. pajamas

Proofread a Questionnaire

Spelling and Run-on Sentences Use proofreading marks to correct **ten** misspelled Basic or Review Words and **two** run-on sentences in this questionnaire.

Example: Pack your ~~pajammas~~ *pajamas* take a vacation!

Answer each question help us plan your vacation.

1. Do you travel a lot, or will this be your first big trip?

2. Would you like to see cowhands lasoo cattle in a roadio, or would you rather sit on a patio and read a magazene?

3. Do you prefer a siesta on a matress or in a hamack?

4. Would you rather photograph a monky or an igwana?

5. Which snack would you order, a vanila ice cream cone or a warm tortilla with beans, sallsa, and chopped tomatoe?

E-mail your responses to Anywhere Excursions we will send you some fabulous travel ideas!

Basic
salsa
mattress
tycoon
burrito
bandanna
tomato
poncho
dungarees
lasso
patio
siesta
cargo
vanilla
tsunami
iguana
plaza
caravan
hammock
pajamas
tortilla

Review
canyon
mirror
magazine
rodeo
monkey

Challenge
mosquito
cathedral
alligator
tambourine
sombrero

Write a Questionnaire

prewrite → draft → revise → proofread → publish

Write some other questions to ask people who want to travel.

• Ask about the **types of places** and **activities** they would enjoy.

• Use some Spelling Words and compound sentences.

• Proofread your work for **spelling** and **sentence punctuation**.

Power Proofreading
www.eduplace.com/kids/sv/

Test Tip Eliminate answer choices that you know are incorrect.

Test Format Practice

Directions For numbers 1 through 8, choose the word that is spelled correctly and best completes the sentence.

Example: I brought a _____ in case it rains.

  A ponsho
  B pancho
  C pantcho
  D poncho

Example:

Ⓐ Ⓑ Ⓒ ●

Answer Sheet

1. Ⓐ Ⓑ Ⓒ Ⓓ
2. Ⓕ Ⓖ Ⓗ Ⓙ
3. Ⓐ Ⓑ Ⓒ Ⓓ
4. Ⓕ Ⓖ Ⓗ Ⓙ
5. Ⓐ Ⓑ Ⓒ Ⓓ
6. Ⓕ Ⓖ Ⓗ Ⓙ
7. Ⓐ Ⓑ Ⓒ Ⓓ
8. Ⓕ Ⓖ Ⓗ Ⓙ

1. My brother has striped _____.

  A pojamas
  B pajamas
  C pejamas
  D pajamis

2. That ship is carrying a _____ of coal.

  F carrgo
  G cargoe
  H kargoe
  J cargo

3. A river runs through the _____.

  A canyon
  B cannyon
  C canion
  D canyen

4. We heard a band playing in the _____.

  F plazza
  G plahza
  H plaza
  J plasa

5. Check the _____ to see how you look.

  A mirorr
  B miror
  C mirrer
  D mirror

6. The mill is owned by a lumber _____.

  F tiecoon
  G tyecoon
  H tycoon
  J tycoun

7. That _____ has twelve camels in it.

  A caravan
  B karavan
  C carevan
  D carivan

8. Don't jump up and down on that _____.

  F matres
  G mattress
  H matress
  J mattres

More Practice

Now write each correctly spelled word on a sheet of paper.

Spelling Games
www.eduplace.com/kids/sv/
Review for your test.

Real-World 🎵 Vocabulary

Music: Music Appreciation

All the words in the box relate to music. Look up these words in your Spelling Dictionary. Write the words to complete the music review.

Spelling Word Link

salsa

harmony
harpsichord
concert
accordion
congas
oboe
quartet
viola

Music Club Performance Offers Contrasts

by Lynn Casey

The Riverlake School Music Club's annual ___(1)___ featured two types of music: classical music and salsa. First, a ___(2)___ of musicians performed music of Bach. Janeece Jones was masterful on the ___(3)___, an early keyboard instrument. John Ita played the ___(4)___, a reed instrument. Shira Lopez played her violin with skill, and Roger Khan excelled on the ___(5)___.

After the intermission, the program featured livelier Latin dance music. The thumping of the ___(6)___ set the rhythm. Ms. Jones, who switched to the smaller keyboard of an ___(7)___, often played the melody. Sometimes several horns would play together in ___(8)___. The program was an unusual mix of styles, but everyone had a wonderful time!

1. _____
2. _____
3. _____
4. _____
5. _____
6. _____
7. _____
8. _____

eWord Game
www.eduplace.com/kids/sv/

Try This
CHALLENGE

Riddles On a separate sheet of paper, write short riddles about musical instruments or types of music. Use some words from the box. Trade riddles with a classmate and try to solve them.

Spelling Review

Unit 19

1. _____

2. _____

3. _____

4. _____

5. _____

6. _____

7. _____

8. _____

9. _____

10. _____

scrubbed	stunned	gathering	beginning	chatting
bothering	scanned	ordered	answered	shrugged

Spelling Strategy For most one-syllable words, double the consonant. For most two-syllable words, do not double the consonant.

     chat + ing = cha**tting**   gather + ing = gather**ing**

Analogies Write the word that best completes each analogy.

1. *Queried* is to *asked* as *commanded* is to _____.

2. *Wiped* is to _____ as *sipped* is to *drank*.

3. *Thrilled* is to *delighted* as _____ is to *shocked*.

4. *Harvesting* is to *planting* as *ending* is to _____.

5. *Threatening* is to *menacing* as *annoying* is to _____.

Context Sentences Write the word that completes each sentence.

6. Everyone stopped _____ when the teacher entered the room.

7. I _____ the sky for a sign of rain.

8. Latrice _____ the teacher's question correctly.

9. David _____ his shoulders as if he didn't remember the score.

10. The children are _____ flowers for the decorations.

Unit 20

11. _____

12. _____

13. _____

14. _____

15. _____

16. _____

17. _____

18. _____

19. _____

20. _____

tiring	borrowed	delivered	losing	decided
related	remarked	attending	amusing	repeated

Spelling Strategy Some words change spelling when an ending is added.

     tire + ing = tir**ing**   deliver + ed = deliver**ed**

Definitions Write the word that fits each meaning.

11. handed over

12. commented

13. determined

14. misplacing

15. exhausting

16. being present at

17. connected

18. humorous

19. took out a loan

20. said again

Unit 21 — Changing Final *y* to *i* — pages 138–143

| duties | earlier | loveliest | terrified | abilities |
| trophies | iciest | drowsier | victories | horrified |

Spelling Strategy When a word ends with a consonant and *y*, change the *y* to *i* when adding *-es*, *-ed*, *-er*, or *-est*.

Word Clues Write the word that fits each clue.

21. prizes people get for winning
22. most beautiful
23. most frozen
24. things you have to do
25. frightened out of your wits
26. synonym for *sleepier*
27. shocked and disgusted
28. ahead of time; sooner
29. skills and talents
30. triumphs or conquests

Unit 22 — Suffixes: *-ful, -ly, -ness, -less, -ment* — pages 144–149

| settlement | watchful | steadily | closeness | countless |
| enjoyment | noisily | forgiveness | harmless | plentiful |

Spelling Strategy A suffix is a word part added to the end of a base word. A suffix adds meaning. The spelling of the base word is usually not changed when the suffix begins with a consonant.

Context Paragraph Write the words that complete this paragraph.

The wagon train wound its way ___(31)___ along the trail. Because of the ___(32)___ of the canyon walls on either side, the pioneers were ___(33)___ for any sign of danger. Finally they could see lights up ahead. The pioneers reached the ___(34)___ just after dark. The inhabitants greeted them ___(35)___, eager for any news. Quickly a feast from the fall's ___(36)___ harvest was prepared for the weary travelers. Eating a meal in their new home brought the settlers great ___(37)___.

Antonyms Write the word that means the opposite of each word below.

38. hurtful
39. blame
40. few

Unit 21
21. _____
22. _____
23. _____
24. _____
25. _____
26. _____
27. _____
28. _____
29. _____
30. _____

Unit 22
31. _____
32. _____
33. _____
34. _____
35. _____
36. _____
37. _____
38. _____
39. _____
40. _____

Spelling Review

Unit 23

41. _____

42. _____

43. _____

44. _____

45. _____

46. _____

47. _____

48. _____

49. _____

50. _____

Unit 23	Words from Other Languages		pages 150–155
mattress	bandanna	tomato	poncho	patio
siesta	vanilla	iguana	plaza	tsunami

Spelling Strategy Breaking unfamiliar words into syllables can help you spell them.

mat / tress   si / es / ta   i / gua / na

Analogies Write the word that best completes each analogy.

41. *Rest* is to *relaxation* as *nap* is to _____.

42. *Headband* is to _____ as *jacket* is to *coat*.

43. *Hallway* is to *corridor* as _____ is to *courtyard*.

44. *Breeze* is to *gale* as *wave* is to _____.

Classifying Write the word that belongs in each group.

45. public square, shopping center, _____

46. raincoat, slicker, _____

47. Gila monster, Komodo dragon, _____

48. bedroll, futon, _____

49. chocolate, strawberry, _____

50. lettuce, avocado, _____

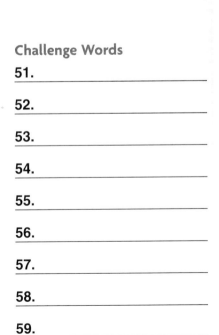

Challenge Words

51. _____

52. _____

53. _____

54. _____

55. _____

56. _____

57. _____

58. _____

59. _____

60. _____

Challenge Words	Units 19–23		pages 126–155
occurred	entertaining	boundaries	merciless	cathedral
canceled	donated	satisfied	seriousness	sombrero

Synonyms Write the word that means the same or almost the same as each word below.

51. church

52. fulfilled

53. amusing

54. happened

55. hat

56. pitiless

57. borders

58. contributed

59. stopped

60. solemnity

Spelling and Writing

Proofread a Personal Narrative

Spelling and Grammar Mixed Review Use proofreading marks to correct **nine** misspelled words, **two** mistakes in using commas, and **one** missing quotation mark in this personal narrative.

Example: "At least you didn't come to school in your ~~pajammas~~ *pajamas*!" she said.

Proofreading Marks	
¶	Indent
∧	Add
⊙	Add a period
⌐	Delete
≡	Capital letter
/	Small letter

Latly I've become very forgetfull and it has been really upseting. Today I even forgot my appointment with Ms. Ross, the school counselor. When I rushed into her office, she looked stern. "I'm glad you came, Vicky. I want to talk to you about your tardyness."

How could I explain that I forgot to set my alarm and forgot our meeting? By then I had whiped myself into a frenzy of suferring. "I'm so sorry, I whispered. "I don't know why I keep forgetting things."

As Ms. Ross quizd me about my life, I suddenly knew what was wrong. I blurted, "My dad's company is moving! We're expekted to sell our house, pack and move to a new city in less than a month! I don't want to leave!"

Ms. Ross told me to think of all the great memorys I would be taking with me to my new school. "I think we've solved your 'remembering' problem," she said.

Write a Personal Narrative

prewrite → draft → revise → proofread → publish

Write a personal narrative about a time when you rushed to arrive somewhere on time and succeeded.

- Use some Spelling Words from Units 19 through 23 in your narrative.
- Proofread your work for **spelling**, the use of **commas**, and the use of **quotation marks**.

Tips
- Brainstorm details about the situation.
- Describe the events in the order they happened.
- Use the first-person pronouns *I, we, me,* and *my.*

Power Proofreading
www.eduplace.com/kids/sv/

Spelling Test Practice

Test Tip Read the directions carefully.

Directions Read each group of sentences. Decide if one of the underlined words is spelled wrong or if there is *No mistake*. Fill in the space for the answer you have chosen.

Example: **A** This <u>mattriss</u> is too soft.
   B The toddler is being <u>naughty</u>.
   C Your book is <u>overdue</u>.
   D No mistake.

Example:

Answer Sheet

1. Ⓐ Ⓑ Ⓒ Ⓓ
2. Ⓕ Ⓖ Ⓗ Ⓙ
3. Ⓐ Ⓑ Ⓒ Ⓓ
4. Ⓕ Ⓖ Ⓗ Ⓙ
5. Ⓐ Ⓑ Ⓒ Ⓓ
6. Ⓕ Ⓖ Ⓗ Ⓙ
7. Ⓐ Ⓑ Ⓒ Ⓓ
8. Ⓕ Ⓖ Ⓗ Ⓙ

More Practice

Now write all the misspelled words correctly on a separate sheet of paper.

www.eduplace.com/kids/sv/
Review for your test.

1. A Hailstones <u>damaiged</u> the windshield.
   B The <u>weather</u> was cloudy.
   C I <u>skimmed</u> the chapter.
   D No mistake

2. F Jill <u>decided</u> to join us.
   G Did you <u>compose</u> that poem?
   H All the leaders are <u>unitted</u>.
   J No mistake

3. A Will you be <u>attending</u> the show?
   B The <u>spider</u> will not hurt you.
   C Dad <u>denyed</u> my request.
   D No mistake

4. F The <u>warehouse</u> is filled with bicycles.
   G The cabin is <u>cozyer</u> with a fire.
   H My favorite flavor is <u>vanilla</u>.
   J No mistake

5. A Skiing is a <u>popular</u> sport.
   B We made <u>tomato</u> soup.
   C I try not to make <u>enemmies</u>.
   D No mistake

6. F If a bee lands on you, act <u>calmly</u>.
   G We made an <u>agreament</u> to meet.
   H May I borrow a <u>quarter</u>?
   J No mistake

7. A This fall the apples are <u>plentyful</u>.
   B The <u>journey</u> to China is long.
   C I enjoy <u>listening</u> to music.
   D No mistake

8. F The <u>carpeting</u> is soft.
   G Please pass the <u>menu</u>.
   H I fell asleep in the <u>hammick</u>.
   J No mistake

Test Tip Be sure to fill in the whole circle.

Directions Find the word that means the <u>opposite</u> of the underlined word.

Example: a <u>cleaner</u> shirt

   A cozier
   B loose
   C dirtier
   D modern

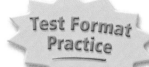

Example:

ⒶⒷ●Ⓓ

Answer Sheet

1. Ⓐ Ⓑ Ⓒ Ⓓ
2. Ⓕ Ⓖ Ⓗ Ⓙ
3. Ⓐ Ⓑ Ⓒ Ⓓ
4. Ⓕ Ⓖ Ⓗ Ⓙ
5. Ⓐ Ⓑ Ⓒ Ⓓ
6. Ⓕ Ⓖ Ⓗ Ⓙ
7. Ⓐ Ⓑ Ⓒ Ⓓ
8. Ⓕ Ⓖ Ⓗ Ⓙ
9. Ⓐ Ⓑ Ⓒ Ⓓ
10. Ⓕ Ⓖ Ⓗ Ⓙ

1. a <u>minor</u> argument
   A legal
   B related
   C normal
   D major

2. a <u>shouted</u> comment
   F whispered
   G cruel
   H further
   J bitter

3. to <u>forbid</u> talking
   A suggest
   B permit
   C publish
   D avoid

4. to <u>fire</u> a worker
   F employ
   G confuse
   H promise
   J greet

5. <u>boiling</u> a liquid
   A knitting
   B upsetting
   C freezing
   D losing

6. a <u>generous</u> person
   F delightful
   G loyal
   H well-known
   J stingy

7. <u>formal</u> clothes
   A borrowed
   B casual
   C damaged
   D violet

8. <u>above</u> the table
   F beneath
   G aboard
   H throughout
   J improve

9. <u>cloudier</u> weather
   A earlier
   B scariest
   C moist
   D sunnier

10. two <u>graceful</u> dancers
   F former
   G barefoot
   H awkward
   J local

Final /n/ or /ən/ Sounds

1. _____
2. _____
3. _____
4. _____
5. _____
6. _____
7. _____

Final /chər/ Sounds

8. _____
9. _____
10. _____
11. _____
12. _____
13. _____
14. _____
15. _____
16. _____
17. _____

Final /zhər/ Sounds

18. _____
19. _____
20. _____

Read the Spelling Words and sentences.

Basic

1.	nature	_nature_	You can study animal habits in **nature**.
2.	certain	_certain_	I am **certain** that bees make honey.
3.	future	_future_	Cara hopes to study law in the **future**.
4.	villain	_villain_	The **villain** in the play was wicked.
5.	mountain	_mountain_	We hiked up the steep **mountain**.
6.	mixture	_mixture_	Stir this **mixture** of ingredients.
7.	pleasure	_pleasure_	Ivan reads mysteries for **pleasure**.
8.	captain	_captain_	The **captain** gives orders to the crew.
9.	departure	_departure_	I saw the train's arrival and **departure**.
10.	surgeon	_surgeon_	The **surgeon** operated on the patient.
11.	texture	_texture_	The walls have a smooth **texture**.
12.	curtain	_curtain_	Does your window need a new **curtain**?
13.	creature	_creature_	What a huge **creature** the blue whale is!
14.	treasure	_treasure_	The **treasure** included gold and jewels.
15.	gesture	_gesture_	A wave of a hand is a friendly **gesture**.
16.	fountain	_fountain_	Did the water **fountain** splash you?
17.	furniture	_furniture_	Greg bought a desk and other **furniture**.
18.	measure	_measure_	Use a yardstick to **measure** the door.
19.	feature	_feature_	A new **feature** is at the movie theater.
20.	adventure	_adventure_	The backpackers began their **adventure**.

Review

21. picture
22. capture
23. surprise
24. receive
25. idea

Challenge

26. leisure
27. sculpture
28. architecture
29. chieftain
30. enclosure

Think and Sort

Each Spelling Word has the final /n/, /ən/, /chər/, or /zhər/ sounds.

/n/ or /ən/ fount**ain**   /chər/ fu**ture**   /zhər/ trea**sure**

⚠ How is the final sound spelled in the Memory Word?

Write each Basic Word under its final sounds.

Word Analysis/Phonics

Write Basic Words to complete the exercises.

21–22. Write two words that have the /j/ sound spelled *g*.

23–24. Write two words that have the /ks/ sound spelled *x*.

Vocabulary: Word Clues

Write a Basic or Review Word that fits each clue.

25. the opposite of *arrival*

26. another name for an animal

27. the opposite of *give away*

28. an image of something

29. what a teaspoon or tablespoon can do

Challenge Words

Write the Challenge Words to complete the paragraph. Use your Spelling Dictionary.

   Near the banks of a river, the tribespeople built wood homes using their traditional form of __(30)__. Around the homes they constructed a long fence as an __(31)__. When they were done, they enjoyed their __(32)__ time. Some people sang, and others told stories. One person began carving a __(33)__. It would be a monument to honor the __(34)__.

Spelling-Meaning Connection

35–36. The words *nature* and *natural* are related in spelling and meaning. Write *nature* and *natural*. Underline the vowel that is the same in both words but spells /ā/ in one word and /ă/ in the other.

n<u>a</u>ture
n<u>a</u>tural

Word Analysis

21. _____

22. _____

23. _____

24. _____

Word Clues

25. _____

26. _____

27. _____

28. _____

29. _____

Challenge Words

30. _____

31. _____

32. _____

33. _____

34. _____

Spelling-Meaning

35. _____

36. _____

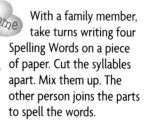

At Home With a family member, take turns writing four Spelling Words on a piece of paper. Cut the syllables apart. Mix them up. The other person joins the parts to spell the words.

163

Vocabulary

1. _____
2. _____
3. _____
4. _____
5. _____
6. _____
7. _____
8. _____

Vocabulary: Analogies

One kind of analogy pairs a noun with an adjective that describes it. Another kind pairs a category with a member of that category.

Example 1: *Skyscraper* is to *tall* as *sugar* is to *sweet*.

Example 2: *Vehicle* is to *tractor* as *clothing* is to *socks*.

Practice Write the word from the box that best completes each analogy. Use your Spelling Dictionary.

dishwasher	helicopter	weaving	piccolo
furniture	nimble	annoying	mountain

1. *Sport* is to *swimming* as *craft* is to _____.
2. *Trough* is to *deep* as _____ is to *lofty*.
3. *Tool* is to *hammer* as *appliance* is to _____.
4. *Cheetah* is to *swift* as *monkey* is to _____.
5. *Aircraft* is to _____ as *boat* is to *canoe*.
6. *Tuba* is to *low* as _____ is to *high*.
7. *Gnat* is to _____ as *puma* is to *dangerous*.
8. *Dwelling* is to *den* as _____ is to *chair*.

Dictionary

9. _____
10. _____
11. _____
12. _____
13. _____
14. _____

Dictionary: Multiple-Meaning Words

Each definition of a multiple-meaning word is numbered.

fea•ture (fē´ chər) *n., pl.* **features 1.** A prominent or distinctive aspect, quality, or characteristic. **2.** A full-length movie.

Practice Write *treasure 1, treasure 2, feature 1,* or *feature 2* to show which meaning of the word best completes each sentence. Use your Spelling Dictionary.

9. The mesa was the most dramatic _____ of the desert.
10. The kindly librarian is a _____ to the community.
11. The movie studio released the first _____ of the summer.
12. The Grand Canyon is a national _____.
13. The cat's blue-gray fur is an unusual _____.
14. The divers found valuable _____ in the sunken ship.

PART 3 Spelling and Writing

Proofread a TV Interview

Spelling and Personal Pronouns Use proofreading marks to correct **ten** misspelled Basic or Review Words and **four** mistakes in the use of *I* and *me, he* and *him,* and *she* and *her* in this TV interview.

Example: Don and ~~me~~ *I* have an ~~idia~~ *idea* for a great science-fiction movie.

INTERVIEWER: Today on *Star Talk,* let's meet Jim Patel, star of the new space advenchure *Planet Ten.* I am sertain the film will be a hit. Tell us about the new feachur, Jim.

JIM: Well, it takes place in the futchur. Me am the captain. My crew and me are looking for treasure on a mounten. The alien villen, a fierce creature, tries to capshure Gloria, the ship's surgen. Her is brave, though.

INTERVIEWER: How does it end? The director won't say.

JIM: I told he I'd keep the ending a sirprize.

INTERVIEWER: Okay! Well, thanks for visiting, Jim.

JIM: It's been my pleshure.

Proofreading Marks
- ¶ Indent
- ∧ Add
- ⊙ Add a period
- ϙ Delete
- ≡ Capital letter
- / Small letter

Basic
nature
certain
future
villain
mountain
mixture
pleasure
captain
departure
surgeon
texture
curtain
creature
treasure
gesture
fountain
furniture
measure
feature
adventure

Review
picture
capture
surprise
receive
idea

Challenge
leisure
sculpture
architecture
chieftain
enclosure

Write a TV Interview

prewrite ➜ draft ➜ revise ➜ proofread ➜ publish

Write the script of an imaginary interview.

- Ask **who, what, where, when,** and **how questions.**
- Use some Spelling Words and at least one of these pronouns: *I, me, he, him, she, her.*
- Proofread for **spelling** and for the correct use of **pronouns.**

Power Proofreading
www.eduplace.com/kids/sv/

> **Test Tip** If you change an answer, erase the first answer completely.

Test Format Practice

Directions Find the phrase containing an underlined word that is <u>not</u> spelled correctly. If all the underlined words are spelled correctly, mark "All correct."

Example: **A** a pretty <u>picture</u>
B a <u>burglar</u> alarm
C to <u>capture</u> the flag
D a friendly <u>jesture</u>
E All correct

Example:

Ⓐ Ⓑ Ⓒ ● Ⓔ

Answer Sheet

1. Ⓐ Ⓑ Ⓒ Ⓓ Ⓔ
2. Ⓕ Ⓖ Ⓗ Ⓙ Ⓚ
3. Ⓐ Ⓑ Ⓒ Ⓓ Ⓔ
4. Ⓕ Ⓖ Ⓗ Ⓙ Ⓚ
5. Ⓐ Ⓑ Ⓒ Ⓓ Ⓔ
6. Ⓕ Ⓖ Ⓗ Ⓙ Ⓚ
7. Ⓐ Ⓑ Ⓒ Ⓓ Ⓔ
8. Ⓕ Ⓖ Ⓗ Ⓙ Ⓚ

1. **A** a <u>pleasure</u> to meet you
B a <u>surprise</u> party
C the final <u>kertain</u>
D to <u>measure</u> the fabric
E All correct

2. **F** a water <u>fownten</u>
G an exciting <u>adventure</u>
H a <u>feature</u> film
J to <u>receive</u> a letter
K All correct

3. **A** a building <u>complex</u>
B to <u>crush</u> a cup
C a sneaky <u>villain</u>
D a snowy <u>mountain</u>
E All correct

4. **F** to read <u>aloud</u>
G a lost <u>treasure</u>
H a new <u>iddea</u>
J a rough <u>texture</u>
K All correct

5. **A** to <u>demand</u> an answer
B to <u>shovel</u> snow
C a <u>sheepish</u> grin
D bedroom <u>furnitchure</u>
E All correct

6. **F** a <u>nachur</u> walk
G a <u>career</u> choice
H a green <u>bandanna</u>
J a <u>delightful</u> concert
K All correct

7. **A** a jigsaw <u>puzzle</u>
B to be in <u>conflict</u>
C a tasty <u>burrito</u>
D to feel <u>certen</u>
E All correct

8. **F** to <u>create</u> an image
G to plan for the <u>fuchur</u>
H to <u>destroy</u> completely
J to <u>select</u> from a group
K All correct

More Practice

Now write all the misspelled words correctly on a separate sheet of paper.

Spelling Games
www.eduplace.com/kids/sv/
Review for your test.

Real-World Vocabulary

Health: Accidents

All the words in the box relate to accidents and medicine. Look up these words in your Spelling Dictionary. Then write the words to complete this news report.

Spelling Word Link

surgeon

ambulance
emergency
recovery
paramedic
physician
specialist
surgery
x-ray

Mountain Rescue

On August 15 Oswald Ruiz fell twenty feet off a ledge in Pacific Crest National Park. The park's search and rescue team came to his aid. The team can handle an ____(1)____ like this anytime. A ranger and the on-duty ____(2)____, a trained medical aide, flew to the scene since it was unreachable by ____(3)____. Ruiz's leg was badly hurt, so they airlifted him to a hospital. There, Ruiz had an ____(4)____ to check for broken bones. A surgeon who was a bone ____(5)____ gave an expert opinion and recommended immediate ____(6)____ to save Ruiz's leg. The operation was a success. Now Ruiz will see his regular ____(7)____ for follow-up care. That doctor will supervise Ruiz's ____(8)____.

1. _____
2. _____
3. _____
4. _____
5. _____
6. _____
7. _____
8. _____

 **eWord Game**
www.eduplace.com/kids/sv/

 **Try This**

CHALLENGE

Questions and Answers Write the word from the box that answers each question.

9. What vehicle is often used to take patients to a hospital?

10. What is a photographic image of bones called?

11. What is a synonym for *operation*?

12. What is the name of a medical worker who responds to a 9-1-1 call?

9. _____
10. _____
11. _____
12. _____

Read the Spelling Words and sentences.

Basic

1. storage	*storage*	We keep our skis in **storage** during May.
2. olive	*olive*	Each tasty **olive** has a pit inside.
3. service	*service*	The hotel staff provides good **service**.
4. relative	*relative*	Is Grandma Anne our oldest **relative**?
5. garbage	*garbage*	Please put the **garbage** in the trash can.
6. courage	*courage*	It takes **courage** to fight a fire.
7. native	*native*	Is this plant **native** to the island?
8. passage	*passage*	Read a **passage** from this book.
9. voyage	*voyage*	Isa went on a **voyage** across the ocean.
10. knowledge	*knowledge*	Lon studied to increase his **knowledge**.
11. image	*image*	The sketch shows an **image** of clouds.
12. creative	*creative*	My **creative** pal writes poems.
13. average	*average*	What is the **average** rainfall for July?
14. justice	*justice*	Lawyers want **justice** for their clients.
15. detective	*detective*	The **detective** likes solving mysteries.
16. postage	*postage*	Laura put extra **postage** on the letter.
17. cowardice	*cowardice*	The hero did not show **cowardice**.
18. adjective	*adjective*	Use an **adjective** to describe a noun.
19. luggage	*luggage*	A suitcase is a piece of **luggage**.
20. language	*language*	Our tour guide speaks our **language**.

Review		**Challenge**	
21. notice	23. package	26. prejudice	28. beverage
22. marriage	24. office	27. cooperative	29. heritage
	25. manage		30. apprentice

Think and Sort

Each Spelling Word has the final /ĭj/, /ĭv/, or /ĭs/ sounds.

/ĭj/ stor**age**   /ĭv/ creat**ive**   /ĭs/ coward**ice**

How are the final /ĭj/ sounds spelled in the Memory Word?

Write each Basic Word under its ending sounds.

Final /ĭj/ Sounds

1. _____

2. _____

3. _____

4. _____

5. _____

6. _____

7. _____

8. _____

9. _____

10. _____

11. _____

Final /ĭv/ Sounds

12. _____

13. _____

14. _____

15. _____

16. _____

17. _____

Final /ĭs/ Sounds

18. _____

19. _____

20. _____

Word Analysis/Phonics

Write the Basic Words that have these base words.

21. pass   **22.** create   **23.** detect   **24.** coward

Vocabulary: Definitions

Write the Basic or Review Word that fits each meaning.

25. a long boat trip to a distant place

26. the condition of living together as husband and wife

27. the part of speech that usually modifies a noun

28. the charge for mailing something

29. facts and ideas; information

Challenge Words

Write the Challenge Word that completes each sentence. Use your Spelling Dictionary.

30. The _____ gardeners shared their seeds with us.

31. Please bring juice or another healthful _____ to the party.

32. The New Year's parade is part of the Chinese cultural _____.

33. The _____ to the carpenter learned how to make a chair.

34. People affected by _____ may not be treated fairly.

Spelling-Meaning Connection

35–36. The silent *e* in *courage* is <u>not</u> dropped when *-ous* is added to form *courageous*. The *e* is needed to retain the soft, or /j/, sound of *g* in both words. Write *courage* and *courageous*. Underline the silent *e* in each word.

courage
courageous

Definitions

25. _____

26. _____

27. _____

28. _____

29. _____

Challenge Words

30. _____

31. _____

32. _____

33. _____

34. _____

Spelling-Meaning

35. _____

36. _____

At Home With a family member, take turns writing the first three letters of a Spelling Word. The other person finishes the word.

Vocabulary

1. _____
2. _____
3. _____
4. _____
5. _____
6. _____
7. _____

Vocabulary: Family Words

Practice Some words for family members help explain how people are related. Write the word from the box that best answers each question. Use your Spelling Dictionary.

relative	ancestor	descendant	stepchild
sibling	husband	son-in-law	

1. Which word has *descend* as its base word?
2. What is the word for a man who is married?
3. What is the name for a man who is related to his mother-in-law by marriage?
4. Which word is a member of the word family that includes *relate* and *relation*?
5. Which word is used for a brother or a sister?
6. What is the word for a spouse's child from a previous marriage?
7. What is a family member from long ago?

Thesaurus

8. _____
9. _____
10. _____
11. _____
12. _____
13. _____
14. _____
15. _____

Thesaurus: Synonyms and Antonyms

A thesaurus entry may list antonyms as well as synonyms.

normal *adj.* of the usual kind. *Today's temperature is* **normal** *for May.*
average typical, usual, or ordinary. *The* **average** *child needs plenty of sleep.*
ordinary everyday; common. *Until the fire alarm went off, it was just another* **ordinary** *school day.*
antonyms: abnormal, unusual, rare, limited

Practice Write a synonym and then an antonym from the box for each word below. Use your Thesaurus to confirm word meanings.

criticism	dull	devoted	lively
informed	disloyal	approval	ignorant

8–9. boring   **10–11.** educated   **12–13.** faithful   **14–15.** praise

Proofread an Informational Handout

Spelling and Personal Pronouns Use proofreading marks to correct **nine** misspelled Basic or Review Words and **three** mistakes in using *we, us, they,* and *them* in this handout.

Example: ~~Us~~ *We* and Aunt Nell took a ~~relatife~~ *relative* on a raft trip.

TO ALL RAFTERS: Please read this notise carefully.

- Do not bring luggige on the raft. Place it in our storeage unit.

- Even if you think you can mannage the rapids, wear a life preserver. Pick one up at the ofise.

- Ask for a guide who speaks your home langwige.

- If you eat lunch on shore, do not disturb natife plants or animals. Them need protection. Also, do not leave garbije behind.

- Go ashore when you see a narrow passage. The rapids are just ahead. Let we check your life preserver and take a photo. You can buy this memorable imije of your voyage later.

- Us and the rest of the staff want to provide excellent service. What can we do for you?

Proofreading Marks

- ¶ Indent
- ∧ Add
- ⊙ Add a period
- ˞ Delete
- ≡ Capital letter
- / Small letter

Basic
storage
olive
service
relative
garbage
courage
native
passage
voyage
knowledge
image
creative
average
justice
detective
postage
cowardice
adjective
luggage
language

Review
notice
marriage
package
office
manage

Challenge
prejudice
cooperative
beverage
heritage
apprentice

Write an Informational Handout

prewrite ➡ draft ➡ revise ➡ proofread ➡ publish

Write a short notice describing the rules for an activity.

- Name the activity. State the rules in **clear, direct language.**
- Use some Spelling Words and *we, us, they,* or *them.*
- Proofread your work for **spelling** and the correct use of **pronouns.**

Power Proofreading
www.eduplace.com/kids/sv/

Test Tip Skip questions that seem hard and go back to them later.

Test Format Practice

Directions Read each group of sentences. Decide if one of the underlined words is spelled wrong or if there is *No mistake*. Fill in the space for the answer you have chosen.

Example: **A** I can print a color <u>image</u>.
B The editor changed an <u>adjective</u>.
C Welsh is the traditional <u>langwige</u> of Wales.
D No mistake

Example:

Ⓐ Ⓑ ● Ⓓ

Answer Sheet

1. Ⓐ Ⓑ Ⓒ Ⓓ
2. Ⓕ Ⓖ Ⓗ Ⓙ
3. Ⓐ Ⓑ Ⓒ Ⓓ
4. Ⓕ Ⓖ Ⓗ Ⓙ
5. Ⓐ Ⓑ Ⓒ Ⓓ
6. Ⓕ Ⓖ Ⓗ Ⓙ
7. Ⓐ Ⓑ Ⓒ Ⓓ
8. Ⓕ Ⓖ Ⓗ Ⓙ

More Practice

Now write all the misspelled words correctly on a separate sheet of paper.

Spelling Games
www.eduplace.com/kids/sv/
Review for your test.

1. **A** Juan is a <u>native</u> of Peru.
B The chef put an <u>olave</u> on the salad.
C Stow your <u>luggage</u> in the closet.
D No mistake

2. **F** The <u>detective</u> dusted for fingerprints.
G We added <u>postage</u> at the post office.
H The food there is just <u>avarege</u>.
J No mistake

3. **A** Glen wrapped the <u>packadge</u> carefully.
B Be <u>creative</u> in your work.
C The experiment added to our <u>knowledge</u>.
D No mistake

4. **F** The <u>voyage</u> was tedious.
G The judge believes in <u>justuce</u> for all.
H We walked through a narrow <u>passage</u>.
J No mistake

5. **A** The lifeguard showed great <u>courage</u>.
B I see a <u>notice</u> in the store window.
C A <u>captain</u> flies a plane.
D No mistake

6. **F** Our <u>office</u> has three new computers.
G The mechanic will <u>serviss</u> our car.
H My favorite <u>relative</u> came to the picnic.
J No mistake

7. **A** Her father is a <u>well-known</u> comic.
B My cousin will <u>manage</u> the team.
C Put the lamp in <u>storige</u>.
D No mistake

8. **F** They applied for a <u>marrige</u> license.
G I will take out the <u>garbage</u> now.
H Alf hit a <u>home run</u>.
J No mistake

Real-World Vocabulary

Math: Analyzing Data

All the words in the box relate to mathematics. Look up these words in your Spelling Dictionary. Then write the words to complete this survey introduction.

Spelling Word Link
average

conclusions
mode
mean
median
results
statistics
survey
tally

Student's Name	Sister	Brother	Sibling's Age
Brian	/		8
Corinne		/	7
David		/	7

My partner and I did a ____(1)____ to collect data about siblings of students in our class. For each sibling, we marked a ____(2)____ under the heading *Sister* or *Brother*. We compiled numerical information, or ____(3)____, about the siblings. Then we analyzed the data. We added all the siblings' ages. Then we divided by the number of siblings to find the ____(4)____, or average, of their ages. Next we found the age in the middle of all the ages—the ____(5)____ age. After that, we found the most common age among the siblings. That number is the ____(6)____. Finally, we looked at the ____(7)____ to draw ____(8)____.

1. _____
2. _____
3. _____
4. _____
5. _____
6. _____
7. _____
8. _____

eWord Game
www.eduplace.com/kids/sv/

Try This CHALLENGE

Yes or No? Answer each question with *yes* or *no*.

9. Is the mode the number that occurs most often in a set?
10. Do you need a calculator to do a class survey?
11. Is a tally a kind of counting mark?
12. Do you use division to find the mean?

9. _____
10. _____
11. _____
12. _____

Read the Spelling Words and sentences.

Basic

1. entry	*entry*	Fill out an **entry** blank for the contest.
2. limit	*limit*	Do not go faster than the speed **limit**.
3. talent	*talent*	Will Jim play guitar in the **talent** show?
4. disturb	*disturb*	Do not **disturb** the sleeping baby.
5. entire	*entire*	We must clean the **entire** house by 5 P.M.
6. wisdom	*wisdom*	**Wisdom** helps you make good decisions.
7. dozen	*dozen*	A **dozen** roses plus one is thirteen.
8. impress	*impress*	Each skater tries to **impress** the judges.
9. respond	*respond*	Please **respond** to the e-mail I sent.
10. fortress	*fortress*	Cannons lined the top of the **fortress**.
11. neglect	*neglect*	Broken floorboards are signs of **neglect**.
12. crystal	*crystal*	Clean the **crystal** glasses carefully.
13. kitchen	*kitchen*	Who is preparing dinner in the **kitchen**?
14. forbid	*forbid*	I **forbid** you to read my diary!
15. pirate	*pirate*	The **pirate** looked for ships to attack.
16. spinach	*spinach*	**Spinach** is a green, leafy vegetable.
17. salute	*salute*	Soldiers **salute** officers to show respect.
18. frighten	*frighten*	Your dog's howls **frighten** children.
19. surround	*surround*	Will you **surround** the yard with a fence?
20. challenge	*challenge*	I **challenge** you to a game of chess.

Review		**Challenge**	
21. honest	23. whether	26. adapt	28. distribute
22. instead	24. event	27. refuge	29. industry
	25. attend		30. somber

VCCV

1. _____
2. _____
3. _____
4. _____
5. _____
6. _____
7. _____
8. _____
9. _____

VCCCV

10. _____
11. _____
12. _____
13. _____
14. _____

VCV

15. _____
16. _____
17. _____
18. _____
19. _____
20. _____

Think and Sort

Each two-syllable word has the VCCV, VCCCV, or VCV syllable pattern. Memorize the spelling of the unstressed syllable.

re / spond (rĭ spŏnd´)   **wis / dom** (wĭz´ dəm)

Write each Basic Word under its syllable pattern. Underline the unstressed syllable. Use your Spelling Dictionary to check your work.

Word Analysis/Phonics

Write the Basic Word that contains the given spelling for each sound.

21. /ch/ spelled *tch*   **23.** /j/ spelled *ge*   **25.** /ī/ spelled *igh*

22. /ī/ spelled *i*   **24.** /ĭ/ spelled *y*

Vocabulary: Analogies

Write the Basic or Review Word that best completes each analogy.

26. *Vegetable* is to _____ as *fruit* is to *lemon*.

27. *Lazy* is to *diligent* as *untruthful* is to _____.

28. *Three* is to *trio* as *twelve* is to _____.

29. *Region* is to *territory* as _____ is to *occurrence*.

Challenge Words

Write the Challenge Word that completes each riddle. Use your Spelling Dictionary.

30. If you are unhappy and gloomy, what are you?

31. If you change in response to situations, what do you do?

32. If you are in a safe area, what kind of place are you in?

33. If you pass something out in portions, what do you do?

34. If you provide a large-scale manufacture of goods, what are you?

Spelling-Meaning Connection

35–36. The words *wise* and *wisdom* are related in spelling and meaning. If you are wise, you have good judgment, or wisdom. Write *wise* and *wisdom*. Underline the vowel that is the same in each but has a different sound.

wise
wisdom

Word Analysis

21. _____

22. _____

23. _____

24. _____

25. _____

Analogies

26. _____

27. _____

28. _____

29. _____

Challenge Words

30. _____

31. _____

32. _____

33. _____

34. _____

Spelling-Meaning

35. _____

36. _____

At Home With a family member, take turns printing the first and last letters of a Spelling Word on a card, with blanks in between. The other person finishes the word.

175

Word Structure

1. _____
2. _____
3. _____
4. _____
5. _____
6. _____
7. _____
8. _____

Word Structure: The Word Root *press*

Practice Each word in the box contains the word root *press*, which means "to press." Write the word for each meaning. Use your Spelling Dictionary.

impress	depress	expressive	suppress
compress	oppressive	decompress	pressurize

1. to press together
2. showing feelings
3. to maintain normal air pressure inside an enclosed space
4. to make sad
5. very harsh or restrictive
6. to have a favorable effect
7. to stop or prevent an activity
8. to relieve pressure

impress

Dictionary

9. _____
10. _____
11. _____
12. _____
13. _____
14. _____

Dictionary: Multiple-Meaning Words

A dictionary entry may include more than one meaning for a word. Each definition is numbered.

crys•tal (krĭs′ təl) *n., pl.* **crystals 1.** A solid piece of matter that has a regular pattern of flat surfaces and angles between the surfaces. **2.** Glass that is clear, colorless, and of high quality.

Practice Write *crystal 1, crystal 2, salute 1, salute 2, entry 1, entry 2,* or *entry 3* to show which meaning of the word makes sense in the sentence. Use your Spelling Dictionary.

9. The store sells expensive <u>crystal</u> and silverware.
10. The soldiers will <u>salute</u> the president of the United States.
11. Marty found a large <u>crystal</u> embedded in the rock.
12. Vince rang the doorbell at the <u>entry</u> of the building.
13. Presidents often <u>salute</u> ambassadors by hosting special dinners.
14. Nate wrote an <u>entry</u> in the hotel guest book.

PART 3 Spelling and Writing

Proofread a Travel Article

Spelling and Possessive Pronouns Use proofreading marks to correct **eight** misspelled Basic or Review Words and **two** mistakes in using possessive pronouns in this travel article.

Example: The Alamo will ~~impres it's~~ *impress its* visitors.

Proofreading Marks
¶	Indent
∧	Add
⊙	Add a period
⌐	Delete
≡	Capital letter
/	Small letter

The Alamo Brings History to Life!

In late 1835, Texans captured a forteress called the Alamo. They wanted Texas to be independent insted of being part of Mexico. They enemy was Santa Anna, a Mexican general. He planned to surrounde and attack the Alamo. His's forces numbered several thousand.

In 1836, fewer than two hundred men held the Alamo. They didn't know wether they could win, but this did not friten them. They were ready to raspond to any challenge. The Texans fought bravely during the final assault, but by March 6, the entyre group had perished. Make plans now to visit the Alamo and atend an event to salute its heroes.

Write a Travel Article

prewrite → draft → revise → proofread → publish

Write a brief travel article about a historical site you want to visit.

- Explain **why the site is important** and **why people should visit it**.
- Use some Spelling Words and possessive pronouns.
- Proofread for **spelling** and correct use of **possessive pronouns**.

Power Proofreading
www.eduplace.com/kids/sv/

Basic
entry
limit
talent
disturb
entire
wisdom
dozen
impress
respond
fortress
neglect
crystal
kitchen
forbid
pirate
spinach
salute
frighten
surround
challenge

Review
honest
instead
whether
event
attend

Challenge
adapt
refuge
distribute
industry
somber

177

Test Tip Read each answer choice before deciding on an answer.

Test Format Practice

Directions For Numbers 1 through 8, choose the word that is spelled correctly and best completes the sentence.

Example: Kent will _____ to the letter.
   A rispond
   B reespond
   C respond
   D raspond

Example:

Ⓐ Ⓑ ● Ⓓ

Answer Sheet

1. Ⓐ Ⓑ Ⓒ Ⓓ

2. Ⓕ Ⓖ Ⓗ Ⓙ

3. Ⓐ Ⓑ Ⓒ Ⓓ

4. Ⓕ Ⓖ Ⓗ Ⓙ

5. Ⓐ Ⓑ Ⓒ Ⓓ

6. Ⓕ Ⓖ Ⓗ Ⓙ

7. Ⓐ Ⓑ Ⓒ Ⓓ

8. Ⓕ Ⓖ Ⓗ Ⓙ

1. Mary Ann has musical _____.
   A talant
   B tallant
   C talent
   D tallent

2. Do not _____ the flower garden.
   F neglect
   G nigleckt
   H naglect
   J nagleckt

3. The time _____ is ten minutes.
   A limmit
   B limit
   C limet
   D limmet

4. Pool rules _____ running.
   F forrbid
   G fourbid
   H forebid
   J forbid

5. Do not _____ the sleeping baby.
   A disturb
   B disterb
   C desturb
   D desterb

6. Will Herman accept the _____?
   F challange
   G challege
   H challenge
   J chalenge

7. The chef is preparing _____.
   A spinnich
   B spinich
   C spinnach
   D spinach

8. Trees _____ our house.
   F saround
   G surround
   H suround
   J sirround

More Practice

Now write each correctly spelled word on a sheet of paper.

Spelling Games
www.eduplace.com/kids/sv/
Review for your test.

178 Unit 27

Real-World Vocabulary

Drama: Summer Theater

All the words in the box relate to the theater. Look them up in your Spelling Dictionary. Then write the words to complete this announcement.

Spelling Word Link
talent

auditorium
musical
backstage
pantomime
theatrical
scenery
skit
spotlight

Summer Theater Workshop at Skyview School

Time: Friday, May 20, 4 P.M.

Place: Skyview School, on the stage in the ___(1)___

We have classes to meet everyone's skills and interests.

- You can play an instrument in a ___(2)___ show.
- You can write and perform a short, funny ___(3)___.
- You can work ___(4)___ to help build the sets and paint the ___(5)___.
- You can join the lighting crew and learn how to aim a ___(6)___.
- You can even learn ___(7)___ and act out a story without using words!

Give the workshop a try! Unless you participate in a theater experience, you will never know if you have ___(8)___ talent!

1. _____
2. _____
3. _____
4. _____
5. _____
6. _____
7. _____
8. _____

eWord Game
www.eduplace.com/kids/sv/

Try This
CHALLENGE

Write About the Theater On a separate sheet of paper, write a few sentences about something you would like to do that is related to the theater. Use at least four of the vocabulary words.

179

Read the Spelling Words and sentences.

Basic

1.	mislead	*mislead*	False advertising can **mislead** people.
2.	dismiss	*dismiss*	The teacher will **dismiss** the class.
3.	insincere	*insincere*	Her hasty apology seemed **insincere**.
4.	unable	*unable*	The sick child is **unable** to play today.
5.	indirect	*indirect*	A detour follows an **indirect** route.
6.	mistreat	*mistreat*	It is cruel to **mistreat** a pet.
7.	disaster	*disaster*	A drought is a **disaster** for farmers.
8.	dishonest	*dishonest*	The **dishonest** clerk overcharged us.
9.	insecure	*insecure*	New students may feel a bit **insecure**.
10.	unknown	*unknown*	The future is **unknown** to us.
11.	incomplete	*incomplete*	A story with no ending is **incomplete**.
12.	unequal	*unequal*	A dime for a dollar is an **unequal** trade.
13.	unstable	*unstable*	Do not stand on that **unstable** chair.
14.	misspell	*misspell*	I don't like to **misspell** words.
15.	disagree	*disagree*	Can we **disagree** and still be friends?
16.	informal	*informal*	He wore shorts to the **informal** event.
17.	discover	*discover*	Scientists still **discover** new species.
18.	unwise	*unwise*	Fools in folktales make **unwise** choices.
19.	mislaid	*mislaid*	I **mislaid** my glass and can't find it!
20.	disgrace	*disgrace*	It is a **disgrace** to be caught lying.

Review
21. untidy
22. disorder
23. mistake
24. uneven
25. dislike

Challenge
26. invisible
27. mishap
28. unfortunate
29. discourage
30. unnecessary

Think and Sort

A **prefix** is a word part added to the beginning of a base word or a word root. The prefixes in this unit can add a negative meaning to base words and word roots.

PREFIX + BASE WORD: **in**sincere, "not sincere"

PREFIX + WORD ROOT: **dis**aster, "something causing great destruction"

Write each Basic Word under its prefix.

un-
1. _____
2. _____
3. _____
4. _____
5. _____

dis-
6. _____
7. _____
8. _____
9. _____
10. _____
11. _____

in-
12. _____
13. _____
14. _____
15. _____
16. _____

mis-
17. _____
18. _____
19. _____
20. _____

Word Analysis/Phonics

Write the Basic Words that have these sounds and spellings.

21. /kw/ spelled *qu*   **22.** /ē/ spelled *ee*   **23.** silent *k*   **24.** silent *h*

Vocabulary: Inferences

Write the Basic or Review Word that best fits each clue.

25. If you find something no one has found before, you do this.

26. Any place that isn't neat can be described as this.

27. If people deliberately harm a living thing, they do this.

28. If you say things you don't really mean, you are this.

29. An event that harms many people is this.

Challenge Words

Write the Challenge Words to complete the paragraph. Use your Spelling Dictionary.

    Mikey waited at the edge of the pool. At the last race, he'd had a _____(30)_____. He had slipped on some _____(31)_____ grease and hurt his knee. It was an _____(32)_____ accident because it had kept him from practicing. Today four strong swimmers were racing against him, but Mikey did not let that fact _____(33)_____ him. He knew he just needed to swim fast and avoid _____(34)_____ movements to win.

Spelling-Meaning Connection

35–36. The word *sincere* comes from a Latin word meaning "pure, clean." Write *sincere*. Then write the Basic Word that is its opposite.

I'm sorry you lost the game.

sincere
insincere

Word Analysis
21. _____
22. _____
23. _____
24. _____

Inferences
25. _____
26. _____
27. _____
28. _____
29. _____

Challenge Words
30. _____
31. _____
32. _____
33. _____
34. _____

Spelling-Meaning
35. _____
36. _____

At Home Make word crosses with a family member. Write one Spelling Word across a page. Take turns writing Spelling Words that cross any word you wrote.

181

Word Structure: Words with Prefixes and Suffixes

Word Structure

1. _____
2. _____
3. _____
4. _____
5. _____
6. _____

Suffixes can be added to words with prefixes to form related words.

Example: unwise + ly → unwisely ("in a way that is foolish")

Practice: Write a word, formed by adding a suffix, to match each meaning. Be sure to use your Spelling Dictionary!

disaster	insincere	-ous	-ful
mistreat	disagree	-ness	-ed
untidy	disgrace	-ment	-ity

1. treated roughly or wrongly
2. a dispute or argument
3. state of not being neat or clean
4. shameful; humiliating
5. having a very bad effect
6. falseness

Dictionary: Prefixes

Dictionary

7. _____
8. _____
9. _____
10. _____
11. _____
12. _____
13. _____
14. _____

A dictionary lists prefixes alphabetically as entries. Look up a base word and a prefix separately. Then combine their meanings.

uni- A prefix that means "one, single": *unicycle.*

Practice Look up the prefix and the base word of each word in the box in your Spelling Dictionary. Then write the word that matches each meaning.

resupply	inexact	recapture	dismount
interact	disallow	interchange	reenter

7. to bring more goods
8. to go into again
9. not precise
10. to catch again
11. to act on one another
12. a freeway connection
13. to get off something
14. not to permit

Proofread an E-mail Message

Spelling and Contractions Use proofreading marks to correct **nine** misspelled Basic or Review Words and **three** apostrophes missing from contractions with pronouns in this part of an e-mail.

Example: *I'm* Im writing an ~~informall~~ *informal* e-mail to my friend Liz.

Proofreading Marks

¶	Indent
∧	Add
⊙	Add a period
⌐	Delete
≡	Capital letter
/	Small letter

Inbox

☹ Liz, have I had a bad day! I hope youve never made this mistaike. My teacher gave us a recipe, but I mislade it. I was unabel to remember the directions. What I wrote down was incompleat. I learned that its unwize to guess when baking. I added too much flour, and I left the counter untidy. The cake came out lumpy and unevin. What a disaster! My teacher took a bite and said, "Sorry, but I deslike the cake." I was in desgrase. When it was time to desmiss us, she said, "Don't feel insecure. You're here to learn. Youll do better tomorrow!" I hope so!

Basic
mislead
dismiss
insincere
unable
indirect
mistreat
disaster
dishonest
insecure
unknown
incomplete
unequal
unstable
misspell
disagree
informal
discover
unwise
mislaid
disgrace

Review
untidy
disorder
mistake
uneven
dislike

Challenge
invisible
mishap
unfortunate
discourage
unnecessary

Write an E-mail Message

prewrite → draft → revise → proofread → publish

Write a short e-mail to a friend about something that happened recently.

- Include interesting **details**.
- Use some Spelling Words and a contraction with a pronoun.
- Proofread your work for **spelling** and for correct use of **apostrophes** in contractions with pronouns.

Power Proofreading
www.eduplace.com/kids/sv/

✓ **Test Tip** Be sure to fill in the whole circle.

Test Format Practice

Directions: For Numbers 1–8, find the phrase containing an underlined word that is <u>not</u> spelled correctly. If all the underlined words are spelled correctly, mark "All correct."

Example: **A** to break a <u>promise</u>
B clear <u>weather</u>
C to make a <u>mestake</u>
D to <u>absorb</u> water
E All correct

Example:

(A) (B) ● (D) (E)

Answer Sheet

1. (A) (B) (C) (D) (E)

2. (F) (G) (H) (J) (K)

3. (A) (B) (C) (D) (E)

4. (F) (G) (H) (J) (K)

5. (A) (B) (C) (D) (E)

6. (F) (G) (H) (J) (K)

7. (A) (B) (C) (D) (E)

8. (F) (G) (H) (J) (K)

1. A an <u>insicure</u> person
B to <u>receive</u> mail
C an interesting <u>subject</u>
D the <u>expected</u> guests
E All correct

2. F to <u>display</u> the artwork
G <u>insincere</u> thanks
H to <u>dislike</u> olives
J to <u>misleed</u> the enemy
K All correct

3. A an <u>uneven</u> hem
B an <u>incomplete</u> puzzle
C an <u>inderect</u> route
D to <u>discover</u> a star
E All correct

4. F <u>unstaibel</u> ground
G a natural <u>disaster</u>
H an <u>untidy</u> closet
J rough <u>texture</u>
K All correct

5. A <u>mislaid</u> keys
B <u>unable</u> to swim
C to feel <u>disgrace</u>
D to <u>mispell</u> a word
E All correct

6. F an <u>unwise</u> decision
G an <u>informel</u> party
H to <u>disagree</u> with
J a <u>dishonest</u> person
K All correct

7. A to <u>gather</u> seashells
B an <u>unknown</u> answer
C a plastic <u>bucket</u>
D a spotless <u>apron</u>
E All correct

8. F a huge <u>machine</u>
G <u>unequal</u> fractions
H a room in <u>dissorder</u>
J a <u>bushel</u> of apples
K All correct

More Practice

Now write all the misspelled words correctly on a separate sheet of paper.

Spelling Games
www.eduplace.com/kids/sv/
Review for your test.

Real-World Vocabulary

Science: The Moon

All the words in the box relate to lunar exploration. Look them up in your Spelling Dictionary. Use them to complete this article.

Spelling Word Link
discover

astronaut
crater
probe
spacecraft
elliptical
hydrogen
revolution
rotation

Earth's Moon

The moon follows an ___(1)___ orbit around Earth. This orbital ___(2)___ lasts about 27.3 days. The moon's ___(3)___ on its axis takes the same length of time. That is why we see only one side of the moon. Scientists want to map each lunar depression, or ___(4)___. The United States has sent several ___(5)___ to the moon to study it. In 1964 an unmanned ___(6)___, or search vehicle, took photos of the moon's surface. Five years later, an ___(7)___ stepped onto the moon. In 1998, scientists detected ___(8)___, an element found in water, on the moon.

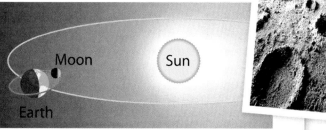

1. _____
2. _____
3. _____
4. _____
5. _____
6. _____
7. _____
8. _____

eWord Game
www.eduplace.com/kids/sv/

Try This

CHALLENGE

Classifying Write a vocabulary word to complete each group.

9. pilot, balloonist, _____
10. oxygen, carbon, _____
11. straight, circular, _____
12. canyon, ditch, _____

9. _____
10. _____
11. _____
12. _____

Read the Spelling Words and sentences.

Basic

1. elect	*elect*	The townspeople will **elect** a new mayor.
2. election	*election*	Did you vote in today's **election**?
3. tense	*tense*	The big game had many **tense** moments.
4. tension	*tension*	Try to relax if you feel **tension**.
5. react	*react*	Our dogs **react** to strangers by barking.
6. reaction	*reaction*	Cass had a happy **reaction** to the victory.
7. confess	*confess*	Did the prisoner **confess** to the crime?
8. confession	*confession*	The guilty person wrote a **confession**.
9. decorate	*decorate*	Let's **decorate** the room with banners.
10. decoration	*decoration*	Make a colorful **decoration** for the party.
11. pollute	*pollute*	Factory smoke can **pollute** the air.
12. pollution	*pollution*	The **pollution** in the air was unpleasant.
13. express	*express*	Joyce can **express** herself through art.
14. expression	*expression*	A smile is a type of facial **expression**.
15. imitate	*imitate*	Parrots **imitate** noises they hear.
16. imitation	*imitation*	Is that a real jewel or an **imitation**?
17. connect	*connect*	Draw lines to **connect** the dots.
18. connection	*connection*	We have a bad phone **connection**!
19. educate	*educate*	Teachers try to **educate** students.
20. education	*education*	Willa hopes to get a college **education**.

Review	23. question	**Challenge**	28. construct
21. camera	24. movie	26. fascinate	29. construction
22. famous	25. minute	27. fascination	

Think and Sort

Each pair of Basic Words includes a verb and a noun. The noun is formed by adding the suffix *-ion* to the verb. When a verb ends with *e*, drop the *e* when adding *-ion*.

connect → connect**ion**   pollut**e** → pollut**ion**

Write each pair of Basic Words under the heading that shows the spelling change when *-ion* is added.

No Spelling Change

1. _____
2. _____
3. _____
4. _____
5. _____
6. _____
7. _____
8. _____
9. _____
10. _____

Final *e* Dropped

11. _____
12. _____
13. _____
14. _____
15. _____
16. _____
17. _____
18. _____
19. _____
20. _____

Word Analysis/Phonics

21–22. Write a pair of Basic Words that have the VV pattern.

23–24. Write a pair of Basic Words in which the letter *x* spells the /ks/ sound.

Vocabulary: Context Paragraph

Write Basic or Review Words to complete the paragraph.

Last night we went to the theater for the opening of the new ___(25)___. One of the stars, a ___(26)___ actress, was supposed to introduce the film. When the curtain went up, however, she was not on stage. Her manager told us, "She'll be here in a ___(27)___." He looked upset and ___(28)___. When she arrived, everyone's ___(29)___ flashed. A reporter tried to ask her a ___(30)___, but the actress hurried past her without answering.

Challenge Words

Write the Challenge Word that best completes each sentence. Use your Spelling Dictionary.

31. Mark will _____ a stone wall.

32. Do science-fiction stories _____ you?

33. When will _____ begin on the new skyscraper?

34. Janice watched the gripping movie with _____.

Spelling-Meaning Connection

35–36. The words *elect* and *election* have the word root *leg*, which is spelled *lec* in these words. This word root can mean "to choose." Write *elect* and *election*. Underline the word root in both words.

elect
election

Word Analysis

21. _____

22. _____

23. _____

24. _____

Context Paragraph

25. _____

26. _____

27. _____

28. _____

29. _____

30. _____

Challenge Words

31. _____

32. _____

33. _____

34. _____

Spelling-Meaning

35. _____

36. _____

At Home With a family member, write each Spelling Word on a small piece of paper. Work together to arrange the words in alphabetical order.

187

Word Structure: The Word Root *ten*

The ancient Latin language is the source of the word root *ten*. This root means "to stretch or to strive."

Practice Write the word from the box that best fits each meaning. Use your Spelling Dictionary.

tension	tendency	tend	tendon	extend
tense	contender	tent	attendant	intend

1. a portable shelter stretched over poles
2. tissue that connects a muscle to its bony attachment
3. anxious or nervous
4. one who strives against difficulties
5. the condition of being stretched
6. an inclination to act in a certain way
7. to look after
8. one who waits on another
9. to stretch or spread out
10. to have in mind

Dictionary: Primary and Secondary Stress

The syllables in a word are said with different levels of stress. In *decorate*, the first syllable is shown in dark print with a dark accent mark ('). It has **primary stress** and is said more strongly. The last syllable has **secondary stress**. It has a light accent mark (') and is said with less emphasis.

dec•o•rate (dĕk´ ə rāt´)

Practice Write each word below in syllables. Circle the syllable with primary stress. Draw a line under the syllable with secondary stress. Use your Spelling Dictionary.

9. educate
10. imitate
11. decoration
12. education
13. imitation
14. hesitate

Word Structure

1. _____
2. _____
3. _____
4. _____
5. _____
6. _____
7. _____
8. _____
9. _____
10. _____

Dictionary

11. _____
12. _____
13. _____
14. _____
15. _____
16. _____

Proofread a Persuasive Letter

Spelling and Abbreviations Use proofreading marks to correct **eight** misspelled Basic or Review Words and **two** mistakes in abbreviations for months and days in this part of a persuasive letter.

Example: Wed., jan 5: I lost my ~~kamera~~ *camera* at the park.

tue., Apr. 4, 2006

Dear Fellow Students:

I must confes something: I used to polute! I hate to make that confesion, but it's true. I left garbage at picnics. Then a park ranger helped edjucate me on the harm done by pollusion in parks. Garbage creates tention between people and animals. What is the connexion? Wild animals eat garbage and learn to like it. The next time they're hungry, they return for more. Imagine the picnickers' reactions! Now I treat parks like my home. So should you! Learn the right way to conekt with nature.
Join the Camel Creek Park cleanup on Sat., mar. 31!

Write a Persuasive Letter

prewrite → draft → revise → proofread → publish

Write a persuasive letter about something you feel strongly about.

• Give **facts** to support your opinion. Include a **call to action.**
• Use some Spelling Words and an abbreviation for a month or day.
• Proofread your work for **spelling** and correct **abbreviations.**

Power Proofreading
www.eduplace.com/kids/sv/

Proofreading Marks

¶ Indent
∧ Add
⊙ Add a period
ℒ Delete
≡ Capital letter
/ Small letter

Basic
elect
election
tense
tension
react
reaction
confess
confession
decorate
decoration
pollute
pollution
express
expression
imitate
imitation
connect
connection
educate
education

Review
camera
famous
question
movie
minute

Challenge
fascinate
fascination
construct
construction

✓ **Test Tip** Read the directions carefully.

Test Format Practice

Example:

Ⓐ Ⓑ ● Ⓓ Ⓔ

Answer Sheet

1. Ⓐ Ⓑ Ⓒ Ⓓ Ⓔ
2. Ⓙ Ⓚ Ⓛ Ⓜ Ⓝ
3. Ⓐ Ⓑ Ⓒ Ⓓ Ⓔ
4. Ⓙ Ⓚ Ⓛ Ⓜ Ⓝ
5. Ⓐ Ⓑ Ⓒ Ⓓ Ⓔ
6. Ⓙ Ⓚ Ⓛ Ⓜ Ⓝ
7. Ⓐ Ⓑ Ⓒ Ⓓ Ⓔ
8. Ⓙ Ⓚ Ⓛ Ⓜ Ⓝ

More Practice

Now write all the misspelled words correctly on a separate sheet of paper.

Spelling Games
www.eduplace.com/kids/sv/
Review for your test.

Directions This test will show how well you can spell.

- Many of the questions in this test have spelling mistakes. Some do not have any mistakes at all.
- Look for mistakes in spelling.
- If there is a mistake, fill in the answer space on your answer sheet that has the same letter as the line with the mistake.
- If there is no mistake, fill in the last answer space.

Example: A settlement
B tension
C minite
D iguana
E *(No mistakes)*

1. A confess
   B realize
   C deckorate
   D pollution
   E *(No mistakes)*

2. J merchant
   K camara
   L election
   M movie
   N *(No mistakes)*

3. A connect
   B edjecation
   C basic
   D custom
   E *(No mistakes)*

4. J imatate
   K molar
   L expression
   M uproar
   N *(No mistakes)*

5. A peddle
   B educate
   C react
   D decaration
   E *(No mistakes)*

6. J question
   K squirm
   L famose
   M connection
   N *(No mistakes)*

7. A apply
   B confession
   C tense
   D express
   E *(No mistakes)*

8. J reaction
   K absorb
   L auction
   M imitasion
   N *(No mistakes)*

Real-World Vocabulary

Math: Learning Algebra

All the words in the box relate to algebra. Look them up in your Spelling Dictionary. Then write the words to complete this textbook chapter overview.

Spelling Word Link

expression

axis
equation
intersect
operations
solution
variable
coordinate
ordered pair

Chapter Overview: Algebra

Part One. An example of an algebra problem is 3 + *n* = 14. Each side of the ____(1)____ has to be equal. The *n* is a ____(2)____ that stands for the unknown number. The answer, or ____(3)____, is written as *n* = 11.

How do you find the value of a phrase like 2 + 3 x 10? You have to know the order of ____(4)____. You multiply and divide before you add and subtract: 2 + 3 x 10 = 2 + 30 = 32

Part Two. An algebraic grid has lines that ____(5)____, or cross. Each *x* or *y* number line is called an ____(6)____. Each location on the grid is written as (*x, y*), a pair of numbers called an ____(7)____. Each number in the pair is called a ____(8)____. For locating a point, the first number (*x*) tells how far to go to the right, and the second number (*y*) tells how far to go up.

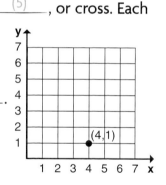

1. _____
2. _____
3. _____
4. _____
5. _____
6. _____
7. _____
8. _____

eWord Game
www.eduplace.com/kids/sv/

Try This
CHALLENGE

True or False? Write whether each statement is true or false.

9. The two sides of an equation can be equal or unequal.

10. An ordered pair contains two coordinates.

11. To solve an equation, you must find the number that the variable stands for.

12. The order of operations tells you what to do first to solve a problem.

9. _____
10. _____
11. _____
12. _____

Spelling Review

Unit 25		Final /n/ or /ən/, /chər/, /zhər/		pages 162–167
mountain	pleasure	future	mixture	ⓘ surgeon
fountain	curtain	creature	furniture	measure

Spelling Strategy

/n/ or /ən/ → **ain, eon**   /chər/ → **ture**   /zhər/ → **sure**

Classifying Write the word that belongs in each group.

1. beast, animal, _____
2. joy, delight, _____
3. blend, combination, _____
4. hill, cliff, _____
5. shade, blinds, _____
6. past, present, _____

Word Clues Write the word that fits each clue.

7. chairs and tables
8. a type of doctor
9. what a yardstick does
10. what you drink water from

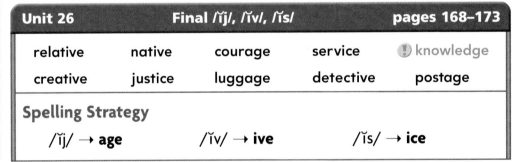

Unit 26		Final /ĭj/, /ĭv/, /ĭs/		pages 168–173
relative	native	courage	service	ⓘ knowledge
creative	justice	luggage	detective	postage

Spelling Strategy

/ĭj/ → **age**   /ĭv/ → **ive**   /ĭs/ → **ice**

Context Sentences Write the word that completes each sentence.

11. The jury helps make sure that _____ is carried out.

12. I visited Grandpa, my favorite _____.

13. Scouts earn awards for _____ to the community.

14. The porter carried the _____ over to the baggage area.

15. Extra reading will increase your _____ of history.

16. The _____ used clues to solve the crime.

17. The brave rescuers showed great _____.

18. Whoever painted that mural is very _____.

19. The _____ people here built their homes into the cliffs.

20. This letter is heavy, so it requires more _____.

Unit 25

1. _____
2. _____
3. _____
4. _____
5. _____
6. _____
7. _____
8. _____
9. _____
10. _____

Unit 26

11. _____
12. _____
13. _____
14. _____
15. _____
16. _____
17. _____
18. _____
19. _____
20. _____

Unit 27 — Unstressed Syllables — pages 174–179

wisdom	entire	dozen	entry	respond
frighten	spinach	challenge	neglect	forbid

Spelling Strategy A two-syllable word has one stressed syllable and one syllable with less stress. Note especially the spelling of the syllable with less stress.

Context Paragraph Write the words that complete this paragraph.

I had bought some milk, a ___(21)___ eggs, a bag of ___(22)___, and other vegetables. Big dogs ___(23)___ me, so when I saw one on my way home, I hurried into my building ___(24)___. No one was home to ___(25)___ to the bell. My parents ___(26)___ leaving the apartment unlocked. It was a ___(27)___ to find my keys. As I searched, I spilled the ___(28)___ bag of groceries! Luckily, only two eggs broke. I'd had the ___(29)___ to put the vegetables in plastic bags, so they were all right. People who ___(30)___ to put produce in bags are just careless!

Unit 28 — Prefixes: *in-, un-, dis-, mis-* — pages 180–185

dismiss	mislead	insecure	unknown	disaster
informal	discover	mislaid	incomplete	unwise

Spelling Strategy Find the prefix and the base word or the word root. Spell the word by parts.

Analogies Write the word that best completes each analogy.

31. *Fascinating* is to *boring* as *familiar* is to _____.
32. *Release* is to _____ as *melt* is to *liquefy*.
33. *Wasteful* is to *efficient* as _____ is to *sensible*.
34. *Detect* is to _____ as *pursue* is to *chase*.

Definitions Write the word that fits each meaning.

35. not finished
36. not confident
37. a calamity
38. casual
39. misplaced
40. deceive

Unit 27

21. _____
22. _____
23. _____
24. _____
25. _____
26. _____
27. _____
28. _____
29. _____
30. _____

Unit 28

31. _____
32. _____
33. _____
34. _____
35. _____
36. _____
37. _____
38. _____
39. _____
40. _____

193

Spelling Review

41. _____

42. _____

43. _____

44. _____

45. _____

46. _____

47. _____

48. _____

49. _____

50. _____

Unit 29		Suffix: *-ion*		pages 186–191
reaction	election	elect	tense	tension
pollution	imitate	connection	educate	expression

Spelling Strategy When a verb ends with *e*, drop the *e* when adding *-ion*. If a verb does not end with *e*, just add *-ion*.

Context Paragraph Write the words that complete this paragraph.

Anh wanted her classmates to ___(41)___ her class president. She felt nervous and ___(42)___ while waiting to speak. When it was her turn, she spoke with a lot of ___(43)___ in her voice. She got a positive ___(44)___ from the students. The ___(45)___ would be close, but now Anh believed she had a chance of winning.

Synonyms Write the word that has the same meaning as each word or phrase.

46. harmful substances

47. to copy

48. to teach

49. a link

50. stress

★ ★ ★ ★ ★
Vote Anh for Class President
★ ★ ★ ★ ★

Challenge

51. _____

52. _____

53. _____

54. _____

55. _____

56. _____

57. _____

58. _____

59. _____

60. _____

Challenge Words		Units 25–29		pages 162–191
refuge	fascinate	invisible	leisure	adapt
unnecessary	construct	cooperative	architecture	heritage

Context Sentences Write the word that completes each sentence.

51. Vacation is a time for _____, not work.

52. To be a good helper, you must be _____.

53. Abandoned animals find _____ at the shelter.

54. The spinning tops really _____ the little children.

55. Students of _____ often photograph buildings.

56. Cutting your sandwich into tiny bits is _____.

57. The way your family celebrates holidays may reflect your _____.

58. A new pet needs time to _____ to its new environment.

59. The snowman quickly became _____ in the snowstorm.

60. The steelworkers will _____ the frame for the new bridge.

Spelling (and) Writing

Proofread a Research Report

Spelling and Grammar Mixed Review Use proofreading marks to correct this report. There are **eight** misspelled Basic Words from the last five units and **four** incorrect usages of personal and possessive pronouns.

Example: He was known for ~~curage~~ *courage*, but was ~~him~~ *he* just ruthless?

Proofreading Marks	
¶	Indent
∧	Add
⊙	Add a period
℘	Delete
≡	Capital letter
/	Small letter

Sir Francis Drake: Hero or Rogue?

The English honored Sir Francis Drake as an explorer who added to they're knowledge of world geography. The Spanish, however, saw him as a pirrate. In 1572 Drake was the captin of a ship that raided a Spanish fortrus and captured thirty tons of silver. This advenchure made he famous in England but infamous in Spain.

In 1577 Drake began a voyaje around the world. Him and his crew sailed through the pasage known as the strait of Magellan. They journeyed to South America, attacking settlements. The Spanish were unabel to stop them. Drake arrived in England late in 1580 with much treasure for Queen Elizabeth. To ixpress her thanks, her made him a knight.

Tips

- Think of a topic you would like to research and write about.

- Write several sentences explaining why this topic interests you.

- Write five questions about the topic you would like to answer in your report.

Plan a Research Report

prewrite → draft → revise → proofread → publish

Describe a topic you would like to do a research report about.

- Use some Spelling Words from Units 25–29.
- Proofread your writing for **spelling** and correct use of **pronouns**.

Power Proofreading
www.eduplace.com/kids/sv/

Spelling Test Practice

Test Tip Eliminate answer choices that you know are incorrect.

Test Format Practice

Directions For Numbers 1 through 8, choose the word that is spelled correctly and best completes the sentence.

Example: What other _____ can you speak?

   A lainguage
   B langwedge
   C language
   D lenguage

Example:

Ⓐ Ⓑ ● Ⓓ

Answer Sheet

1. Ⓐ Ⓑ Ⓒ Ⓓ
2. Ⓕ Ⓖ Ⓗ Ⓙ
3. Ⓐ Ⓑ Ⓒ Ⓓ
4. Ⓕ Ⓖ Ⓗ Ⓙ
5. Ⓐ Ⓑ Ⓒ Ⓓ
6. Ⓕ Ⓖ Ⓗ Ⓙ
7. Ⓐ Ⓑ Ⓒ Ⓓ
8. Ⓕ Ⓖ Ⓗ Ⓙ

More Practice

Now write each correctly spelled word on a sheet of paper.

Spelling Games
www.eduplace.com/kids/sv/
Review for your test.

1. Do not _____ any customer.
   A mistreat
   B misstreet
   C misstreat
   D misstrete

2. Cars should not _____.
   F palute
   G pollute
   H polute
   J pillute

3. We use our basement shelves for _____.
   A storrage
   B storaje
   C storage
   D stoarage

4. When is the train's first _____ today?
   F departure
   G deparchore
   H deparchur
   J deeparture

5. The rocks on the hillside are _____.
   A unnstable
   B unstable
   C unstabel
   D unstayble

6. Will has a _____ to make.
   F confesion
   G confeshun
   H confestion
   J confession

7. We plan to hike on a _____ trail.
   A naycher
   B natcher
   C nature
   D natchur

8. An _____ is a descriptive word.
   F adjecteve
   G ajective
   H adjective
   J ajicteve

Test Tip Try each answer. Read the sentence to yourself. Fill in the blank with a different answer choice each time.

Directions For Numbers 1–6, find the words that best complete the paragraph.

Test Format Practice

Example: "The _____ in this restaurant is terrible," Dad complained. "The waiter forgot the menu, spilled the soup, and _____ the wrong meal!"

1. A decoration
   B service
   C salsa
   D odor

2. F burnt
   G expected
   H terrified
   J delivered

Example:

1. Ⓐ ● Ⓒ Ⓓ

2. Ⓕ Ⓖ Ⓗ ●

Answer Sheet

1. Ⓐ Ⓑ Ⓒ Ⓓ

2. Ⓕ Ⓖ Ⓗ Ⓙ

3. Ⓐ Ⓑ Ⓒ Ⓓ

4. Ⓕ Ⓖ Ⓗ Ⓙ

5. Ⓐ Ⓑ Ⓒ Ⓓ

6. Ⓕ Ⓖ Ⓗ Ⓙ

Without warning, the chef announced that he'd run out of every _____ on the menu! The waiter suddenly felt _____.

1. A feather
   B olive
   C mixture
   D item

2. F wonder
   G panic
   H joy
   J strength

Tameka and her brother rode a river _____ in Holland. "That trip was a great _____!" she said happily when it was over.

3. A barge
   B caravan
   C passenger
   D bicycle

4. F hazard
   G haunt
   H adventure
   J headache

At last Tristan was certain that the stranger he'd encountered in the cave was a _____. The man had vanished, and he'd stolen every bit of the _____!

5. A villain
   B surgeon
   C relative
   D detective

6. F horses
   G music
   H memories
   J treasure

Read the Spelling Words and sentences.

Basic

1. produce	*produce*	Those factories **produce** auto parts.
2. company	*company*	This **company** employs eight people.
3. protect	*protect*	Use sunscreen to **protect** your skin.
4. preview	*preview*	We saw a **preview** of a comedy film.
5. contain	*contain*	Does that jar **contain** many marbles?
6. combat	*combat*	Sleep can help you **combat** an illness.
7. prejudge	*prejudge*	Don't **prejudge** the new principal.
8. commotion	*commotion*	The sirens made a loud **commotion**.
9. contest	*contest*	Who will win the dance **contest**?
10. prefix	*prefix*	Add the **prefix** *un-* to this word.
11. progress	*progress*	A new airport is a sign of **progress**.
12. computer	*computer*	I use my **computer** to write reports.
13. confide	*confide*	My pals **confide** their ideas to me.
14. convince	*convince*	Did I **convince** you to join the team?
15. prospect	*prospect*	Do we have any **prospect** of winning?
16. confirm	*confirm*	The agent will **confirm** our tickets.
17. preflight	*preflight*	Eat a **preflight** meal before traveling.
18. provide	*provide*	Will the camp **provide** lunch for us?
19. propose	*propose*	I **propose** a change to the plan.
20. promotion	*promotion*	Ty's boss gave him a nice **promotion**.

Review	23. protest	**Challenge**	28. commercial
21. complete	24. pretend	26. concurrent	29. compete
22. continue	25. prepare	27. conscious	30. conversation

Think and Sort

A prefix is a word part that is added to the beginning of a word root or base word. Prefixes and word roots cannot stand alone. A base word can stand alone.

Prefix + Word Root:	**con**vince	**com**pany
Prefix + Base Word:	**pre**view	**con**test

Write each Basic Word under its prefix.

com-

1. _____
2. _____
3. _____
4. _____

con-

5. _____
6. _____
7. _____
8. _____
9. _____

pre-

10. _____
11. _____
12. _____
13. _____

pro-

14. _____
15. _____
16. _____
17. _____
18. _____
19. _____
20. _____

Word Analysis/Phonics

Write the Basic Words that have these elements.

21–22. /shən/ spelled *tion*   24. /ā/ spelled *ai*

23. /ī/ spelled *igh*   25. /yo͞o/ spelled *iew*

Vocabulary: Analogies

Write the Basic or Review Word that best completes each analogy.

26. *Whisper* is to *shout* as *deny* is to _____.

27. *Giggle* is to *weep* as *endanger* is to _____.

28. *Open* is to *close* as _____ is to *pause*.

29. *Squeeze* is to *compress* as *finish* is to _____.

Challenge Words

Write the Challenge Word that best completes each sentence. Use your Spelling Dictionary.

30. Our soccer team will _____ for the city championship.

31. Pilar can attend only one of the two _____ events.

32. I had a _____ with a friend about my hobby, rock collecting.

33. Would you buy the product shown in that TV _____?

34. I try not to be _____ of the weather when I run.

Spelling-Meaning Connection

35–36. How can you remember how to spell the /ə/ sound in the first syllable of *contestant*? Think of the /ŏ/ sound in the related noun *contest*. Write *contestant* and *contest*. Underline the letter that spells /ə/ in one and /ŏ/ in the other.

contest contestant

At Home With a family member, take turns writing four Spelling Words on a piece of paper. Cut the prefix off each word. Mix up the parts of the words. The other person puts the parts together to spell the words.

Word Analysis

21. _____

22. _____

23. _____

24. _____

25. _____

Analogies

26. _____

27. _____

28. _____

29. _____

Challenge Words

30. _____

31. _____

32. _____

33. _____

34. _____

Spelling-Meaning

35. _____

36. _____

Vocabulary

1. _____
2. _____
3. _____
4. _____
5. _____
6. _____

Vocabulary: Analogies

Some analogies compare workers and their tasks. Others compare people's jobs and the equipment they use.

Example 1: *Watchman* is to *guard* as *teacher* is to *educate*.

Example 2: *Artist* is to *paintbrush* as *programmer* is to *computer*.

Practice Write the word from the box that best completes each analogy. Use your Spelling Dictionary.

> combat   represent   locomotive   loom   mason   potter

1. *Paver* is to *asphalt* as _____ is to *clay*.
2. *Carpenter* is to *lumber* as _____ is to *bricks*.
3. *Athlete* is to *compete* as *attorney* is to _____.
4. *Doctor* is to *surgery* as *soldier* is to _____.
5. *Pilot* is to *airplane* as *engineer* is to _____.
6. *Firefighter* is to *hose* as *weaver* is to _____.

Dictionary

7. _____
8. _____
9. _____
10. _____
11. _____
12. _____
13. _____
14. _____

Dictionary: Different Pronunciations

Remember that some words, such as *contest*, have different pronunciations when used as different parts of speech.

> **con•test** (kŏn′ tĕst′) *n.* A competition rated by judges. —(kən tĕst′) *or* (kŏn′ tĕst′) *v.* **1.** To complete or strive for. **2.** To dispute; challenge.

Practice Write *noun* or *verb* to show how each underlined word is being used, followed by *first* or *second* to show which syllable receives the primary stress. Use your Spelling Dictionary.

7. We must <u>combat</u> our fears.
8. Diplomacy may prevent <u>combat</u>.
9. Jon holds the <u>record</u> in that race.
10. When will she <u>record</u> her new CD?
11. I am making great <u>progress</u> in math.
12. Study hard and you will <u>progress</u>.
13. People <u>object</u> to being rushed.
14. What is that <u>object</u> in the sand?

Proofread a Letter

Spelling and Abbreviations in Addresses Use proofreading marks to correct **ten** misspelled Basic or Review Words and **two** mistakes in abbreviations in addresses in this part of a letter.

Example: Please complete our survey; mail it to 10 Tower dr ⊙

25 S. Magnolia ave

Austin, TX 78704

Dear Business Owner:

Since our computir company opened last year, we have made real progress. We now pruduce the best machines you can buy. They contane more memory than similar products. As a sales promotion, I would like to propos a free trial. We will pruvide you with our machine for one month. You can then return it or buy it at a special price. I hope I can convinse you to accept my offer. Don't pruhtend you aren't interested. Don't prowtest! Just call to conferm your interest. I will prepair the paperwork.

Proofreading Marks	
¶	Indent
∧	Add
⊙	Add a period
℔	Delete
≡	Capital letter
/	Small letter

Basic
produce
company
protect
preview
contain
combat
prejudge
commotion
contest
prefix
progress
computer
confide
convince
prospect
confirm
preflight
provide
propose
promotion

Review
complete
continue
protest
pretend
prepare

Challenge
concurrent
conscious
commercial
compete
conversation

Write a Letter

prewrite → draft → revise → proofread → publish

Write a short letter in response to the one above.

- Write your **reaction** and include an **address** in the heading.
- Use some Spelling Words and an abbreviation in an address.
- Proofread for **spelling** and correct **abbreviations in addresses.**

Power Proofreading
www.eduplace.com/kids/sv/

201

PART 4 Spelling Test Practice

Test Tip Read every answer choice before deciding on an answer.

Test Format Practice

Directions Choose the word that is spelled correctly and best completes the sentence.

Example: Dorothy hopes for a job _____.
- **A** promosion
- **B** promoshun
- **C** promotion
- **D** promotian

Example:

Ⓐ Ⓑ ● Ⓓ

Answer Sheet

1. Ⓐ Ⓑ Ⓒ Ⓓ
2. Ⓕ Ⓖ Ⓗ Ⓙ
3. Ⓐ Ⓑ Ⓒ Ⓓ
4. Ⓕ Ⓖ Ⓗ Ⓙ
5. Ⓐ Ⓑ Ⓒ Ⓓ
6. Ⓕ Ⓖ Ⓗ Ⓙ
7. Ⓐ Ⓑ Ⓒ Ⓓ
8. Ⓕ Ⓖ Ⓗ Ⓙ

1. How can I _____ you to join us?
- **A** convinse
- **B** convince
- **C** cunvince
- **D** convins

2. The word part *con-* is a _____.
- **F** perfix
- **G** prifix
- **H** preefix
- **J** prefix

3. My dad plans to start his own _____.
- **A** company
- **B** companie
- **C** cumpany
- **D** cumpeny

4. We have a good _____ of winning.
- **F** prospecked
- **G** prospeckt
- **H** prospect
- **J** prospecket

5. Do not _____ a new student.
- **A** prejudge
- **B** prijudge
- **C** preejudge
- **D** prejuge

6. Try to make steady _____ on your homework.
- **F** progress
- **G** pregress
- **H** proggres
- **J** progres

7. The host will _____ snacks.
- **A** pervide
- **B** previde
- **C** provide
- **D** previed

8. I will _____ a secret to you.
- **F** confied
- **G** confide
- **H** confiede
- **J** confyd

More Practice

Now write each correctly spelled word on a sheet of paper.

Spelling Games
www.eduplace.com/kids/sv/
Review for your test.

Real-World Vocabulary

Social Studies: Aircraft

All the words in the box relate to flight. Look up these words in your Spelling Dictionary. Then write the words to complete this science fair display.

Spelling Word Link
preflight

altitude
ascend
aviator
biplane
cockpit
descend
taxi
turbulence

The History of Flight

Before airplanes, people flew in hot-air balloons. They could ___(1)___ to a high ___(2)___, but steering was a problem. Sometimes they would ___(3)___ into trees.

Heavier-than-air flight began with the Wright brothers' ___(4)___, a flying machine with upper and lower wings. Orville sat on the lower wing. There was no ___(5)___. He was the first ___(6)___ to make a successful powered flight.

Today, jets ___(7)___ down the runway every few minutes. Air ___(8)___ can make a flight uncomfortable, but flying on commercial jets is one of the safest ways to travel.

1. _____
2. _____
3. _____
4. _____
5. _____
6. _____
7. _____
8. _____

eWord Game
www.eduplace.com/kids/sv/

Try This CHALLENGE

Yes or No? Answer each question about flight with *yes* or *no*.

9. Is the cockpit part of a jet engine?

10. Is an airline pilot an aviator?

11. Does a plane ascend as it gets ready to land?

12. Is altitude a measurement of height?

9. _____
10. _____
11. _____
12. _____

-ent, -ence, -ency

1. _____
2. _____
3. _____
4. _____
5. _____
6. _____
7. _____
8. _____

-ant, -ance, -ancy

9. _____
10. _____
11. _____
12. _____
13. _____
14. _____
15. _____
16. _____

-able

17. _____
18. _____

-ible

19. _____
20. _____

Read the Spelling Words and sentences.

Basic

1.	vacant	*vacant*	Has the **vacant** lot been empty long?
2.	vacancy	*vacancy*	The hotel has one **vacancy** tonight.
3.	possible	*possible*	A victory is **possible** but not likely.
4.	different	*different*	I have two **different** hats for school.
5.	difference	*difference*	The **difference** is in the style.
6.	honorable	*honorable*	Her **honorable** deeds won praise.
7.	distant	*distant*	I took a long flight to a **distant** land.
8.	distance	*distance*	She can run for a long **distance**.
9.	urgent	*urgent*	Hurry—the situation is **urgent**!
10.	urgency	*urgency*	Scared rabbits run with **urgency**.
11.	comfortable	*comfortable*	This soft chair is **comfortable**.
12.	absent	*absent*	I was **absent** today because I am ill.
13.	absence	*absence*	My **absence** from class was excused.
14.	infant	*infant*	My baby brother is still an **infant**.
15.	infancy	*infancy*	Children cry a lot during **infancy**.
16.	terrible	*terrible*	Rotten eggs smell **terrible**.
17.	frequent	*frequent*	The train made **frequent** stops.
18.	frequency	*frequency*	Cows eat with great **frequency**.
19.	radiant	*radiant*	The sunlight was strong and **radiant**.
20.	radiance	*radiance*	Bright lights shine with **radiance**.

Review	23. becoming		**Challenge**	28. occupant
21. president	24. cheerful		26. evident	29. occupancy
22. important	25. illness		27. evidence	30. capable

Think and Sort

Each Basic Word ends with *-ent, -ence, -ency, -ant, -ance, -ancy, -able,* or *-ible.* All of these endings have a schwa sound. Since that sound can be spelled different ways, the spelling of each word's ending must be remembered.

/ənt/ vac**ant**, urg**ent**   /ə bəl/ poss**ible**, comfort**able**

Write each Basic Word under the correct heading.

Word Analysis/Phonics

21–24. Write the Basic Words in which the /ā/ sound is spelled *a*.

Vocabulary: Definitions

Write the Basic or Review Word that fits each definition.

25. a baby
26. very bad
27. far away
28. needing immediate attention
29. happy

Challenge Words

Write the Challenge Words to complete the paragraph. Use your Spelling Dictionary.

The Queen of Hearts has presented solid ___(30)___ that the knave stole her strawberry tarts. Another ___(31)___ of the castle has also identified the knave as the thief. The attorney is ___(32)___ of convincing the jury of the knave's guilt. He says the knave's guilt will be ___(33)___ to all. The dungeon has been prepared for ___(34)___.

Spelling-Meaning Connection

35–36. *Possible, impossible,* and *possibility* are related in spelling and meaning. Write *possible* and *possibility*. Draw a line under the letter that spells the schwa sound in the second syllable of each word. Memorize the spelling.

possible
impossible
possibility

Definitions
25.
26.
27.
28.
29.

Challenge Words
30.
31.
32.
33.
34.

Spelling-Meaning
35.
36.

At Home With a family member, write each Spelling Word on a small piece of paper. Work together to arrange the words in alphabetical order.

205

Vocabulary

1. _____
2. _____
3. _____
4. _____
5. _____
6. _____
7. _____
8. _____

Vocabulary: Words About Frequency

Many words tell about frequency, or how often something happens.

Example: I **sometimes** swim after school but **never** before.

Practice Write the word from the box that best matches each meaning. Use your Spelling Dictionary.

frequent	occasionally	annually	usually
continuously	sporadically	periodically	rarely

1. not very often
2. occurring or appearing often
3. in routine, predictable cycles
4. sometimes
5. in the way that most often happens
6. randomly, with no pattern
7. without interruption
8. once a year

Thesaurus

9. _____
10. _____
11. _____
12. _____
13. _____
14. _____

Thesaurus: Synonyms and Antonyms

A thesaurus entry may list antonyms as well as synonyms.

terrible _adj._ causing great fear; dreadful. _We feared the crops would be destroyed by the **terrible** drought._
awful very bad; horrible. _The car's engine began smoking and making an **awful** noise._
unpleasant not pleasing; disagreeable. _The burning rubber created an **unpleasant** odor._
antonyms: wonderful, terrific, marvelous

Practice Write a synonym and then an antonym from the box for each word below. Use your Thesaurus to confirm your answers.

fickle	appreciative	careless
cautious	trustworthy	ungrateful

9–10. careful   **11–12.** thankful   **13–14.** reliable

✏ Proofread an Announcement

Spelling and Dates Use proofreading marks to correct **ten** misspelled Basic or Review Words and **two** mistakes in the capitalization and punctuation of a date in this announcement.

Example: ~~Freequant~~ *Frequent* reminders will be posted starting october 30.

Remember to Vote

WHEN: november 15 2006

WHERE: Lakebridge School Cafeteria

WHY: The election for student body prezident is very importent! Right now this office is vackant. We need the strongest leader possable to fill this vacancy. Each of the three candidates has a diffrent plan. Vote for the person you think is the most honorible and capable, not just the most cheerful. Unless you have a terrible ilness, do not be absint on election day! Keep a sense of urgensy—your vote will make a differance!

Proofreading Marks

¶ Indent
∧ Add
⊙ Add a period
ℐ Delete
≡ Capital letter
/ Small letter

Basic
vacant
vacancy
possible
different
difference
honorable
distant
distance
urgent
urgency
comfortable
absent
absence
infant
infancy
terrible
frequent
frequency
radiant
radiance

Review
president
important
becoming
cheerful
illness

Challenge
evident
evidence
occupant
occupancy
capable

✏ Write an Announcement

prewrite → draft → revise → proofread → publish

Write an announcement for an election or other school event.
- Tell **when** the event is and **why** students should participate.
- Use some Spelling Words and at least one date.
- Proofread your work for **spelling** and **correct capitalization and punctuation of dates.**

✓ **Test Tip** Read the directions carefully.

Test Format Practice

Example:

Ⓐ Ⓑ ● Ⓓ Ⓔ

Answer Sheet

1. Ⓐ Ⓑ Ⓒ Ⓓ Ⓔ
2. Ⓕ Ⓖ Ⓗ Ⓙ Ⓚ
3. Ⓐ Ⓑ Ⓒ Ⓓ Ⓔ
4. Ⓕ Ⓖ Ⓗ Ⓙ Ⓚ
5. Ⓐ Ⓑ Ⓒ Ⓓ Ⓔ
6. Ⓕ Ⓖ Ⓗ Ⓙ Ⓚ
7. Ⓐ Ⓑ Ⓒ Ⓓ Ⓔ
8. Ⓕ Ⓖ Ⓗ Ⓙ Ⓚ

More Practice

Now write all the misspelled words correctly on a separate sheet of paper.

Directions Find the phrase containing an underlined word that is <u>not</u> spelled correctly. If all the underlined words are spelled correctly, mark "All correct."

Example: **A** <u>radiant</u> sunlight
B <u>different</u> types
C an <u>urjent</u> message
D a serious <u>illness</u>
E All correct

1. **A** a former <u>president</u>
   B still in his <u>infincy</u>
   C to <u>bury</u> treasure
   D a sudden <u>movement</u>
   E All correct

2. **F** a <u>vacant</u> room
   G a <u>comfortible</u> chair
   H an <u>important</u> day
   J a painful <u>blister</u>
   K All correct

3. **A** an <u>honorable</u> person
   B a <u>frantic</u> gesture
   C shining <u>radiance</u>
   D <u>becuming</u> wiser
   E All correct

4. **F** no <u>vacancy</u>
   G a <u>solid</u> wall
   H the ship's <u>captain</u>
   J an unexcused <u>absense</u>
   K All correct

5. **A** increased <u>frequency</u>
   B a major <u>difference</u>
   C a vast <u>distence</u>
   D an <u>absent</u> student
   E All correct

6. **F** to sing a <u>hymn</u>
   G to <u>greet</u> a friend
   H <u>frequant</u> visits
   J an accurate <u>scale</u>
   K All correct

7. **A** a <u>possable</u> solution
   B a <u>terrible</u> noise
   C to <u>excite</u> the crowd
   D to <u>scowl</u> at someone
   E All correct

8. **F** a crying <u>infent</u>
   G to <u>perform</u> on stage
   H to be <u>certain</u>
   J to <u>compete</u> fairly
   K All correct

Spelling Games
www.eduplace.com/kids/sv/
Review for your test.

Real-World Vocabulary

Health: Exercise

All the words in the box relate to health and exercise. Look up these words in your Spelling Dictionary. Then write the words to complete this bulletin board notice.

Spelling Word Link
distance

endurance
fatigue
accelerates
heartbeat
marathon
nutrition
strength
workout

Join the New Family Gym

Does your family lack energy on weekends? Do you all experience ____(1)____ around the dinner table? Then it's time to join our gym and work on physical fitness. To help you become fit, our trainers will design a ____(2)____ for each member of the family that ____(3)____ the ____(4)____ just the right amount. Your parents can lift weights to improve ____(5)____ while you learn facts about diet and ____(6)____. Regular workouts will improve your ____(7)____, and you'll be able to exercise longer and longer! Some day, you may even be ready to run a ____(8)____!

1. _____
2. _____
3. _____
4. _____
5. _____
6. _____
7. _____
8. _____

eWord Game
www.eduplace.com/kids/sv/

Try This — CHALLENGE

Write Health Tips On a separate sheet of paper, write two tips on how to become healthier. Use at least four vocabulary words.

PART 1 Spelling and Phonics

graph
1. _____
2. _____
3. _____
4. _____
5. _____
6. _____
7. _____

phone
8. _____
9. _____
10. _____
11. _____
12. _____
13. _____

micro
14. _____
15. _____
16. _____

Other Greek Word Parts
17. _____
18. _____
19. _____
20. _____

Read the Spelling Words and sentences.

Basic

1.	telephone	*telephone*	The **telephone** rang loudly.
2.	autograph	*autograph*	Did he **autograph** the book for you?
3.	microscope	*microscope*	Use a **microscope** to see the cells.
4.	photograph	*photograph*	Put that **photograph** in the album.
5.	televise	*televise*	We **televise** our school ball games.
6.	biology	*biology*	We study living things in **biology.**
7.	microphone	*microphone*	Jonelle sang into the **microphone.**
8.	paragraph	*paragraph*	Read the introductory **paragraph.**
9.	symphony	*symphony*	The **symphony** played lovely music.
10.	telegraph	*telegraph*	Use the **telegraph** to send a message.
11.	megaphone	*megaphone*	Use a **megaphone** so all can hear.
12.	microwave	*microwave*	A **microwave** oven heats food fast.
13.	photocopy	*photocopy*	I will **photocopy** this letter for you.
14.	biography	*biography*	Has Al read a **biography** of Lincoln?
15.	saxophone	*saxophone*	She plays **saxophone** in a jazz band.
16.	telescope	*telescope*	We saw stars through a **telescope.**
17.	calligraphy	*calligraphy*	Is **calligraphy** beautiful writing?
18.	xylophone	*xylophone*	You play a **xylophone** with mallets.
19.	homophone	*homophone*	A **homophone** can be tricky to spell.
20.	homograph	*homograph*	*Tear* is a **homograph** of *tear.*

Review
21. athlete
22. history
23. melody
24. type
25. topic

Challenge
26. telecommute
27. bibliography
28. phonetic
29. microbe
30. autobiography

Think and Sort

Many English words contain word parts from the ancient Greek language. Knowing Greek word parts can help you learn the meanings and spellings of words that contain them.

bio ("life") → **bio**logy, **bio**graphy

Write each Basic Word under its correct Greek word part. Write *microphone* under *micro.*

Word Analysis/Phonics

Write the Basic Words that have these elements.

21. /ĭ/ spelled *y*   **23.** /z/ spelled *x*

22. /ĭ/ spelled *i*   **24.** /f/ spelled *ph* at the beginning and end

Vocabulary: Context Paragraph

Use Basic and Review Words to complete the paragraph.

The Olympic Games may be the world's greatest athletic competition. Each ____(25)____ of event requires different skills. The games have a ____(26)____ that goes back to ancient times. TV stations throughout the world ____(27)____ the events. When people hear the familiar ____(28)____ of the Olympics theme song, they rush to the TV screen. They cheer if a favorite ____(29)____ is competing.

Challenge Words

Write the Challenge Word that fits each meaning. Use your Spelling Dictionary.

30. to use a home computer connected to an office

31. representing the sounds of speech with symbols

32. an account of a person's life, written by that person

33. a list of books

34. a tiny life form

Spelling-Meaning Connection

35–36. The /ŏ/ sound in the second syllable of *photography* will help you remember how to spell the /ə/ sound in the related word *photograph*. Write these two words. Underline the second *o* in each word.

photograph
photography

Word Analysis

21. _____

22. _____

23. _____

24. _____

Context Paragraph

25. _____

26. _____

27. _____

28. _____

29. _____

Challenge Words

30. _____

31. _____

32. _____

33. _____

34. _____

Spelling-Meaning

35. _____

36. _____

At Home With a family member, take turns writing two Spelling Words on a piece of paper. Cut the letters apart. Mix them up. The other person uses the letters to spell the words.

Vocabulary

1. _____

2. _____

3. _____

4. _____

5. _____

6. _____

Vocabulary: Words from Names

Many English words come from the names of the people who inspired the words. Knowing the origins of these words can help you remember their meanings.

Practice Write the word from the box that best matches each definition. Use your Spelling Dictionary.

saxophone	pasteurize	leotard
diesel	watt	maverick

1. a person who is independent in thought and action; named after Samuel Maverick, a cattleman who refused to brand his calves

2. to heat food or drink to a certain temperature to kill bacteria that can cause spoilage; named after the inventor of the process, Louis Pasteur

3. a musical instrument invented by Adolph Sax

4. a unit of power; named after James Watt, a Scottish engineer

5. a one-piece garment worn by dancers or gymnasts; invented by Jules Léotard, a French aerialist

6. a type of engine; named after Rudolph Diesel, a German engineer

Dictionary: Shortened Forms of Words

Dictionary

7. _____

8. _____

9. _____

10. _____

11. _____

12. _____

13. _____

14. _____

Some short words are actually shortened forms of longer words. When you look up a shortened word in a dictionary, it will tell you the longer word it came from.

phone (fōn) *n.* a telephone: *Use the phone to call me.* [Short for *telephone.*]

Practice Look up each of these shortened words in your Spelling Dictionary. Write the longer word that it comes from.

7. limo   9. gym   11. ad   13. fridge

8. photo   10. hippo   12. deli   14. pants

✏️ Proofread a Journal Entry

Spelling and Book Titles Use proofreading marks to correct **eleven** misspelled Basic or Review Words and **three** mistakes in a book title in this journal entry.

Example: The author of <u>Science for Kids</u> was a famous ~~athalete~~. *athlete*

March 3, 2006

    Last month I read a series of books called Great minds of sight and Sound. The topicks included how the mycroscope and the teloscope were invented, and how the telefone replaced the telligraph. There was even a diagram comparing a mikrophone and a megophone! I wrote a letter to the author in my finest calligraphy, promising to buy her new biogriphy of Einstein when it came out. Today she sent me a photecopy of the first chapter, along with her autagraph, a photograph, and a short parograph thanking me!

✏️ Write a Journal Entry

prewrite → draft → revise → proofread → publish

Write a journal entry about an idea for a book you would like to write.

- Write the **date,** describe your **book** idea, and suggest a **title.**
- Use some Spelling Words and include at least one book title.
- Proofread for **spelling** and correct treatment of the **book title.**

Power Proofreading
www.eduplace.com/kids/sv/

Basic
telephone
autograph
microscope
photograph
televise
biology
microphone
paragraph
symphony
telegraph
megaphone
microwave
photocopy
biography
saxophone
telescope
calligraphy
xylophone
homophone
homograph

Review
athlete
history
melody
type
topic

Challenge
telecommute
bibliography
phonetic
microbe
autobiography

✓ **Test Tip** Watch the time. Don't spend too much time on one question.

 *Test Format Practice*

Directions Read each group of sentences. Decide if one of the underlined words is spelled wrong or if there is *No mistake*. Fill in space for the answer you have chosen.

Example:

Ⓐ ● Ⓒ Ⓓ

Example: **A** Will you <u>photocopy</u> this paper?
B I can play a simple <u>meludy</u> on the piano.
C Loreta teaches the art of <u>calligraphy</u>.
D No mistake

Answer Sheet

1. Ⓐ Ⓑ Ⓒ Ⓓ
2. Ⓕ Ⓖ Ⓗ Ⓙ
3. Ⓐ Ⓑ Ⓒ Ⓓ
4. Ⓕ Ⓖ Ⓗ Ⓙ
5. Ⓐ Ⓑ Ⓒ Ⓓ
6. Ⓕ Ⓖ Ⓗ Ⓙ
7. Ⓐ Ⓑ Ⓒ Ⓓ
8. Ⓕ Ⓖ Ⓗ Ⓙ

1. **A** The <u>simphony</u> was enjoyable.
B Pick up the <u>telephone</u>!
C The <u>athlete</u> won the race.
D No mistake

2. **F** Will they <u>televise</u> the game?
G William plays the <u>saxophone</u>.
H May I have your <u>autagraph</u>?
J No mistake

3. **A** My favorite subject is <u>biology</u>.
B I make popcorn in a <u>microwaive</u>.
C Who was <u>absent</u>?
D No mistake

4. **F** Use the <u>microphone</u>.
G What <u>type</u> of pizza is best?
H Tam shouted into the <u>megaphone</u>.
J No mistake

5. **A** I lost my <u>history</u> book.
B Kit read a new <u>biography</u>.
C The word *fair* is a <u>homagraph</u>.
D No mistake

6. **F** The <u>microscope</u> is in the science lab.
G My camera took a great <u>photograf</u>.
H The <u>xylophone</u> is easy to play.
J No mistake

7. **A** *Flee* is a <u>homofone</u>.
B You can see stars with a <u>telescope</u>.
C The <u>telegraph</u> transmits messages.
D No mistake

8. **F** Read this <u>paragraph</u>.
G I need a <u>topic</u> for my paper.
H The official is an <u>honerable</u> person.
J No mistake

More Practice
Now write all the misspelled words correctly on a separate sheet of paper.

 **Spelling Games**
www.eduplace.com/kids/sv/
Review for your test.

Real-World Vocabulary

Technology: Communication

All the words in the box relate to communication. Look them up in your Spelling Dictionary. Then write the words to complete this magazine article.

Fast Communication: Then and Now

In the early 1860s, a person in a hurry to ___(1)___ a message across the country would hand an ___(2)___ to a rider with the pony express. Soon, though, the telegraph system could send messages over long distances much faster. These messages were called ___(3)___. Not long after, the ___(4)___ Alexander Graham Bell developed the telephone. Recently, portable ___(5)___ phones have become popular. Some people use a headset with their portable phone for ___(6)___ communication. People also use phones to leave ___(7)___. Another new form of communication is ___(8)___ mail, or e-mail. Communication that once took days now takes seconds!

Spelling Word Link

telephone

cellular
electronic
envelope
inventor
dispatch
hands-free
telegrams
voice mail

1. _____
2. _____
3. _____
4. _____
5. _____
6. _____
7. _____
8. _____

Try This CHALLENGE

True or False? Write *true* if the sentence is true. Write *false* if it is false.

9. Hands-free communication was perfected by Bell.

10. Voice mail is a message you send through the post office.

11. Telegrams are messages sent by telegraph.

12. In the nineteenth century, people often traveled on the pony express.

9. _____
10. _____
11. _____
12. _____

PART 1 Spelling and Phonics

spect

1. _____
2. _____
3. _____
4. _____

port

5. _____
6. _____
7. _____
8. _____
9. _____
10. _____
11. _____

dict

12. _____
13. _____
14. _____
15. _____
16. _____

rupt

17. _____
18. _____
19. _____
20. _____

Read the Spelling Words and sentences.

Basic

1.	inspect	*inspect*	Airport guards must **inspect** luggage.
2.	export	*export*	We **export** products to Peru and Chile.
3.	erupt	*erupt*	That smoking volcano may **erupt** soon.
4.	predict	*predict*	I **predict** that tomorrow will be sunny.
5.	respect	*respect*	I show **respect** by obeying my parents.
6.	bankrupt	*bankrupt*	Did that vacant store go **bankrupt**?
7.	dictate	*dictate*	Speak clearly if you **dictate** a letter.
8.	porter	*porter*	Will the **porter** carry our bags?
9.	report	*report*	Lisa has written a **report** about frogs.
10.	spectacle	*spectacle*	A circus show is quite a **spectacle.**
11.	deport	*deport*	To **deport** is to expel from a country.
12.	interrupt	*interrupt*	Don't **interrupt** when he is speaking.
13.	dictator	*dictator*	A country's **dictator** is all-powerful.
14.	import	*import*	Many firms **import** goods from Asia.
15.	disrupt	*disrupt*	Rain might **disrupt** our picnic plans.
16.	portable	*portable*	My computer is a **portable** model.
17.	transport	*transport*	Boats **transport** people across the lake.
18.	spectator	*spectator*	A **spectator** caught the foul ball.
19.	verdict	*verdict*	Did the jury reach a **verdict** of guilty?
20.	dictionary	*dictionary*	Find word meanings in a **dictionary**.

Review		Challenge	
21. support	23. polite	26. spectacular	28. corrupt
22. hospital	24. recent	27. contradict	29. retrospect
	25. memory		30. rupture

Think and Sort

Many English words contain Latin word roots. Becoming familiar with Latin word roots can help you remember the spellings and meanings of the words that contain them.

spect ("to see") → in**spect**

Write each Basic Word under its Latin word root.

Word Analysis/Phonics

Write the Basic Words that contain these elements.

21–23. the VCCCV pattern   **24.** the prefix *ex-*   **25.** the prefix *de-*

Vocabulary: Context Paragraph

Write the Basic or Review Words that best complete the paragraph.

Rupa is in the ___(26)___ with a broken arm. She fell off her bicycle on a ___(27)___ ride in the park. Rupa asked her doctor to ___(28)___ how long it might take for her arm to heal, and he said six weeks. Since Rupa temporarily cannot write, she will ___(29)___ a thank-you note to the doctors and nurses, and her sister will write it.

Challenge Words

Write the Challenge Word that best fits each clue. Use your Spelling Dictionary.

30. a review of past events   **33.** an antonym for *honest*

31. an antonym for *confirm*   **34.** a synonym for *burst*

32. a synonym for *wonderful*

Spelling-Meaning Connection

35–36. To remember how to spell the /ə/ sound in the second syllable of *spectacle*, think of the /ă/ sound in the related word *spectacular*. Write *both words*. Underline the *a* in the second syllable of each word.

spect<u>a</u>cle
spect<u>a</u>cular

Word Analysis

21. _____

22. _____

23. _____

24. _____

25. _____

Context Paragraph

26. _____

27. _____

28. _____

29. _____

Challenge Words

30. _____

31. _____

32. _____

33. _____

34. _____

Spelling-Meaning

35. _____

36. _____

At Home With a family member, take turns writing a Spelling Word on a card, leaving blanks for the letters that form the Latin root. Have the other person write the missing letters.

217

Vocabulary

1. _____
2. _____
3. _____
4. _____
5. _____
6. _____
7. _____
8. _____

Vocabulary: Words About the Law

Some words related to the law have Latin roots.

Example: ver + dict, ("to say") = ver**dict**

　　　　　jur ("law") + y = **jur**y

Practice Use the words in the box to complete each sentence. Check your work in your Spelling Dictionary.

verdict	indict	defendant	attorney
plaintiff	jury	prosecute	sentence

1. The _____ in this case says that her bicycle was stolen.
2. The _____ has entered a plea of not guilty.
3. Another name for a lawyer is an _____.
4. Twelve people will make up the _____.
5. The court will _____ the defendant on charges of theft.
6. A district attorney will _____ the case.
7. The jury will try to reach a _____.
8. If the defendant is found guilty, the judge will _____ her.

Dictionary

9. _____
10. _____
11. _____
12. _____
13. _____
14. _____

Dictionary: Multiple-Meaning Words

As you know, a dictionary entry may include more than one numbered definition.

Practice For each sentence, write the part of speech and definition number that corresponds to the meaning of the underlined word. Use your Spelling Dictionary.

9. I read a news <u>report</u> about the heat wave.
10. Nina <u>reported</u> for duty at the volunteer center.
11. Each club must write an annual <u>report</u> about its activities.
12. Jamie has excellent <u>balance</u> and can walk on a tightrope.
13. The clown will <u>balance</u> a basket of apples on his head.
14. Use the <u>balance</u> to weigh this chemical.

PART 3 Spelling and Writing

Proofread a Newspaper Article

Spelling and Titles Use proofreading marks to correct **ten** misspelled Basic or Review Words and **four** mistakes in the capitalization and punctuation of titles in this article.

Example: I used a ~~dicsionery~~ *dictionary* to proofread "School Days.

Thoughts of a Professional Journalist

Here are some highlights from a recent presentation by noted journalist Alex Gumas.

- I rispect everyone I interview. Instead of barking orders like a dictater, I ask questions in a polight tone and try not to interupt.

- I usually dictait my articles into a portible tape recorder because I can't rely on my memry.

- The best article I ever read was called Power Outages Do Not Dissrupt Local Hospitle," written in suport of the medical staff. My favorite interview was with the author of the poem Dreaming of better Days.

Write a Newspaper Article

prewrite → draft → revise → proofread → publish

Write a newspaper article about something interesting that has happened in your community lately.

- Tell **who, what, when, where,** and **why.**
- Use some Spelling Words and include a title of a poem or article.
- Proofread for **spelling, capitalization,** and **punctuation.**

Basic
inspect
export
erupt
predict
respect
bankrupt
dictate
porter
report
spectacle
deport
interrupt
dictator
import
disrupt
portable
transport
spectator
verdict
dictionary

Review
support
hospital
polite
recent
memory

Challenge
spectacular
contradict
corrupt
retrospect
rupture

Power Proofreading
www.eduplace.com/kids/sv/

Test Tip Skip questions that seem hard and go back to them later.

Directions This test will show how well you can spell.

- Many of the questions in this test have spelling mistakes. Some do not have any mistakes at all.
- Look for mistakes in spelling.
- If there is a mistake, fill in the answer space on your answer sheet that has the same letter as the **line** with the mistake.
- If there is no mistake, fill in the last answer space.

Example:

1. Ⓐ ● Ⓒ Ⓓ Ⓔ

Answer Sheet

1. Ⓐ Ⓑ Ⓒ Ⓓ Ⓔ
2. Ⓙ Ⓚ Ⓛ Ⓜ Ⓝ
3. Ⓐ Ⓑ Ⓒ Ⓓ Ⓔ
4. Ⓙ Ⓚ Ⓛ Ⓜ Ⓝ
5. Ⓐ Ⓑ Ⓒ Ⓓ Ⓔ
6. Ⓙ Ⓚ Ⓛ Ⓜ Ⓝ
7. Ⓐ Ⓑ Ⓒ Ⓓ Ⓔ
8. Ⓙ Ⓚ Ⓛ Ⓜ Ⓝ

Example:
- **A** struggle
- **B** virdict
- **C** dismiss
- **D** export
- **E** *(No mistakes)*

1.
- **A** transport
- **B** riport
- **C** polite
- **D** microphone
- **E** *(No mistakes)*

2.
- **J** televise
- **K** hospital
- **L** emport
- **M** dictate
- **N** *(No mistakes)*

3.
- **A** eerupt
- **B** spectacle
- **C** photocopy
- **D** predict
- **E** *(No mistakes)*

4.
- **J** disrupt
- **K** homophone
- **L** symphony
- **M** spectater
- **N** *(No mistakes)*

5.
- **A** calligraphy
- **B** deport
- **C** megaphone
- **D** dictionarry
- **E** *(No mistakes)*

6.
- **J** portor
- **K** dictator
- **L** express
- **M** recent
- **N** *(No mistakes)*

7.
- **A** portable
- **B** paragraph
- **C** inspeckt
- **D** support
- **E** *(No mistakes)*

8.
- **J** memory
- **K** rispect
- **L** bankrupt
- **M** biography
- **N** *(No mistakes)*

More Practice

Now write all the misspelled words correctly on a separate sheet of paper.

Spelling Games
www.eduplace.com/kids/sv/
Review for your test.

Real-World Vocabulary

Social Studies: Weather Around the Globe

All the words in the box relate to weather. Look up these words in your Spelling Dictionary. Then write the words to complete this weather report.

World Weather Brief

In Thailand, rain poured down in a record ___(1)___ during the wet ___(2)___ season. In the Indian Ocean, a storm is gathering force and may develop into a ___(3)___. In northern Africa, a severe ___(4)___, or lack of precipitation, continues, causing problems in the ___(5)___ desert areas.

Here in North America, the Midwest is sweltering through a ___(6)___, while in the Pacific Northwest, sudden ___(7)___ are making it dangerous to sail. In the Northeast, the weather continues to be ___(8)___, and more rain is predicted.

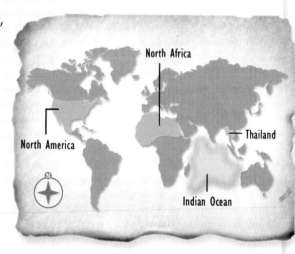

1. _____
2. _____
3. _____
4. _____
5. _____
6. _____
7. _____
8. _____

Try This CHALLENGE

Write Clues Write clues for at least four words from the box on a separate sheet of paper. For example, "It happens when there is no rain for months" could be a clue for *drought*. Exchange papers with a partner and write the answers.

PART 1 Spelling and Phonics

French

1. _____
2. _____
3. _____
4. _____
5. _____
6. _____
7. _____
8. _____
9. _____
10. _____
11. _____
12. _____
13. _____
14. _____
15. _____

Other Languages

16. _____
17. _____
18. _____
19. _____
20. _____

Read the Spelling Words and sentences.

Basic

1. ballet	*ballet*	**Ballet** is a form of dance.
2. echo	*echo*	My voice has an **echo** in this huge hall.
3. bouquet	*bouquet*	That is a beautiful **bouquet** of flowers!
4. cassette	*cassette*	I recorded a song on a **cassette**.
5. coupon	*coupon*	This **coupon** saves us 25 cents on soap.
6. safari	*safari*	Did you see any lions on the **safari**?
7. portrait	*portrait*	Ross painted a **portrait** of his mom.
8. barrette	*barrette*	Maya bought a green **barrette** for her hair.
9. depot	*depot*	Two trains pulled into the **depot**.
10. courtesy	*courtesy*	Show **courtesy** by introducing yourself.
11. petite	*petite*	I bought a small dress for my **petite** sister.
12. denim	*denim*	That blue **denim** jacket matches my jeans.
13. brunette	*brunette*	A person with brown hair is a **brunette**.
14. buffet	*buffet*	What foods did you try at the **buffet** lunch?
15. gazette	*gazette*	Trevor reads the school's daily **gazette**.
16. khaki	*khaki*	My **khaki** pants are a light brown color.
17. crochet	*crochet*	Tina likes to **crochet** warm sweaters.
18. chorus	*chorus*	The **chorus** sang together beautifully.
19. essay	*essay*	I am writing an **essay** about freedom.
20. alphabet	*alphabet*	We spell words using the **alphabet**.

Review
21. routine
22. rescue
23. crayon
24. amuse
25. reason

Challenge
26. encore
27. collage
28. matinee
29. premiere
30. embarrass

Think and Sort

Knowing the language an English word was borrowed from can help you figure out how to spell and pronounce the word.

ball**et** (from French)   brun**ette** (from French)

Write each Basic Word under the language from which it was borrowed. Use your Spelling Dictionary. Look for the first language listed in the Word History for each word.

Word Analysis/Phonics

21–24. Write the four Basic Words that include a double *t*.

Vocabulary: Context Sentences

Write the Basic or Review Word that best completes each sentence.

25. The artist will paint a _____ of my family.

26. Grace's little sister colored her paper with a _____.

27. Written English uses the twenty-six letters called the Roman _____.

28. With this _____ we can buy two pizzas for the price of one.

29. The _____ on the mantel had roses and daisies in it.

Challenge Words

Write the Challenge Words to complete the paragraph. Use your Spelling Dictionary.

Our class went to a ___(30)___, a performance in the middle of the day. It was the world ___(31)___ of a new piece of music. We all listened quietly because we did not want to ___(32)___ our teacher. We loved the concert! The audience cheered so loudly at the end that the musicians played an ___(33)___. Back at school, we put together a ___(34)___ of photos we took before and after the event.

Spelling-Meaning Connection

35–36. You can remember how to spell the /ĭ/ sound in *courtesy* by thinking about the /ē/ sound in the word *courteous*. Write *courtesy* and *courteous*. Underline the letter that has the /ĭ/ sound in one word and the /ē/ sound in the other word.

courtesy
courteous

Word Analysis

21. _____

22. _____

23. _____

24. _____

Context Sentences

25. _____

26. _____

27. _____

28. _____

29. _____

Challenge Words

30. _____

31. _____

32. _____

33. _____

34. _____

Spelling-Meaning

35. _____

36. _____

At Home Make word crosses with a family member. Write one Spelling Word across a page. Take turns writing Spelling Words that cross any word you wrote.

223

Vocabulary

1. _____
2. _____
3. _____
4. _____
5. _____
6. _____
7. _____
8. _____

Vocabulary: Words from Place Names

Practice Write the word from the box that matches each definition. Use your Spelling Dictionary.

denim	jersey	cheddar	cologne
Dalmatian	frankfurter	rhinestone	cashmere

1. a cheese named after the English town of Cheddar
2. an artificial gem named after the Rhine River in Germany
3. cloth used to make jeans; named for the French town of Nîmes
4. a spotted dog first bred in Dalmatia, an area in Croatia
5. a scented liquid; named after the German city of Cologne
6. a sausage made of beef or pork; named after the German city of Frankfurt
7. a soft fabric made from goat's wool; named after the Kashmir region in India
8. a soft, stretchy fabric, produced on the Isle of Jersey in the United Kingdom

Thesaurus

9. _____
10. _____
11. _____
12. _____
13. _____
14. _____

Thesaurus: Exact Words for *small*

Practice Look up *small* in your Thesaurus. Write a word from the box to replace *small* in each sentence.

compact	miniature	microscopic	petite	cramped	undersized

9. The peaches we bought were <u>small</u> but delicious.
10. The dancer easily lifted the <u>small</u> ballerina.
11. Adding ten guests made our dining room feel <u>small</u>.
12. Bacteria are <u>small</u> organisms, invisible to the naked eye.
13. These parking spaces are for <u>small</u> cars only.
14. Mom has an antique locket with a <u>small</u> painting inside.

Proofread a Travel Diary

Spelling and Titles Use proofreading marks to correct **ten** misspelled Basic or Review Words and **two** mistakes in the capitalization and underlining of titles in this travel diary entry.

Example: I used a *coopon* to buy the magazine animals Today.

Proofreading Marks
¶ Indent
∧ Add
⊙ Add a period
⌐ Delete
≡ Capital letter
/ Small letter

July 12, 2006

Today we began our safary! The reasin we are here is that my parents are wildlife portrait painters. We arrived at the deppot by train. A park ranger wearing khacki pants and a denim vest met us. Just inside the park, we saw elephants crossing the road. Elephants really amyoose me! We watched wildlife all day and then had a buffette dinner. Later I read an esay in a magazine called In the Wild. My father read the local gazette, The Kenyan times, and my petete mother began to croshet a scarf. We could hear the ecko of lions roaring all night.

Write a Travel Diary

prewrite → draft → revise → proofread → publish

Write a travel diary entry about a trip you took or want to take.

- Tell **when** and **where** you went, and give details about the trip.
- Use some Spelling Words and a newspaper or magazine title.
- Proofread for **spelling, capitalization,** and **punctuation.**

Basic
ballet
echo
bouquet
cassette
coupon
safari
portrait
barrette
depot
courtesy
petite
denim
brunette
buffet
gazette
khaki
crochet
chorus
essay
alphabet

Review
routine
rescue
crayon
amuse
reason

Challenge
encore
collage
matinee
premiere
embarrass

Power Proofreading
www.eduplace.com/kids/sv/

Test Tip Eliminate answer choices that you know are incorrect.

Directions For Numbers 1 through 8, choose the word that is spelled correctly and best completes the sentence.

Example: I have brown hair, so I am a _____.

   A brunnete
   B brunet
   C brunette
   D broonett

Example:

Ⓐ Ⓑ ● Ⓓ

Answer Sheet

1. Ⓐ Ⓑ Ⓒ Ⓓ

2. Ⓕ Ⓖ Ⓗ Ⓙ

3. Ⓐ Ⓑ Ⓒ Ⓓ

4. Ⓕ Ⓖ Ⓗ Ⓙ

5. Ⓐ Ⓑ Ⓒ Ⓓ

6. Ⓕ Ⓖ Ⓗ Ⓙ

7. Ⓐ Ⓑ Ⓒ Ⓓ

8. Ⓕ Ⓖ Ⓗ Ⓙ

1. Tanya wants to audition for the _____.
   A balet
   B ballet
   C balett
   D ballett

2. Judy received a _____ of roses for her birthday.
   F bouqet
   G boukay
   H booquet
   J bouquet

3. Dwight sings in the school _____.
   A corus
   B corrus
   C corace
   D chorus

4. Let's record a song on a _____.
   F cassete
   G casette
   H cassette
   J cassett

5. My morning _____ is efficient.
   A routeen
   B routene
   C routine
   D rooteen

6. You must show _____ at the table.
   F courtesy
   G curtesy
   H courtisy
   J courtesee

7. Firefighters _____ many animals.
   A rescue
   B rescew
   C reskew
   D resscew

8. The queen's _____ hangs in a gallery.
   F portrit
   G portrait
   H portrate
   J portriat

More Practice
Now write each correctly spelled word on a sheet of paper.

Spelling Games
www.eduplace.com/kids/sv/
Review for your test.

Real-World ★ Vocabulary

Careers: Photography

All the words in the box relate to photography. Look them up in your Spelling Dictionary. Then write the words to complete these course descriptions for photography classes.

ART CLASSES, *Photography*

Electronic Photography. (Mondays, 6:00–9:00 P.M.) You will learn how to use a ____(1)____ camera and photo editing software. The software allows you to change or ____(2)____ images before you ____(3)____ them. You can ____(4)____ the photo to cut off parts you don't like, or you can ____(5)____ it to create a poster.

Black and White Photography. (Wednesdays, 5:00–8:00 P.M.) In this class, you will use a traditional camera. You will learn how to ____(6)____ it manually to get the clearest shot and how to measure light using the ____(7)____. You will also learn how to ____(8)____ your own photographs in a darkroom.

e Word Game
www.eduplace.com/kids/sv/

Spelling Word Link

portrait

crop
digital
enlarge
focus
light meter
manipulate
print
develop

1. _____
2. _____
3. _____
4. _____
5. _____
6. _____
7. _____
8. _____

Try This CHALLENGE

Questions and Answers Write the word from the box that answers each queston.

9. Which word means "to arrange, operate, or control"?
10. Which word means "to make bigger"?
11. What measures the intensity of light?
12. What kind of photos can you edit using computer software?

9. _____
10. _____
11. _____
12. _____

Unit 31

1. _____
2. _____
3. _____
4. _____
5. _____
6. _____
7. _____
8. _____
9. _____
10. _____

Unit 31	Prefixes: *com-, con-, pre-, pro-*			pages 198–203
preview	company	protect	contain	prejudge
confirm	computer	provide	confide	preflight

Spelling Strategy A prefix is a word part added to the beginning of a base word or word root. It adds meaning to a word.

pre + view = **pre**view   **com** + motion = **com**motion

Word Clues Write the word that fits each clue.

1. to share a secret
2. a place you might work
3. to judge too soon
4. to watch in advance
5. to keep from harm
6. a very useful machine
7. to verify
8. before you fly
9. to hold in
10. to give

Unit 32

11. _____
12. _____
13. _____
14. _____
15. _____
16. _____
17. _____
18. _____
19. _____
20. _____

Unit 32	Suffixes: *-ent, -ant, -able, -ible*			pages 204–209
vacant	different	urgency	possible	honorable
terrible	comfortable	absent	infant	radiance

Spelling Strategy

/ənt/ → differ**ent**, vac**ant**   ə bəl/ → comfort**able**, terr**ible**

Analogies Write the word that best completes each analogy.

11. *Open* is to *closed* as _____ is to *occupied*.
12. *Fearless* is to *courageous* as *noble* is to _____.
13. *Awake* is to *asleep* as _____ is to *wonderful*.
14. *Certain* is to *impossible* as *same* is to _____.
15. *Baby* is to _____ as *stove* is to *range*.

Context Sentences Write the word that best completes each sentence.

16. The sun's _____ was strongest at midday.
17. The operator heard _____ in the caller's voice.
18. I feel most _____ around my friends.
19. It is not _____ to get tickets to the movie anymore.
20. When the teacher was _____, we had a substitute.

Unit 33   Greek Word Parts   pages 210–215

| autograph | photograph | televise | microphone | symphony |
| microwave | photocopy | biography | saxophone | telescope |

Spelling Strategy

    graph ("something written") → auto**graph**, bio**graph**y

Context Paragraph Write the words that complete this paragraph.

    Today we went to see the ___(21)___ orchestra perform. I knew that a TV station was going to ___(22)___ the performance, but I didn't know why. When we got there, I found out that a famous pop singer was performing with the orchestra. As the musicians played, she sang into a ___(23)___. I wanted to take a ___(24)___ of her, but I forgot my camera. So instead, I asked her to ___(25)___ my program.

Classifying Write the word that belongs in each group.

26. piano, violin, _____
27. stove, oven, _____
28. microscope, binoculars, _____
29. poem, novel, _____
30. print, duplicate, _____

Unit 33
21. _____
22. _____
23. _____
24. _____
25. _____
26. _____
27. _____
28. _____
29. _____
30. _____

Unit 34   Latin Word Roots   pages 216–221

| export | respect | bankrupt | dictate | spectacle |
| import | disrupt | portable | verdict | spectator |

Spelling Strategy

    spect ("to see") → **spect**acle, **spect**ator

Definitions Write the word that best fits each meaning.

31. to throw into disorder
32. financially ruined
33. to say for someone to write
34. a person who watches
35. admiration
36. carried easily
37. to bring in from another country
38. the decision of a jury
39. an impressive public event
40. to send out to another place

Unit 34
31. _____
32. _____
33. _____
34. _____
35. _____
36. _____
37. _____
38. _____
39. _____
40. _____

Spelling Review

Unit 35
41. _____
42. _____
43. _____
44. _____
45. _____
46. _____
47. _____
48. _____
49. _____
50. _____

Unit 35 More Words from Other Languages   pages 222–227

ballet	bouquet	safari	portrait	depot
petite	brunette	gazette	crochet	essay

Spelling Strategy Knowing the language a word comes from can help you remember how to spell that word.

Analogies Write the word that best completes each analogy.

41. *Goalie* is to *soccer* as *ballerina* is to _____.
42. *Smart* is to *intelligent* as _____ is to *small*.
43. *Sculptor* is to *bust* as *painter* is to _____.
44. *Omelet* is to *egg* as _____ is to *flower*.

Word Clues Write the word that fits each clue.

45. a newspaper
46. a trip to see wild animals
47. a way to make mittens
48. a paper on one subject
49. a place to catch the train
50. a brown-haired person

Challenge Words
51. _____
52. _____
53. _____
54. _____
55. _____
56. _____
57. _____
58. _____
59. _____
60. _____

Challenge Words   Units 31–35   pages 198–227

commercial	autobiography	contradict	occupant	matinee
evidence	retrospect	conversation	embarrass	bibliography

Context Sentences Write the word that best completes each sentence.

51. The _____ of that apartment is not at home.
52. The jury considered all the _____ in the case.
53. A famous swimmer wrote an _____ about her life.
54. We should see the _____ at noon today.
55. Don't _____ me in front of my friends.
56. That company has a new _____ on TV.
57. I don't like it when you _____ what I say.
58. In _____, Emilio regretted his action.
59. The teacher and I had a good _____.
60. Include a _____ at the end of a report.

Proofread a Persuasive Essay

Spelling and Grammar Mixed Review Use proofreading marks to correct this essay. There are **nine** misspelled Basic Words from the last five units. There is **one** error in the punctuation of a date and **two** errors involving the title of an article.

Example: The fair will offer a great ~~buffay~~ *buffet* dinner on July 19 2006.

Let's Stop the Confusion!

I perpose that workers at the Coast County Fair all dress in kakhi and dennum. Identical outfits will make it easy to tell the differince between workers and visitors. I prodict that workers will be treated with greater courtesy if people can identify them at a distence—and all workers, from biolagy experts to waiters, deserve polite treatment. Also, people will no longer interupt visitors with frequent questions, mistaking them for workers. This matter deserves urjant attention. My article, "County Fair workers Need Uniforms, will appear in our newspaper on June 27 2005. Please support my proposal.

Mike Yoshida

Proofreading Marks

¶ Indent
∧ Add
⊙ Add a period
⌇ Delete
= Capital letter
/ Small letter

Write a Persuasive Essay

prewrite → draft → revise → proofread → publish

Write an essay that persuades others to do or believe something.

- Use some Spelling Words from Units 31–35 in your essay.
- Proofread for **spelling** and correct capitalization and punctuation of **dates** and **titles**.

Tips

- Think about something you would like to persuade others to do or believe.
- Brainstorm some reasons that might persuade your audience.
- Support each reason with one fact or example.

Power Proofreading
www.eduplace.com/kids/sv/

231

Student's Handbook

Contents

Unit 1   Short Vowels   pages 18–23

closet	crush	direct	promise	fund
demand	swift	bundle	solid	weather

Spelling Strategy Remember that a short vowel sound is usually spelled by a single vowel and followed by a consonant sound.

Definitions Write the word that fits each meaning.

1. a place to store belongings
2. fast-moving
3. a package
4. to crumple

Context Sentences Write the word that completes each sentence.

5. We gave money to a _____ that helps disadvantaged children.

6. The _____ will be cold and rainy.

7. A cube and a cylinder are _____ shapes.

8. Our teachers _____ that we get to class on time.

9. He will _____ you so you don't get lost.

10. Please _____ not to tell anyone my secret.

Unit 1

1. _____
2. _____
3. _____
4. _____
5. _____
6. _____
7. _____
8. _____
9. _____
10. _____

Unit 2   Long *a* and Long *e*   pages 24–29

awake	feast	greet	repeat	display
sheepish	release	remain	sway	brain

Spelling Strategy

/ā/ → **a**-consonant-**e, ai, ay**   /ē/ → **ea, ee**

Word Clues Write the word that fits each clue.

11. show
12. stay behind
13. fancy meal
14. let go
15. embarrassed
16. used to think
17. back and forth
18. hello
19. over and over
20. alarm clock

Unit 2

11. _____
12. _____
13. _____
14. _____
15. _____
16. _____
17. _____
18. _____
19. _____
20. _____

235

Cycle 1 Extra Practice and Review

Unit 3

21. _____

22. _____

23. _____

24. _____

25. _____

26. _____

27. _____

28. _____

29. _____

30. _____

Unit 3		Long *i* and Long *o*		pages 30–35
sign	groan	strike	mighty	stroll
apply	slight	odor	silent	approach

Spelling Strategy

/ī/ → **i**-consonant-**e**, **igh**, **i**, **y**

/ō/ → **o**-consonant-**e**, **o**, **oa**, **ow**

Word Completion Write the word by adding the missing letters.

21. ap _ _ y

22. str _ _ l

23. str _ _ e

24. a _ _ roach

25. sli _ _ t

26. si _ _

Analogies Write the word that best completes each analogy.

27. *Weak* is to *powerless* as *strong* is to _____.

28. *Enormous* is to *tiny* as *noisy* is to _____.

29. *Joyful* is to *laugh* as *disturbed* is to _____.

30. *Sound* is to *noise* as *smell* is to _____.

Unit 4		Vowel Sounds: /o͞o/, /yo͞o/		pages 36–41
glue	flute	accuse	stew	loose
confuse	cruise	route	include	assume

Spelling Strategy

/o͞o/ and /yo͞o/ → **u**-consonant-**e**, **oo**, **ue**, **ew**, **ui**, **ou**

Unit 4

31. _____

32. _____

33. _____

34. _____

35. _____

36. _____

37. _____

38. _____

39. _____

40. _____

Context Sentences Write the word that completes each sentence.

31. If everyone talks at once, it will _____ him.

32. My brother plays the _____.

33. Mom made beef _____ for dinner.

34. We are going to travel on a _____ ship.

35. The dog escaped because its collar was _____.

36. Do not _____ me of looking at your paper!

37. The quickest _____ to his house is past the park.

38. Does the model kit _____ everything we need?

39. Why did they _____ that we would wait for them?

40. I need to _____ the picture to my report cover.

Cycle 1

Unit 5		Vowel Sounds: /ou/, /ô/, /oi/		pages 42–47
sprawl	launch	loyal	avoid	haunt
saucer	pounce	August	royal	coward

Spelling Strategy

/ou/ → **ou, ow**   /ô/ → **aw, au, a** before **l**   /oi/ → **oi, oy**

Word Clues Write the word that fits each clue.

41. not a hero
42. summer month
43. small plate
44. king or queen
45. spread out
46. send aloft
47. what ghosts do
48. jump on
49. dodge
50. faithful

Challenge Words		Units 1–5		pages 18–47
instruct	betray	reproach	conclude	poise
distress	motivate	defy	intrude	exhaust
physical	upheaval	plight	presume	alternate

Context Sentences Write the word that completes each sentence.

51. When I didn't throw the ball, my dog gave me a look of _____.
52. Running is a form of _____ exercise.
53. My father promised to _____ me in the game of golf.
54. A soldier is not allowed to _____ orders.
55. The girl's bad behavior will _____ her parents.
56. The story will _____ in next month's magazine.
57. A good friend will never _____ you.
58. Climbing the mountain would _____ most people.
59. The mountain was formed by an _____ of the earth.
60. He knocked before entering because he didn't want to _____.
61. I _____ you know each other since you are neighbors.
62. The _____ of flood victims is terrible.
63. She showed great _____ singing for an audience.
64. Did his speech _____ you to try harder?
65. Let's _____ turns playing Ping-Pong.

Unit 5

41. _____
42. _____
43. _____
44. _____
45. _____
46. _____
47. _____
48. _____
49. _____
50. _____

Challenge Words

51. _____
52. _____
53. _____
54. _____
55. _____
56. _____
57. _____
58. _____
59. _____
60. _____
61. _____
62. _____
63. _____
64. _____
65. _____

237

Unit 7

1. _____
2. _____
3. _____
4. _____
5. _____
6. _____
7. _____
8. _____
9. _____
10. _____

Unit 7	Vowel + /r/ Sounds		pages 54–59
glory	carton	adore	dairy	pardon
barely	soar	beware	armor	former

Spelling Strategy

/ôr/ → **or, oar, ore**   /âr/ → **are, air**   /är/ → **ar**

Context Sentences Write the words that complete the sentences.

1. I know Mr. Sing because he is my _____ baseball coach.
2. The sign warned drivers to _____ of falling rocks.
3. She packed the dishes in a large _____.
4. The music was so soft that we could _____ hear it.
5. The children all _____ their grandmother.
6. We watched the hawk _____ through the air.
7. The knight wore a suit of _____.
8. I beg your _____, but I need to ask a question.
9. We went to the _____ to get some ice cream.
10. The athlete enjoyed the _____ of winning.

Unit 8

11. _____
12. _____
13. _____
14. _____
15. _____
16. _____
17. _____
18. _____
19. _____
20. _____

Unit 8	More Vowel + /r/ Sounds		pages 60–65
earth	burnt	smear	further	nerve
squirm	weary	alert	worship	volunteer

Spelling Strategy

/ûr/ → **ir, ur, er, ear, or**   /îr/ → **eer, ear**

Context Paragraph Write the words to complete the paragraph.

Mario started to ___(11)___ restlessly. He stopped abruptly and tried to shrink into his seat when his teacher said, "I need a ___(12)___ to give the first speech." His baby sister had been up for hours during the night, and Mario was very ___(13)___. He knew he wasn't ___(14)___ enough to do a good job on his speech.

Word Completion Write the word by adding the missing letters.

15. f _ _ ther   17. n _ _ ve   19. b _ _ nt
16. w _ _ ship   18. e _ _ th   20. sm _ _ r

238

Unit 9 — Homophones — pages 66–71

steel	manor	lesson	hanger	whose
steal	manner	lessen	hangar	overdo

Spelling Strategy Remember that homophones are words that sound alike but have different spellings and meanings.

Definitions Write the word that fits each meaning.

21. way something is done
22. do more than necessary
23. take from someone
24. airplane garage
25. belonging to whom

26. something learned
27. kind of metal
28. large, fancy house
29. become less
30. device for hanging

Unit 10 — Compound Words — pages 72–77

wildlife	home run	teammate	wheelchair	well-known
barefoot	warehouse	overboard	outspoken	newscast

Spelling Strategy Remember that a compound word is made of two or more smaller words. A compound word may be written as one word, a hyphenated word, or separate words.

Analogies Write the word that completes each analogy.

31. *Honest* is to *dishonest* as *slippered* is to _____.
32. *Interior* is to *exterior* as *quiet* is to _____.
33. *Computer* is to *technology* as *tiger* is to _____.
34. *Admired* is to *well-liked* as *famous* is to _____.

Context Sentences Write the word that completes each sentence.

35. The catcher threw the ball to his _____.
36. The furniture company uses that building as a _____.
37. We won the game when Tanya hit a _____.
38. I heard the story on the evening _____.
39. After breaking her hip, my grandmother had to use a _____ to get around.
40. The sailor threw the life jacket _____ to a swimmer.

Unit 9

21. _____
22. _____
23. _____
24. _____
25. _____
26. _____
27. _____
28. _____
29. _____
30. _____

Unit 10

31. _____
32. _____
33. _____
34. _____
35. _____
36. _____
37. _____
38. _____
39. _____
40. _____

239

Unit 11

41. _____

42. _____

43. _____

44. _____

45. _____

46. _____

47. _____

48. _____

49. _____

50. _____

Challenge Words

51. _____

52. _____

53. _____

54. _____

55. _____

56. _____

57. _____

58. _____

59. _____

60. _____

61. _____

62. _____

63. _____

64. _____

65. _____

Unit 11	Final Schwa + /r/ Sounds			pages 78–83
cellar	chapter	mayor	major	popular
tractor	thunder	messenger	calendar	quarter

Spelling Strategy

/ər/ → **er, or, ar**

Classifying Write the word that belongs in each group.

41. president, governor, _____

42. rain, lightning, _____

43. page, paragraph, _____

44. daybook, reminder, _____

45. courier, runner, _____

46. half, third, _____

47. attic, first floor, _____

48. important, big, _____

49. beloved, well-liked, _____

50. reaper, truck, _____

Challenge Words	Units 7–11			pages 54–83
forfeit	yearn	canvas	overseas	clamor
orchestra	engineer	canvass	quick-witted	circular
hoard	dreary	sight	bulletin board	adviser

Context Sentences Write the word that completes each sentence.

51. Wolves have a keen sense of _____.

52. At night, many people _____ for peace and quiet.

53. The _____ of the subway train made it hard to hear.

54. The racers ran around a _____ track.

55. He plays the violin in the school _____.

56. The teacher put a notice on the _____.

57. Her father is an _____ who works with the space program.

58. The class _____ helped us plan the school trip.

59. We will _____ every class for the survey.

60. My parents are going _____ on their vacation.

61. The artist put a layer of paint on the _____.

62. It is no fun to play outside on a cold, _____ day.

63. A miser will often _____ his money.

64. The _____ boy easily solved the puzzle.

65. We will _____ the game if we are late.

Unit 13   VCCV Pattern   pages 90–95

bargain	object	suppose	shoulder	tunnel
custom	suggest	perhaps	timber	common

Spelling Strategy To spell a word with the VCCV pattern, divide the word between the consonants. Look for patterns you have learned, and spell the word by syllables.

Analogies Write the word that best completes each analogy.

1. *Pleasant* is to *nasty* as *rare* is to _____.

2. *Know* is to *recognize* as *guess* is to _____.

3. *Allow* is to *permit* as *protest* is to _____.

4. *Leg* is to *hip* as *arm* is to _____.

Context Sentences Write the word that completes each sentence.

5. Pablo knows the area, so he can _____ a good restaurant.

6. The rain dance is a traditional Native American _____.

7. I got a great _____ at the clearance sale.

8. The train disappeared into the _____.

9. It may rain today, but _____ it won't start till tomorrow.

10. Excellent _____ comes from Maine's forests.

Unit 14   VCV Pattern   pages 96–101

human	exact	basic	vivid	nation
panic	select	item	police	menu

Spelling Strategy Divide a VCV word into syllables before or after the consonant. Note carefully the spelling of the unstressed syllable. Spell the word by syllables.

Word Clues Write the word that fits each clue.

11. colorful   **14.** country   **17.** simple   **19.** lawmen

12. choose   **15.** thing   **18.** food list   **20.** perfect

13. person   **16.** terror

Unit 13

1. _____

2. _____

3. _____

4. _____

5. _____

6. _____

7. _____

8. _____

9. _____

10. _____

Unit 14

11. _____

12. _____

13. _____

14. _____

15. _____

16. _____

17. _____

18. _____

19. _____

20. _____

241

Unit 15

21. _____

22. _____

23. _____

24. _____

25. _____

26. _____

27. _____

28. _____

29. _____

30. _____

Unit 15		VCCCV Pattern		pages 102–107
orphan	complex	burglar	laundry	employ
merchant	freckles	purchase	dolphin	partner

Spelling Strategy When two consonants in a VCCCV pattern spell one sound or form a cluster, divide the word into syllables before or after those two consonants. Look for patterns you have learned, and spell the word by syllables.

Word Clues Write the word that fits each clue.

21. not simple
22. person who steals
23. one with no parents
24. ocean mammal
25. dirty clothing

26. found on the face
27. teammate
28. storekeeper
29. buy
30. make use of

Unit 16

31. _____

32. _____

33. _____

34. _____

35. _____

36. _____

37. _____

38. _____

39. _____

40. _____

Unit 16		VV Pattern		pages 108–113
patriot	diet	museum	pioneer	visual
create	audio	dial	theater	violet

Spelling Strategy When two vowels in a VV pattern spell two vowel sounds, divide the word into syllables between the vowels. Look for patterns you have learned. Spell the word by syllables.

Context Paragraph Write the words to complete the paragraph.

Elena studied the exhibit on the early United States at the history __(31)__. When she turned the __(32)__ on the display about settling the frontier, a voice began to explain what life was like in __(33)__ days. Elena listened carefully to the __(34)__ presentation. Then she went into the __(35)__ with her family to watch a movie about George Washington, an American __(36)__.

Syllable Search Write a word by adding the missing syllable.

37. vi / ___ / let
38. ___ / su / al

39. di / ___
40. ___ / ate

Unit 17   Final Schwa + /l/ Sounds   pages 114–119

central	legal	angle	needle	angel
struggle	bicycle	channel	global	article

Spelling Strategy

The final /əl/ sounds can be spelled **al, el,** and **le.**

Classifying Write the word that belongs in each group.

41. thread, scissors, _____
42. skates, wagon, _____
43. cherub, spirit, _____
44. lawful, legitimate, _____
45. difficulty, hardship, _____
46. national, international, _____
47. line, circle, _____

48. river, canal, _____
49. noun, verb, _____
50. middle, main, _____

Challenge Words   Units 13–17   pages 90–119

attempt	autumn	function	diagnose	mineral
collide	column	conscience	media	colonel
ignore	laser	apostrophe	society	artificial

Word Completion Write the word by adding the missing letters.

51. col _ _ el
52. art _ fic _ _ _
53. _ _ tum _
54. di _ g _ ose

55. _ _ _ ct _ _ _
56. apo _ _ _ o _ _ e
57. _ _ _ scien _ _
58. la _ er

Context Sentences Write a word to complete each sentence.

59. One _____ on our porch was damaged in the storm.
60. Radio and television are both types of _____.
61. Inez will make one more _____ to learn the song.
62. Tony tried to _____ the noise of the lawnmower.
63. The geologist did a test to identify the _____ in the rock.
64. José joined a _____ of artists and musicians.
65. The skaters went the same direction so they wouldn't _____.

Unit 17

41. _____
42. _____
43. _____
44. _____
45. _____
46. _____
47. _____
48. _____
49. _____
50. _____

Challenge Words

51. _____
52. _____
53. _____
54. _____
55. _____
56. _____
57. _____
58. _____
59. _____
60. _____
61. _____
62. _____
63. _____
64. _____
65. _____

Unit 19

1. _____
2. _____
3. _____
4. _____
5. _____
6. _____
7. _____
8. _____
9. _____
10. _____

Unit 19		Words with *-ed* or *-ing*		pages 126–131
listening	knitting	carpeting	wandered	skimmed
whipped	quizzed	suffering	totaled	upsetting

Spelling Strategy

ONE-SYLLABLE WORDS: knit + ing = kni**tting**

TWO-SYLLABLE WORDS: total + ed = total**ed**

Word Clues Write the word that fits each clue.

1. added
2. disturbing
3. questioned
4. walked around
5. hearing
6. floor covering
7. using yarn
8. scanned
9. did to cream
10. misery

Unit 20		More Words with *-ed* or *-ing*		pages 132–137
freezing	whispered	amazing	performing	resulting
damaged	practicing	supported	united	expected

Spelling Strategy

freeze - e + ing = freez**ing**   expect + ed = expect**ed**

Unit 20

11. _____
12. _____
13. _____
14. _____
15. _____
16. _____
17. _____
18. _____
19. _____
20. _____

Context Paragraph Write the words to complete the paragraph.

Our school marching band will be ____(11)____ at the state fair this year. It's a big honor, and we have been ____(12)____ for months! Three weeks ago, a small but smoky fire in the music room ____(13)____ some uniforms. The whole town ____(14)____ to help raise money for new uniforms. If people hadn't ____(15)____ us, the band wouldn't be going to the fair.

Word Completion Write a word by adding the missing letters.

16. _ xp _ ct _ d
17. _ m _ z _ ng
18. wh _ sp _ r _ d
19. r _ s _ lt _ ng
20. fr _ _ z _ ng

Unit 21   Changing Final *y* to *i*   pages 138–143

| denied | ferries | sunnier | dirtier | scariest |
| cozier | enemies | greediest | memories | strategies |

Spelling Strategy When a word ends with a consonant and *y*, change the *y* to *i* when adding *-es, -ed, -er,* or *-est*.

Analogies Write the word that completes each analogy.

21. *Taller* is to *higher* as *snugger* is to _____.
22. *Allies* are to *friends* as *foes* are to _____.
23. *Medals* are to *trophies* as *plans* are to _____.
24. *Cried* is to *laughed* as *admitted* is to _____.

Word Clues Write the word that fits each clue.

25. brighter
26. things recalled from the past
27. boats that transport people
28. most frightening
29. less clean
30. least generous

Unit 22   Suffixes: *-ful, -ly, -ness, -less, -ment*   pages 144–149

| lately | calmly | government | agreement | cloudiness |
| delightful | tardiness | forgetful | appointment | effortless |

Spelling Strategy A **suffix** is a word part added to the end of a base word. A suffix adds meaning. The spelling of the base word doesn't change when the suffix begins with a consonant.

Context Sentences Write the word that completes each sentence.

31. The ice was so smooth that skating on it seemed _____.
32. We were in _____ about what movie to see.
33. I don't want to be late for my doctor's _____.
34. Everyone likes Tony because he is _____ to be with.
35. I had to remind him because he is _____.
36. The weather has been very wet _____.
37. The United States Capitol is a _____ building.
38. I can't be late because my teacher doesn't put up with _____.
39. He couldn't see the stars because of the _____.
40. Speak _____ to the frightened puppy.

Unit 21
21.
22.
23.
24.
25.
26.
27.
28.
29.
30.

Unit 22
31.
32.
33.
34.
35.
36.
37.
38.
39.
40.

245

Cycle 4 Extra Practice and Review

Unit 23

41. _____

42. _____

43. _____

44. _____

45. _____

46. _____

47. _____

48. _____

49. _____

50. _____

Challenge Words

51. _____

52. _____

53. _____

54. _____

55. _____

56. _____

57. _____

58. _____

59. _____

60. _____

61. _____

62. _____

63. _____

64. _____

65. _____

Unit 23		Words from Other Languages		pages 150–155
salsa	tycoon	burrito	dungarees	lasso
cargo	caravan	hammock	pajamas	tortilla

Spelling Strategy Saying the words and breaking them into syllables will help you to spell words from other languages.

Classifying Write the word that belongs in each group.

41. ketchup, relish, _____   43. procession, parade, _____

42. chair, swing, _____   44. millionaire, executive, _____

Syllable Search Write a word by adding the missing syllable.

45. ___ / ja / mas   47. bur / ri / ___   49. dun ___ / rees

46. las / ___   48. car / ___   50. ___ / til / la

Challenge Words		Units 19–23		pages 126–155
compelling	assigned	unified	suspenseful	mosquito
deposited	operated	dictionaries	contentment	alligator
threatening	rehearsing	tragedies	suspiciously	tambourine

Context Sentences Write the word that completes each sentence.

51. The kitten purred to show its _____.

52. The mystery story was very _____.

53. The band was _____ for the concert.

54. Juan slapped a _____ before it bit him.

55. Our teacher _____ a lot of homework today.

56. He _____ his money in a bank account.

57. Two teams were _____ to form one large one.

58. Just before a thunderstorm, the sky looks _____.

59. The play was so _____ that we were enthralled.

60. The doctor washed his hands before he _____.

61. He eyed the bruised fruit _____ before tasting it.

62. Everyone looked up the definitions in their _____.

63. The _____ slipped off the bank into the swamp.

64. The Civil War is one of the great _____ in America's history.

65. The baby likes to shake her toy _____.

Unit 25   Final /n/ or /ən/, /chər/, /zhər/   pages 162–167

nature	certain	villain	captain	departure
texture	treasure	gesture	feature	adventure

Spelling Strategy

/n/ or /ən/ → **ain, eon**   /chər/ → **ture**   /zhər/ → **sure**

Context Sentences   Write the word that completes each sentence.

1. Small classes are one _____ of our school.
2. Are you _____ you can get there?
3. Sandpaper has a rough _____.
4. The ship's _____ stood on the deck.
5. Rafting down the river was a bold _____.
6. Gardeners are people who enjoy _____.
7. The pirates buried a chest full of _____.
8. In the story, the _____ stole everyone's money.
9. The plane's _____ time has been delayed.
10. He made a _____ with his arm to move us along.

Unit 25

1. _____
2. _____
3. _____
4. _____
5. _____
6. _____
7. _____
8. _____
9. _____
10. _____

Unit 26   Final /ĭj/, /ĭv/, /ĭs/   pages 168–173

storage	olive	garbage	passage	voyage
image	average	cowardice	adjective	language

Spelling Strategy

/ĭj/ → **age**   /ĭv/ → **ive**   /ĭs/ → **ice**

Word Clues   Write the word that fits each clue.

11. communication
12. boat trip
13. opposite of *bravery*
14. not outstanding
15. descriptive word
16. a tunnel is one type

Word Completion   Write a word by adding the missing letters.

17. gar _ _ _ e
18. st _ _ age
19. im _ _ _
20. _ liv_

Unit 26

11. _____
12. _____
13. _____
14. _____
15. _____
16. _____
17. _____
18. _____
19. _____
20. _____

247

Unit 27

21. _____

22. _____

23. _____

24. _____

25. _____

26. _____

27. _____

28. _____

29. _____

30. _____

Unit 27		Unstressed Syllables		pages 174–179
limit	talent	disturb	impress	fortress
crystal	kitchen	pirate	salute	surround

Spelling Strategy To spell a two-syllable word, divide it into syllables. Spell the word by syllables, noting carefully the spelling of the unstressed syllable.

Syllable Search Write a word by adding the missing syllable.

21. pi / ___   23. ___ / round   25. lim / ___

22. sa / ___   24. ___ / tress

Context Paragraph Write the words to complete the paragraph.

Tonya wanted to enter the school ___(26)___ contest. She could juggle, which she thought would ___(27)___ the judges. Tonya went into the ___(28)___, where no one would ___(29)___ her, to practice with some oranges. A few minutes later, disaster struck. "Oh no," groaned Tonya. "An orange shattered Mom's ___(30)___ pitcher! Maybe I should dance with my hoops instead."

Unit 28

31. _____

32. _____

33. _____

34. _____

35. _____

36. _____

37. _____

38. _____

39. _____

40. _____

Unit 28		Prefixes: *in-, un-, dis, mis-*		pages 180–185
insincere	unable	indirect	mistreat	dishonest
unequal	unstable	misspell	disagree	disgrace

Spelling Strategy

PREFIX + BASE WORD → **un**able, **mis**spell

PREFIX + WORD ROOT → **dis**grace

Word Clues Write the word that fits each clue.

31. not the same

32. antonym for *capable*

33. wobbly

34. write incorrectly

35. argue

36. untruthful

37. abuse

38. cause shame

39. not genuine

40. not straight

Unit 29   Suffix: *-ion*   pages 186–191

react	confess	confession	decorate	decoration
pollute	express	imitation	connect	education

Spelling Strategy

VERB → confess   decorate
NOUN → confess**ion**   decorat**ion**

Word Clues Write the word that fits each clue.

41. put together   **45.** to make dirty   **49.** admission of
42. fake   **46.** to admit the truth   wrongdoing
43. say   **47.** respond   **50.** ornament
44. schooling   **48.** beautify

Challenge Words   Units 25–29   pages 162–191

sculpture	prejudice	distribute	mishap	fascination
chieftain	beverage	industry	unfortunate	construction
enclosure	apprentice	somber	discourage	

Analogies Write the word that completes each analogy.

51. *Fondness* is to *adoration* as *interest* is to _____.
52. *Dishonest* is to *honest* as *joyful* is to _____.
53. *Grin* is to *smile* as *accident* is to _____.
54. *Praise* is to *criticize* as *cheer* is to _____.
55. *Eat* is to *food* as *drink* is to _____.
56. *Content* is to *unhappy* as *lucky* is to _____.
57. *Writer* is to *novel* as *artist* is to _____.
58. *Teacher* is to *student* as *master* is to _____.

Word Completion Write the word by adding
the missing letters.

59. in _ _ _ try   **62.** _ _ _ tribute
60. _ _ clo _ _ _ _   **63.** pre _ u _ ice
61. ch _ _ _ t _ _ n   **64.** _ _ _ struct _ _ _

Unit 29

41. _____
42. _____
43. _____
44. _____
45. _____
46. _____
47. _____
48. _____
49. _____
50. _____

Challenge Words

51. _____
52. _____
53. _____
54. _____
55. _____
56. _____
57. _____
58. _____
59. _____
60. _____
61. _____
62. _____
63. _____
64. _____

Unit 31

1. _____
2. _____
3. _____
4. _____
5. _____
6. _____
7. _____
8. _____
9. _____
10. _____

Unit 31	Prefixes: *com-, con-, pre-, pro-*	pages 198–203

produce	combat	commotion	contest	prefix
progress	convince	prospect	propose	promotion

Spelling Strategy A **prefix** is a word part added to the beginning of a base word or word root. It adds meaning to a word. Find the prefix and the base word or word root. Spell the word by parts.

Definitions Write the word that matches each definition.

1. advertising campaign
2. to suggest
3. to make
4. to fight against
5. uproar
6. word part
7. forward motion
8. competition
9. to persuade
10. possibility

LINCOLN SCHOOL
PRESENTS ITS
WINTER MUSIC FESTIVAL
School Auditorium
February 5ᵗʰ - 7:30 P.M.

Unit 32

11. _____
12. _____
13. _____
14. _____
15. _____
16. _____
17. _____
18. _____
19. _____
20. _____

Unit 32	Suffixes: *-ent, -ant, -able, -ible*	pages 204–209

vacancy	difference	distant	distance	urgent
absence	infancy	frequent	frequency	radiant

Spelling Strategy

/ənt/ → **-ent**, **-ant**,   /əbəl/ → **-able**, **-ible**

Analogies Write the word that completes each analogy.

11. *Scary* is to *frightening* as *glowing* is to _____.
12. *Greedy* is to *generous* as *rare* is to _____.
13. *Dirtiness* is to *cleanliness* as *presence* is to _____.
14. *Slow* is to *fast* as *unimportant* is to _____.
15. *Near* is to *close* as *far* is to _____.
16. *Surety* is to *uncertainty* as *similarity* is to _____.

Word Completion Write a word by adding the missing letters.

17. v _ c _ nc _
18. fr_ q _ _ ncy
19. in _ _ _ cy
20. dist _ _ _ e

Unit 33 — Greek Word Parts — pages 210–215

| telephone | microscope | biology | paragraph | telegraph |
| megaphone | calligraphy | xylophone | homophone | homograph |

Spelling Strategy Knowing the Greek word parts *phone* ("sound"), *scope* ("watch"), and *graph* ("write") can help you spell and understand words with these parts.

Context Sentences Write the word that completes each sentence.

21. As soon as the _____ rang, Maria answered it.

22. I have to write a _____ about what I did this weekend.

23. The cheerleader used a _____ to lead the spectators in cheers.

24. The scientist studied the sample under the _____.

25. The word *rein* is a _____ for the word *rain*.

26. The _____ is an interesting instrument to play.

27. The study of living things is called _____.

28. A _____ has the same spelling but a different meaning.

29. Morse code is used to send messages by _____.

30. My aunt writes in beautiful _____.

Unit 33

21. _____

22. _____

23. _____

24. _____

25. _____

26. _____

27. _____

28. _____

29. _____

30. _____

Unit 34 — Latin Word Roots — pages 216–221

| inspect | erupt | predict | porter | report |
| deport | interrupt | dictator | transport | dictionary |

Spelling Strategy Knowing the Latin word roots *spect* ("see"), *port* ("carry"), *dict* ("say"), and *rupt* ("break") can help you spell and understand words with these roots.

Context Paragraph Write the words to complete the paragraph.

Tony wrote a ___(31)___ on volcanoes. He said that scientists often ___(32)___ volcanoes for signs of increasing activity. This helps them to ___(33)___ when a volcano might ___(34)___ next.

Word Clues Write the word that fits each clue.

35. to break in on   37. to send away   39. book of words

36. to convey   38. one who carries   40. tyrant

Unit 34

31. _____

32. _____

33. _____

34. _____

35. _____

36. _____

37. _____

38. _____

39. _____

40. _____

Unit 35

41. _____
42. _____
43. _____
44. _____
45. _____
46. _____
47. _____
48. _____
49. _____
50. _____

Challenge Words

51. _____
52. _____
53. _____
54. _____
55. _____
56. _____
57. _____
58. _____
59. _____
60. _____
61. _____
62. _____
63. _____
64. _____
65. _____

Unit 35	More Words from Other Languages		pages 222–227	
echo	cassette	coupon	barrette	courtesy
denim	buffet	khaki	chorus	alphabet

Spelling Strategy Knowing the language a word comes from can help you remember how to spell the word.

Context Sentences Write the word that completes each sentence.

41. I listened to that _____ so often that the tape wore out.
42. The _____ director asked Maria to sing a solo.
43. Tony ate so much at the _____ that he felt sick.
44. Holding the door for someone is a common _____.
45. My sister used a _____ to keep her hair out of her eyes.
46. We heard the _____ of voices across the canyon.
47. Blue jeans are made from _____ cloth.
48. The kindergarteners sang the _____ song at the assembly.
49. The _____ tent was nearly invisible in the dense woods.
50. I used a _____ to save money when I bought bread.

Challenge Words		Units 31–35		pages 198–227
concurrent	evident	telecommute	spectacular	encore
conscious	occupancy	phonetic	corrupt	collage
compete	capable	microbe	rupture	premiere

Analogies Write the word that completes each analogy.

51. *Salary* is to *bonus* as *performance* is to _____.
52. *Bright* is to *sparkly* as *obvious* is to _____.
53. *Different* is to *similar* as *boring* is to _____.
54. *Vacant* is to *empty* as *crooked* is to _____.

Syllable Search Write a word by adding the missing syllable.

55. pre / __
56. __ / scious
57. tel / e / __ / mute
58. __ / net / ic
59. rup / __
60. __ / lage
61. con / __ / rent
62. __ / pete
63. ca / pa / __
64. oc / cu/ __ / cy
65. mi / __

Capitalization and Punctuation Guide

Abbreviations

Abbreviations are shortened forms of words. Most abbreviations begin with a capital letter and end with a period.

Titles

Mr. *(Mister)* Mr. Juan Albano   Sr. *(Senior)* John Helt Sr.
Mrs. *(Mistress)* Mrs. Frances Wong   Jr. *(Junior)* John Helt Jr.
Ms. Leslie Clark   Dr. *(Doctor)* Dr. Janice Dodd

Note: *Miss* is not an abbreviation and does not end with a period.

Words used in addresses

St. *(Street)*   Blvd. *(Boulevard)*   Pkwy. *(Parkway)*
Rd. *(Road)*   Rt. *(Route)*   Mt. *(Mount or Mountain)*
Ave. *(Avenue)*   Apt. *(Apartment)*   Expy. *(Expressway)*
Dr. *(Drive)*

Words used in business

Co. *(Company)*   Inc. *(Incorporated)*
Corp. *(Corporation)* Ltd. *(Limited)*

Other abbreviations

Some abbreviations are written in all capital letters, with a letter standing for each important word.

PD *(Police Department)*   PO *(Post Office)*
JP *(Justice of the Peace)*   RN *(Registered Nurse)*

The United States Postal Service uses two capital letters and no period in each of its state abbreviations.

AL *(Alabama)*	IN *(Indiana)*	NE *(Nebraska)*
AK *(Alaska)*	IA *(Iowa)*	NV *(Nevada)*
AZ *(Arizona)*	KS *(Kansas)*	NH *(New Hampshire)*
AR *(Arkansas)*	KY *(Kentucky)*	NJ *(New Jersey)*
CA *(California)*	LA *(Louisiana)*	NM *(New Mexico)*
CO *(Colorado)*	ME *(Maine)*	NY *(New York)*
CT *(Connecticut)*	MD *(Maryland)*	NC *(North Carolina)*
DE *(Delaware)*	MA *(Massachusetts)*	ND *(North Dakota)*
FL *(Florida)*	MI *(Michigan)*	OH *(Ohio)*
GA *(Georgia)*	MN *(Minnesota)*	OK *(Oklahoma)*
HI *(Hawaii)*	MS *(Mississippi)*	OR *(Oregon)*
ID *(Idaho)*	MO *(Missouri)*	PA *(Pennsylvania)*
IL *(Illinois)*	MT *(Montana)*	*(continued)*

Capitalization and Punctuation Guide

Other abbreviations *(continued)*			
RI *(Rhode Island)*	TX *(Texas)*	WA *(Washington)*
SC *(South Carolina)*	UT *(Utah)*	WV *(West Virginia)*
SD *(South Dakota)*	VT *(Vermont)*	WI *(Wisconsin)*
TN *(Tennessee)*	VA *(Virginia)*	WY *(Wyoming)*

Initials are abbreviations that stand for a person's first or middle name. Some names have both a first and a middle initial.

E. B. White *(Elwyn Brooks White)*
T. James Carey *(Thomas James Carey)*
Mr. John M. Gordon *(Mister John Morris Gordon)*

Titles

Underlining

Titles of books, magazines, TV shows, movies, and newspapers are underlined. In computer documents they are shown in italic type.

Oliver Twist *(book)*   Treasure Island *(movie)*
Cricket *(magazine)*   The Phoenix Express *(newspaper)*
Nova *(TV show)*   *The Phoenix Express*

Quotation marks with titles

Titles of short stories, songs, articles, book chapters, and most poems are set off by quotation marks.

"The Necklace" *(short story)*   "The Human Brain" *(chapter)*
"Home on the Range" *(song)*   "Deer at Dusk" *(poem)*
"Three Days in the Sahara" *(article)*

Quotations

Quotation marks with commas and periods

Quotation marks are used to set off a speaker's exact words. The first word of a quotation begins with a capital letter. Punctuation belongs inside the closing quotation marks. Commas separate a quotation from the rest of the sentence.

"Where," asked the stranger, "is the post office?"
"Please put away your books now," said Mr. Emory.
Linda whispered, "What time is it?"
"It's late," replied Bill. "Let's go!"

Capitalize the first word of every sentence.

What an unusual color the roses are!

Capitalize the pronoun *I*.

What should I do next?

Capitalize proper nouns. If a proper noun is made up of more than one word, capitalize each important word.

Emily G. Messe   District of Columbia   Lincoln Memorial

Capitalize titles or their abbreviations when used with a person's name.

Governor Bradford   Senator Smith   Dr. Ling

Capitalize proper adjectives.

We ate at a French restaurant.
She is French.
That is a North American custom.

Capitalize the names of days, months, and holidays.

My birthday is on the last Monday in March.
We watched the parade on the Fourth of July.

Capitalize the names of buildings and companies.

Empire State Building
Central School
Able Supply Company

Capitalize the first, last, and all important words in a title. Do not capitalize words such as *a*, *in*, *and*, *or*, and *the* unless they begin or end a title.

From Earth to the Moon   "The Rainbow Connection"
The New York Times   "Growing Up in the South"

Capitalization and Punctuation Guide

Rules for capitalization *(continued)*

Capitalize the first word of each main topic and subtopic in an outline.

I. Types of libraries *(main topic)*
   A. Large public library *(subtopic)*
   B. Bookmobile *(subtopic)*

Capitalize the first word in the greeting and the closing of a letter.

Dear Marcia,   Yours truly,

Punctuation

End marks

There are three end marks. A period (.) ends a declarative or imperative sentence. A question mark (?) follows an interrogative sentence. An exclamation point (!) follows an exclamatory sentence.

The scissors are on my desk. *(declarative)*
Look up the spelling of that word. *(imperative)*
How is the word spelled? *(interrogative)*
This is your best poem so far! *(exclamatory)*

Apostrophe

To form the possessive of a singular noun, add an apostrophe and s.

doctor's   teacher's   grandmother's   family's

For a plural noun that ends in s, add only an apostrophe.

sisters'   families'   Smiths'   hound dogs'

For a plural noun that does not end in s, add an apostrophe and s to form the plural possessive.

women's   mice's   children's   geese's

Use an apostrophe in contractions in place of dropped letters. Do not use contractions in formal writing.

isn't *(is not)*   don't *(do not)*   wasn't *(was not)*
can't *(cannot)*   won't *(will not)*   we're *(we are)*
it's *(it is)*   they've *(they have)*   could've *(could have)*
I'm *(I am)*   they'll *(they will)*   would've *(would have)*

Colon	**Use a colon after the greeting in a business letter.**
	Dear Mrs. Trimby<u>:</u> Dear Realty Homes<u>:</u>
Comma	**A comma tells your reader where to pause. For three or more items in a series, put a comma after each item except the last.**
	Clyde asked if we had any apples<u>,</u> peaches<u>,</u> or grapes.
	Use commas to separate two or more adjectives that are listed together unless one adjective tells how many.
	The fresh<u>,</u> ripe fruit was placed in a bowl.
	One red apple was especially shiny.
	Use a comma before the conjunction in a compound sentence.
	Some students were at lunch<u>,</u> but others were studying.
	Use commas after words such as *Yes*, *No*, *Oh*, and *Well* when they begin a sentence.
	Well<u>,</u> it's just too cold out. No<u>,</u> it isn't six o'clock yet.
	Use a comma to set off a noun in direct address.
	Jean<u>,</u> help me fix this tire.
	How was your trip<u>,</u> Grandpa?
	Can you see<u>,</u> Joe<u>,</u> where I left my glasses?
	Use a comma between the names of a city and a state.
	Chicago<u>,</u> Illinois Miami<u>,</u> Florida
	Use a comma after the greeting in a friendly letter.
	Dear Deena<u>,</u> Dear Uncle Rudolph<u>,</u>
	Use a comma after the closing in a letter.
	Your nephew<u>,</u> Sincerely yours<u>,</u>

Using the Thesaurus

Why Use a Thesaurus?

A **thesaurus** is a reference that can help you make your writing clearer and more interesting. Use it to find a word to replace an overused word or to find an exact word to say what you mean.

How to Use This Thesaurus

This thesaurus includes main entries for words you often use. The **main entry words** appear in purple and are in alphabetical order. The main entry for *perfect* is shown below. Each main entry includes

- the **part of speech,** a **definition,** and a **sample sentence** for the main entry word;

- several **subentry words** that could be used in place of the main entry word, with a definition and a sample sentence for each one;

- **antonyms,** or opposites, for the main entry word.

For example How would you decide which subentry to use to replace *perfect* in this sentence?

*I think it is a **perfect** solution.*

① Find each subentry word listed below *perfect*. The subentries are *excellent, ideal,* and *total.*

② Read the definition and the sample sentence for each subentry. Decide which subentry fits the meaning of the sentence most closely.

*I think it is an **ideal** solution.*

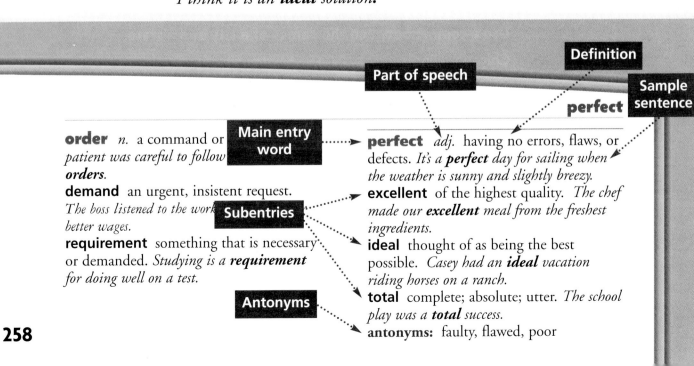

Definition

Part of speech

Sample sentence

perfect

Main entry word

Subentries

Antonyms

order *n.* a command or patient was careful to follow **orders**.
demand an urgent, insistent request. *The boss listened to the work... better wages.*
requirement something that is necessary or demanded. *Studying is a **requirement** for doing well on a test.*

perfect *adj.* having no errors, flaws, or defects. *It's a **perfect** day for sailing when the weather is sunny and slightly breezy.*
excellent of the highest quality. *The chef made our **excellent** meal from the freshest ingredients.*
ideal thought of as being the best possible. *Casey had an **ideal** vacation riding horses on a ranch.*
total complete; absolute; utter. *The school play was a **total** success.*
antonyms: faulty, flawed, poor

Using the Thesaurus Index

The Thesaurus Index will help you find a word in this Thesaurus. The Thesaurus Index lists **all** of the main entry words, the subentries, and any antonyms included in the Thesaurus. The words in the Thesaurus Index are in alphabetical order.

When you look in the Thesaurus Index, you will see that words are shown in three ways.

Main entry words are shown in purple. For example, the word *perfect* is a main entry word.

Subentries are shown in dark type. For example, *pleasure* is a subentry.

Antonyms are shown in regular type. For example, *poor* is an antonym.

P

perfect *adj.*
perilous **dangerous** *adj.*
petite **small** *adj.*
place **put** *v.*
placid **peaceful** *adj.*
pleased **angry** *adj.*
pleasure **happiness** *n.*
ponder **think** *v.*
poor **perfect** *adj.*
praise *n.*
praise **complain** *v.*

Practice Look up each word below in the Thesaurus Index. Write the main entry word for each word.

1. distressed   **2.** chortle   **3.** startled   **4.** informed   **5.** comical

Use the Thesaurus to choose a more exact word to replace each underlined word. Rewrite each sentence, using the new word.

6. Mario will <u>get</u> ten dollars for mowing the lawn.

7. The old shirt was <u>damaged</u>.

8. Did you <u>see</u> the bicycle accident?

9. Kim wore a visor to <u>protect</u> her eyes from the sun.

10. She was <u>thankful</u> that they saved her dog.

Thesaurus Index

A

abnormal **normal** *adj.*
aboveboard **candid** *adj.*
accept **give** *v.*
accumulate **gather** *v.*
acquire **get** *v.*
active **lively** *adj.*
address **speech** *n.*
admirable **worthy** *adj.*
admiration **praise** *n.*
agitated **peaceful** *adj.*
agreeable **angry** *adj.*
alarm **warning** *n.*
alarming **scary** *adj.*
alert **warning** *n.*
amusing **funny** *adj.*
angry *adj.*
anguish **sorrow** *n.*
antiseptic **dirty** *adj.*
anxious **peaceful** *adj.*
appreciative **thankful** *adj.*
approval **praise** *n.*
artless **candid** *adj.*
assemble **gather** *v.*
astonished **surprised** *adj.*
average **normal** *adj.*
aware **educated** *adj.*
awareness **knowledge** *n.*
awestruck **surprised** *adj.*
awful **terrible** *adj.*

B

believe **think** *v.*
blend **mixture** *n.*
blunt **candid** *adj.*
boast *v.*
boring *adj.*
brag **boast** *v.*
bruised **damaged** *adj.*
brusque **candid** *adj.*
bunch **gather** *v.*
bury **hide** *v.*
buy **get** *v.*

C

calm **angry** *adj.*
calm **peaceful** *adj.*
candid *adj.*
careful *adj.*
careless **careful** *adj.*
cast **throw** *v.*
cause **create** *v.*
cause **effect** *n.*
caution **warning** *n.*
cautious **careful** *adj.*
censure **complain** *v.*
changeable **faithful** *adj.*
cheer **happiness** *n.*
chipper **lively** *adj.*
choose **decide** *v.*
chortle **laugh** *v.*
chuck **throw** *v.*
chuckle **laugh** *v.*
clean **dirty** *adj.*
cluster **gather** *v.*
collect **gather** *v.*
combine **join** *v.*
comforting **scary** *adj.*
comical **funny** *adj.*
common **regular** *adj.*
compact **small** *adj.*
complain *v.*
compliment **complain** *v.*
conceal **hide** *v.*
connect **join** *v.*
consequence **effect** *n.*
consider **think** *v.*
constant **faithful** *adj.*
construct **create** *v.*
contaminated **dirty** *adj.*
cover **hide** *v.*
crack up **laugh** *v.*
cramped **small** *adj.*
create *v.*
criticism **praise** *n.*
cross **angry** *adj.*
crow **boast** *v.*
cry **laugh** *v.*

D

damaged *adj.*
dangerous *adj.*
deceitful **candid** *adj.*
decide *v.*
decrease **increase** *v.*
delight **happiness** *n.*
demand **order** *n.*
demolish **create** *v.*
demonstration **display** *n.*
dented **damaged** *adj.*
deplore **complain** *v.*
deposit **put** *v.*
depression **happiness** *n.*
deserve *v.*
design **create** *v.*
destroy **create** *v.*
determine **decide** *v.*
devoted **faithful** *adj.*
different *adj.*
dingy **dirty** *adj.*
direct **candid** *adj.*
dirty *adj.*
disapproval **praise** *n.*
dishonest **candid** *adj.*

disinfected **dirty** *adj.*
disloyal **faithful** *adj.*
display *n.*
display **hide** *v.*
dissent complain *v.*
distress sorrow *n.*
distressed **peaceful** *adj.*
double-crossing **faithful** *adj.*
dream think *v.*
dreary boring *adj.*
dry boring *adj.*
dull boring *adj.*
dull **lively** *adj.*
dusty dirty *adj.*

E

earn deserve *v.*
earn get *v.*
earnest **funny** *adj.*
edgy **peaceful** *adj.*
educated *adj.*
effect *n.*
endanger **protect** *v.*
endorse **complain** *v.*
energetic lively *adj.*
enjoyment happiness *n.*
enlarge increase *v.*
enormous **small** *adj.*
establish create *v.*
evasive **candid** *adj.*
excellent perfect *adj.*
exciting **boring** *adj.*
exhibit display *n.*
exhibit **hide** *v.*
expand increase *v.*
expose **hide** *v.*
extend increase *v.*

F

faithful *adj.*
faithful reliable *adj.*
faithless **faithful** *adj.*
false **candid** *adj.*
false **faithful** *adj.*
fast quick *adj.*
faulty **perfect** *adj.*
fickle **reliable** *adj.*
filthy dirty *adj.*
fire throw *v.*
flawed **perfect** *adj.*
fling throw *v.*
flip throw *v.*
forbidding scary *adj.*
forfeit **get** *v.*
forgiving **angry** *adj.*
forthright candid *adj.*
frank candid *adj.*
frightening scary *adj.*
frisky lively *adj.*
funny *adj.*
furious angry *adj.*
furnish give *v.*
fuss complain *v.*

G

gather *v.*
genuine candid *adj.*
get *v.*
giant **small** *adj.*
giggle laugh *v.*
give *v.*
gladness **sorrow** *n.*

grateful thankful *adj.*
grief sorrow *n.*
grimy dirty *adj.*
gripe complain *v.*
grumble complain *v.*
grungy dirty *adj.*
guard protect *v.*
guffaw laugh *v.*

H

happiness *n.*
happiness **sorrow** *n.*
harmless **dangerous** *adj.*
harmonious peaceful *adj.*
hasty quick *adj.*
hazardous dangerous *adj.*
heave throw *v.*
heedful careful *adj.*
hide *v.*
honorable worthy *adj.*
huge **small** *adj.*
humorous funny *adj.*
hurl throw *v.*
hygienic **dirty** *adj.*

I

ideal perfect *adj.*
idle **lively** *adj.*
ignorant **educated** *adj.*
ignore **see** *v.*
imagine think *v.*
immaculate **dirty** *adj.*
impure dirty *adj.*

complain

make to create or produce. *The children* **make** *a lot of noise.*

manufacture to make a product by hand or machine. *That factory* **manufactures** *automobiles.*

antonyms: demolish, destroy

Shades of Meaning

complain *v.*

1. to express unhappiness or discontent:
deplore	gripe	squawk
fuss	grumble	whine

2. to make a formal accusation or charge:
censure	object	reproach
dissent	protest	

antonyms: **1.** compliment *v.*, praise *v.*
2. endorse, laud *v.*

D

damaged *adj.* harmed or injured. *That door will not shut because the hinge is* **damaged.**

bruised made discolored as a result of an injury that does not break the skin. *Gregory's leg was* **bruised** *from a bad fall.*

dented having a hollow in the surface caused by pressure or a blow. *The tin pan would not lie flat because the bottom was* **dented.**

scratched having a thin, shallow cut or mark made by or as if by a sharp tool. *We sanded and waxed the* **scratched** *wooden floor.*

shattered broken suddenly into many small pieces; smashed. *Pieces of the* **shattered** *window lay on the floor.*

tattered having torn and hanging pieces; shredded; ragged. *The* **tattered** *dress could no longer be mended.*

antonyms: overhauled *adj.*, patched *adj.*, repaired *adj.*

dangerous *adj.* full of danger; risky. *Riding a bicycle on a busy street is* **dangerous.**

hazardous able or likely to cause harm. *Breathing polluted air can be* **hazardous** *to your health.*

perilous very dangerous. *Climbing the steep mountain was a* **perilous** *adventure.*

risky involving the possibility of suffering harm or loss. *Crossing the shaky old bridge was* **risky,** *but we had no choice.*

treacherous not to be trusted; dangerous. *Driving was difficult on the* **treacherous** *roads.*

antonyms: harmless, safe *adj.*

decide *v.* to make up one's mind. *I* **decided** *to buy the red bike instead of the blue one.*

choose to pick out, especially on the basis of what one wants and thinks best. *I* **chose** *to spend my vacation with my grandmother.*

determine to make a firm decision. *Dr. Tsao* **determined** *to do all that he could to save the injured cat.*

resolve to make a firm decision (to do something). *I* **resolve** *to eat a good breakfast every day from now on.*

settle to arrange or decide by agreement. *They finally* **settled** *on a place to have the picnic.*

deserve *v.* to be worthy of or have a right to. *An animal lover like Paul* **deserves** *a pet of his own.*

earn to deserve as a result of effort or behavior. *The hard-working crew had* **earned** *a good long rest.*

merit to be worthy of; deserve. *June's courage* **merits** *the highest praise.*

rate to be good or valuable enough to receive. *The television show was too silly to* **rate** *much interest from the viewers.*

different *adj.* not identical. *David and Emily live in* **different** *parts of the country.*

separate individual or independent. *Each of the cats eats from a* **separate** *bowl.*

unusual not usual, common, or ordinary. *Maura wears her hair in a very* **unusual** *style.*

dirty *adj.*

1. full of or covered with dirt; not clean:

dingy	messy	soiled
dusty	muddy	sooty
filthy	murky	stained
grimy	smudged	tarnished
grungy		

2. polluted:

contaminated	unclean	unsterile
impure	unsanitary	

antonyms: **1.** clean *adj.*, immaculate, spotless, washed *adj.* **2.** antiseptic *adj.*, disinfected *adj.*, hygienic, pure, sanitary, sterile

---

display *n.* a public showing. *The science fair included a* ***display*** *of lovely seashells.*
demonstration a show and explanation of the operation of something for sale. *The salesperson gave us a* ***demonstration*** *of what the computer can do.*
exhibit something put on display, as at a museum or gallery. *At the crafts shop Mario saw an* ***exhibit*** *of Native American pottery.*

E

educated *adj.* provided with formal instruction. *All college professors are highly* ***educated*** *people.*
aware having knowledge. *One purpose of a newspaper is to make the public* ***aware*** *of world events.*
informed having, displaying, or using information. ***Informed*** *shoppers judge a product before making a purchase.*

knowledgeable well-informed. *Because the speaker was* ***knowledgeable,*** *he was able to answer all of our questions.*
learned having or showing much knowledge or learning. *The* ***learned*** *professor had many books on Greek and Roman history.*
antonyms: ignorant, unaware, unschooled

---

effect *n.* something brought about by a cause. *The* ***effect*** *of too much eating can be a stomachache.*
consequence a direct outcome of something. *The musicians' fine performance was a* ***consequence*** *of their hard work.*
outcome something that happens as a result. *The* ***outcome*** *of the trial was a surprise to everyone.*
result something that happens because of something else. *The broken branches are the* ***result*** *of last night's storm.*
upshot the final result; outcome. *The* ***upshot*** *of our meeting was that we decided to put on a play.*
antonyms: cause *n.*, reason *n.*, source

F

faithful *adj.* worthy of trust. *Theresa was a* ***faithful*** *friend who stood by her promises.*
constant firm in loyalty and affection; faithful. *Jonah and Dan have been* ***constant*** *friends since the day they met.*
devoted feeling or showing strong affection or attachment. *My dog is my* ***devoted*** *companion and would follow me anywhere.*
loyal firm in supporting a person, country, or cause. *Ben was a* ***loyal*** *customer at his neighborhood market.*
true trustworthy and devoted. *Ariel was a* ***true*** *friend when I needed her.*
antonyms: changeable, disloyal, double-crossing, faithless, false

funny

funny *adj.* causing laughter or amusement. *I laughed long and hard at Sal's* **funny** *story.*
amusing pleasantly entertaining. *The juggler on stilts was* **amusing.**
comical causing much laughter. *Three-legged races are always* **comical** *to watch.*
humorous characterized by or expressing what is funny. *Ron told a* **humorous** *story about a chicken.*
laughable amusing or ridiculous. *Maria did a* **laughable** *imitation of a cow.*
antonyms: earnest, serious

G

gather *v.* to bring or come together into one place. *They* **gathered** *around the campfire and sang songs.*
accumulate to gather together; pile up. *Chen has* **accumulated** *stacks of science fiction magazines.*
assemble to bring or come together as a group (of related things or people). *The museum will* **assemble** *medieval manuscripts to place in an exhibit.*
bunch to gather into a group of like things. *Mom* **bunched** *flowers into a bouquet.*
cluster to grow or gather in a close group. *The fans* **clustered** *around the singer to ask for her autograph.*
collect to gather as a hobby or for study. *Jamal* **collects** *baseball cards of the players in the old Negro Leagues.*
antonyms: scatter, separate *v.*

get *v.* to receive. *Did you* **get** *any payment for your work in the garden?*
acquire to gain by one's own efforts. *Ed worked many hours to* **acquire** *his skill in typing.*
buy to gain by paying a price for. *Ana used her allowance to* **buy** *a gift for her mother.*

earn to gain by working or supplying a service. *Jason* **earns** *money by baby-sitting for families in his neighborhood.*
obtain to gain by means of planning or effort. *Dara wants to know how she can* **obtain** *a driver's license in this state.*
win to receive as a prize or reward. *Did Joe* **win** *a prize in the school essay contest?*
antonyms: forfeit, lose *v.*

give *v.* to hand over to another. *Sara* **gave** *her sister a beautiful music box for her birthday.*
furnish to supply; give. *A hardware store* **furnished** *hoses and buckets for the fifth-grade car wash.*
offer to put forward to be accepted or refused. *Katie* **offered** *Ina half of a turkey sandwich.*
present to make a gift or award to. *Coach Hart* **presented** *a trophy to our baseball team.*
provide to give something needed or useful. *The City Hotel* **provides** *breakfast for its guests.*
supply to make available something that is needed. *The blood* **supplies** *oxygen to the brain.*
antonyms: accept, receive, take *v.*

H

happiness *n.* pleasure or joy. *Marta smiled with* **happiness** *as she told me the news.*
cheer good spirits; happiness. *The holiday celebration filled us with* **cheer.**
delight great pleasure. *The playful kittens made him laugh with* **delight.**
enjoyment a form or source of pleasure; joy. *Reading brings Kris great* **enjoyment.**
pleasure a feeling of happiness or enjoyment; delight. *Josh gazed at the lovely scene with* **pleasure.**
antonyms: depression, misery, sadness, sorrow *n.*, suffering *n.*

hide *v.* to keep or put out of sight. *The cat* **hid** *under the bed until the company left.*

bury to hide by placing in the ground and covering with earth. *The dog* **buried** *another bone under the rose bush.*

conceal to keep from being seen or known. *Allen* **concealed** *his sadness behind a happy face.*

cover to put something over or on. *The turtle* **covered** *her eggs with sand.*

mask to cover or hide. *They used vines and branches to* **mask** *the opening of the cave.*

antonyms: display *v.*, exhibit *v.*, expose, reveal, show *v.*

I

increase *v.* to make or become greater or larger. *The thin cattle were given extra food to* **increase** *their weight.*

enlarge to make or become larger. *The photographer* **enlarged** *the snapshots.*

expand to make or become larger in size, volume, or amount. *The Dashos* **expanded** *their house by adding a second floor.*

extend to increase in length. *Road workers* **extended** *the road another mile.*

magnify to enlarge the appearance of. *The microscope* **magnified** *the cells so that they could be seen by the human eye.*

antonyms: decrease *v.*, reduce, shrink

J

join *v.* to bring or come together, as by fastening. *Liz used electrical tape to* **join** *the two pieces of wire.*

combine to bring or come together into a single whole or substance. *The colors blue and yellow* **combine** *to make green.*

connect to link or come together. *We had to* **connect** *the computer to the new printer.*

knowledge *n.* understanding; awareness. *Philip's* **knowledge** *of animal behavior comes from raising many kinds of pets over the years.*

awareness consciousness of something. *Her trip to Asia gave Ann a new* **awareness** *of other ways of life.*

wisdom intelligence and good judgment in knowing what to do and being able to tell the difference between good and bad and right and wrong. *People often ask my aunt for advice because she is known for her* **wisdom.**

Shades of Meaning

laugh *v.*

1. to make a sound that expresses amusement or joy:

| chortle | crack up | guffaw |
| chuckle | giggle | |

2. to express amusement at the expense of another:

| jeer | ridicule | snicker |
| mock | scoff | snigger |

antonyms: 1. cry *v.*, sob *v.* weep
2. sympathize

lively *adj.* full of energy; active. *The **lively** baby kept climbing out of the crib.*
active busy. *My baby sister is very **active**.*
chipper full of cheer. *Ike felt **chipper** on this lovely morning.*
energetic full of energy; vigorous. *I've been watching those **energetic** children on the swings.*
frisky energetic, lively, and playful. *The **frisky** colt leaped around the pasture.*
spirited full of life. *Our team put on a **spirited** performance.*
antonyms: dull *adj.*, idle *adj.*, inactive, lazy, lifeless, sluggish

M

mixture *n.* any combination of different ingredients, things, or kinds. *The sand was a **mixture** of crushed rocks and shells.*
blend a mixture in which the parts are combined. *The sauce was a **blend** of spices.*
jumble a group of things mixed together without any order. *The tool box contained a **jumble** of nails, screws, nuts, and bolts.*

N

normal *adj.* of the usual kind. *Today's temperature is **normal** for May.*
average typical, usual, or ordinary. *The **average** child needs plenty of sleep.*
ordinary everyday; common. *Until the fire alarm went off, it was just another **ordinary** school day.*
typical showing the special traits or characteristics of a group, kind, or class; ordinary. *A **typical** circus includes clowns, acrobats, and wild animals.*

usual happening at regular intervals or all of the time; customary. *Nicole took a shortcut instead of going to school the **usual** way.*
antonyms: abnormal, rare, strange, unusual

O

order *n.* a command or rule. *The patient was careful to follow the doctor's **orders**.*
demand an urgent, insistent request. *The boss listened to the workers' **demands** for better wages.*
requirement something that is necessary or demanded. *Studying is a **requirement** for doing well on a test.*

P

Word Bank

peaceful *adj.* marked by peace and calmness.

calm	relaxed	tranquil
harmonious	restful	undisturbed
placid	serene	unruffled
quiet	soothing	untroubled

antonyms: agitated *adj.*, anxious, distressed *adj.*, edgy, nervous, restless, tense *adj.*, troubled *adj.*, uneasy, unsettled, upset *adj.*, worried *adj.*

perfect *adj.* having no errors, flaws, or defects. *It's a **perfect** day for sailing when the weather is sunny and slightly breezy.*
excellent of the highest quality. *The chef made our **excellent** meal from the freshest ingredients.*

ideal thought of as being the best possible. *Casey had an **ideal** vacation riding horses on a ranch.*
total complete; absolute; utter. *The school play was a **total** success.*
antonyms: faulty, flawed, poor *adj.*

praise *n.* approval or admiration. *The teacher's words of **praise** made Alex beam with pride.*
admiration an expression of pleasure, wonder, and approval. *Lisa's singing won the **admiration** of her classmates.*
approval favorable judgment. *Pablo's suggestion met with everyone's **approval.***
antonyms: criticism, disapproval, scorn *n.*

protect *v.* to keep safe from harm, attack, or injury. *A helmet can **protect** a cyclist's head.*
guard to defend or keep safe from danger. *The police **guarded** the museum against theft.*
shield to protect or cover. *Cowhands used kerchiefs to **shield** their faces from the dust.*
antonyms: endanger, threaten

put *v.* to cause to be in a particular position. ***Put** your bike in the shed.*
deposit to lay or put down. *I **deposited** a package on your front steps.*
lay to put or set down. *Be gentle when you **lay** the baby in the crib.*
locate to place or situate. *A sunny spot is certainly the best place to **locate** your garden.*
place to lay something in a certain space. ***Place** your hands on your hips.*
set to cause to be in a particular location. ***Set** the books on the kitchen table before you go to your room.*
antonyms: remove, take away

Q

quick *adj.* done or happening without delay. *We took a **quick** trip to the store.*
fast moving or acting with speed. *Traveling by plane is **faster** than traveling by car.*

hasty in a hurried way. *Jim scribbled a **hasty** note and then ran out the door.*
rapid marked by speed. *The **rapid** subway train zoomed through the dark.*
speedy able to get from one place to another in a short time. *A **speedy** rabbit outran my dog.*
swift moving or able to move very fast. *Charlie is very **swift** on his feet.*
antonyms: leisurely *adj.*, slack *adj.*, slow *adj.*

R

regular *adj.* appearing again and again. *Exercise should be a **regular** part of one's life.*
common found or occurring often. *Blizzards are **common** in North Dakota.*
routine done as part of a regular procedure. *Amanda made an appointment for a **routine** eye examination.*

reliable *adj.* dependable; responsible. *Mr. Johnson asked Becky to take the message because he knew she was **reliable**.*
faithful loyal. *Tom is a **faithful** friend.*
trustworthy honest, honorable. *We need to choose a **trustworthy** club treasurer.*
antonyms: fickle, irresponsible

S

scary *adj.* causing fear. *Your story was so **scary** that I was afraid to walk home.*
alarming causing a feeling of approaching danger. *The police siren was **alarming** to the drivers on the highway.*
forbidding threatening, dangerous, or unfriendly in nature or appearance; frightening. *Brian trembled as he entered the dark, **forbidding** forest.*
frightening causing sudden, great fear. *He told us that the **frightening** crash was only thunder.*

271

Thesaurus

terrifying causing overpowering fright. *The **terrifying** noise made me freeze in my tracks.*
antonyms: comforting *adj.,* reassuring *adj.,* soothing *adj.*

see *v.* to take in with the eyes. *Julie stared at the tree, but she could not **see** the bird.*
notice to take note of; pay attention to. *Noah entered quietly, but everyone **noticed** that he was late.*
observe to watch carefully. *The cat **observed** the bird in the tree.*
regard to look at. *The artist stood back from the easel to **regard** her work.*
spot to find or locate. *The sunbathers **spotted** dolphins not far from shore.*
view to look at. *We **viewed** the entire city from the top of the skyscraper.*
witness to be a witness of; see. *Several passers-by had **witnessed** the accident.*
antonyms: ignore, miss *v.,* overlook *v.*

small *adj.* little in size, amount, or extent. *A **small** dog sat on the girl's lap.*
compact occupying a small amount of space. *Dad likes **compact** cars because they are easy to park.*
cramped too small for what it holds. *I could barely fit all of my books into my **cramped** backpack.*
microscopic capable of being seen only through a microscope. *The book contained an enlarged photograph of a **microscopic** plant cell.*
miniature much smaller than the usual size. *I gave my sister a **miniature** living room set for her doll house.*
petite small and slender; dainty. *I look tall when I stand next to my **petite** sister.*
undersized smaller than the usual, required, or expected. *The **undersized** shirt did not fit me.*
antonyms: enormous, giant *adj.,* huge, major *adj.,* tremendous

sorrow *n.* sadness caused by loss or injury. *Ethan felt deep **sorrow** when his old dog died.*
anguish intense sorrow or pain. *The women's wailing expressed their **anguish**.*
distress pain or suffering of the mind or body. *The bad news caused him some **distress**.*

grief sadness. *They felt **grief over their friend's accident**.*
antonyms: gladness, happiness, joy

speech *n.* a public talk. *The writer gave a **speech** at the high school.*
address a formal speech. *We listened to the President's **address**.*
lecture a speech providing information on a subject, given before a class. *The class heard a **lecture** about the planets.*

surprised *adj.* filled with wonder or amazement, as at something unexpected. *The **surprised** child gaped at the enormous chocolate cake.*
astonished overwhelmed with wonder and amazement. *The professor was **astonished** when the class gave her an ovation.*
awestruck full of wonder, fear, and respect. *The **awestruck** hikers marveled at the majestic mountain peaks.*
shocked surprised and disturbed greatly. *I was **shocked** when I realized the ring I'd been given was a fake.*
startled alarmed, frightened, or surprised suddenly. *The **startled** guests huddled together when the lights suddenly went out.*

T

terrible *adj.* causing great fear; dreadful. *We feared the crops would be destroyed by the **terrible** drought.*
awful very bad; horrible. *The car's engine began smoking and making an **awful** noise.*
unpleasant not pleasing; disagreeable. *The burning rubber created an **unpleasant** odor.*
antonyms: marvelous, terrific, wonderful

thankful *adj.* pleased; glad. *We were **thankful** when it finally stopped raining.*
appreciative filled with gratitude or admiration. *At the end of the concert, the room rang with **appreciative** applause.*

grateful filled with gratitude; thankful. *The flood victims felt **grateful** toward the rescue workers.*
antonyms: thankless, ungrateful

think *v.* to use one's mind to form ideas and make decisions. *You should **think** carefully before you answer the question.*
believe to expect or suppose. *I **believe** that it is going to rain.*
consider to think about before deciding. *Ellie **considered** moving to the city.*
dream to think or believe possible. *Daniel never **dreamed** that he could be so lucky.*
imagine to form a mental picture or idea of. *Try to **imagine** what life was like a hundred years ago.*
ponder to think about carefully. *Max had **pondered** the problem for hours but still had found no solution.*

Word Bank

throw *v.* to send through the air with a fast motion of the arm.

cast	heave	propel
chuck	hurl	shoot
fire	launch	sling
fling	lob	toss
flip	pelt	

W

warning *n.* something that urges one to watch out for danger. *The sign was a **warning** to drivers about a curve ahead.*
alarm a bell or light that alerts one to danger. *The fire **alarm** clanged as smoke filled the attic.*
alert a warning signal of attack or danger. *When a tornado is coming, the weather station sends out a special **alert.***
caution a warning against possible trouble or danger. *The label on the can included a **caution** against improper use.*
signal a sign, gesture, or device that gives a command, a warning, or other information. *As the traffic **signal** turned from yellow to red, the cars came to a stop.*

worthy *adj.* having worth, merit, or value. *A cleanup drive for the park is a **worthy** cause.*
admirable deserving of respect. *Her hard work and devotion are most **admirable.***
honorable deserving honor or respect. *The firefighter was rewarded for his years of **honorable** service.*
valuable of great importance, use, or service. *A hammer is a **valuable** tool to a carpenter.*
antonyms: undeserving, unimportant, useless, worthless

Spelling-Meaning Index

This Spelling-Meaning Index contains words related in spelling and meaning. The Index has three sections: Consonant Changes, Vowel Changes, and Word Parts. The first two sections contain related word pairs and other words in the same word families. The last section contains a list of Latin word roots, Greek word parts, and words that contain these word parts. The words in each section of this Index are in alphabetical order.

Consonant Changes

The letters in dark print show that the spelling stays the same even though the sound changes.

Consonant Changes: Silent to Sounded

Sometimes you can remember how to spell a word with a silent consonant by thinking of a related word in which the letter is pronounced.

bomb-bombard

bombarded, bombarder, bombardier, bombarding, bombardment, bombards, bombed, bomber, bombing, bombs

column-columnist

columnar, columned, columnists, columns

heir-inherit

inherit, heir, heirs, heritage, inheritance, inherited, inheriting, inherits

moisten-moist

moistened, moistening, moistens, moister, moistest, moistness

muscle-muscular

muscled, muscles, muscling, musculature

receipt-reception

receipts, receptacle, receptionist, receptions, receptive

sign-signal

signaled, signaler, signaling, signals, signature, signed, signer, signify, signing, signs

Consonant Changes: The Sound of c

The /k/ sound spelled c may change to the /s/ sound in some words. Thinking of a related word can help you remember that the /s/ sound is spelled c.

critic-criticize

critical, critically, criticism, criticized, criticizer, criticizes, criticizing, critics, uncritical

practical-practice

impractical, impracticality, impractically, practicality, practically, practiced, practices, practicing, unpracticed

Consonant Changes: The Sound of t

The sound of a final t may change to the /sh/ or the /ch/ sound when an ending or a suffix is added. Thinking of a related word can help you remember that those sounds are spelled t.

affect-affection

affected, affecting, affectionate, affectionately, affective, affects, disaffected, unaffected

create-creature

created, creates, creating, creation, creative, creatively, creativity, creator, creatures, noncreative, re-create

depart-departure

departer, departed, departing, departs, departures

except-exception

excepted, excepting, exceptional, exceptionally, exceptions, excepts, unexceptional, unexceptionally

fact-factual

facts, factually

graduate-graduation

graduated, graduates, graduating, graduations, postgraduate, undergraduate

habit-habitual

habits, habitually

instruct-instruction

instructed, instructing, instructional, instructions, instructive, instructor, instructorship, instructs, uninstructive

invent-invention

invented, inventing, inventions, inventive, inventively, inventiveness, inventor, invents

moist-moisture

moister, moistest, moistness, moisturize, moisturizer

object-objection

objected, objecting, objectionable, objectionably

part-partial

parted, partially, particle, parting, partition, partly

regulate-regulation

regulated, regulates, regulating, regulations, regulator, regulatory, unregulated

suggest-suggestion

suggested, suggestible, suggesting, suggestions, suggestive, suggests

Vowel Changes

The letters in dark print show that the spelling stays the same even though the sound changes.

Vowel Changes: Long to Short Vowel Sound

Words that are related in meaning are often related in spelling, even though one word has a long vowel sound and the other word has a short vowel sound.

breathe-breath

breathable, breathed, breather, breathes, breathily, breathiness, breathing, breathless, breathlessly, breathlessness, breaths, breathtaking

cave-cavity

caved, cavern, cavernous, caves, caving, cavities

clean-cleanse

cleanable, cleaned, cleaner, cleanest, cleaning, cleanliness, cleanly, cleanness, cleans, cleansed, cleanser, cleanses, cleansing, unclean, uncleanness

cycle-bicycle

bicycled, bicycles, bicycling, bicyclist, cycled, cycler, cycles, cyclical, cycling, cyclist, recycle, tricycle, unicycle, unicyclist

Spelling-Meaning Index

deal-dealt

dealer, dealership, dealing, deals

decided-decision

decisive, indecision, indecisive, undecided

dream-dreamt

dreamed, dreamer, dreamily, dreaminess, dreaming, dreamless, dreamlike, dreams, dreamy

heal-health

healed, healer, healing, heals, healthful, healthfully, healthfulness, healthily, healthiness, healthy, unhealthy

mean-meant

meaning, meaningful, meaningless, means, unmeant

minus-minimum

minimal, minimize, minimums, minuscule

mute-mutter

muted, mutely, muteness, mutes, muting, muttered, muttering, mutters

nation-national

denationalize, international, nationalism, nationalist, nationalistic, nationality, nationalize, nationally, nationals, nationhood, nationwide

nature-natural

naturalized, naturally, natured, unnatural

page-paginate

paged, pages, paginated, paginates, paginating, pagination, paging

pale-pallid

paled, paleness, paler, pales, palest, paling, pallor

sole-solitary

solely, solitarily, solitariness, solitude, solo, soloist

steal-stealth

stealer, stealing, stealthily, stealthiness, stealthy

unite-unity

reunite, unit, united, uniting

wise-wisdom

wisely, wiser, wisest

Vowel Changes: Schwa to Long Vowel Sound

You can remember how to spell the schwa sound in some words by thinking of a related word with a long vowel sound spelled the same way.

ability-able

abilities, abler, ablest, ably, disability, disable, inability, unable

equaled-equation

equal, equaling, equality, equalize, equals, equate, equations, equator, inequality, unequal

proposition-propose

proposal, proposed, proposer, proposes, proposing, propositions

Vowel Changes: Schwa to Short Vowel Sound

You can remember how to spell the schwa sound in some words by thinking of a related word with a short vowel sound spelled the same way.

adore-adoration

adorable, adored, adoring, adoringly

angel-angelic

angelical, angelically, angels

compete-competition

competed, compctes, competing, competitions, competitive, competitively, competitiveness, competitor

democracy-democratic

democracies, democrat, democratically, democratization, democratize, undemocratic

formal-formality

form, formalism, formalist, formalities, formalize, formally, format, formula, informal, informality, informally

general-generality

generalist, generalities, generalization, generalize, generally, generalness

history-historical

historian, historic, historically, histories, prehistory

individual-individuality

individualism, individualist, individualistic, individualities, individualize, individually, individuals

legal-legality

illegal, illegality, illegally, legalese, legalism, legalities, legalize, legally

local-locality

locale, localism, localities, localize, locally

major-majority

majorities

medal-medallion

medalist, medallions, medals

mental-mentality

mentalities, mentally

metal-metallic

metallically, metallography, metallurgy, metals

method-methodical

methodic, methodically, methodicalness, methods

moral-morality

immoral, morale, moralism, moralist, moralistic, moralities, moralize, morally, morals

mortal-mortality

immortal, mortalities, mortally, mortals

normal-normality

abnormal, abnormalities, norm, normalcy, normalize, normally

patriot-patriotic

compatriot, patriotically, patriotism, unpatriotic

personal-personality

impersonal, interpersonal, person, personalism, personalities, personalize, personally

photograph-photography

photocopy, photogenic, photographic

poem-poetic

poems, poct, poetical, poetically, poetics, poetry

regular-regularity

irregular, regularities, regularize, regularly

reside-resident

resided, residence, residency, residential, residentially, resides, residing

Spelling-Meaning Index

similar-similarity

dissimilar, dissimilarity, similarities, similarly

spectacle-spectacular

spectacles, spectacularity, spectacularly

total-totality

totaled, totaling, totalitarian, totalities, totally, totals

Word Parts

Words with the same Latin word root or the same Greek word part are related in spelling and meaning. Knowing the meaning of a word part can help you understand and spell the words in that family. The letters in dark print highlight the word part.

Latin Word Roots

aud, "to hear"

audible	audit
audience	audition
audio	auditorium
audio-visual	auditory

cred, "to believe"

credence	credulity
credentials	discredit
credibility	incredible
credit	incredulous

dict, "to tell"

contradict	dictionary
dictate	predict
dictator	valedictorian
diction	verdict

fin, "to limit"

affinity	finish
confined	finite
definable	infinite
define	infinitesimal
definite	infinity
final	

ject, "to throw"

adjective	project
deject	projector
inject	reject
interject	subject
object	subjective
objective	

loc, "place"

allocate	locate
dislocate	location
local	locomotion
locale	locomotive
locality	relocate

mit, "to send"

admit	permit
commit	submit
committee	transmit

ped, "foot"

centipede	pedestrian
millipede	pedigree
pedal	pedometer
pedestal	

port, "to carry"

deport	porter
export	report
import	support
important	transport
portable	

pose, "to put"

compose	positive
depose	posture
dispose	propose
expose	repose
oppose	suppose
opposite	transpose
position	

press, "to press"

compress	express
decompress	expression
depress	impress
depressed	impressive

scribe or script, "to write"

describe	description
inscribe	descriptive
prescribe	inscription
scribble	manuscript
scribe	prescription
subscribe	subscription
transcribe	transcription

sist, "to stand"

assist	irresistable
assistance	persist
consist	persistent
consistent	resist
insist	resistance
insistence	

sol, "alone"

desolate	solitary
isolate	solitude
isolation	solo
sole	soloist

spect, "to look"

aspect	respect
circumspect	respectable
inspect	spectacle
inspection	spectacular
inspector	spectator
perspective	specter
prospect	spectrum
prospector	suspect

ten, "to stretch"

attend	portend
attentive	pretend
contend	tendon
extend	tension
extension	

tract, "to pull"

abstract	extract
attract	protract
attraction	retract
attractive	subtract
contract	tract
detract	traction
distract	tractor

vac, "to be empty"

evacuate	vacate
vacancy	vacuum
vacant	

ven, "to come"

advent	eventual
adventure	intervene
avenue	intervention
circumvent	invent
convene	invention
convention	prevent
event	prevention

Spelling-Meaning Index

vers or vert, "to turn"

adverse	avert
anniversary	convert
aversion	divert
controversy	introvert
conversion	invert
inverse	revert
irreversible	vertigo
perverse	
reverse	
universe	
versatile	

vict, "to conquer"

convict	victor
conviction	victories
evict	victorious
victim	victory
victimize	

vid, "to see"

evidence	video
evident	videocassette
provide	videotape

vis, "to see"

advise	visage
audio-visual	visible
improvise	vision
provision	visit
revise	visor
supervise	vista
televise	visual
visa	visualize

Greek Word Parts

ast, "star"

aster	astronaut
asterisk	astronomer
asteroid	astronomy
astrology	disaster

phys, "nature"

physical	physics
physician	physique

poli, "city"; "government"

Acropolis	police
cosmopolitan	policy
megalopolis	politician
metropolis	politics
metropolitan	

tele, "far off, distant"

telecast	telescope
telegram	telethon
telegraph	televise
telepathy	television
telephone	

Spelling Table

This Spelling Table shows many of the letter combinations that spell the same sounds in different words. Use this table for help in looking up words that you do not know how to spell.

Sounds	Spellings	Sample Words
/ă/	a, au	have, bat, laugh
/ā/	a, ai, ay, ea	made, later, rain, play, great
/âr/	air, ar, are, eir, ere	fair, scarce, care, their, where
/ä/	a, al	father, calm
/är/	ar, ear	art, heart
/b/	b, bb	bus, rabbit
/ch/	ch, tch, tu	chin, match, culture
/d/	d, dd	dark, sudden
/ĕ/	a, ai, ay, e, ea, ie	any, said, says, went, head, friend
/ē/	e, ea, ee, ei, ey, i, ie, y	these, we, beast, fleet, receive, honey, ski, magazine, chief, bumpy
/f/	f, ff, gh, ph	funny, off, enough, phone
/g/	g, gg, gu	get, egg, guide
/h/	h, wh	hat, who
/hw/	wh	whoop

Sounds	Spellings	Sample Words
/ĭ/	a, e, ee, i, ia, u, ui, y	cottage, before, been, mix, give, carriage, busy, build, gym
/ī/	ei, i, ie, igh, y	height, time, mind, pie, fight, try, type
/îr/	ear, eer, eir, ier	near, deer, weird, pier
/j/	dge, g, ge, j	judge, gem, range, jet
/k/	c, ch, ck, k	picnic, school, tick, key
/kw/	qu	quick
/l/	l, ll	last, all
/m/	m, mb, mm, mn	mop, bomb, summer, column
/n/	gn, kn, n, nn	sign, knee, no, inn
/ng/	n, ng	think, ring
/ŏ/	a, ho, o	was, honor, pond
/ō/	o, oa, ough, ow	most, hope, float, though, row

Spelling Dictionary

Sounds	Spellings	Sample Words
/ô/	**a, al, au, aw, o, ough**	wall, talk, haunt, lawn, soft, brought
/ôr/	**oar, oor, or, ore, our**	roar, door, storm, store, court
/oi/	**oi, oy**	join, toy
/ou/	**ou, ough, ow**	loud, bough, now
/ o͝o /	**oo, ou, u**	good, could, put
/ o͞o /	**ew, o, oe, oo, ou, u, ue, ui**	flew, do, lose, shoe, spoon, you, truth, blue, juice
/p/	**p, pp**	paint, happen
/r/	**r, rh, rr, wr**	rub, rhyme, borrow, write
/s/	**c, ce, ps, s, sc, ss**	city, fence, psychology, same, scent, lesson
/sh/	**ce, ch, ci, s, sh, ss, ti**	ocean, machine, special, sure, sheep, mission, nation

Sounds	Spellings	Sample Words
/t/	**ed, t, tt**	stopped, talk, little
/th/	**th**	they, other
/th/	**th**	thin, teeth
/ŭ/	**o, oe, oo, ou, u**	front, come, does, flood, tough, sun
/yo͞o/	**eau, ew, iew, u, ue**	beauty, few, view, fuse, fuel, cue
/ûr/	**ear, er, ir, or, ur**	learn, herd, girl, word, turn
/v/	**f, v**	of, very
/w/	**o, w, wh**	one, way, whale
/y/	**i, y**	million, yes
/z/	**s, z, zz**	rise, zoo, fizz
/zh/	**ge, s**	garage, usual
/ə/	**a, ai, e, eo, i, o, ou, u**	about, captain, silent, surgeon, pencil, lemon, famous, circus

How to Use a Dictionary

Finding an Entry Word

Guide Words

The word you want to find in a dictionary is listed in alphabetical order. To find it quickly, turn to the part of the dictionary that has words with the same first letter. Use the guide words at the top of each page. Guide words name the first and last entries on the page.

Base Words

To find a word ending in **-ed** or **-ing**, you must usually look up its base word. To find **deserved** or **deserving**, for example, look up the base word **deserve**.

Homographs

Homographs have separate, numbered entries. For example, **object** meaning "something that can be seen" is listed as **object¹**. **Object** meaning "to be against" is **object²**.

Reading an Entry

Read the dictionary entry below. Note the purpose of each part.

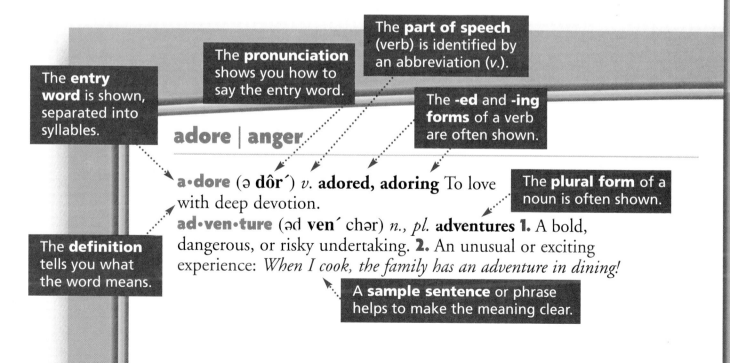

The **entry word** is shown, separated into syllables.

The **pronunciation** shows you how to say the entry word.

The **part of speech** (verb) is identified by an abbreviation (*v.*).

The **-ed** and **-ing** forms of a verb are often shown.

The **plural form** of a noun is often shown.

The **definition** tells you what the word means.

adore | anger

a·dore (ə dôr´) *v.* **adored, adoring** To love with deep devotion.

ad·ven·ture (əd ven´ chər) *n., pl.* **adventures 1.** A bold, dangerous, or risky undertaking. **2.** An unusual or exciting experience: *When I cook, the family has an adventure in dining!*

A **sample sentence** or phrase helps to make the meaning clear.

Spelling Dictionary

ab·do·men (ăb´ də mən) *n., pl.* **abdomens**
In humans and other mammals, the front or lower part of the body from below the chest to about where the legs join, containing the stomach, intestines, and other vital organs.

a·bil·i·ty (ə bĭl´ ĭ tē) *n., pl.* **abilities**
1. The quality of being able to do something; power. **2.** Power to do something, especially as a result of practice; skill.

a·ble (ā´ bəl) *adj.* **abler, ablest** Having the power or ability to do something.

-able A suffix that forms adjectives and means: **1.** Capable of; able to: *breakable*. **2.** Worthy of: *lovable*.

a·board (ə bôrd´) *adv.* On, onto, or in a ship, train, or other passenger vehicle.

ab·sence (ăb´ səns) *n., pl.* **absences**
The period during which one is away.

ab·sent (ăb´ sənt) *adj.* Not present in a place or with someone.

ab·sorb (əb sôrb´) *v.* **absorbed, absorbing**
To take in; soak up.

ac·cel·er·ate (ăk sĕl´ ə rāt´) *v.* **accelerated, accelerating** To go or cause to go faster.

ac·cor·di·on (ə kôr´ dē ən) *n., pl.* **accordions** A wind instrument with keys and a bellows from which air can be forced to pass over reeds that create tones.

accordian

ac·cuse (ə kyo͞oz´) *v.* **accused, accusing**
To blame for wrongdoing.

act (ăkt) *v.* **acted, acting 1.** To conduct oneself; behave. **2.** To perform a part, especially in a play or movie.

ac·tu·al (ăk´ cho͞o əl) *adj.* Existing or happening in fact; real: *The actual time was 6:38 P.M.*

a·cute an·gle (ə kyo͞ot´ ăng´ gəl) *n., pl.* **acute angles** An angle whose measure in degrees is between 0° and 90°: *That narrow space makes an acute angle.*

ad (ăd) *n., pl.* **ads** A public notice, as in newspaper or on television, designed to call attention to a product, meeting, or event. [Short for **advertisement.**]

a·dapt (ə dăpt´) *v.* **adapted, adapting**
To change so as to be suitable for a different condition or purpose.

ad·jec·tive (ăj´ ĭk tĭv) *n., pl.* **adjectives**
The part of speech that modifies a noun by describing it or limiting or adding to its meaning.

a·dor·a·ble (ə dôr´ ə bəl) *adj.* Delightful, lovable, charming.

ad·o·ra·tion (ăd´ ə rā´ shən) *n.* Great and devoted love.

a·dore (ə dôr´) *v.* **adored, adoring** To love with deep devotion: *I adore my baby brother.*

ad·ven·ture (əd vĕn´ chər) *n., pl.* **adventures**
1. A bold, dangerous, or risky undertaking.
2. An unusual or exciting experience: *When I cook, the family has an adventure in dining!*

ad·ver·si·ty (ăd vûr´ sĭ tē) *n., pl.* **adversities**
Great misfortune; hardship.

ad·vis·er (ăd vī´ zər) *n., pl.* **advisers**
A person who offers advice, especially officially or professionally.

a·fraid (ə frād´) *adj.* **1.** Filled with fear; fearful: *afraid of snakes*. **2.** Reluctant; hesitant. **3.** Full of concern; regretful.

a·gree·ment (ə grē´ mənt) *n., pl.* **agreements** Harmony of opinion.

a·lert (ə lûrt´) *adj.* Watchful; attentive; vigilant. —*n.* A warning signal against danger or attack. —*v.* **alerted, alerting** To make aware of.

al·ge·bra (ăl´ jə brə) *n.* A branch of mathematics that deals with the relations and properties of quantities by the use of letters and other symbols to represent unknown numbers, especially in equations, in order to solve problems.

all right (ôl´ rīt) *adj.* and *adv.* Satisfactory but not excellent; good enough.

al·li·ga·tor (ăl´ ĭ gā´ tər) *n., pl.* **alligators** A large reptile having tough skin, sharp teeth, and powerful jaws. ➤ **Word History:** from the Spanish words *el lagarto,* "the lizard," from the Latin words *ille,* "that," *legarto,* "lizard."

al·lo·cate (ăl´ ə kāt´) *v.* **allocated, allocating** To set aside for a particular purpose; allot: *We've allocated this money for bus trips.*

al·low (ə lou´) *v.* **allowed, allowing 1.** To let do or happen; permit. **2.** To permit to have; let have.

♦ *These sound alike* **allowed, aloud.**

a·loud (ə loud´) *adv.* With the voice.

♦ *These sound alike* **aloud, allowed.**

al·pha·bet (ăl´ fə bĕt´) *n., pl.* **alphabets** The letters used to represent the different sounds of a language, arranged in a set order. ➤ **Word History:** from the first two letters in the Greek alphabet: *alpha,* "a," and *bēta,* "b."

al·ter·nate (ôl´ tər nāt´) *v.* **alternated, alternating** To act or proceed by turns.

al·though (ôl *th*ō´) *conj.* Even though.

al·ti·tude (ăl´ tĭ tōōd´) *n., pl.* **altitudes** The height of a thing above a reference level, usually above sea level or the earth's surface: *Planes fly at a high altitude.*

a·maz·ing (ə mā´ zing) *adj.* Causing great surprise or wonder; astonishing.

am·bu·lance (ăm´ byə ləns) *n., pl.* **ambulances** A specially equipped vehicle used to transport sick and injured patients.

a·mount (ə mount´) *n., pl.* **amounts** A quantity.

a·muse (ə myōōz´) *v.* **amused, amusing** To give enjoyment to; entertain pleasantly: *Playing checkers always amuses me.*

an·ces·tor (ăn´ sĕs´ tər) *n., pl.* **ancestors** A person from whom one is descended.

an·chor (ăng´ kər) *n., pl.* **anchors** A heavy object attached to a boat or ship by a cable and dropped overboard to keep the vessel in place, either by its weight or by catching on the bottom of a body of water.

an·gel (ān´ jəl) *n., pl.* **angels 1.** A spiritual being. **2.** A kind and lovable person.

an·ger (ăng´ gər) *n.* A feeling of great displeasure or hostility toward someone or something; rage; wrath. —*v.* **angered, angering** To make or become angry: *I was angered by his rudeness. She angers slowly.*

an·gle (ăng´ gəl) *n., pl.* **angles** The figure made by two lines that begin at the same point.

alligator

Spelling Dictionary

an·ni·ver·sa·ry (ăn´ ə vûr´ sə rē) *n., pl.*
anniversaries The yearly returning date of an
event that happened in an earlier year.
an·nounce (ə nouns´) *v.* **announced,**
announcing To bring to public notice.
an·noy·ing (ə noi´ ĭng) *adj.* Troublesome
or irritating.
an·nu·al (ăn´ yōō əl) *adj.* Happening every
year; yearly: *We throw an annual pool party
every June. —adv.* **annually** *We celebrate
birthdays annually.*
an·swer (ăn´ sər) *v.* **answered, answering**
To respond in words or action. *—n., pl.*
answers Something said or written in return
to a question, statement, request, or letter; reply.
-ant A suffix that forms nouns and adjectives:
occupant.
an·them (ăn´ thəm) *n., pl.* **anthems** A song of
praise or loyalty: *A national anthem praises its
country.*
an·ti·dote (ăn´ tĭ dōt´) *n., pl.* **antidotes**
A substance that counteracts the effects of
poison.
an·y·one (ĕn´ ē wŭn) *pron.* Any person;
anybody.
a·pos·tro·phe (ə pŏs´ trə fē) *n., pl.*
apostrophes A mark (') used to indicate the
omission of a letter or letters from a word
or phrase, as in *aren't,* or to show the possessive
case, as in *Tom's hat,* or certain plurals, such
as those of single letters, as in *A's.*
ap·pear (ə pîr´) *v.* **appeared, appearing**
To come into view.
ap·ply (ə plī´) *v.* **applied, applying 1.** To put
on, upon, or to: *I should apply some hair gel
before I leave.* **2.** To put into action: *Apply
the rocket's thrusters now.* **3.** To devote (oneself
or one's efforts) to something: *You must apply
yourself to your homework.*
ap·point·ment (ə point´ mənt) *n., pl.*
appointments An arrangement for a meeting
at a particular time or place.
ap·pre·ci·ate (ə prē´ shē āt´) *v.* **appreciated,**
appreciating 1. To enjoy and understand:
I appreciate books. **2.** To be thankful for:
I appreciated your help.
ap·pren·tice (ə prĕn´ tĭs) *n., pl.* **apprentices**
A person who is learning a craft
or trade by working for a skilled worker.

ap·proach (ə prōch´) *v.* **approached,**
approaching To move near or nearer.
—n., pl., **approaches 1.** The act of moving
near or nearer: *We planned our approach
carefully.* **2.** A way of beginning to deal with or
work on something.
a·pri·cot (ăp´ rĭ kŏt´) *or* (ā´ prĭ kŏt´)
n. A yellowish orange: *I painted the wall
a yellow-orange color called apricot.*
aq·ua·ma·rine (ăk´ wə mə rēn´) *or*
(ä´ kwə mə rēn´) *n.* A pale blue to light
greenish blue.
ar·chi·tect (är´ kĭ tĕkt´) *n., pl.* **architects**
A person who designs and directs the
construction of buildings and other large
structures.
ar·chi·tec·ture (är´ kĭ tĕk´ chər) *n.*
1. The art and occupation of designing and
directing the construction of buildings and
other large structures. **2.** A style of building.
arc·tic (ärk´ tĭk) *or* (är´ tĭk) *adj.* Extremely
cold; frigid. *—n.* A region between the North
Pole and the northern timberlines of North
America and Eurasia.
ar·e·a (âr´ ē ə) *n., pl.* **areas** A region, as
of land.
ar·gue (är´ gyōō) *v.* **argued, arguing** To give
reasons for or against something.
ar·mor (är´ mər) *n.* A covering worn to
protect the body in battle.
ar·rive (ə rīv´) *v.* **arrived, arriving** To reach
a place.
ar·ti·cle (är´ tĭ kəl) *n., pl.* **articles**
1. An individual thing; item: *Which article
of clothing would you like?* **2.** A written piece
that forms an independent part of a
publication; a report; an essay: *Which
newspaper article should I write?*

apricot

286

ar·ti·fi·cial (är´ tə **fĭsh´** əl) *adj.* Made by humans rather than occurring in nature: *artificial pearls.*

as·cend (ə sĕnd´) *v.* **ascended, ascending** To go or move upward; rise: *Ascend the staircase and turn to your right.*

a·shamed (ə shāmd´) *adj.* Feeling shame or guilt; not proud.

as·sault (ə sôlt´) *n., pl.* **assaults** A violent physical or verbal attack.

as·sign (ə sīn´) *v.* **assigned, assigning** To give out a task; allot.

as·sume (ə soom´) *v.* **assumed, assuming** To take for granted; suppose.

a·stound (ə stound´) *v.* **astounded, astounding** To astonish and bewilder.

as·tro·naut (ăs´ trə nôt´) *n., pl.* **astronauts** A person trained to travel in a spacecraft.

ath·lete (ăth´ lēt´) *n., pl.* **athletes** A person who is trained for or naturally good at sports requiring physical strength, endurance, and coordination.

at·tempt (ə tĕmpt´) *v.* **attempted, attempting 1.** To try (to do something). **2.** To try to perform, make, or achieve: *She will attempt to turn a cartwheel.*

at·tend (ə tĕnd´) *v.* **attended, attending** To be present at.

at·ten·dant (ə tĕn´ dənt) *n., pl.* **attendants** A person who attends or waits on another.

at·tor·ney (ə tûr´ nē) *n., pl.* **attorneys** A person, especially a lawyer, legally appointed to act as an agent for another.

auc·tion (ôk´ shən) *n., pl.* **auctions** A public sale in which goods are sold to the highest bidder.

au·di·o (ô´ dē ō´) *adj.* Of or relating to sound or hearing.

au·di·to·ri·um (ô´ dĭ tôr´ ē əm) *n., pl.* **auditoriums** A room to seat a large audience in a building, such as a school.

Au·gust (ô´ gəst) *n.* The eighth month of the year, having 31 days. ➤ **Word History:** from the Roman emperor Augustus.

Pronunciation Key

ă	pat	ŏ	pot	ûr	fur
ā	pay	ō	go	*th*	**the**
âr	care	ô	paw	th	**thin**
ä	father	ôr	for	hw	**wh**oop
är	farm	oi	**oil**	zh	usual
ĕ	pet	ŏŏ	book	ə	ago, item,
e	be	ōō	boot		pencil,
ĭ	pit	yōō	cute		atom,
ī	ice	ou	**out**		circus
îr	near	ŭ	cut	ər	butter

au·to·bi·og·ra·phy (ô´ tō bī ŏg´ rə fē) *n., pl.* **autobiographies** The story of a person's life written by that person. ➤ **Word History:** from the Greek words *auto-,* "self," and *biographia,* "a writing of a life": *bio-,* "life," and *graphein,* "to write."

au·to·graph (ô´ tə grăf´) *n., pl.* **autographs** A signature, usually of a famous person, that is saved by an admirer or collector: *The famous swimmer signed her autograph for me.* —*v.* **autographed, autographing** To write one's name or signature. ➤ **Word History:** ultimately from the Greek word *autographos,* "written with one's own hand": *auto-,* "self," and *graphein,* "to write."

au·tumn (ô´ təm) *n.* The season of the year between summer and winter. —*adj.* Of, occurring in, or appropriate to the season of autumn.

autumn leaves

Spelling Dictionary

av·e·nue (ăv′ ə noo′) *n., pl.* **avenues**
A usually wide street.

av·er·age (ăv′ ər ĭj) *or* (ăv′ rĭj) *n., pl.*
averages 1. A number, especially an arithmetic mean, that is derived from and considered typical or representative of a set of numbers. **2.** A typical kind or usual level or degree: *That musician's abilities are above average.*

a·vert (ə vûrt′) *v.* **averted, averting** To turn away or aside: *Avert your eyes if you don't want to see the accident.*

a·vi·a·tor (ā′ vē ā′ tər) *n., pl.* **aviators**
A person who flies an aircraft; a pilot.

a·void (ə void′) *v.* **avoided, avoiding**
To keep away from; to steer clear of.

a·wake (ə wāk′) *adj.* Not asleep.

a·ward (ə wôrd′) *n., pl.* **awards** Something, such as a prize or medal, awarded for outstanding performance or quality.

a·ware (ə wâr′) *adj.* Conscious of something.

awe·struck (ô′ strŭk′) *adj.* Full of awe or wonder.

awk·ward (ôk′ wərd) *adj.* Not graceful; clumsy.

ax·is (ăk′ sĭs) *n., pl.* **axes** A straight line around which an object rotates or can be imagined to rotate.

B

back·stage (băk′ stāj′) *adv.* In or toward the area of a theater that is behind the area where the performance takes place.

bal·ance (băl′ əns) *n., pl.* **balances**
1. A weighing device with a beam in the center and two pans on either side. **2.** A state of stability. —*v.* **balanced, balancing 1.** To keep something stable. **2.** To equalize amounts.

bal·let (bă lā′) *or* (băl′ ā′) *n., pl.* **ballets**
An artistic form of dance characterized by very precise, graceful movements based on established steps, poses, and gestures.
► **Word History:** from French, from the Italian word *balletto,* a form of the word *ballo,* "dance," from *ballare,* "to dance."

ballet

ban·dan·na (băn dăn′ ə) *n., pl.* **bandannas**
A large, brightly colored handkerchief, often having a printed pattern on a red or blue background. ► **Word History:** from the Hindi word *bāndhnū,* "to tie."

bank·rupt (băngk′ rŭpt′) *adj.* Completely without money; financially ruined. ► **Word History:** from the Italian word *bancarotta,* "broken counter" (from the practice of breaking the tables of bankrupt moneychangers).

bare·foot (bâr′ foot′) *adj.* and *adv.* Without shoes or other covering on the feet.

bare·ly (bâr′ lē) *adv.* By very little; hardly; just: *We barely made it to the bus stop on time.*

bar·gain (bär′ gĭn) *n., pl.* **bargains**
Something offered or bought at a low price.

barge (bärj) *n., pl.* **barges** A large boat with a flat bottom, used to carry freight on rivers and canals.

bar·rette (bə rĕt′) *n., pl.* **barrettes** A bar-shaped or oval clip used to hold the hair in place.
► **Word History:** from French, from a form of the word *barre,* "bar."

bar·ter (bär′ tər) *v.* **bartered, bartering**
To trade goods or services without using money.

ba·sic (bā′ sĭk) *adj.* Main; essential; primary.

bat·tle·field (băt′ l fēld′) *n., pl.* **battlefields**
A field or area where a battle is or was fought.

beam (bēm) *v.* **beamed, beaming** To smile broadly.

be·come (bĭ kŭm′) *v.* **became, become, becoming** To grow or come to be.

be·gin (bĭ gĭn´) *v.* **began, begun, beginning**
To take the first step in doing something; start.
be·gin·ning (bĭ gĭn´ ĭng) *n., pl.* **beginnings**
The place where something begins or is begun; an initial section, division, or part.
be·have (bĭ hāv´) *v.* **behaved, behaving**
To act in a given way.
be·lief (bĭ lēf´) *n., pl.* **beliefs 1.** Mental conviction of the truth or existence of something. **2.** Something believed or accepted as true, especially by a group of people.
be·neath (bĭ nēth´) *adv.* In a lower place; below.
ben·e·fi·cial (bĕn´ ə fĭsh´ əl) *adj.* Bringing benefit; advantageous.
ben·e·fit (bĕn´ ə fĭt) *n., pl.* **benefits**
A payment or favorable allowance made in accordance with a wage agreement, insurance policy, or public assistance program.
ber·ry (bĕr´ ē) *n., pl.* **berries** A usually small, juicy fruit that has many seeds.
♦ *These sound alike* **berry, bury.**
be·tray (bĭ trā´) *v.* **betrayed, betraying**
To give help or information to an enemy.
bev·er·age (bĕv´ ər ĭj) *or* (bĕv´ rĭj) *n., pl.*
beverages A liquid for drinking, such as milk, tea, or juice.
be·ware (bĭ wâr´) *v.* **bewared, bewaring**
To be careful; look out.
bi- A prefix that means: **1.** Two: *bifocal.*
2. Both sides or parts. **3.** Occurring at intervals of two: *bicentennial.*
bib·li·og·ra·phy (bĭb´ lē ŏg´ rə fē) *n., pl.*
bibliographies 1. A list of the works of a specific author or publisher: *a bibliography of works by the poet Robert Frost.* **2.** A list of works used by an author in preparing a particular work. ➤ **Word History:** from the Greek words *biblion,* "book," and *graphein,* "to write."
bi·cen·ten·ni·al (bī´ sĕn tĕn´ ē əl) *n., pl.*
bicentennials Occurring once every 200 years: *a bicentennial celebration.*
bi·cy·cle (bī´ sĭk´ əl) *or* (bī´ sī´ kəl) *n., pl.*
bicycles A vehicle consisting of a light metal frame mounted on two wheels, one behind the other, and having a seat for the rider, who steers the front wheel by handlebars and pushes pedals that drive the rear wheel.

bi·fo·cals (bī fō´ kəlz) *or* (bī´ fō´ kəlz) *pl. n.,*
A pair of glasses having lenses that correct both near and distant vision.
bi·lin·gual (bī lĭng´ gwəl) *adj.* Able to use two languages equally well.
bi·og·ra·phy (bī ŏg´ rə fē) *n., pl.*
biographies An account of a person's life written by someone else. ➤ **Word History:** from the Greek *biographiā,* "a writing of a life": *bio-,* "life," and *graphein,* "to write."
bi·ol·o·gy (bī ŏl´ ə jē) *n., pl.* **biologies**
The scientific study of life and of living organisms, including growth, structure, and reproduction. ➤ **Word History:** from the German word *Biologie,* from the Greek *bio-,* "life," and *logiā,* "study."

bicycle

Spelling Dictionary

bi·ped (bī′ pĕd′) *n., pl.* **bipeds** An animal having two feet, such as a bird or human.

bi·plane (bī′ plān′) *n., pl.* **biplanes** An airplane having two sets of wings, one above the other.

bit·ter (bĭt′ ər) *adj.* Having or being a taste that is sharp or unpleasant.

blis·ter (blĭs′ tər) *n., pl.* **blisters 1.** A thin, fluid-filled sac that forms on the skin as a result of rubbing or a burn. **2.** A raised bubble, as on a painted surface. —*v.* **blistered, blistering** To form or cause a blister.

boar (bôr) *n., pl.* **boars** A male pig.
♦ *These sound alike* **boar, bore.**

board (bôrd) *v.* **boarded, boarding** To go aboard.

boast (bōst) *v.* **boasted, boasting** To praise oneself, one's belongings, or one's actions; brag.

bore (bôr) *v.* **bored, boring 1.** To cause to feel that one has had enough, as by seeming dull or uninteresting. **2.** To make (a hole, tunnel, or well) by drilling or digging: *Use a drill to bore a hole into the rock.* —*n., pl.* **bores** An uninteresting person or thing: *Only a bore would make us listen to the same story eight times.*
♦ *These sound alike* **bore, boar.**

bor·row (bŏr′ ō) *v.* **borrowed, borrowing** To get from someone else with the understanding that what is gotten will be returned or replaced; to take on loan.

both·er (bŏth′ ər) *v.* **bothered, bothering** To disturb or anger; annoy.

bough (bou) *n., pl.* **boughs** A large or main branch of a tree.

bound·a·ry (boun′ də rē) *or* (boun′ drē) *n., pl.* **boundaries** A border or limit: *a boundary line.*

bouquet

bou·quet (bō kā′) *or* (boo kā′) *n., pl.* **bouquets** A bunch of flowers. ➤ **Word History:** from French, from the Old French word *bosquet,* "thicket," a form of the word *bosc,* "forest."

brain (brān) *n., pl.* **brains** The main organ of the nervous system in humans and other animals with backbones. The brain controls voluntary actions, such as speaking, and many involuntary actions, such as breathing. In humans the brain is the center of memory, learning, and emotion.

breath (brĕth) *n., pl.* **breaths** The air taken into the lungs and forced out when a person breathes.

breathe (brēth) *v.* **breathed, breathing** To take air into the lungs and force it out; inhale and exhale.

brief (brēf) *adj.* **1.** Short in time or duration. **2.** Short in length or extent.

bright·en (brīt′ n) *v.* **brightened, brightening** To make or become more filled with light.

bruise (brooz) *n., pl.* **bruises** An injury that leaves a mark on the skin but does not break it.

bru·nette (broo nĕt′) *n., pl.* **brunettes** Someone with dark or brown hair. ➤ **Word History:** from French, the feminine of *brunet,* a diminutive form of *brun,* "brown."

buff·er (bŭf′ ər) *n., pl.* **buffers** A soft pad or tool used to polish or shine objects: *Use a buffer to make the wood polish shine.*

buf·fet (bə fā′) *or* (boo fā′) *n., pl.* **buffets** A meal at which guests serve themselves from dishes arranged on a table or counter. —*adj.* Being a meal where diners serve themselves: *a buffet lunch.* ➤ **Word History:** French

bul·le·tin board (bool ĭ tn bôrd) *n., pl.* **bulletin boards** A board on which notices are posted.

bunch (bŭnch) *n., pl.* **bunches** A group of things of the same kind that are growing, fastened, or placed together.

bun·dle (bŭn′ dl) *n., pl.* **bundles 1.** A group of objects tied or gathered together. **2.** package. —*v.* **bundled, bundling 1.** To tie or wrap together. **2.** To dress warmly.

bur·den (bûr′ dn) *n., pl.* **burdens** Something that is carried; a load.

bur·glar (bûr′ glər) *n., pl.* **burglars** A person who breaks into a building to steal; a thief.

burn (bûrn) *v.* **burned** or **burnt, burning** To damage or injure by fire, heat, chemicals, or some other means.

burnt (bûrnt) *v.* A past tense and past participle of **burn.** —*adj.* Damaged by heat.

bur·ri·to (boo rē′ tō) *n., pl.* **burritos** A dish consisting of a flour tortilla wrapped around a filling, as of beef, beans, or cheese. ➤ **Word History:** American Spanish, from the diminutive of the Spanish word *burro,* "donkey."

bur·ro (bûr′ ō) *or* (boor ō) *n., pl.* **burros** A small donkey, usually used for carrying loads. ➤ **Word History:** Spanish, from the Spanish word *borrico,* "donkey," from Late Latin *burricus,* "small horse."

bur·row (bûr′ ō) *v.* **burrowed, burrowing** To dig a hole or tunnel in the ground.

bur·y (bĕr′ ē) *v.* **buried, burying 1.** To place in the ground. **2.** To hide (something).
♦ *These sound alike* **bury, berry.**

cal·en·dar (kăl′ ən dər) *n., pl.* **calendars** A chart showing the months, weeks, and days of a certain year.

cal·lig·ra·phy (kə lĭg′ rə fē) *n.* The art of fine handwriting. ➤ **Word History:** from the French word *calligraphie,* from the Greek word *kalligraphiā,* "beautiful writing."

calm (käm) *adj.* Peacefully quiet; not excited; composed. —*adv.* **calmly** *The mother calmly rocked the baby to sleep.*

cam·er·a (kăm′ ər ə) *or* (kăm′ rə) *n., pl.* **cameras** A device for taking photographs or motion pictures.

can·cel (kăn səl) *v.* **canceled, canceling** To make invalid; call off.

can·vas (kăn′ vəs) *n., pl.* **canvases** A heavy, coarse cloth of cotton, hemp, or flax that is used for making tents and sails and is the material on which artists make paintings.
♦ *These sound alike* **canvas, canvass.**

can·vass (kăn′ vəs) *v.* **canvassed, canvassing** To visit (a person or region) to get votes, hear opinions, or make sales; to poll or survey.
♦ *These sound alike* **canvass, canvas.**

can·yon (kăn′ yən) *n., pl.* **canyons** A deep, narrow valley with steep cliff walls, cut into the earth by running water; a gorge. ➤ **Word History:** from the Spanish word *cañon,* from the Latin word *canna,* "tube" or "reed."

ca·pa·ble (kā′ pə bəl) *adj.* Having capacity or ability; able; competent.

cap·tain (kăp′ tən) *n., pl.* **captains** **1.** The leader of a group; chief. **2.** The person in command of a ship. **3.** An Army, Air Force, or Marine Corps officer ranking below a major.

camera

cap·ture (kăp´ chər) *v.* **captured, capturing**
To seize and hold, as by force or skill.

car·a·van (kăr´ ə văn´) *n., pl.* **caravans**
A group of travelers or pack of animals
journeying together for safety in hostile regions
such as the desert. ➤ **Word History:** from
the French word *caravane* or the Italian word
carovane, both from the Persian word *kārvān*.

ca·reer (kə rîr´) *n., pl.* **careers** A profession
that a person chooses as a life's work.

car·go (kär´ gō) *n., pl.* **cargoes** or **cargos**
The freight carried by a ship, airplane, or other
vehicle. ➤ **Word History:** from the Spanish
word *cargar,* "to load," from the Latin word
carrus, for a type of wagon.

car·i·bou (kăr´ ə bōō´) *n., pl.* **caribou** or
caribous Any of several deer of arctic regions
of North America, having large spreading
antlers in both males and females.

car·pet (kär´ pĭt) *n., pl.* **carpets** A thick,
heavy covering for a floor, usually made of
woven wool or synthetic fibers; a rug.

car·pet·ing (kär´ pĭ tĭng) *n.* Material or
fabric used for carpets.

car·ti·lage (kär´ tl ĭj) *n.* A tough, white
connective tissue that forms a large part of
the skeleton of humans and other vertebrates.
It is more flexible than bone but not as hard.

car·tog·ra·pher (kär tŏg´ rə fər) *n., pl.*
cartographers Person who makes maps or
charts: *The cartographer finished drawing the map.*

caribou

car·ton (kär´ tn) *n., pl.* **cartons** A cardboard
or plastic box made in various sizes.

car·toon (kär tōōn´) *n., pl.* **cartoons**
A drawing, often appearing with a caption,
showing a humorous situation.

cash·mere (kăzh´ mîr´) *or* (kăsh´ mîr´) *n., pl.*
cashmeres Fine, soft wool growing beneath the
outer hair of a goat native to the mountains of
India and Tibet. ➤ **Word History:** from
Kashmir, a region in India where these goats live.

cas·sette (kə sĕt´) *n., pl.* **cassettes** A magnetic
tape contained in a plastic case and used to make
audio or video recordings and to store data
in digital form. ➤ **Word History:** from the
French word *cassette,* "small box," from the Old
French word *casse,* "case."

ca·su·al (kăzh´ ōō əl) *adj.* **1.** Suited for
everyday wear; informal. **2.** Not thought about
beforehand; passing.

ca·the·dral (kə thē´ drəl) *n., pl.* **cathedrals**
1. The principal church of a bishop's diocese.
2. A large or important church.
➤ **Word History:** from the Medieval Latin
word *cathedrāis,* "of a bishop's see
[jurisdiction]," from the Latin word *cathedra,*
"chair."

cause (kôz) *n., pl.* **causes** Someone or
something that makes something happen. —*v.*
caused, causing To make something happen.

cav·al·ry (kăv´ əl rē) *n., pl.* **cavalries** Troops
trained to fight on horseback.

cel·lar (sĕl´ ər) *n., pl.* **cellars** A room or
rooms under a building where things are
stored; basement.

cel·lu·lar (sĕl´ yə lər) *adj.* A mobile telephone
that sends and receives calls through a network of
short-range radio transmitters and a relay station
that makes connections to telephone lines.

cen·tral (sĕn´ trəl) *adj.* Situated at, near,
or in the center.

cer·e·mo·ny (sĕr´ ə mō´ nē) *n., pl.*
ceremonies A formal act or set of acts performed
in honor or celebration of an occasion.

cer·tain (sûr´ tn) *adj.* Established beyond
doubt.

chal·lenge (chăl´ ənj) *n., pl.* **challenges**
Something that tests a person's skills, efforts,
or resources. —*v.* **challenged, challenging**
To call to engage in a contest or fight.

change (chānj) *v.* **changed, changing**
To cause to be different.

chan·nel (chăn´ əl) *n., pl.* **channels**
1. A band of radio waves used for broadcasting, as on television: *Change the channel so I can watch my favorite TV show.* **2.** A part of a river or harbor deep enough for ships to pass through.

chaps (chăps) *pl. n.* Heavy trouser fronts worn by cowboys. ➤ **Word History:** short for the American Spanish word *chaparreras,* from the Spanish word *chaparro,* "chaparral," a dense thicket of shrubs and small trees.

chap·ter (chăp´ tər) *n., pl.* **chapters** A main division in a book.

chat (chăt) *v.* **chatted, chatting** To converse in a relaxed, friendly, informal manner.

check (chĕk) *v.* **checked, checking** To test or examine to find out if something is correct or in good condition.

ched·dar (chĕd´ ər) *n., pl.* **cheddars** A firm, smooth, yellowish cheese. ➤ **Word History:** after Cheddar, a village of southwest England, where the cheese was first made.

cheer (chîr) *v.* **cheered, cheering** To shout in happiness, approval, encouragement, or enthusiasm.

cheer·ful (chîr´ fəl) *adj.* Showing or full of cheer; happy; not gloomy.

chief·tain (chēf´ tən) *n., pl.* **chieftains** The leader or head of a group, especially of a clan or tribe.

chis·el (chĭz´ əl) *n., pl.* **chisels** A metal tool with a sharp beveled edge across the end of a thick blade, used to cut or chip and shape stone, wood, or metal.

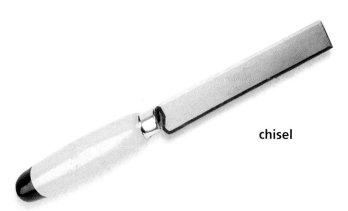

chisel

choose (cho͞oz) *v.* **chose, chosen, choosing** To pick out, especially on the basis of what one wants and thinks best.

cho·rus (kôr´ əs) *n., pl.* **choruses** An organized group of singers who perform together. ➤ **Word History:** from the Latin word for a choral dance, from the Greek word *khoros,* "dancing ground," "dance," or "dramatic chorus."

cir·cu·lar (sûr´ kyə lər) *adj.* Forming or moving in a circle.

ci·ta·tion (sī tā´ shən) *n., pl.* **citations** A summons to appear in court.

cite (sīt) *v.* **cited, citing 1.** To quote as an authority or example. **2.** To mention or bring forward as support, illustration, or proof.
♦ *These sound alike* **cite, sight, site.**

clam·or (klăm´ ər) *n., pl.* **clamors** A loud noise, as of a crowd shouting; a great uproar.

cli·mate (klī´ mĭt) *n., pl.* **climates** The general or average weather conditions of a certain region, including temperature, rainfall, and wind.

cli·max (klī´ măks´) *n., pl.* **climaxes** The point in a series of events that is of greatest intensity or effect, usually occurring near the end.

close (klōs) *adj.* **closer, closest 1.** Near in space or time. **2.** Near in relationship; intimate —*n.* **closeness** *There was a fond closeness between Cheryl and her grandfather.*

clos·et (klŏz´ ĭt) *n., pl.* **closets** A small room in which clothes or household supplies can be kept.

cloudy | complex

cloud·y (klou´ dē) *adj.* **cloudier, cloudiest**
Full or covered with clouds; overcast. —*n.*
cloudiness *We couldn't see the sun because
of the sky's cloudiness.*

clum·sy (klŭm´ zē) *adj.* **clumsier, clumsiest**
Lack of grace or deftness; awkward. —*n.*
clumsiness *Her clumsiness prevented her from
dancing well.*

cock·pit (kŏk´ pĭt´) *n., pl.* **cockpits**
The space in an airplane that has seats for
the pilot and copilot and sometimes passengers:
*The pilot quickly took her place in the plane's
cockpit.*

col·lage (kə läzh´) *n., pl.* **collages** A work
of art made by pasting materials or objects
onto a surface.

col·lar (kŏl´ ər) *n., pl.* **collars** The part of
a garment that fits around the neck.

col·lide (kə līd´) *v.* **collided, colliding**
To strike together with force; crash.

co·logne (kə lōn´) *n., pl.* **cologne** A scented
liquid made of alcohol and fragrant oils, used
as light perfume. ➤ **Word History:** from the
French words *eau de Cologne,* "water from
Cologne," after the German city of Cologne,
where the perfume was first made.

colo·nel (kûr´ nəl) *n., pl.* **colonels** An officer
in the U.S. Army, Air Force, or Marine Corps
ranking below a brigadier general and above
a major.

col·umn (kŏl´ əm) *n., pl.* **columns**
1. An article that appears regularly in
a newspaper or magazine: *the sports column.*
2. One or more vertical sections of a page,
lying side by side but separated from each
other, in which lines of print are arranged:
The columns of words on my paper are not even.

com- A prefix that means "together" or
"with": *compete.*

com·bat (kəm băt´) *v.* **combated, combating**
1. To oppose in battle. **2.** To fight or struggle
against: *new drugs that combat infection.*
—*n.* (kŏm´ băt´) Armed conflict; battle: *The
soldier prepared for combat.*

com·fort·a·ble (kŭm´ fər tə bəl) *adj.* Giving
comfort.

com·ic (kŏm´ ĭk) *adj.* Humorous, amusing.
—*n., pl.* **comics** Person who is funny.

com·mer·cial (kə mûr´ shəl) *n., pl.*
commercials An advertisement on television
or radio.

com·mon (kŏm´ ən) *adj.* **1.** Belonging
to or shared equally by everybody. **2.** Found
or occurring often; widespread.

com·mo·tion (kə mō´ shən) *n., pl.*
commotions A disturbance or tumult.

com·pa·ny (kŭm´ pə nē) *n., pl.* **companies**
A business enterprise; firm.

com·pare (kəm pâr´) *v.* **compared,
comparing 1.** To represent as similar; liken.
2. To study in order to note similarities and
differences.

com·pass rose (kŭm´ pəs rōz´) *n., pl.*
compass roses Symbol on a map that indicates
direction.

com·pel·ling (kəm pĕl´ ĭng) *adj.* Having
a very strong influence or effect; powerful.

com·pete (kəm pēt´) *v.* **competed,
competing** To strive against another or others
to attain a goal.

com·plain (kəm plān´) *v.* **complained,
complaining** To express discontent.

com·ple·men·ta·ry co·lor (kŏm´ plə mĕn´
tə rē kŭl´ ər) *n.* One of two colors, such as red
and green, that produce white (light) or gray
(pigment) when mixed in the proper amounts.

com·plete (kəm plēt´) *v.* **completed,
completing 1.** To add what is missing.
2. To bring to an end.

com·plex (kəm plĕks´) *or* (kŏm´ plĕks´) *adj.*
Difficult to understand; not simple: *Computers
can solve complex mathematical problems.*

a cloudy sky

com·plex·i·ty (kəm **plĕk´** sĭ tē) *n., pl.*
complexities The condition of being complex.
com·pose (kəm **pōz´**) *v.* **composed,**
composing To make or create by putting
together parts or elements.
com·po·si·tion (kŏm´ pə **zĭsh´** ən) *n., pl.*
compositions 1. The act of composing.
2. A work created by such a process, as
a musical work or a short essay.
com·po·sure (kəm **pō´** zhər) *n.* Control over
one's emotions; calmness.
com·press (kəm **prĕs´**) *v.* **compressed,**
compressing To squeeze or press together.
com·put·er (kəm **pyōō´** tər) *n., pl.*
computers A complex electronic machine that
can accept information, work on the
information to solve a problem, and produce
an answer or result.
con- See **com-.**
con·cert (**kŏn´** sərt) *n., pl.* **concerts**
A musical performance usually given by one
or more singers or instrumentalists or both.
con·clude (kən **klōōd´**) *v.* **concluded,**
concluding To bring to an end.
con·clu·sion (kən **klōō´** zhən) *n., pl.*
conclusions A judgment or decision reached
by reasoning.
con·cur·rent (kən **kûr´** ənt) *adj.* Happening
at the same time.
con·dense (kən **dĕns´**) *v.* **condensed,**
condensing To change from a gas to a liquid.
con·fess (kən **fĕs´**) *v.* **confessed, confessing**
To admit that one has done something bad
or illegal.
con·fes·sion (kən **fĕsh´** ən) *n., pl.*
confessions The act of admitting guilt.
con·fide (kən **fīd´**) *v.* **confided, confiding**
To tell confidentially: *You can confide in me.*
con·firm (kən **fûrm´**) *v.* **confirmed,**
confirming 1. To support or establish the
certainty of. **2.** To make firmer, strengthen.
con·flict (**kŏn´** flĭkt´) *n., pl.* **conflicts**
1. A state of disagreement, as between persons,
ideas, or interests: *If we agree, we may avoid
conflict.* **2.** A state of fighting; a battle or war.
con·fuse (kən **fyōōz´**) *v.* **confused, confusing**
To cause to be unable to understand or think
clearly.

con·ga (**kŏng´** gə) *n., pl.* **congas** A tall, usually
tapering single-headed drum typically played
by beating with the hands.
con·nect (kə **nĕkt´**) *v.* **connected,**
connecting To join or fasten together; link.
con·nec·tion (kə **nĕk´** shən) *n., pl.*
connections An association or relationship.
con·science (**kŏn´** shəns) *n., pl.* **consciences**
Inner feelings and ideas that tell a person what
is right and what is wrong.
con·scious (**kŏn´** shəs) *adj.* Able to perceive
what is happening around oneself.
con·se·quence (**kŏn´** sĭ kwĕns´) *n., pl.*
consequences Something that follows from
an action or condition; an effect; a result:
*I broke my arm as a consequence of falling off my
skateboard.*

computer

Spelling Dictionary

con·strict (kən strĭkt´) *v.* **constricted, constricting** To make or become smaller or narrower, as by contracting; compress.

con·struct (kən strŭkt´) *v.* **constructed, constructing** To build or put together.

con·struc·tion (kən strŭk´ shən) *n.* The act or process of building or putting together.

con·struc·tive (kən strŭk´ tĭv) *adj.* Serving to help or increase: *Studying is a constructive way to spend your time.*

con·tain (kən tān´) *v.* **contained, containing** **1.** To have within itself; hold: *Orange juice contains vitamins.* **2.** To consist of or include.

con·tend·er (kən tĕnd´ ər) *n., pl.* **contenders** One who struggles against difficulties.

con·tent·ment (kən tĕnt´ mənt) *n.* Happiness and satisfaction; peace of mind.

con·test (kŏn´ tĕst´) *n., pl.* **contests** **1.** A struggle for victory or superiority between rivals. **2.** A competition rated by judges. —*v.* (kən tĕst´) *or* (kŏn´ tĕst´) **contesting, contested 1.** To compete or strive for. **2.** To dispute; challenge.

con·tes·tant (kən tĕs´ tənt) *or* (kŏn´ tĕs´ tənt) *n., pl.* **contestants** A person who takes part in a contest.

con·tin·ue (kən tĭn´ yōo) *v.* **continued, continuing** To keep on or persist in.

con·tin·u·ous (kən tĭn´ yōo əs) *adj. and adv.* **continuously** Continuing without interruption; unbroken.

con·tra·dict (kŏn´ trə dĭkt´) *v.* **contradicted, contradicting** To assert or express the opposite of (a statement). ➤ **Word History:** from the Latin word *contrādīcere: contrā-,* "against," and *dīcere,* "to speak."

con·trol (kən trōl´) *v.* **controlled, controlling** To manage or regulate. —*n., pl.* **controls** A device used to set or run a machine.

con·ver·sa·tion (kŏn´ vər sā´ shən) *n., pl.* **conversations** A spoken exchange of thoughts and feelings; a talk.

con·vince (kən vĭns´) *v.* **convinced, convincing** To persuade to do or believe.

cool (kōol) *v.* **cooled, cooling** To make or become less warm.

costume

co·op·er·a·tive (kō ŏp´ ər ə tĭv) *or* (kō ŏp´ rə tĭv) *adj.* Willing to help or cooperate: *The nurse said you are a cooperative patient.*

co·or·di·nate (kō ôr´ dn āt´) *or* (kō ôr´ dn ĭt) *n., pl.* **coordinates** One of a set of numbers that determines the position of a point.

cor·rupt (kə rŭpt´) *adj.* Immoral; wicked; depraved. ➤ **Word History:** from the Latin word *corruptus,* the past participle of *corrumpere,* "to destroy": *com-,* an intensive prefix, and *rumpere,* "to break."

cos·tume (kŏs´ tōōm´) *n., pl.* **costumes** An outfit or disguise worn on special occasions.

count (kount) *v.* **counted, counting** To name the numbers in order up to and including (a particular number).

count·er (koun´ tər) *n., pl.* **counters** A flat surface where food is prepared, usually on top of a low kitchen cabinet.

count·less (kount´ lĭs) *adj.* Too many to count.

coun·try (kŭn´ trē) *n., pl.* **countries** A land in which people live under a single government; nation.

cou·pon (kōō´ pŏn´) *or* (kyōō´ pŏn´) *n., pl.* **coupons** A printed form to be used to order something or to obtain a discount. ➤ **Word History:** from the Old French word *colpon,* "a piece cut off."

cour·age (kûr´ ĭj) *n.* The quality of mind or spirit that enables one to face danger or hardship with confidence; bravery.

cou·ra·geous (kə rā´ jəs) *adj.* Having or displaying courage; brave.

cour·te·ous (kûr´ tē əs) *adj.* Considerate toward others; gracious; polite. ➤ **Word History:** from the Middle English word *corteis,* "courtly," from the Old French word *cort,* "court."

cour·te·sy (kûr´ tĭ sē) *n., pl.* **courtesies** Polite behavior: *As a courtesy, he showed us the way to our new classroom.* ➤ **Word History:** from the Old French word *corteis,* "courtly." It was borrowed into Middle English and became *courtesie.*

court·room (kôrt´ rōōm´) *n., pl.* **courtrooms** A room in which the proceedings of a court of law are carried on.

cous·in (kŭz´ ĭn) *n., pl.* **cousins** A child of one's aunt or uncle: *Your aunt's daughter is your cousin.*

cow·ard (kou´ ərd) *n., pl.* **cowards** A person who has no courage.

cow·ard·ice (kou´ ər dĭs) *n.* Lack of courage or a shameful show of fear when facing danger or pain.

co·zy (kō´ zē) *adj.* **cozier, coziest** Snug and comfortable.

cramped (krămpt) *adj.* Crowded into limited space.

cra·ter (krā´ tər) *n., pl.* **craters** A shallow, bowl-shaped hole in a surface.

cray·on (krā´ ŏn´) *or* (krā´ ən) *n., pl.* **crayons** A stick of colored wax used for drawing.

cre·ate (krē āt´) *v.* **created, creating** To bring into being; invent.

crater

Pronunciation Key

ă	pat	ŏ	pot	ûr	fur
ā	pay	ō	go	*th*	**the**
âr	care	ô	paw	th	thin
ä	father	ôr	for	hw	whoop
är	farm	oi	oil	zh	usual
ĕ	pet	ŏŏ	book	ə	ago, item,
ē	be	ōō	boot		pencil,
ĭ	pit	yōō	cute		atom,
ī	ice	ou	out		circus
îr	near	ŭ	cut	ər	butter

cre·a·tive (krē ā´ tĭv) *adj.* Having the ability or power to create things; original.

crea·ture (krē´ chər) *n., pl.* **creatures** A living being, especially an animal.

cre·dence (krēd´ ns) *n.* Acceptance as true; belief.

cre·den·tial (krĭ dĕn´ shəl) *n., pl.* **credentials** Letters or written evidence of a person's qualifications or status: *He has the right credentials for the job.*

cred·i·ble (krĕd´ ə bəl) *adj.* Worthy of confidence or belief; believable.

cred·it (krĕd´ ĭt) *n., pl.* **credits 1.** Belief or confidence in the truth of something; trust: *I gave full credit to what you told me.* **2.** A system of buying things and paying for them later.

cred·it·a·ble (krĕd´ ĭ tə bəl) *adj.* Deserving praise or credit.

cred·i·tor (krĕd´ ĭ tər) *n., pl.* **creditors** A person or firm to whom money is owed: *Our creditor gave us time to pay what we owe.*

cre·do (krē´ dō) *or* (krā´ dō) *n., pl.* **credos** A statement of belief; a creed: *She lives by the credo of treating others fairly.*

cre·du·li·ty (krĭ dōō´ lĭ tē) *n.* The tendency to believe too readily; gullibility: *His credulity makes him easy to trick.*

cro·chet (krō shā´) *v.* **crocheted, crocheting** To make by looping thread or yarn into connected links with a hooked needle. ➤ **Word History:** from the French word *crocheter,* from the Old French word *crochet,* "hook."

Spelling Dictionary

crop (krŏp) *v.* **cropped, cropping** To trim.

crow·bar (krō´ bär´) *n.* A straight iron or steel bar, usually having one edge bent with a wedge-shaped edge, used as a lever for lifting or prying.

cru·el (krōō´ əl) *adj.* **crueler, cruelest** Liking to cause pain or suffering; unkind.

cruise (krōōz) *n., pl.* **cruises** A sea voyage for pleasure. —*v.* **cruised, cruising** To take a voyage by boat.

crush (krŭsh) *v.* **crushed, crushing** To press, squeeze, or bear down on with enough force to break or injure; crumple.

crys·tal (krĭs´ təl) *n., pl.* **crystals 1.** A solid piece of matter that has a regular pattern of flat surfaces and angles between the surfaces. **2.** Glass that is clear, colorless, and of high quality.

cul·ture (kŭl´ chər) *n., pl.* **cultures** The arts, beliefs, customs, institutions, and all other products of human work and thought at a particular time.

cur·rent (kûr´ ənt) *adj.* Belonging to the present time.

cur·tain (kûr´ tn) *n., pl.* **curtains** A piece of material hanging in a window or other opening.

cus·tom (kŭs´ təm) *n., pl.* **customs** An accepted practice or usual way followed by people of a particular group or religion.

cy·clone (sī´ klōn´) *n., pl.* **cyclones** A storm or wind moving around and toward a calm center of low pressure.

D

dair·y (dâr´ ē) *n., pl.* **dairies 1.** A room or building where milk and cream are stored, prepared for use, or made into butter and cheese. **2.** A business or store that prepares or sells milk and milk products.

Dal·ma·tian (dăl mā´ shən) *n., pl.* **Dalmatians** A large dog having a short smooth white coat with many small black spots.
➤ **Word History:** from Dalmatia, an area in Croatia, where the dogs were first bred.

Dalmation

dam·age (dăm´ ĭj) *v.* **damaged, damaging** To harm or injure: *Some insects damage plants.*

dan·ger (dān´ jər) *n., pl.* **dangers** The chance or risk of harm or destruction: *Some people get goose bumps when they sense danger.*

dare (dâr) *v.* **dared, daring** To be brave or bold enough.

dec·ade (dĕk´ ād´) *n., pl.* **decades** A period of ten years.

de·cide (dĭ sīd´) *v.* **decided, deciding** To make up one's mind.

de·ci·sion (dĭ sĭzh´ ən) *n., pl.* **decisions** The act of deciding or making up one's mind.

de·com·press (dē´ kəm prĕs´) *v.* **decompressed, decompressing** To bring (a person exposed to increased pressure) gradually to normal atmospheric pressure.

dec·o·rate (dĕk´ ə rāt´) *v.* **decorated, decorating** To furnish with something attractive or beautiful; beautify; adorn.

dec·o·ra·tion (dĕk´ ə rā´ shən) *n., pl.* **decorations** Something that decorates; ornament.

de·fen·dant (dĭ fĕn´ dənt) *n., pl.* **defendants** The person or party against which a legal action or claim is brought.

de·fine (dĭ fīn´) *v.* **defined, defining** To give the meaning of.

de·fy (dĭ fī´) *v.* **defied, defying** To dare; challenge.

a train depot

Pronunciation Key

ă	pat	ŏ	pot	ûr	fur
ā	pay	ō	go	th	the
âr	care	ô	paw	th	thin
ä	father	ôr	for	hw	whoop
är	farm	oi	oil	zh	usual
ĕ	pet	ŏŏ	book	ə	ago, item,
ē	be	ōō	boot		pencil,
ĭ	pit	yōō	cute		atom,
ī	ice	ou	out		circus
îr	near	ŭ	cut	ər	butter

del·i (dĕl´ ē) *n., pl.* **delis** A store that sells cooked or prepared foods ready for serving, such as cheeses, salads, and smoked meats: *Let's get a sandwich at the deli.* [Short for **delicatessen.**]

de·light·ful (dĭ līt´ fəl) *adj.* Very pleasing.

de·liv·er (dĭ lĭv´ ər) *v.* **delivered, delivering** To take and turn over to the proper person or at the proper destination; bring to.

del·uge (dĕl´ yōōj) *or* (dā´ lōōj) *n., pl.* **deluge** A great flood or heavy downpour.

de·mand (dĭ mănd´) *v.* **demanded, demanding** To ask for in a firm or definite way. —*n., pl.* **demands** A requirement or need.

den·im (dĕn´ ĭm) *n.* A coarse, twilled, cotton cloth, usually used for jeans, overalls, and work uniforms. ➤ **Word History:** from the French *(serge) de Nîmes*, after Nîmes, a city in France where the cloth was first made.

den·si·ty (dĕn´ sĭ tē) *n., pl.* **densities** The mass (amount of matter) per unit of volume of a substance: *Lead has greater density than water.*

de·ny (dĭ nī´) *v.* **denied, denying 1.** To decline to grant or allow. **2.** To declare to be untrue; contradict: *She denied taking the volleyball.*

de·par·ture (dĭ pär´ chər) *n., pl.* **departures** The act of going away.

de·port (dĭ pôrt´) *v.* **deported, deporting** To expel from a country. ➤ **Word History:** from the French word *déporter,* "to banish," from the Latin word *dēportāre,* "to carry away": *dē-,* "off" or "away," and *portāre,* "to carry."

de·pos·it (dĭ pŏz´ ĭt) *v.* **deposited, depositing** To put or set down; place: *Deposit these books in the library box.*

de·pot (dē´ pō) *or* (dĕp´ ō) *n., pl.* **depots** A railroad or bus station. ➤ **Word History:** from the French word *dépôt,* from the Old French word *depost,* from the Latin word *dēpositum,* "something deposited," a form of the word *dēpōnere,* "to put down or deposit."

de·press (dĭ prĕs´) *v.* **depressed, depressing** To lower the spirits.

de·scend (dĭ sĕnd´) *v.* **descended, descending** To move from a higher to a lower place; go or come down.

de·scen·dant (dĭ sĕn´ dənt) *n., pl.* **descendants** A person or animal descended from specified ancestors.

de·serve (dĭ zûrv´) *v.* **deserved, deserving** To be worthy of or have a right to.

de·sign (dĭ zīn´) *n., pl.* **designs** A decorative pattern.

de·sign·er (dĭ zī´ nər) *n., pl.* **designers** A person who creates ideas for clothing and stage settings.

des·ti·na·tion (dĕs´ tə nā´ shən) *n., pl.* **destinations** The place to which a person or thing is going or is sent.

de·stroy (dĭ stroi´) *v.* **destroyed, destroying** To completely ruin.

de·struc·tive (dĭ strŭk´ tĭv) *adj.* Causing something to be destroyed or damaged: *An earthquake is a destructive force.*

a detective's badge

de·tec·tive (dĭ tĕk´ tĭv) *n., pl.* **detectives** A person whose work is to get information about crimes and try to solve them.

det·ri·men·tal (dĕt´ rə mĕn´ tl) *adj.* Causing damage or harm; injurious: *Not getting enough exercise is detrimental to your health.*

de·vel·op (dĭ vĕl´ əp) *v.* **developed, developing** To treat (photographic film) with chemicals to make images recorded on it appear.

di·ag·nose (dī´ əg nōs´) *or* (dī´ əg nōz´) *v.* **diagnosed, diagnosing** To make careful examination of; identify and study.

di·al (dī´ əl) *v.* **dialed, dialing** To make a telephone call to (a specific number). —*n., pl.* **dials 1.** A graduated surface or face on which a measurement, as of speed or time, is indicated by a moving needle or pointer: *This clock dial is broken.* **2.** The control that selects the station to which a radio or television is tuned: *Turn the dial on that old radio.*

di·a·logue (dī´ ə lôg´) *n., pl.* **dialogues** The words spoken in conversation by the characters of a written work, as a play.

dic·tate (dĭk´ tāt´) *or* (dĭk tāt´) *v.* **dictated, dictating** To say or read aloud for another person to write down on a machine to record.
➤ **Word History:** from the Latin word *dictāre*, from *dīcere,* "to say."

dic·ta·tor (dĭk´ tā´ tər) *or* (dĭk tā´ tər) *n., pl.* **dictators 1.** An absolute ruler. **2.** A tyrant.
➤ **Word History:** from the Latin word *dictāre,* from *dīcere,* "to say," and -*or,* "one who."

dic·tion·ar·y (dĭk´ shə nĕr´ ē) *n., pl.* **dictionaries** A reference book containing an alphabetical list of words with information given for each word. ➤ **Word History:** from the Medieval Latin word *dictiōnārium,* from the Latin word *dictiō,* "diction."

die·sel (dē´ zəl) *or* (dē´ səl) *n.* A diesel engine. ➤ **Word History:** after Rudolph Diesel, a German engineer who invented the diesel engine.

di·et (dī´ ĭt) *n., pl.* **diets** The usual food and drink taken in by a person or an animal.

dif·fer·ence (dĭf´ ər əns) *or* (dĭf´ rəns) *n., pl.* **differences** The quality or condition of being unlike or dissimilar.

dif·fer·ent (dĭf´ ər ənt) *adj.* Partly or completely unlike another.

dig·i·tal (dĭj´ ĭ tl) *adj.* Characterized by widespread use of computers.

di·lute (dī lo͞ot´) *or* (dĭ lo͞ot´) *v.* **diluted, diluting** To make thinner or less concentrated.

dim (dĭm) *v.* **dimmed, dimming 1.** To make or become darker. **2.** Not favorable: *Our chances for winning dimmed as we missed another goal.*

di·men·sion (dĭ mĕn´ shən) *n., pl.* **dimensions** A measurement of length, width, or thickness: *Measure the dimensions of the square.*

di·rect (dĭ rĕkt´) *v.* **directed, directing 1.** To aim, point, or guide to or toward. **2.** To be in charge of; manage. —*adj.* In a straight line, in the shortest way. —*adv.* **directly** *The bus takes me directly to school.*

di·rec·tion (dĭ rĕk´ shən) *n., pl.* **directions 1.** The line or course along which someone or something aims, points, or moves. **2.** An instruction or order.

di·rec·tor (dĭ rĕk´ tər) *n., pl.* **directors** A person who supervises and guides the performers and others involved in a dramatic production, film, or other performance.

di·rec·to·ry (dĭ rĕk´ tə rē) *n., pl.* **directories** A book containing a list of names and information.

dirt·y (dûr´ tē) *adj.* **dirtier, dirtiest** Full of or covered with dirt; not clean.

dis- A prefix that means: **1.** Not: *dishonest.* **2.** Absence of: *disinterest.* **3.** Opposite of: *disfavor.*

dis·a·gree (dĭs´ ə grē´) *v.* **disagreed, disagreeing 1.** To fail to agree; be different. **2.** To dispute or quarrel. —*n.* **disagreement** *The students' disagreement kept them from working together.*

dis·as·ter (dĭ zăs´ tər) *n., pl.* **disasters** Something that causes great destruction. —*adj.* **disastrous** *The flood was disastrous.*

dis·card (dĭ skärd´) *v.* **discarded, discarding** To throw away; reject.

dis·count (dĭs´ kount´) *n., pl.* **discounts** A reduction from the full amount of a price or debt.

dis·cour·age (dĭ skûr´ ĭj) *v.* **discouraged, discouraging** To make less hopeful.

dis·cov·er (dĭ skŭv´ ər) *v.* **discovered, discovering** To find out; learn.

dis·ease (dĭ zēz´) *n., pl.* **diseases** Sickness; a condition that makes a living thing unable to function properly: *The flu is a serious disease.*

dis·grace (dĭs grās´) *n., pl.* **disgraces** Loss of honor or respect; shame. —*adj.* **disgraceful** *I'm embarrassed by your disgraceful behavior.*

dis·hon·est (dĭs ŏn´ ĭst) *adj.* **1.** Inclined to lie, cheat, or deceive. **2.** Showing or resulting in falseness.

dish·wash·er (dĭsh´ wŏsh´ ər) *n., pl.* **dishwashers** A machine that washes dishes.

dis·like (dĭs līk´) *v.* **disliked, disliking** To have a feeling of not liking.

dis·lo·cate (dĭs´ lō kāt´) *v.* **dislocated, dislocating** To put or force out of a normal position.

dis·miss (dĭs mĭs´) *v.* **dismissed, dismissing** To allow or ask to leave.

dis·or·der (dĭs ôr´ dər) *n., pl.* **disorders** Lack of order; confusion.

dis·patch (dĭ spăch´) *v.* **dispatched, dispatching** To send off to a specific destination or on specific business: *Dispatch this message to your leader.*

dis·play (dĭ splā´) *n., pl.* **displays** A public exhibition.

dis·pos·al (dĭ spō´ zəl) *n., pl.* **disposals** The act of getting rid of something.

Pronunciation Key

ă	pat	ŏ	pot	ûr	fur
ā	pay	ō	go	*th*	**the**
âr	care	ô	paw	th	**thin**
ä	father	ôr	for	hw	**whoop**
är	farm	oi	**oil**	zh	usual
ĕ	pet	ŏŏ	book	ə	ago, item,
ē	be	ōō	boot		pencil,
ĭ	pit	yōō	cute		atom,
ī	ice	ou	**out**		circus
îr	near	ŭ	cut	ər	butter

dis·rupt (dĭs rŭpt´) *v.* **disrupted, disrupting** To throw into confusion or disorder. ➤ **Word History:** from the Latin word *disrumpere,* "to break apart": *dis-,* "part," and *rumpere,* "to break."

dis·sect (dĭ sĕkt´) *or* (dī sĕkt´) *or* (dī´ sĕkt´) *v.* **dissected, dissecting 1.** To cut apart or separate for study. **2.** To examine or analyze in detail.

dis·tance (dĭs´ təns) *n., pl.* **distances** The amount of space between two places, things, or points.

dis·tant (dĭs´ tənt) *adj.* Far away; remote.

dis·tress (dĭ strĕs´) *n.* State of being in need of help.

dis·trib·ute (dĭ strĭb´ yōōt) *v.* **distributed, distributing** To divide and give out in portions.

dis·trict (dĭs´ trĭkt) *n., pl.* **districts** An area that has a particular characteristic or function.

disaster: a flood

foolish | fuzzy

fool·ish (foo′ lĭsh) *adj.* Lacking in good sense or judgment.

for·bid (fôr bĭd′) *v.* **forbade** or **forbad, forbidden** or **forbid, forbidding 1.** To command (someone) not to do something. **2.** To prohibit.

for·ev·er (fər ĕv′ ər) *adv.* For everlasting time; eternally.

for·feit (fôr′ fĭt) *v.* **forfeited, forfeiting** Something surrendered or paid as a penalty.

for·get·ful (fər gĕt′ fəl) *adj.* Apt to forget.

for·give·ness (fôr gĭv′ nĭs) *n.* The act of forgiving; pardon: *I hurt her feelings but later asked for forgiveness.*

for·mer (fôr′ mər) *adj.* Of, relating to, or taking place in the past.

fort·night (fôrt′ nīt′) *n., pl.* **fortnights** A period of two weeks.

for·tress (fôr′ trĭs) *n., pl.* **fortresses** A fortified place, especially a large military stronghold.

fos·sil (fŏs′ əl) *n., pl.* **fossils** The remains or traces of a plant or animal of an earlier age, embedded in rock or in the earth's crust.

foun·tain (foun′ tən) *n., pl.* **fountains** A stream or jet of water, as for drinking or for decoration.

frank (frăngk) *adj.* **franker, frankest** Open and sincere; straightforward.

frank·furt·er (frăngk′ fər tər) *n., pl.* **frankfurters** A sausage usually made of beef or beef and pork. ➤ **Word History:** after the city of Frankfurt, Germany.

fossil

fran·tic (frăn′ tĭk) *adj.* Very excited and fearful or worried; desperate. —*adv.* **frantically** In a frantic way.

freck·le (frĕk′ əl) *n., pl.* **freckles** A small spot of dark pigment in the skin, often caused by exposure to the sun.

free·dom (frē′ dəm) *n., pl.* **freedoms** The right to use or enjoy something freely.

freeze (frēz) *v.* **froze, frozen, freezing 1.** To be or make uncomfortably cold. **2.** To be at that degree of temperature at which ice forms.

fre·quen·cy (frē′ kwən sē) *n., pl.* **frequencies** The condition of occurring repeatedly at short intervals.

fre·quent (frē′ kwənt) *adj.* Occurring or appearing quite often or at close intervals.

fridge (frĭj) *n., pl.* **fridges** An appliance used for storing food or other substances at a low temperature. [Short for **refrigerator**.]

fright·en (frīt′ n) *v.* **frightened, frightening** To fill with fear.

frig·id (frĭj′ ĭd) *adj.* Extremely cold.

fruit (froot) *n., pl.* **fruits** A seed-bearing plant part that is fleshy or juicy, eaten as food. Apples, oranges, grapes, strawberries, and bananas are fruits.

-ful A suffix that forms adjectives and means: **1.** Full of: *beautiful.* **2.** Able or apt to: *forgetful.* **3.** An amount that fills: *cupful; handful.*

func·tion (fŭngk′ shən) *n., pl.* **functions** The proper activity; purpose or use.

fund (fŭnd) *n., pl.* **funds** A sum of money raised or kept for a certain purpose.

fur·ni·ture (fûr′ nĭ chər) *n.* The movable objects that are needed to make a room or office fit for living or working. Chairs, tables, and beds are pieces of furniture.

fur·ther (fûr′ thər) *v.* **furthered, furthering** To help the progress of; advance.

fu·ry (fyoor′ ē) *n., pl.* **furies** Violent anger; rage.

fu·ture (fyoo′ chər) *n., pl.* **futures** The time that is to come.

fuzz·y (fŭz′ ē) *adj.* **fuzzier, fuzziest** Covered with soft, short fibers or hairs.

G

gar·bage (gär´ bĭj) *n.* Food wastes, as from a kitchen.

gar·ment (gär´ mənt) *n., pl.* **garments** An article of clothing.

gas·e·ous (găs´ ē əs) *or* (găsh´ əs) *adj.* Of, relating to, or existing as a gas: *The air we breathe is gaseous.*

gath·er (gă*th*´ ər) *v.* **gathered, gathering** 1. To bring or come together into one place; collect. 2. To pick up from many sources.

ga·zette (gə zĕt´) *n., pl.* **gazettes** A newspaper: *Kim writes stories for the town's gazette.*

➤ Word History: French, from the Italian word *gazzetta*, probably from the Italian word *gazeta*, "a small coin" (possibly from the price).

gen·u·ine (jĕn´ yo͞o ĭn) *adj.* Not false; real or pure.

ges·ture (jĕs´ chər) *n., pl.* **gestures** Movement of the limbs, head, or body to express meaning.

gin·ger (jĭn´ jər) *n.* A topical plant having a root with a sharp spicy flavor.

gla·cier (glā´ shər) *n., pl.* **glaciers** A large mass of ice slowly moving over a mountain or through a valley, formed over many years from packed snow in areas where snow builds up faster than it melts.

glare (glâr) *v.* **glared, glaring** To stare angrily.

glob·al (glō´ bəl) *adj.* Of the entire earth; worldwide.

glacier

Pronunciation Key

ă	pat	ŏ	pot	ûr	fur	
ā	pay	ō	go	*th*	the	
âr	care	ô	paw	th	thin	
ä	father	ôr	for	hw	whoop	
är	farm	oi	oil	zh	usual	
ĕ	pet	oͦo	book	ə	ago, item,	
ē	be	oͦo	boot		pencil,	
ĭ	pit	yoͦo	cute		atom,	
ī	ice	ou	out		circus	
îr	near	ŭ	cut	ər	butter	

glo·ry (glôr´ ē) *n., pl.* **glories** Great honor or praise given by others; fame; renown.

glue (gloͦo) *n., pl.* **glues** A thick, sticky substance used to join things together.

good·bye (goͦod bī´) *n., pl.* **goodbyes** An acknowledgment of parting.

gov·ern (gŭv´ ərn) *v.* **governed, governing** To direct the public affairs of a country or state.

gov·ern·ment (gŭv´ ərn mənt) *n., pl.* **governments** A form or system by which a political unit, as a country, is governed.

gov·er·nor (gŭv´ ər nər) *n., pl.* **governors** A person who is appointed to govern a colony or territory.

gown (goun) *n., pl.* **gowns** A long, loose, flowing garment.

gra·cious (grā´ shəs) *adj.* Characterized by kindness and courtesy.

grasp (grăsp) *v.* **grasped, grasping** To grab and hold firmly with or as if with the hand.

greed·y (grē´ dē) *adj.* **greedier, greediest** Filled with greed; wanting more than one needs or deserves.

greet (grēt) *v.* **greeted, greeting** To welcome or speak to in a friendly or polite way.

grim·ace (grĭm´ ĭs) *v.* **grimaced, grimacing** to contort the face, as in showing pain

groan (grōn) *v.* **groaned, groaning** To make a deep, low sound that expresses pain, sorrow, or good-natured disapproval.

group (groͦop) *n., pl.* **groups** A number of persons or things gathered together.

Spelling Dictionary

guilt·y (gĭl´ tē) *adj.* **guiltier, guiltiest** Having done wrong; deserving of blame.

gym (jĭm) *n., pl.* **gyms** A room or building equipped for indoor sports. [Short for **gymnasium**.]

H

ham·mer (hăm´ ər) *v.* **hammered, hammering** To hit, especially with or as if with a hammer.

ham·mock (hăm´ ək) *n., pl.* **hammocks** A hanging bed or couch made of canvas or heavy netting and suspended by cords between two trees or other supports: *I napped outside in the hammock.* ➤ **Word History:** from the Spanish word *hamaca,* from the Taino word.

hands-free (hăndz´ frē´) *adj.* Something that can be used without use of the hands: *With this tiny microphone, I can make hands-free calls.*

han·gar (hăng ər) *n., pl.* **hangars** A building used for housing or repairing aircraft: *Pilots moved their small planes into hangars as the hurricane approached.*
♦ *These sound alike* **hangar, hanger.**

hang·er (hăng´ ər) *n., pl.* **hangers** A frame or hook on which an article of clothing can be hung.
♦ *These sound alike* **hanger, hangar.**

hap·py (hăp´ ē) *adj.* **happier, happiest** Having, showing, or marked by a feeling of joy or pleasure.

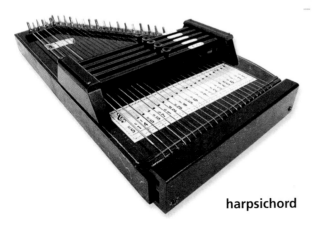

harpsichord

har·bor (här´ bər) *n., pl.* **harbors** A sheltered part of a body of water deep enough to serve as a port for ships.

harm·less (härm´ lĭs) *adj.* Incapable of causing harm.

har·mo·ny (här´ mə nē) *n., pl.* **harmonies** The sounding together of musical notes in a chord.

harp·si·chord (härp´ sĭ kôrd´) *n., pl.* **harpsichords** A keyboard instrument that resembles a piano, having strings that are plucked by means of quills or leather picks.

har·vest (här´ vĭst) *v.* **harvested, harvesting** To gather a crop.

haunt (hônt) *v.* **haunted, haunting** To come continually to the mind of; obsess. —*n., pl.* **haunts** A favorite place: *The arcade is one of my favorite haunts.*

head·ache (hĕd´ āk´) *n., pl.* **headaches** A pain in the head.

heart·beat (härt´ bēt´) *n., pl.* **heartbeats** A single cycle of contraction and relaxation of the heart.

heat wave (hēt´ wāv´) *n., pl.* **heat waves** A period of unusually hot weather.

height (hīt) *n., pl.* **heights 1.** The distance from bottom to top: *The height of the flagpole is twenty feet.* **2.** The distance from foot to head: *My height increased two inches this year.* **3.** The highest point; peak: *The height of the storm.*

hel·i·cop·ter (hĕl´ ĭ kŏp´ tər) *n., pl.* **helicopters** A wingless aircraft that is lifted by blades that rotate horizontally above the aircraft.

hem·i·sphere (hĕm´ ĭ sfîr´) *n., pl.* **hemispheres** Either of the halves into which the earth's surface is divided by the equator or a meridian: *The United States is in the Northern Hemisphere.*

her·i·tage (hĕr´ ĭ tĭj) *n., pl.* **heritages** Something handed down to later generations from earlier generations: *Freedom of speech is part of our national heritage.*

hes·i·tate (hĕz´ ĭ tāt´) *v.* **hesitated, hesitating** To pause or hold back because of feeling unsure.

hip·po (hĭp´ ō) *n., pl.* **hippos** A large, heavy African mammal having dark, almost hairless thick skin, short legs, a broad snout, and a wide mouth. It lives in and near rivers and lakes. [Short for **hippopotamus.**]

his·to·ry (hĭs´ tə rē) *n., pl.* **histories** **1.** The continuing events of the past leading up to the present. **2.** The study of past events as a special field of knowledge.

hoard (hôrd) *n., pl.* **hoards** A supply that is stored away, often secretly. —*v.* **hoarded, hoarding** To save and store away.

home run (hōm´ rŭn´) *n., pl.* **home runs** In baseball, a hit that allows the batter to touch all the bases and score a run.

hom·o·graph (hŏm´ ə grăf´) *or* (hō´ mə grăf´) *n., pl.* **homographs** A word that has the same spelling as another word but differs in meaning, origin, and sometimes in pronunciation. For example, *ring* (circle) and *ring* (sound). ➤ **Word History:** from the Greek words *homos,* "same," and *graphein,* "to write."

hom·o·phone (hŏm´ ə fōn´) *or* (hō´ mə fōn´) *n., pl.* **homophones** A word that has the same sound as another word but differs in spelling, meaning, and origin. For example, **steel** and **steal.** ➤ **Word History:** from the Greek words *homos,* "same," and *phōnē,* "sound."

hon·est (ŏn´ ĭst) *adj.* Not lying, cheating, or stealing; trustworthy.

hon·or (ŏn´ ər) *n., pl.* **honors 1.** Special respect or high regard: *We display the flag to show honor to the United States.* **2.** A special privilege or mark of excellence. —*v.* **honored, honoring** To show respect or recognition to: *We honored the volunteers with a party.*

hon·or·a·ble (ŏn´ ər ə bəl) *adj.* Having or showing a strong sense of what is right or just.

hor·ri·fy (hôr´ ə fī´) *v.* **horrified, horrifying** To surprise unpleasantly; shock.

hos·pi·tal (hŏs´ pĭ tl) *n., pl.* **hospitals** A medical institution that treats sick and injured people.

hua·ra·che (wə rä´ chē) *or* (hə rä´ chē) *n., pl.* **huaraches** A flat-heeled sandal with an upper part made from leather strips. ➤ **Word History:** from the American Spanish word *huarache,* or *guarache,* from the Tarascan word *huarache.*

hue (hyo͞o) *n., pl.* **hues** A shade or tint of color.

hu·man (hyo͞o´ mən) *adj.* Of or characteristic of people. —*n., pl.* **humans** A person.

hu·mor (hyo͞o´ mər) *n.* The quality of being comical or funny.

hun·dred (hŭn´ drĭd) *n., pl.* **hundreds** The number, written 100, that is equal to the product of 10×10.

hurl (hûrl) *v.* **hurled, hurling 1.** To throw with great force. **2.** To utter forcefully.

hus·band (hŭz´ bənd) *n., pl.* **husbands** A man married to a woman.

hy·dro·gen (hī´ drə jən) *n., pl.* **hydrogens** A colorless, odorless gas.

hippo

Spelling Dictionary

hymn (hĭm) *n., pl.* **hymns** A song of praise or joy, often sung as part of a religious service.

hy·pot·e·nuse (hī pŏt´ n ōōs´) *n., pl.* **hypotenuses** The side of a right triangle opposite the right angle.

I

-ible A form of the suffix **-able**.

ic·y (ī´ sē) *adj.* **icier, iciest** Containing or covered with ice.

i·de·a (ī dē´ ə) *n., pl.* **ideas** A thought or plan carefully formed in the mind.

i·den·ti·cal (ī dĕn´ tĭ kəl) *adj.* Exactly equal and alike.

ig·nore (ĭg nôr´) *v.* **ignored, ignoring** To pay no attention to; disregard.

i·gua·na (ĭ gwä´ nə) *n., pl.* **iguanas** Any of various large tropical American lizards having a ridge of spines along the back. ➤ **Word History:** Spanish, from the Arawak word *iwana*.

il·le·gal (ĭ lē´ gəl) *adj.* Against the law.

ill·ness (ĭl´ nĭs) *n., pl.* **illnesses** A sickness or disease.

il·lu·sion (ĭ lōō´ zhən) *n., pl.* **illusions** An unreal or misleading appearance or image.

il·lus·trate (ĭl´ ə strāt´) *or* (ĭ lŭs´ trāt´) *v.* **illustrated, illustrating** To provide pictures or diagrams that explain or adorn.

im·age (ĭm´ ĭj) *n., pl.* **images** A representation of a person or thing, especially a picture or statue.

im·i·tate (ĭm´ ĭ tāt´) *v.* **imitated, imitating** To copy the actions, looks, or sounds of.

im·i·ta·tion (ĭm´ ĭ tā´ shən) *n., pl.* **imitations** Something made to look or seem just like something else; a copy.

im·pact (ĭm´ păkt´) *n., pl.* **impacts** The effect or impression of something.

im·port (ĭm pôrt´) *or* (ĭm´ pôrt´) *v.* **imported, importing** To bring in (goods) from a foreign country for sale or use. ➤ **Word History:** from the Latin word *importāre,* "to carry in."

im·por·tant (ĭm pôr´ tnt) *adj.* Strongly affecting the course of events or the nature of things; significant.

im·pose (ĭm pōz´) *v.* **imposed, imposing** To force oneself upon another; to take unfair advantage.

im·pos·si·ble (ĭm pŏs´ ə bəl) *adj.* Not capable of happening or existing.

im·press (ĭm prĕs´) *v.* **impressed, impressing** To have a strong, often favorable effect on the mind or feelings of.

im·prove (ĭm prōōv´) *v.* **improved, improving** To make or become better.

im·pro·vise (ĭm´ prə vīz´) *v.* **improvised, improvising** To invent, compose, or perform without preparation: *We didn't have script to read, so we had to improvise on stage.*

in-¹ A prefix that means "not": inactive

in-² A prefix that means "in," "within," or "into."

in·clem·ent (ĭn klĕm´ ənt) *adj.* Stormy, rough: *inclement weather.*

in·clude (ĭn klōōd´) *v.* **included, including** To have as a part or a member; contain.

in·com·plete (ĭn´ kəm plēt´) *adj.* Not complete.

in·cred·i·ble (ĭn krĕd´ ə bəl) *adj.* Hard to believe; unbelievable.

in·cred·u·lous (ĭn krĕj´ ə ləs) *adj.* Disbelieving or doubtful; skeptical: *Her incredulous look told me she doubted my words.*

iguana

in·dict (ĭn dīt´) *v.* **indicted, indicting**
To accuse of wrongdoing; charge: *The grand jury will indict the suspects.*

in·di·go (ĭn´ dĭ gō´) *adj.* A dark violet blue.

in·di·rect (ĭn´ dĭ rĕkt´) *or* (ĭn´ dī rĕkt´) *adj.*
Not following a direct course.

in·dus·try (ĭn´ də strē) *n., pl.* **industries**
A large-scale enterprise that provides a product or service.

in·fan·cy (ĭn´ fən sē) *n., pl.* **infancies** The earliest period of childhood, especially before being able to walk.

in·fant (ĭn´ fənt) *n., pl.* **infants** A child in the earliest period of life, especially before being able to walk.

in·fan·try (ĭn´ fən trē) *n., pl.* **infantries** Soldiers armed and trained to fight on foot.

in·for·mal (ĭn fôr´ məl) *adj.* Suitable for everyday use or casual occasions.

in·no·cent (ĭn´ ə sənt) *adj.* Free of evil or wrongdoing; not guilty of a crime or sin.

in·se·cure (ĭn´ sĭ kyŏor´) *adj.* Not sure or certain.

in·sin·cere (ĭn´ sĭn sîr´) *adj.* Not sincere; not heartfelt. —*n.* **insincerity** The condition of being insincere; hypocrisy.

in·spect (ĭn spĕkt´) *v.* **inspected, inspecting**
To look over carefully. ➤ **Word History:** from the Latin word *īnspicere,* "to see in."

in·stant (ĭn´ stənt) *n., pl.* **instants** A period of time almost too brief to detect. —*adj.* Prepared by a manufacturer for quick preparation by the consumer.

in·stead (ĭn stĕd´) *adv.* In place of something previously mentioned.

in·struct (ĭn strŭkt´) *v.* **instructed, instructing** **1.** To teach or give information. **2.** To give orders to.

inter- A prefix that means: **1.** Between; among. **2.** Together.

in·te·ri·or (ĭn tîr´ ē ər) *adj.* Of or located in the inside; inner. —*n., pl.* **interiors**
The inner part of something; the inside.

in·ter·mis·sion (ĭn´ tər mĭsh´ ən) *n., pl.*
intermissions An interval between periods of activity; a pause.

in·ter·pret (ĭn tûr´ prĭt) *v.* **interpreted, interpreting** To tell the meaning or importance of; explain; translate.

in·ter·rupt (ĭn´ tə rŭpt´) *v.* **interrupted, interrupting** To do something that hinders or stops the action or conversation of; break in on: *Should we interrupt them while they are talking?*
➤ **Word History:** from the Latin word *interrumpere,* "to break off."

in·ter·sect (ĭn´ tər sĕkt´) *v.* **intersected, intersecting** To cut across or through.

in·ter·view (ĭn´ tər vyōō´) *n., pl.* **interviews**
A face-to-face meeting for a specified purpose.

in·tes·tine (ĭn tĕs´ tĭn) *n., pl.* **intestines** The part of the alimentary canal that extends below the stomach, consisting of the large intestine and small intestine.

in·trude (ĭn trōōd´) *v.* **intruded, intruding**
To break, come, or force in without being wanted or asked; trespass; invade.

infant

Spelling Dictionary

in·ven·tor (ĭn vĕn´ tər) *n.*, *pl.* **inventors**
A person who produces or creates new ideas, things, or methods.

in·vis·i·ble (ĭn vĭz´ ə bəl) *adj.* Impossible to see.

-ion A suffix that forms nouns and means "an act or process" or "the outcome of an act": *election.*

i·tem (ī´ təm) *n.*, *pl.* **items 1.** A single thing or unit. **2.** A piece of news or information.

-ity A suffix that forms nouns and means "a state or quality of": *possibility.*

kayak

J

Jan·u·ar·y (jăn´ yoo ĕr´ ē) *n.*, *pl.* **Januaries** The first month of the year, having 31 days. ➤ **Word History:** from the Greek god Janus, the protector of doorways and gates.

jer·sey (jûr´ zē) *n.*, *pl.* **jerseys** A soft, elastic fabric of knitted wool, cotton, or rayon, used for clothing. ➤ **Word History:** after the island of Jersey in the United Kingdom, where the cloth was first produced.

jew·el (joo´ əl) *n.*, *pl.* **jewels 1.** A precious stone; gem. **2.** A valuable ornament, as a ring or necklace, especially one made of precious metal and set with gems. **3.** A person or thing that is greatly admired or valued.

jour·ney (jûr´ nē) *n.*, *pl.* **journeys** A trip, especially one over a great distance.

ju·ry (joor´ ē) *n.*, *pl.* **juries** A body of citizens who hear evidence in a case as presented in a court of law and hand down a verdict on the basis of the evidence according to the law.

jus·tice (jŭs´ tĭs) *n.* The carrying out of the law or the way in which the law is carried out: *The courts make sure that justice is achieved.*

K

kay·ak (kī´ ăk´) *n.*, *pl.* **kayaks** A boat consisting of a light wooden frame covered with watertight skins, with only a small opening for the paddler.

khak·i (kăk´ ē) *or* (kä´ kē) *n.*, *pl.* **khakis 1.** A yellowish brown. **2.** A strong, heavy, khaki-colored cloth. —*adj.* Of a yellowish brown color. ➤ **Word History:** from the Persian word *khāk*, "dust."

kitch·en (kĭch´ ən) *n.*, *pl.* **kitchens** A room or area where food is prepared or cooked.

knit (nĭt) *v.* **knitted, knitting** To make by forming yarn or thread into interlocked loops either by hand with special needles or by machine.

knowl·edge (nŏl´ ĭj) *n.* **1.** Facts and ideas; information. **2.** Understanding; awareness.

L

la·bel (lā´ bəl) *n.*, *pl.* **labels** A tag or sticker that is attached to something to tell what it is or what it contains.

la·bor (lā´ bər) *v.* **labored, laboring** To work: *Workers labored in the field picking beans.*

land (lănd) *v.* **landed, landing** To come down or bring to rest on a surface.

land·form (lănd´ fôrm) *n., pl.* **landforms**
A feature of the earth's surface, such as a plain, valley, or mountain.

lan·guage (lăng´ gwĭj) *n., pl.* **languages**
A system of words and expressions shared by a people: *What is your native language?*

la·ser (lā´ zər) *n., pl.* **lasers** A device that sends out a very narrow and extremely powerful beam of light. Laser beams are used to cut through steel and perform surgery.

las·so (lăs´ ō) *or* (lă sōō´) *n., pl.* **lassos** or **lassoes** A long rope with a loop at one end, used especially to catch horses and cattle.
➤ **Word History:** from the Spanish word *lazo,* from the Vulgar Latin word *laceum,* "noose."

late·ly (lāt´ lē) *adv.* In the near past; recently; not long ago.

lat·i·tude (lăt´ ĭ tōōd´) *n. pl.* **latitudes**
Distance north or south of the equator measured in degrees: *Canada and Mexico are at different latitudes.*

laugh·ter (lăf´ tər) *n.* The act or sound of laughing.

launch (lônch) *or* (länch) *n., pl.* **launches** The act of putting something, such as a rocket or a ship, into motion.

laun·dry (lôn´ drē) *or* (län´ drē) *n.* Clothes and linens that have just been or will be washed.

law·yer (lô´ yər) *n., pl.* **lawyers** A person who is trained and qualified to give legal advice to clients and represent them in a court of law; an attorney.

lay (lā) *v.* **laid, laying 1.** To place or put, especially on a flat surface. **2.** To put in place. **3.** To spread over a surface.

le·gal (lē´ gəl) *adj.* Based on or authorized by law; lawful.

le·gal·i·ty (lē găl´ ĭ tē) *n., pl.* **legalities** The state of being legal; lawfulness.

leg·end (lĕj´ ənd) *n., pl.* **legends** A story handed down from earlier times, often believed to be historically true.

lei·sure (lē´ zhər) *or* (lĕzh´ ər) *n.* Free time in which to relax and do as one pleases.

le·o·tard (lē´ ə tärd´) *n., pl.* **leotards** A tight-fitting garment, sometimes with sleeves, originally worn by dancers and acrobats.
➤ **Word History:** after Jules Léotard (1830–1870), a French aerialist.

Pronunciation Key

ă	pat	ŏ	pot	ûr	fur
ā	pay	ō	go	*th*	the
âr	care	ô	paw	th	thin
ä	father	ôr	for	hw	whoop
är	farm	oi	oil	zh	usual
ĕ	pet	ŏŏ	book	ə	ago, item,
ē	be	ōō	boot		pencil,
ĭ	pit	yōō	cute		atom,
ī	ice	ou	out		circus
îr	near	ŭ	cut	ər	butter

-less A suffix that forms adjectives and means "not having" or "without": *harmless; shoeless.*

less·en (lĕs´ ən) *v.* **lessened, lessening** To make or become less.
♦ *These sound alike* **lessen, lesson.**

les·son (lĕs´ ən) *n., pl.* **lessons** Something to be learned, especially an assignment or exercise in which something is studied or taught.
♦ *These sound alike* **lesson, lessen.**

lev·el (lĕv´ əl) *adj.* Having a flat, even surface; not tilted.
◊ **Idioms** **(one's) level best** The best one could do in those circumstances. **on the level** Honest; without any dishonesty.

lie (lī) *v.* **lay, lain, lying 1.** To place oneself in a flat or resting position. **2.** To be or rest on a surface.

life·guard (līf´ gärd´) *n., pl.* **lifeguards** A person hired to look out for the safety of bathers at a beach or pool.

lifeguard

313

ligament | magazine

lig·a·ment (lĭg´ ə mənt) *n., pl.* **ligaments**
A sheet or band of tough, fibrous tissue that connects two bones or holds an organ of the body in place.

light bulb (līt´ bŭlb´) *n., pl.* **light bulbs**
A glass-covered electric light source in which a wire is heated by an electric current so that it gives off light.

light me·ter (līt´ mē´ tər) *n., pl.* **light meters**
A device that measures the intensity of light, used especially in photography.

like·li·hood (līk´ lē hŏŏd´) *n.* The chance of a thing happening; probability.

lim·it (lĭm´ ĭt) *n., pl.* **limits** The greatest amount of something allowed.

lim·o (lĭm´ ō) *n., pl.* **limos** A large, luxurious vehicle driven by a chauffeur. [Short for **limousine.**]

lin·en (lĭn´ ən) *adj.* Strong, smooth cloth made of flax fibers.

liq·uid (lĭk´ wĭd) *n., pl.* **liquids** A substance that is neither a solid nor a gas. A liquid moves freely within the container in which it is put.

lis·ten (lĭs´ ən) *v.* **listened, listening** To try to hear something.

lo·cal (lō´ kəl) *adj.* Of a certain limited area or place. —*n., pl.* **locals** A person who lives in a certain region or neighborhood.

lo·cale (lō kăl´) *n., pl.* **locales** A place, especially with reference to a particular event or circumstance: *The basketball tournament is held at a different locale every year.*

lo·cal·ize (lō´ kə līz´) *v.* **localized, localizing** To confine or become restricted to a particular area: *Let's localize the search and keep it in town.*

lo·cate (lō´ kāt´) *v.* **located, locating** To find and show the position of.

lo·co·mo·tive (lō´ kə mō´ tĭv´) *n., pl.* **locomotives** An engine that moves on its own power and is used to pull or push railroad cars.

log·ic (lŏj´ ĭk) *n.* Rational thought; sound reasoning.

loi·ter (loi´ tər) *v.* **loitered, loitering** To stand about idly; to linger.

lone·ly (lōn´ lē) *adj.* **lonelier, loneliest** Sad at being alone.

lon·gi·tude (lŏn´ jĭ tōōd´) *n., pl.* **longitudes** Distance measured in degrees east or west of the meridian at Greenwich, a city in England: *I found the longitude of Memphis on a map.*

loom (lōōm) *n., pl.* **looms** A machine or frame on which threads or yarns are woven to make cloth.

loose (lōōs) *adj.* **looser, loosest** Not fastened tightly.

lose (lōōz) *v.* **lost, losing 1.** To be unable to find; mislay **2.** To be deprived of (something one has had). **3.** To fail to win.

love·ly (lŭv´ lē) *adj.* **lovelier, loveliest** Having attractive qualities of character or appearance; beautiful or endearing.

loy·al (loi´ əl) *adj.* Firm in supporting a person, country, or cause; faithful; true.

lug·gage (lŭg´ ĭj) *n.* Bags and suitcases that a person takes on a trip; baggage.

lu·nar (lōō´ nər) *adj.* Of, on, or having to do with the moon.

-ly A suffix that forms adverbs and means "in a certain way": *accidentally, happily.*

M

mag·a·zine (măg´ ə zēn´) *or* (măg´ ə zēn´) *n., pl.* **magazines** A publication that is issued regularly, as every week or month. ➤ **Word History:** from the Arabic word *mahāzin,* "storehouse."

luggage

ma·jor (mā′ jər) *adj.* Larger, greater, or more important.

mal·let (măl′ ĭt) *n., pl.* **mallets** A hammer with a wooden head and a short handle, used to drive a chisel or wedge.

man·age (măn′ ĭj) *v.* **managed, managing** To have control over; direct: *Who will manage the business while your parents are away?*

ma·nip·u·late (mə nĭp′ yə lāt′) *v.* **manipulated, manipulating** To arrange, operate, or control by the hands or by mechanical means.

man·ner (măn′ ər) *n., pl.* **manners** A way of acting; behavior.
♦ *These sound alike* **manner, manor.**

man·or (măn′ ər) *n., pl.* **manors** The main house on an estate.
♦ *These sound alike* **manor, manner.**

man·til·la (măn tē′ yə) *or* (măn tĭl′ ə) *n., pl.* **mantillas** A lace scarf worn over the head. Often seen in Spain and Latin America.
➤ **Word History:** from the Spanish word *manta,* "cape."

mar·a·thon (măr′ ə thŏn′) *n., pl.* **marathons** A race for runners over a distance of 26 miles, 385 yards.

mar·riage (măr′ ĭj) *n., pl.* **marriages** The state of living together as husband and wife.

ma·son (mā′ sən) *n., pl.* **masons** A person who builds or works with stone or brick.

mas·sive (măs′ ĭv) *adj.* Heavy and solid.

mast (măst) *n., pl.* **masts** The tall, upright pole that supports the sails and rigging of a ship or boat.

mast

mat·i·nee (măt′ n ā′) *n., pl.* **matinees** A theatrical performance or movie that is given or shown in the afternoon.

mat·ter (măt′ ər) *n.* Something that occupies space, has mass, and can exist ordinarily as a solid, liquid, or gas.

mat·tress (măt′ rĭs) *n., pl.* **mattresses** A pad of heavy cloth filled with soft material or a group of springs, used on or as a bed.
➤ **Word History:** from an Arabic word meaning "place where something is thrown," and "mat" or "cushion," from a word meaning "to throw." In the Middle Ages, Europeans borrowed the Arab custom of sleeping on cushions thrown on the floor.

mav·er·ick (măv′ ər ĭk) *or* (măv′ rĭk) *n., pl.* **mavericks** A person who refuses to go along with the policies or views of a group: *I call him a maverick because he does everything his own way.*
➤ **Word History:** possibly after Samuel Augustus Maverick (1803–1870), an American cattleman who did not brand the calves in his herd.

may·or (mā′ ər) *n., pl.* **mayors** The chief government official of a city or town.

mean (mēn) *n., pl.* **means** A number or quantity that is intermediate between other numbers.

me·an·der (mē ăn′ dər) *v.* **meandered, meandering** To wander aimlessly and idly.

meas·ure (mĕzh′ ər) *v.* **measured, measuring** To find the size, amount, capacity, or degree of.

me·di·a (mē´ dē ə) *pl. n.* A plural of **medium.**

me·di·an (mē´ dē ən) *n., pl.* **medians** In mathematics, the middle number of a sequence having an odd number of values or the average of the two middle values if the sequence has an even number of values. For example, in the sequence 3, 4, 5, 6, 7, the median is 5; in the sequence 4, 8, 12, 16, the median is 10.

me·di·um (mē´ dē əm) *n., pl.* **media** A means for sending information to large numbers of people.

meg·a·phone (měg´ ə fōn´) *n., pl.* **megaphones** A large funnel-shaped horn, used to direct and amplify the voice. ➤ **Word History:** from the Greek words *megas,* "great," and *phōnē,* "sound."

mel·o·dy (měl´ ə dē) *n., pl.* **melodies** A pleasant arrangement of sounds.

mem·o·ry (měm´ ə rē) *n., pl.* **memories** **1.** The power or ability to remember. **2.** Something that is remembered.

-ment A suffix that forms nouns and means: **1.** Action or process: *government.* **2.** The result of an action or process: *measurement.*

men·tor (měn´ tôr´) *n., pl.* **mentors** A wise and trusted advisor.

men·u (měn´ yōō) *n., pl.* **menus** A list of foods and drinks available or served, as at a restaurant.

mer·chant (mûr´ chənt) *n., pl.* **merchants** A person who buys and sells goods, especially a person who runs a store.

mer·ci·less (mûr´ sĭ lĭs) *adj.* Having or showing no mercy; cruel.

me·rid·i·an (mə rĭd´ ē ən) *n., pl.* **meridians** An imaginary half circle on the earth's surface running from the North Pole to the South Pole.

mes·sen·ger (měs´ ən jər) *n., pl.* **messengers** A person who carries messages or runs errands.

mess·y (měs´ ē) *adj.* **messier, messiest** Disorderly and dirty: *a messy bedroom.*

mi·crobe (mī´ krōb´) *n., pl.* **microbes** A microorganism, especially a bacterium that causes disease. ➤ **Word History:** from the Greek words *mīkros,* "small," and *bios,* "life."

mi·cro·phone (mī´ krə fōn´) *n., pl.* **microphones** A device that converts sound waves into electric current, as in recording or radio broadcasting. ➤ **Word History:** from the Greek words *mīkros,* "small," and *phōnē,* "sound."

mi·cro·scope (mī´ krə skōp´) *n., pl.* **microscopes** An instrument with a special lens for making a very small object appear larger, especially objects too small to be seen by the naked eye. ➤ **Word History:** from the Greek words *mīkros,* "small," and *skopein,* "to see."

mi·cro·wave (mī´ krō wāv´) *n., pl.* **microwaves** An oven that uses high-frequency electromagnetic waves. ➤ **Word History:** from the Greek word *mīkros,* "small," and the Middle English word *waven,* from the Old English word *wafian,* "to move (the hand) up and down."

mid·night sun (mĭd´ nīt´ sŭn´) *n., pl.* **midnight suns** The sun as seen at midnight during the summer within the Arctic or Antarctic Circle.

might·y (mī´ tē) *adj.* **mightier, mightiest** **1.** Having or showing great power, strength, or force: *a mighty army.* **2.** Great in size, importance, or effect. —*adv.* Very; extremely: *mighty important.*

mil·i·tar·y (mĭl´ ĭ tĕr´ ē) *n., pl.* **militaries** Of, relating to, or characteristic of the armed forces.

microscope

mil·len·ni·um (mə lĕn´ ē əm) *n., pl.*
millenniums or **millennia** A period of one
thousand years.

min·er·al (mĭn´ ər əl) *n., pl.* **minerals**
A natural substance, such as a diamond or salt,
that is not of plant or animal origin.

min·ing (mī´ nĭng) *n.* The work, process,
or business of extracting coal, minerals, or ore
from the earth.

min·ute (mĭn´ ĭt) *n., pl.* **minutes** A unit of
time equal to sixty seconds.

mir·ror (mĭr´ ər) *n., pl.* **mirrors** A surface,
as of glass, that reflects the image of an object
placed in front of it. ➤ **Word History:** from
the Old French word *mireor,* from *mirer,*
"to look at."

mis- A prefix that means: **1.** Error or
wrongness: *misspell.* **2.** Badness or impropriety:
misbehave. **3.** Failure or lack of: *misfire, mistrust.*

mis·chief (mĭs´ chĭf) *n.* **1.** Naughty or bad
behavior. **2.** Harm or damage caused by
someone or something.

mis·count (mĭs kount´) *v.* **miscounted,**
miscounting To count incorrectly.

mis·hap (mĭs´ hăp´) *or* (mĭs hăp´) *n., pl.*
mishaps An unfortunate accident.

mis·lay (mĭs lā´) *v.* **mislaid, mislaying**
To lay or put down in a place one cannot
remember.

mis·lead (mĭs lēd´) *v.* **misled, misleading**
1. To lead in the wrong direction. **2.** To lead
into error of thought or wrongdoing.

mis·spell (mĭs spĕl´) *v.* **misspelled,**
misspelling To spell incorrectly.

mis·take (mĭ stāk´) *n., pl.*
mistakes Something that is thought up, done,
or figured out in an incorrect way.

mis·treat (mĭs trēt´) *v.* **mistreated,**
mistreating To treat badly. —*n.* **mistreatment**
Rough or unkind treatment.

mix·ture (mĭks´ chər) *n., pl.* **mixtures** Any
combination of different ingredients, things,
or kinds; blend.

mode (mōd) *n., pl.* **modes** The number that
occurs most frequently in a data set. For
example, in the series 125, 140, 172, 164, 140,
and 110, 140 is the mode.

Pronunciation Key					
ă	pat	ŏ	pot	ûr	fur
ā	pay	ō	go	*th*	the
âr	care	ô	paw	th	thin
ä	father	ôr	for	hw	whoop
är	farm	oi	oil	zh	usual
ĕ	pet	o͝o	book	ə	ago, item,
ē	be	o͞o	boot		pencil,
ĭ	pit	yo͞o	cute		atom,
ī	ice	ou	out		circus
îr	near	ŭ	cut	ər	butter

mod·el (mŏd´ l) *n., pl.* **models 1.** A small
copy: *a model of a train.* **2.** A person hired
to display merchandise, such as clothing.
3. A person or thing that is a good example.
—*v.* **modeled, modeling** To display by
wearing. —*adj.* Serving as a standard of
excellence: *a model student.*

mod·ern (mŏd´ ərn) *adj.* Of or relating
to a recently developed style, technique, or
technology.

moist (moist) *adj.* **moister, moistest** Slightly
wet; damp.

mois·ten (moi´ sən) *v.* **moistened,**
moistening To make moist; to dampen.

mois·ture (mois´ chər) *n.* Wetness.

mo·lar (mō´ lər) *n., pl.* **molars** Any of the
teeth located toward the back of the jaws,
having broad crowns for grinding food.

mineral: amethyst

Spelling Dictionary

Mon·day (mŭn´ dē) *or* (mŭn´ dā´) *n., pl.*
Mondays The second day of the week.
➤ Word History: from the Old English word
Mōnandag, "moon's day": *mōna,* "moon," and
dag, "day."

mon·key (mŭng´ kē) *n., pl.* **monkeys** Any of
various medium-sized primates having long
tails and hands and feet that are adapted for
grasping. ➤ Word History: probably from
Low German; akin to Old Spanish word *mona,*
"monkey."

mon·soon (mŏn soon´) *n., pl.* **monsoons**
A system of winds that influences the climate
of a large area in certain seasons, especially the
wind system that produces the wet and dry
seasons in southern Asia.

mood·y (moo´ dē) *adj.* **moodier, moodiest**
Gloomy: *a moody expression.*

mos·qui·to (mə skē´ tō) *n., pl.* **mosquitoes**
or **mosquitos** A small flying insect. The
female mosquito bites and sucks blood from
animals and human beings. ➤ Word
History: from the diminutive of the Spanish
word *mosca,* "fly," from the Latin word
musca.

mo·ti·vate (mō´ tə vāt´) *v.* **motivated,
motivating** To provide with a reason or
purpose; move to action: *Our coach's speech
motivated us to try harder.*

mo·tor·cy·cle (mō´ tər sī´ kəl) *n., pl.*
motorcycles A vehicle with two wheels, similar
to a bicycle but larger and heavier, propelled by
an engine.

motorcycle

mot·to (mŏt´ ō) *n., pl.* **mottoes** or **mottos**
A brief expression of a guiding principle;
a slogan.

mount (mount) *v.* **mounted, mounting**
To get up on.

moun·tain (moun´ tən) *n., pl.* **mountains**
An area of land that rises to a great height.

move·ment (moov´ mənt) *n., pl.* **movements**
The act or process of changing position.

mov·ie (moo´ vē) *n., pl.* **movies** A motion
picture.

mur·mur (mûr´ mər) *n., pl.* **murmurs** A low,
continuous sound. —*v.* **murmured, murmuring**
To speak or complain in an undertone.

mus·cle (mŭs´ əl) *n., pl.* **muscles** A type of
body tissue that can be contracted and relaxed
to cause movement or exert force.

mu·se·um (myoo zē´ əm) *n., pl.* **museums**
A building in which objects of artistic,
historical, or scientific interest are exhibited.

mu·si·cal (myoo´ zĭ kəl) *adj.* Of, involving,
or used in producing music. —*n., pl.* **musicals**
A play or movie in which songs are included
along with dialogue.

myth (mĭth) *n., pl.* **myths** A traditional story
dealing with ancestors, heroes, or supernatural
beings, and usually making an attempt to
explain a belief, practice, or natural
phenomenon.

N

nar·rate (năr´ āt´) *or* (nă rāt´) *v.* **narrated,
narrating** To tell (a story, for example) in
speech or writing or by means of images.

nar·row (năr´ ō) *adj.* **narrower, narrowest**
Small or limited in width, especially in
comparison with length.

na·tion (nā´ shən) *n., pl.* **nations** A group of
people who share the same territory and are
organized under a single government; country.

na·tion·al (năsh´ ə nəl) *adj.* Of, having to do
with, or belonging to a nation.

na·tion·al·i·ty (năsh´ ə **năl´** ĭ tē) *n., pl.*
nationalities The condition of belonging
to a particular nation. Children born in the
United States are of American nationality.
na·tive (**nā´** tĭv) *adj.* **1.** Belonging to a person
because of the person's place of birth: *native
language.* **2.** Originally living, grown, or
produced in a particular place: *a plant native
to Asia.* —*n., pl.* **natives** A person born in
a certain place or country: *a native of Ohio.*
nat·u·ral (**năch´** ər əl) *or* (**năch´** rəl) *adj.*
Present in or produced by nature; not artificial
or synthetic.
na·ture (**nā´** chər) *n.* The world of living
things and the outdoors; wildlife and natural
scenery.
naugh·ty (**nô´** tē) *adj.* **naughtier, naughtiest**
Disobedient; mischievous.
nav·i·ga·tion (năv´ ĭ **gā´** shən) *n.* The
practice of plotting and controlling the course
of a ship or aircraft.
nee·dle (**nēd´** l) *n., pl.* **needles** A small,
slender sewing tool made of polished steel,
pointed at one end and having an eye at the
other through which a length of thread is
passed and held.
◇ *Idiom* **on pins and needles** In a state of
anxiety; nervous.
ne·glect (nĭ **glĕkt´**) *v.* **neglected,
neglecting** To fail to give proper care and
attention to.
nerve (nûrv) *n., pl.* **nerves 1.** Any of the
bundles of fibers that carry messages between
the brain or spinal cord and other parts of the
body. **2.** Courage or daring: *It took all my nerve
to jump that high fence.*
-ness A suffix that forms nouns and means
"condition" or "quality": *emptiness.*
news·cast (**nōōz´** kăst´) *n., pl.* **newscasts**
A broadcast of news on radio or television.
nick·el (**nĭk´** əl) *n., pl.* **nickels** A United
States or Canadian coin worth five cents.
niece (nēs) *n., pl.* **nieces** The daughter of
one's brother or sister or of the brother or sister
of one's spouse.
nim·ble (**nĭm´** bəl) *adj.* **nimbler, nimblest**
Quick and light in movement: *nimble fingers.*

Pronunciation Key

ă	pat	ŏ	pot	ûr	fur
ā	pay	ō	go	*th*	**the**
âr	care	ô	paw	th	**thin**
ä	father	ôr	for	hw	**whoop**
är	farm	oi	**oil**	zh	usual
ĕ	pet	ōō	book	ə	**a**go, item,
ē	be	ōō	boot		pencil,
ĭ	pit	yōō	cute		atom,
ī	ice	ou	**out**		circus
îr	near	ŭ	cut	ər	butter

nois·y (**noi´** zē) *adj.* **noisier, noisiest** Making
a lot of noise. —*adv.* **noisily** *She sneezed noisily.*
nor·mal (**nôr´** məl) *adj.* Of the usual or
regular kind.
no·tice (**nō´** tĭs) *n., pl.* **notices** A published or
displayed announcement: *Post a notice on
the bulletin board.*
nour·ish (**nûr´** ĭsh) *v.* **nourished, nourishing**
To provide (a living thing) with the food or
other substances necessary for life and growth.
nov·el¹ (**nŏv´** əl) *adj.* Very new, unusual, or
different.
nov·el² (**nŏv´** əl) *n., pl.* **novels** A made-up
story that is long enough to fill a book.
nui·sance (**nōō´** səns) *n., pl.* **nuisances**
Someone or something that is annoying; a pest:
A mosquito can be a nuisance.
nu·tri·tion (nōō **trĭsh´** ən) *n.* Nourishment;
diet: *Having good nutrition is important for
good health.*

nickel

Spelling Dictionary

ob·ject[1] (ŏb´ jĕkt´) *n., pl.* **objects**
1. Something that has shape and can be felt or seen. **2.** A purpose; goal.
ob·ject[2] (əb jĕkt´) *v.* **objected, objecting**
To express an opposing view or argument; to be against; disapprove of.
ob·jec·tion (əb jĕk´ shən) *n., pl.* **objections**
The expression of an opposing point of view or argument.
o·boe (ō´ bō) *n., pl.* **oboes** A woodwind instrument with a thin conical shape and mouthpiece with a double reed. It is played by pressing keys that uncover holes in its body.
ob·tuse an·gle (əb tōōs´ ăng´ gəl) *n., pl.*
obtuse angles An angle whose measure in degrees is between 90° and 180°: *A large angle is obtuse.*
oc·ca·sion·al·ly (ə kā´ zhə nə lē) *adv.* From time to time; now and then.
oc·cu·pan·cy (ŏk´ yə pən sē) *n., pl.*
occupancies The period during which a person or group stays in, rents, or uses certain premises or land.
oc·cu·pant (ŏk´ yə pənt) *n., pl.* **occupants**
A person or thing occupying a place or position.
oc·cur (ə kûr´) *v.* **occurred, occurring**
To take place; come about; happen.
odd (ŏd) *adj.* **odder, oddest** Not ordinary or usual; peculiar.
o·dor (ō´ dər) *n., pl.* **odors** Smell; scent.
of·fer (ô´ fər) *v.* **offered, offering 1.** To show readiness to do; volunteer. **2.** To put forward to be accepted or refused.
of·fice (ô´ fĭs) *n., pl.* **offices** A place, as a room or series of rooms, in which the work of a business or profession is carried on.
ol·ive (ŏl´ ĭv) *n., pl.* **olives** The small, oval green or black fruit that grows in warm regions.
op·er·ate (ŏp´ ə rāt´) *v.* **operated, operating**
1. To perform surgery. **2.** To perform a function; work.

orchestra

op·er·a·tion (ŏp´ ə rā´ shən) *n., pl.*
operations 1. A mathematical process or action performed in a specific way according to specific rules. **2.** Surgery.
op·po·nent (ə pō´ nənt) *n., pl.* **opponents**
A person or group that opposes another in a battle, contest, or other event.
op·pose (ə pōz´) *v.* **opposed, opposing**
To offer resistance to or contend against.
op·pres·sive (ə prĕs´ ĭv) *adj.* Difficult to bear; harsh and unjust.
op·tion (ŏp´ shən) *n., pl.* **options** A choice.
o·ral (ôr´ əl) *adj.* Spoken rather than written.
or·ches·tra (ôr´ kĭ strə) *n., pl.* **orchestras**
A large group of musicians who play together on various instruments, including string, woodwind, brass, and percussion instruments.
or·der (ôr´ dər) *v.* **ordered, ordering**
1. To give a command to: *The captain ordered the crew to drop anchor.* **2.** To place an order: *order a book.* —*n., pl.* **orders** A command.
or·dered pair (ôr´ dərd pâr) *n., pl.* **ordered pairs** A pair of numbers in a specific order and usually written in parentheses, such as *(3, 5).*
or·di·nance (ôr´ dn əns) *n., pl.* **ordinances**
A statute or regulation, especially one enacted by a city government.
or·gan (ôr´ gən) *n., pl.* **organs** A distinct part of an organism, adapted for a specific function.
or·gan·ism (ôr´ gə nĭz´ əm) *n., pl.* **organisms**
An individual form of life that is capable of growing and reproducing.

or·phan (ôr´ fən) *n., pl.* **orphans** A child whose parents are dead.

ounce (ouns) *n., pl.* **ounces** A unit of weight and mass equal to 1/16 pound.

-ous A suffix that means "possessing" or "characterized by": *wondrous.*

out·come (out´ kŭm´) *n., pl.* **outcomes** An end result; a consequence.

out·spo·ken (out spō´ kən) *adj.* Spoken without reserve; frank and honest; bold.

o·va·tion (ō vā´ shən) *n., pl.* **ovations** A loud and enthusiastic display of approval, usually in the form of shouting or hearty applause.

o·ver (ō´ vər) *adv., prep.,* and *adj.* Higher than; above: *He put a hand over her head.*
◇ *Idioms* **cry over spilled milk** To be upset about things you can't change: *It's better to look to the future than to cry over spilled milk.* **go over** To review: *I want to go over my recipe before I bake the cake.* **go overboard** Do or use too much: *Don't go overboard when you use perfume.* **once-over** A quick but thorough look or review: *He gave the book the once-over before deciding to buy it.* **over and above** In addition to: *We paid a fee over and above the regular charge.* **over and over** Again and again; repeatedly: *My sister listened to the same song over and over.* **over my head** Difficult to understand: *That scientific explanation was over my head.* **over the top** Beyond the normal bounds; excessive: *His wild reaction to a small problem was over the top.*

o·ver·board (ō´ vər bôrd´) *adv.* Over the side of a boat.

package

o·ver·do (ō´ vər dōō´) *v.* **overdid, overdone, overdoing** To do or use to excess; carry too far.
♦ *These sound alike* **overdo, overdue.**

o·ver·due (ō´ vər dōō´) *adj.* Unpaid after being due.
♦ *These sound alike* **overdue, overdo.**

o·ver·seas (ō´ vər sēz´) *adv.* Across the seas; abroad: *Jane lived overseas in Europe for years.*

P

pack·age (păk´ ĭj) *n., pl.* **packages** A wrapped or boxed object; a parcel.

pa·ja·mas (pə jä´ məz) *or* (pə jăm´ əz) *pl. n.* A loose-fitting outfit consisting of a shirt and pants, worn to sleep in or for lounging.
➤ **Word History:** from the Hindi word *pāījma,* "loose-fitting trousers," from the Persian words *pāī,* "leg," and *jāmah,* "garment."

pan·ic (păn´ ĭk) *v.* **panicked, panicking** A sudden overwhelming terror: *People sometimes panic when they are frightened.*

pan·to·mime (păn´ tə mīm´) *n., pl.* **pantomimes** Acting that consists mostly of gestures and other body movement without speech.

pan·try (păn´ trē) *n., pl.* **pantries** A small room or closet, usually next to the kitchen, where items such as dry goods and silverware are stored.

Spelling Dictionary

pants (pănts) *pl. n.* An outer garment for covering the body from the waist to the ankles, divided into sections to fit each leg separately. [Short for **pantaloons.**]

par·a·graph (păr´ ə grăf´) *n., pl.* **paragraphs** A division of a piece of writing that begins on a new, usually indented line and that consists of one or more sentences on a single idea or aspect of the subject. ➤ **Word History:** from the Greek word *paragraphein,* "to write beside."

par·al·lel (păr´ ə lĕl´) *adj.* Lying the same distance apart at all points: *road parallel to the river.* —*n., pl.* **parallels** Any of the lines considered to encircle the earth parallel to the equator, used to represent degrees of latitude.

par·a·med·ic (păr´ ə **mĕd**´ ĭk) *n., pl.* **paramedics** A person who is trained to give emergency treatment or to assist medical professionals.

par·don (pär´ dn) *v.* **pardoned, pardoning** To make allowance for; excuse.

par·ti·cle (pär´ tĭ kəl) *n., pl.* **particles** A very small piece of solid matter; a speck: *particles of dust.*

part·ner (pärt´ nər) *n., pl.* **partners** One of two or more persons associated in business.

part-time (pärt´ tīm´) *adj.* For or during only part of the usual or standard working time.

pas·sage (păs´ ĭj) *n., pl.* **passages 1.** A narrow path or channel. **2.** A part of a written work or piece of music.

pas·sen·ger (păs´ ən jər) *n., pl.* **passengers** A person riding in or on a vehicle or vessel.

pas·teur·ize (păs´ chə rīz´) *v.* **pasteurized, pasteurizing** To treat (a liquid) by heat in order to kill bacteria. ➤ **Word History:** after Louis Pasteur, the scientist who invented the treatment.

pas·try (pā´ strē) *n., pl.* **pastries** Baked foods, such as pie or tarts, made from a dough of flour, water, shortening, and other ingredients.

pat·i·o (păt´ ē ō´) *n., pl.* **patios** An outdoor space for dining or recreation, next to a house or apartment. ➤ **Word History:** from Spanish, possibly from a word meaning "pasture."

paramedics

pa·tri·ot (pā´ trē ət) *n., pl.* **patriots** A person who loves, supports, and defends his or her country.

pa·tri·ot·ic (pā´ trē ŏt´ ĭk) *adj.* Feeling or expressing love for one's country.

pat·tern (păt´ ərn) *n., pl.* **patterns** An artistic design used for decoration.

pave·ment (pāv´ mənt) *n., pl.* **pavements** A hard, smooth surface of concrete, asphalt, brick, or a similar material, as for a road or sidewalk.

ped·al (pĕd´ l) *n., pl.* **pedals** A lever, as on a piano, that is worked by the foot. —*v.* **pedaled, pedaling** To ride a bicycle or tricycle. ♦ *These sound alike* **pedal, peddle.**

ped·dle (pĕd´ l) *v.* **peddled, peddling, peddles** To travel about selling (goods): *We peddle magazines to raise money for our team.* ♦ *These sound alike* **peddle, pedal** (lever).

ped·es·tal (pĕd´ ĭ stəl) *n., pl.* **pedestals** A support or base, as for a column or statue.

pe·des·tri·an (pə dĕs´ trē ən) *n., pl.* **pedestrians** A person traveling on foot.

pe·dom·e·ter (pĭ dŏm´ ĭ tər) *n., pl.* **pedometers** An instrument that measures the approximate distance a person takes on foot by keeping track of the number of steps taken.

peer (pîr) *v.* **peered, peering** To look intently, closely, or with difficulty: *peer through a window.* ♦ *These sound alike* **peer, pier.**

pen·ni·less (pĕn´ ē lĭs) *adj.* Having no money or very little; very poor.

per·cent·age (pər sĕn´ tĭj) *n., pl.* **percentages** A fraction that has 100 understood as its denominator.

per·fect (**pûr´** fĭkt) *adj.* Having no flaws, mistakes, or defects.

per·form (pər **fôrm´**) *v.* **performed, performing** To present or enact before an audience.

per·haps (pər **hăps´**) *adv.* Maybe but not definitely; possibly.

pe·ri·od (**pĭr´** ē əd) *n., pl.* **periods** An interval or portion of time.

pe·ri·od·ic (pĭr´ ē **ŏd´** ĭk) *adj.* and *adv.* **periodically** Having or repeating at regular intervals; cyclic.

per·ma·frost (**pûr´** mə frôst´) *n.* A layer of permanently frozen subsoil found throughout most of the arctic regions.

per·mit (pər **mĭt´**) *v.* **permitted, permitting** To give permission to; allow. —*n., pl.* **permits** (**pûr´** mĭt) *or* (pər **mĭt´**) A written certificate of permission, such as a license.

pes·tle (**pĕs´** əl) *or* (**pĕs´** təl) *n., pl.* **pestles** A heavy tool, often with a rounded end, used for mashing substances.

pe·tite (pə **tēt´**) *adj.* Small and slender; dainty. ➤ **Word History:** from the French word *petite,* the feminine form of *petit,* "small."

phone (fōn) *n., pl.* **phones** A telephone: *Use the phone to call me.* [Short for **telephone.**]

pho·net·ic (fə **nĕt´** ĭk) *adj.* Representing the sounds of speech with a set of symbols, each denoting a single sound. ➤ **Word History:** from the Latin word *phōnēticus,* "speech sounds," from the Greek *phōnētikos,* "vocal," ultimately from *phōnē,* "sound, voice."

photograph

pho·to (**fō´** tō) *n., pl.* **photos** An image produced by a camera. [Short for **photograph.**]

pho·to·cop·y (**fō´** tə kŏp´ ē) *v.* **photocopied, photocopying** To make a photographic reproduction of (printed, written, or graphic material). ➤ **Word History:** from the Greek word *phot-,* "light," and the Medieval Latin word *cōpia,* "transcript."

pho·to·graph (**fō´** tə grăf´) *n., pl.* **photographs** An image formed on a light-sensitive surface by a camera and developed by chemical means to produce a positive print: *a yearbook photograph* —*v.* **photographed, photographing** To take a photograph of: *to photograph the moon.* ➤ **Word History:** from the Greek words *phōt-,* "light," and *graphein,* "to write."

pho·tog·ra·phy (fə **tŏg´** rə fē) *n.* The art or process of creating images on light-sensitive surfaces.

phys·i·cal (**fĭz´** ĭ kəl) *adj.* Having to do with the body or bodily activity.

phy·si·cian (fĭ **zĭsh´** ən) *n., pl.* **physicians** A medical doctor.

pic·co·lo (**pĭk´** ə lō´) *n., pl.* **piccolos** A small flute with a range an octave above that of an ordinary flute.

pic·ture (**pĭk´** chər) *n., pl.* **pictures** A painting, drawing, or photograph of a person or thing.

pier (pîr) *n., pl.* **piers** A platform that extends into water. A pier can be used to protect a harbor or serve as a landing place for ships and boats; a dock; wharf. ♦ *These sound alike* **pier, peer.**

Spelling Dictionary

pil·lar (pĭl´ ər) *n., pl.* **pillars** An upright structure that serves as a support, as for a bridge or a building, or stands alone as a monument; column.

pi·o·neer (pī´ ə nîr´) *n., pl.* **pioneers** A person who opens up new areas of research, thought, or development. —*adj.* Leading the way; trailblazing: *a pioneer program.*

pi·rate (pī´ rĭt) *n., pl.* **pirates** A person who robs ships at sea.

plain·tiff (plān´ tĭf) *n., pl.* **plaintiffs** The party that institutes a suit in a court of law.

pla·za (plä´ zə) *or* (plăz´ ə) *n., pl.* **plazas** **1.** A public square or similar open area in a town or city. **2.** A shopping center. ➤ **Word History:** Spanish, from the Latin word *platea,* "broad street."

pleas·ant (plĕz´ ənt) *adj.* **1.** Enjoyable. **2.** Nice; agreeable.

please (plēz) *v.* **pleased, pleasing** To give (someone or something) pleasure or satisfaction.

pleas·ing (plē´ zĭng) *adj.* Giving pleasure or enjoyment; agreeable.

pleas·ure (plĕzh´ ər) *n., pl.* **pleasures** A feeling of happiness or enjoyment; delight.

plen·ti·ful (plĕn´ tĭ fəl) *adj.* In abundant supply; ample.

plight (plīt) *n., pl.* **plights** A situation of difficulty.

pluck (plŭk) *v.* **plucked, plucking** To detach by pulling with the fingers.

poise (poiz) *n.* Sureness and confidence of manner: *The child recited the poem with poise.*

poi·son (poi´ zən) *n., pl.* **poisons** A substance that causes injury, sickness, or death. —*v.* **poisoned, poisoning** To put poison on or into.

poi·son·ous (poi´ zə nəs) *adj.* Having effects like that of poison.

po·lice (pə lēs´) *n.* The department of government established to maintain order, enforce the law, and prevent and detect crime.

po·lite (pə līt´) *adj.* **politer, politest** Having or showing good manners; courteous.

pol·lute (pə lōōt´) *v.* **polluted, polluting** To make dirty or impure; contaminate.

pol·lu·tion (pə lōō´ shən) *n.* **1.** The contamination of air, water, or soil by harmful substances. **2.** Something that pollutes.

pol·y·gon (pŏl´ ē gŏn´) *n., pl.* **polygons** A flat, closed geometric figure bounded by three or more line segments: *How many sides does that polygon have?*

pon·cho (pŏn´ chō) *n., pl.* **ponchos** A cloak with a hole for a head in its center. ➤ **Word History:** American Spanish, from Spanish, "cape," perhaps a variant of *pocho,* "faded," "discolored."

pop·u·lar (pŏp´ yə lər) *adj.* Enjoyed or liked by many or most people.

pop·u·lar·i·ty (pŏp yə lăr´ ĭ tē) *n.* The quality of being popular; the state of being liked by many people.

pore (pôr) *v.* **pored, poring** To examine with great care and attention: *I pored over the book.* ♦ *These sound alike* **pore, pour.**

por·ta·ble (pôr´ tə bəl) *adj.* Capable of being carried or moved: *We bought a portable radio to take to the beach.* ➤ **Word History:** from the Latin word *portāre,* "to carry."

por·ter (pôr´ tər) *n., pl.* **porters** A person hired to carry baggage, as at a railroad station. ➤ **Word History:** from the Latin word *portāre,* "to carry."

por·trait (pôr´ trĭt) *or* (pôr´ trāt´) *n., pl.* **portraits** A painting, photograph, or other likeness of a person, especially one showing the face. ➤ **Word History:** from French, from the Old French word meaning "image," from a form of the word *portraire,* "to portray."

poncho

pos·si·bil·i·ty (pŏs´ ə bĭl´ ĭ tē) *n., pl.*
possibilities Something that is possible.
pos·si·ble (pŏs´ ə bəl) *adj.* Capable of
happening or being done.
post of·fice (pōst´ ô´ fĭs) *n., pl.* **post offices**
1. A government department or agency
responsible for sending and delivering mail.
2. A local office where mail is received, sorted,
and sent out.
post·age (pō´ stĭj) *n.* The charge for mailing
something.
pot·ter (pŏt´ ər) *n., pl.* **potters** A person who
makes pottery.
pounce (pouns) *v.* **pounced, pouncing**
To spring or swoop suddenly so as to seize
something.
pour (pôr) *v.* **poured, pouring** To flow
or cause to flow in a steady stream.
♦ *These sound alike* **pour, pore.**
pout (pout) *v.* **pouted, pouting** To show
disappointment or displeasure.
prac·tice (prăk´ tĭs) *v.* **practiced,**
practicing To do or work over and over
in order to acquire skill.
praise (prāz) *v.* **praised, praising** To express
approval or admiration for.
praise·wor·thy (prāz´ wûr´ thē) *adj.*
Deserving of praise: *Her work for the charity
is praiseworthy.*
pre- A prefix that means "earlier," "before,"
or "in advance": *preview.*
pre·cise (prĭ sīs´) *adj.* Exact.
pre·dict (prĭ dĭkt´) *v.* **predicted,**
predicting To tell about in advance. ➤ **Word**
History: from the Latin word *praedict: prae,*
"before," + *dīcere,* "to say."
pre·fer (prĭ fûr´) *v.* **preferred, preferring**
To like better.
pre·fix (prē´ fĭks) *n., pl.* **prefixes** A word part
added to the beginning of a base word
to change the meaning of the word. For
example, word parts *dis-* in *dislike, re-* in *repeat,*
and *un-* in *unable* are prefixes.
pre·flight (prē´ flīt´) *adj.* Occurring before
flight.
pre·heat (prē hēt´) *v.* **preheated, preheating**
To heat (an oven, for example) beforehand.

pre·judge (prē jŭj´) *v.* **prejudged, prejudging**
To judge beforehand without adequate evidence.
prej·u·dice (prĕj ə dĭs) *n., pl.* **prejudices**
A strong feeling or opinion formed unfairly or
without knowing all the facts.
pre·miere (prĭ mîr´) *or* (prĭ myâr´) *n., pl.*
premieres The first public performance, as of
a movie or a play.
pre·pare (prĭ pâr´) *v.* **prepared, preparing**
To make ready beforehand for some purpose,
task, or event.
prep·o·si·tion (prĕp´ ə zĭsh´ ən) *n., pl.*
prepositions A word or phrase placed before
a noun or pronoun that shows the relationship
between that noun or pronoun and another
word. Some common English prepositions are
at, by, from, in, of, on, to, and *with.*
pres·i·dent (prĕz´ ĭ dənt) *n., pl.* **presidents**
1. The chief executive of a republic, such as the
United States. **2.** The chief officer of a
company, organization, or institution.

potter

pressurize | pupil

pres·sur·ize (prĕsh´ ə rīz´) *v.* **pressurized, pressurizing** To keep an enclosed space at normal air pressure.

pre·sume (prĭ zōōm´) *v.* **presumed, presuming** To assume to be true in the absence of proof; to take for granted.

pre·tend (prĭ tĕnd´) *v.* **pretended, pretending 1.** To claim insincerely or falsely. **2.** To make believe.

pre·view (prē´ vyōō´) *n., pl.* **previews** A showing of something, as a movie, to an invited audience before presenting it to the public.

pri·mar·y co·lor (prī´ mĕr´ ē kŭl ər) *n.* Any of the three colors of pigment, red, blue, and yellow, from which pigment of any color can be made by mixing.

print (prĭnt) *v.* **printed, printing** To produce on a paper surface by means of pressed type, an electronic printer, or similar means.

pri·or (prī´ ər) *adj.* Preceding in time or order.

prize (prīz) *n., pl.* **prizes** Something offered or won as an award for superiority or victory.

pro-[1] A prefix that means: **1.** Favor or support: *propose.* **2.** Acting as; substituting for: *pronoun.*

pro-[2] A prefix that means "before; in front of": *proceed.*

prob·a·ble (prŏb´ ə bəl) *adj.* Likely but not certain to happen or be true.

probe (prōb) *n., pl.* **probes** An action, expedition, or device designed to research or investigate an unknown region: *a space probe.*

proc·ess (prŏs´ ĕs´) *n., pl.* **processes** A series of steps, actions, motions, or operations that bring about or lead to a result: *Making a movie is a long process.*

pro·duce (prə dōōs´) *v.* **produced, producing 1.** To bring forth; yield. **2.** To create by mental or physical effort: *to produce a poem* —(prŏd´ ōōs) *or* (prō´ dōōs´) *n.* Farm products: *Zack bought some fresh produce at the farm stand.*

prog·ress (prŏg´ rĕs´) *or* (prŏg´ rəs) *n.* **1.** Steady improvement: *He has made good progress learning piano.* **2.** Onward improvement; advance. —(prə grĕs´) *v.* **progressed, progressing** To move along; advance; proceed.

prom·ise (prŏm´ ĭs) *n., pl.* **promises** A statement that one will or will not do something; a vow. —*v.* **promised, promising** To say as a promise; pledge.

pro·mo·tion (prə mō´ shən) *n., pl.* **promotions 1.** Advancement in rank, position, or class: *a job promotion.* **2.** Advertising.

prop·er (prŏp´ ər) *adj.* Suitable; appropriate.

pro·po·sal (prə pō´ zəl) *n., pl.* **proposals 1.** The act of proposing an offer. **2.** A plan or scheme offered for consideration.

pro·pose (prə pōz´) *v.* **proposed, proposing** To put forward for consideration; suggest.

pros·e·cute (prŏs´ ĭ kyōōt´) *v.* **prosecuted, prosecuting** To initiate or conduct a legal action against (someone).

pros·pect (prŏs´ pĕkt´) *n., pl.* **prospects** Something expected or foreseen; a possibility —*v.* **prospected, prospecting** To explore (a region) in search of mineral deposits or oil.

pro·tect (prə tĕkt´) *v.* **protected, protecting** To keep safe from harm, attack, or injury; guard.

pro·test (prə tĕst´) *or* (prō´ tĕst´) *v.* **protested, protesting** To express strong objections to (something), as in a formal statement or public demonstration.

pro·vide (prə vīd´) *v.* **provided, providing** To give something needed or useful; supply.

pub·lish (pŭb´ lĭsh) *v.* **published, publishing** To print and offer for public sale or distribution.

pu·pil (pyōō´ pəl) *n., pl.* **pupils** A student receiving instruction from a teacher.

produce

pur·chase (pûr´ chǐs) *v.* **purchased, purchasing** To buy.

pur·suit (pər sōot´) *n., pl.* **pursuits** The act of chasing.

puz·zle (pǔz´ əl) *n., pl.* **puzzles 1.** Something that is hard to understand; mystery. **2.** A problem, toy, or game that makes one think and tests one's skill.

Q

quad·ru·ped (kwŏd´ rə pĕd´) *n., pl.* **quadrupeds** An animal having four feet, such as most reptiles and mammals.

quar·rel (kwôr´ əl) *n., pl.* **quarrels** An angry argument or dispute.

quar·ter (kwôr´ tər) *n., pl.* **quarters 1.** Any of four equal parts into which something can be divided. **2.** A coin of the United States or Canada that is worth twenty-five cents.

quar·tet (kwôr tĕt´) *n., pl.* **quartets** A group of four singers or four instrumentalists.

ques·tion (kwĕs´ chən) *n., pl.* **questions** Something that is asked.

quick-wit·ted (kwĭk´ wĭt´ ĭd) *adj.* Mentally alert; clever.

qui·et (kwī´ ĭt) *adj.* **quieter, quietest** Making little or no noise: *quiet neighbors.*

quiz (kwĭz) *v.* **quizzed, quizzing 1.** To question closely; interrogate. **2.** To test the knowledge of by asking questions.

quarter

Pronunciation Key

ă	pat	ŏ	pot	ûr	fur
ā	pay	ō	go	*th*	**the**
âr	care	ô	paw	th	thin
ä	father	ôr	for	hw	whoop
är	farm	oi	oil	zh	usual
ĕ	pet	ŏŏ	book	ə	ago, item,
ē	be	ōō	boot		pencil,
ĭ	pit	yōō	cute		atom,
ī	ice	ou	out		circus
îr	near	ŭ	cut	ər	butter

R

ra·di·ance (rā´ dē əns) *n.* The quality or state of being radiant.

ra·di·ant (rā´ dē ənt) *adj.* Filled with brightness; beaming.

raise (rāz) *v.* **raised, raising 1.** To move to a higher position; lift. **2.** To increase.

rare·ly (râr´ lē) *adv.* Infrequently; seldom.

ra·tio (rā´ shō) *or* (rā´ shē ō´) *n., pl.* **ratios** A relationship in amount, number, or size of two things. For example, if there are ten students and one teacher in a room, the ratio of students to teachers is ten to one or 10:1.

re- A prefix that means: **1.** Again. **2.** Back; backward.

re·act (rē ăkt´) *v.* **reacted, reacting** To act in response, as to an experience or the behavior of another.

re·ac·tion (rē ăk´ shən) *n., pl.* **reactions** A response to something.

re·al es·tate (rē´ əl ĭ stāt´) *or* (rēl´ ĭ stāt´) *n.* Land, including all the permanent buildings and natural resources on it.

re·al·ize (rē´ ə līz´) *v.* **realized, realizing** To understand completely or correctly; grasp.

reap (rēp) *v.* **reaped, reaping 1.** To cut (grain or a similar crop) for harvest, as with a scythe: *reap wheat.* **2.** A To gain as a result of effort.

rear (rêr) *n.* The area or direction closest to or at the back.

rea·son (rē´ zən) *n., pl.* **reasons** A fact or cause that explains why something exists or occurs.

re·ceive (rĭ sēv´) *v.* **received, receiving** To get or acquire (something given, offered, or transmitted).

re·cent (rē´ sənt) *adj.* Of, belonging to, or occurring at a time immediately before the present.

re·cord (rĭ kôrd´) *v.* **recorded, recording** To store (sound or images) in some permanent form. —*n.* (rĕk´ ərd´) *pl.* **records** The highest or lowest measurement known, as in a sports event or weather readings.

re·count (rĭ kount´) *v.* **recounted, recounting** To count again.

re·cov·er·y (rĭ kŭv´ ə rē) *n., pl.* **recoveries** A return to a normal condition, as of health.

rec·tan·gle (rĕk´ tăng´ gəl) *n., pl.* **rectangles** A four-sided plane figure with four right angles.

re·di·rect (rē dĭ rĕkt´) *v.* **redirected, redirecting** To change the course or direction of.

ref·uge (rĕf´ yōōj) *n., pl.* **refuges** Protection or shelter from danger or trouble.

re·fuse (rĭ fyōōz´) *v.* **refused, refusing** To turn down.

re·gal (rē´ gəl) *adj.* **1.** Of or relating to a king; royal. **2.** Befitting a king: *The king gave a regal wave to his subjects.*

reg·i·ment (rĕj´ ə mənt) *n., pl.* **regiments** A unit of soldiers, composed of two or more battalions.

re·hears·al (rĭ hûr´ səl) *n., pl.* **rehearsals** A private practicing, as of a play, in preparation for a public performance.

re·hearse (rĭ hûrs´) *v.* **rehearsed, rehearsing** To practice in preparation for a performance.

re·la·ted (rĭ lā´ tĭd) *adj.* Connected by kinship, marriage, or common origin.

rel·a·tive (rĕl´ ə tĭv) *n., pl.* **relatives** A person related to another by family.

re·lease (rĭ lēs´) *v.* **released, releasing** To set free; let go.

re·lo·cate (rē lō´ kāt) *v.* **relocated, relocating** To establish or become established in a new place.

re·main (rĭ mān´) *v.* **remained, remaining** To continue to be in the same state or condition.

re·mark (rĭ märk´) *v.* **remarked, remarking** To express as a comment.

re·mote (rĭ mōt´) *adj.* **remoter, remotest** **1.** Far away: *a remote island.* **2.** Distant in time or relationship: *The story takes place in the remote past.*

re·pair (rĭ pâr´) *v.* **repaired, repairing** To put back into proper or useful condition; fix; mend.

re·peat (rĭ pēt´) *v.* **repeated, repeating** To say, do, or go through again.

re·ply (rĭ plī´) *v.* **replied, replying** To give an answer.

re·port (rĭ pôrt´) *n., pl.* **reports** **1.** A spoken or written description: *weather report.* **2.** A formal account of the activities of a group. —*v.* **reported, reporting** **1.** To provide an account for publication. **2.** To present oneself.
➤ **Word History:** from the Latin word *reportāre*, "to report": *re-*, "back," and *portāre*, "to carry."

rep·re·sent (rĕp´ rĭ zĕnt´) *v.* **represented, representing** To act for: *Lawyers represent their clients in court.*

re·proach (rĭ prōch´) *v.* **reproached, reproaching** To express disapproval of.

re·quire (rĭ kwīr´) *v.* **required, requiring** **1.** To need or call for. **2.** To demand; order: *The form requires two signatures.*

res·cue (rĕs´ kyōō) *v.* **rescued, rescuing** **1.** To save from danger or harm. **2.** To set free, as from danger or imprisonment; save.

re·search (rĭ sûrch´) *n.* Careful study of a given subject, field, or problem, undertaken to discover facts or principles.

repair

re·spect (rĭ **spĕkt´**) *v.* **respected, respecting**
To avoid violation of or interference with. —*n.*
Willingness to show consideration or appreciation.
➤ **Word History:** from the Latin word
respicere, "to look back at."

re·spond (rĭ **spŏnd´**) *v.* **responded,
responding** To make a reply; answer.

re·sult (rĭ **zŭlt´**) *v.* **resulted, resulting**
To come about as a consequence. —*n., pl.*
results The consequence of a particular action
or course; an outcome.

re·treat (rĭ **trēt´**) *v.* **retreated, retreating**
To fall or draw back.

ret·ro·spect (**rĕt´** rə spĕkt´) *n.* A review,
survey, or contemplation of things in the past.
➤ **Word History:** from the Latin word
retrōspectus, "to look back at."
◇ *Idiom* **in retrospect** Looking backward
or reviewing the past: *In retrospect, last year was
pretty good.*

re·verse (rĭ **vûrs´**) *v.* **reversed, reversing**
To turn around to the opposite direction.

re·vert (rĭ **vûrt´**) *v.* **reverted, reverting**
To return or go back to a former condition,
belief, or interest.

re·vise (rĭ **vīz´**) *v.* **revised, revising**
To prepare a newly edited version of (a text).

rev·o·lu·tion (rĕv´ ə **lōō´** shən) *n., pl.*
revolutions A single complete cycle of motion
around a point in a closed path, as of a planet
around the sun.

rhine·stone (**rīn´** stōn´) *n., pl.* **rhinestones**
A colorless artificial gem of glass or paste
having facets in imitation of a diamond.
➤ **Word History:** after the Rhine, a river
in Germany.

rhom·bus (**rŏm´** bəs) *n., pl.* **rhombuses**
or **rhombi** A figure with four equal sides whose
opposite sides are parallel.

rig·ging (**rĭg´** ĭng) *n.* The system of ropes,
chains, and tackle used to support and control
the masts, sails, and yards of a sailing vessel.

right an·gle (**rīt´** ăng´ gəl) *n., pl.* **right angles**
An angle formed by the perpendicular
intersection of two straight lines; an angle of 90°.

ri·ot (**rī´** ət) *n., pl.* **riots** Disturbance created
by a large number of people. —*v.* **rioted,
rioting** To take part in a riot.

rise (rīz) *v.* **rose, rising 1.** To move from
a lower to higher position; ascend **2.** To stand
after sitting or lying. **3.** To increase in size,
volume, or level.

rit·u·al (**rĭch´** ōō əl) *n., pl.* **rituals** Being part
of a routine.

ro·bot (**rō´** bŏt´) *n., pl.* **robots** A machine
that can perform human tasks or imitate
human actions. A robot has a computer that
processes information, such as commands.

ro·de·o (**rō´** dē ō´) *n., pl.* **rodeos** A show in
which cowhands display their skill in riding
horses and bulls and compete in events such as
roping cattle. ➤ **Word History:** from the
Spanish word *rodeo,* "corral," from the Latin
word *rota,* "wheel."

ro·ta·tion (rō tā´ shən) *n., pl.* **rotations**
The act or process of turning around a center
or axis: *the rotation of Earth.*

rhinestone

rough (rŭf) *adj.* **rougher, roughest 1.** Bumpy or uneven; not smooth. **2.** Not calm.

route (rōōt) *or* (rout) *n., pl.* **routes** A road or course for traveling from one place to another.

rou·tine (rōō tēn´) *n., pl.* **routines** A series of activities performed or meant to be performed regularly; a standard or usual procedure.

row·dy (rou´ dē) *adj.* **rowdier, rowdiest** Disorderly, rough.

roy·al (roi´ əl) *adj.* Of or having to do with a queen or king.

ru·in (rōō´ ĭn) *v.* **ruined, ruining** To damage beyond repair; wreck.

rup·ture (rŭp´ chər) *v.* **ruptured, rupturing** The process or an instance of breaking open or bursting. ➤ **Word History:** from the Latin word *ruptūra,* from *rumpere,* "to break."

S

sa·fa·ri (sə fär´ ē) *n., pl.* **safaris** A hunting trip or journey of exploration, especially in Africa: *We took pictures of zebras while on safari.* ➤ **Word History:** from the Arabic word *safarīya,* "journey."

sail·or (sā´ lər) *n., pl.* **sailors** A person who is a member of a ship's crew or who serves in a navy.

sal·sa (säl´ sə) *n., pl.* **salsas 1.** A spicy sauce of chopped, usually uncooked vegetables or fruit, especially tomatoes, onions, and chili peppers.

saxophone

2. A form of Latin American dance music. ➤ **Word History:** American Spanish, from the Spanish word meaning "sauce."

sa·lute (sə lōōt´) *v.* **saluted, saluting 1.** To show respect by raising the right hand stiffly to the forehead. **2.** To honor formally. —*n., pl.* **salutes** An act of saluting.

sat·is·fy (săt´ ĭs fī´) *v.* **satisfied, satisfying** To fulfill (a need) and give satisfaction.

Sat·ur·day (săt´ ər dē´) *or* (săt´ ər dā) *n., pl.* **Saturdays** The seventh day of the week. ➤ **Word History:** from the Roman god Saturn, the god of agriculture.

sau·cer (sô´ sər) *n., pl.* **saucers** A small, shallow dish for holding a cup.

sax·o·phone (săk´ sə fōn´) *n., pl.* **saxophones** A wind instrument having a single-reed mouthpiece, a curved conical body made of metal, and keys operated by the player's fingers: *He is learning to play a saxophone.* ➤ **Word History:** after Adolph Sax, a Belgian who invented the instrument.

scale (skāl) *n., pl.* **scales** Device for measuring weight. —*v.* **scaled, scaling** To climb up or over: *The climbers scaled the steep mountain.*

scan (skăn) *v.* **scanned, scanning** To look (something) over quickly and systematically.

scar·y (skâr´ ē) *adj.* **scarier, scariest** Causing fright or alarm.

scen·er·y (sē´ nə rē) *n., pl.* **sceneries** Backdrops, furnishings, and other items on a stage that create the setting for a theatrical production.

sched·ule (skĕj´ ōōl) *n., pl.* **schedules** A plan or program of upcoming appointments.

sci·ence (sī´ əns) *n., pl.* **sciences** The study and explanation of things that happen in nature and the universe.

scis·sors (sĭz´ ərz) *n.* A cutting tool consisting of two blades, each with a ring-shaped handle, joined on a pivot that allows the cutting edges to close against each other.

scowl (skoul) *v.* **scowled, scowling** To wrinkle or contract the brow as an expression of anger or disapproval.

scrub (skrŭb) *v.* **scrubbed, scrubbing** To rub hard in order to clean.

sculp·ture (skŭlp´ chər) *n., pl.* **sculptures**
A work of art created by shaping or making figures or designs by carving wood, chiseling stone, or casting metal.

scythe (sīth) *n., pl.* **scythes** A tool with a long curved blade and a long bent handle, used for mowing or reaping.

se·lect (sĭ lĕkt´) *v.* **selected, selecting**
To choose from among several; pick out: *Select a good book to read.*

sen·a·tor (sĕn´ ə tər) *n., pl.* **senators**
A member of a senate: *Do you know the names of the senators from your state?*

sen·tence (sĕn´ təns) *v.* **sentenced, sentencing**
The judgment of a court of law; a verdict.

se·ra·pe (sə rä´ pē) *n., pl.* **serapes** A woolen cloak with a head-hole and open sides.
➤ **Word History:** from the American Spanish word *sarape.*

se·ri·ous (sîr´ ē əs) *adj.* Grave; not humorous: *a serious mistake.* —*n.* **seriousness**
Gravity: *the seriousness of the problem.*

ser·vice (sûr´ vĭs) *n., pl.* **services 1.** The act or work of helping others; aid: *They spend their lives in service to the poor.* **2.** The act or manner of satisfying customers' requests: *The service at that restaurant is very slow.*

set (sĕt) *v.* **set, setting 1.** To put in a specific position; place. **2.** To arrange. **3.** To establish.

set·tle·ment (sĕt´ l mənt) *n., pl.* **settlements**
1. An adjustment or understanding reached, as in financial matters or business proceedings.
2. A small community; village.

sharp (shärp) *adj.* **sharper, sharpest**
Not rounded or blunt; pointed.

shovel

Pronunciation Key

ă	pat	ŏ	pot	ûr	fur
ā	pay	ō	go	*th*	the
âr	care	ô	paw	th	thin
ä	father	ôr	for	hw	whoop
är	farm	oi	oil	zh	usual
ĕ	pet	o͝o	book	ə	ago, item,
ē	be	o͞o	boot		pencil,
ĭ	pit	yo͞o	cute		atom,
ī	ice	ou	out		circus
îr	near	ŭ	cut	ər	butter

sheep·ish (shē´ pĭsh) *adj.* Embarrassed; ashamed.

shoul·der (shōl´ dər) *n., pl.* **shoulders**
The part of the human body between the neck and the upper arm.

shov·el (shŭv´ əl) *n., pl.* **shovels** A tool with a long handle and a flattened scoop. —*v.*
shoveled, shoveling To pick up or move with a shovel.

show (shō) *v.* **showed, shown** or **showed, showing** To cause or allow to be seen.

shown (shōn) *v.* A past participle of **show.**

shrink (shrĭngk) *v.* **shrank** or **shrunk, shrunk** or **shrunken** To become smaller.

shrug (shrŭg) *v.* **shrugged, shrugging**
To raise (the shoulders), especially to show doubt, disdain, or indifference.

sib·ling (sĭb´ lĭng) *n., pl.* **siblings** One of two or more people having one or both parents in common; a brother or a sister.

si·es·ta (sē ĕs´ tə) *n., pl.* **siestas** A rest or nap after the midday meal. ➤ **Word History:**
Spanish, from the Latin word *sexta (hōra)*, "sixth (hour)," or "midday."

sift (sĭft) *v.* **sifted, sifting** To put through a sieve or other straining device to separate fine from coarse particles.

sigh (sī) *v.* **sighed, sighing** To let out a long, deep breath because of fatigue, sorrow, or relief.

sight (sīt) *n., pl.* **sights 1.** The ability to see.
2. The field of vision: *out of our sight.*
♦ *These sound alike* **sight, cite, site.**

Spelling Dictionary

sombrero

sign (sīn) *n., pl.* **signs** Something, such as a poster, that conveys information.

si·lent (sī´ lənt) *adj.* Making or having no sound; quiet.

sim·ple (sĭm´ pəl) *adj.* **simpler, simplest** Not complicated; easy.

sim·ply (sĭm´ plē) *adv.* **1.** In an uncomplicated or easy way; plainly. **2.** Merely; just.

sin·cere (sĭn sîr´) *adj.* Not lying or pretending; honest; genuine.

sit (sĭt) *v.* **sat, sitting 1.** To rest on the lower part of the body where the hips and legs join. **2.** To be situated; lie. **3.** To lie or rest.

site (sīt) *n., pl.* **sites** A position or location.
♦ *These sound alike* **site, cite, sight.**

skel·e·ton (skĕl´ ĭ tn) *n., pl.* **skeletons** The internal structure composed of bone and cartilage that supports and protects the soft organs of a vertebrate.

skim (skĭm) *v.* **skimmed, skimming 1.** To remove (floating matter) from a liquid. **2.** To throw so as to bounce or slide. **3.** To glide or pass quickly and lightly over or along a surface. **4.** To read quickly, skipping over parts.

skir·mish (skûr´ mĭsh) *n., pl.* **skirmishes** A minor battle between small bodies of troops.

skit (skĭt) *n., pl.* **skits** A short, usually humorous theatrical sketch.

sleeve (slēv) *n., pl.* **sleeves** The part of a piece of clothing that covers all or part of the arm.

slight (slīt) *adj.* **slighter, slightest** Small in amount or degree.

slith·er (slĭ*th*´ ər) *v.* **slithered, slithering** To glide or slide like a snake.

smear (smîr) *v.* **smeared, smearing** To cover or spread with a sticky or greasy substance. —*n., pl.* **smears 1.** A stain or blotch. **2.** A substance or preparation placed on a slide for microscopic study.

smirk (smûrk) *v.* **smirked, smirking** To smile in an annoying manner that expresses too much approval of oneself.

snap (snăp) *v.* **snapped, snapping 1.** To make or cause to make a sharp cracking sound. **2.** To bite, seize, or grasp at suddenly and eagerly.

sneer (snîr) *v.* **sneered, sneering** To show contempt or scorn by raising one corner of the upper lip slightly.

soar (sôr) *v.* **soared, soaring** To rise, fly, or glide high in the air.

so·ci·e·ty (sə sī´ ĭ tē) *n., pl.* **societies** An organization or association of people sharing common interests or activities.

sol·id (sŏl´ ĭd) *adj.* **1.** Having a definite shape; not liquid or gaseous. **2.** Firm or compact.

so·lu·tion (sə lōō´ shən) *n., pl.* **solutions 1.** An answer to a problem. **2.** The method or procedure used in solving an equation or problem.

som·ber (sŏm´ bər) *adj.* **1.** Dark and dull; gloomy: *The somber sky was the first sign of the approaching storm.* **2.** Serious: *The bad news put us in a somber mood.*

som·bre·ro (sŏm brâr´ ō) *n., pl.* **sombreros** A large straw hat with round, upcurled brim.
➤ **Word History:** from the Spanish word *sombra,* "shade," perhaps from the Latin word *subumbrāre,* "to cast a shadow."

some·bod·y (sŭm´ bŏ dē) *pron.* An unspecified or unknown person; someone.

son-in-law (sŭn´ ĭn lô´) *n., pl.* **sons-in-law** The husband of one's daughter.

sor·row (sŏr´ ō) *n., pl.* **sorrows** Grief or sadness caused by loss or injury.

sou·ve·nir (sōō´ və nîr´) *or* (sōō´ və nîr´) *n., pl.* **souvenirs** A token kept as a remembrance, as of a place or event.

space·craft (spās´ krăft´) *n., pl.* **spacecraft** A vehicle designed for space travel.

spat·u·la (spăch´ ə lə) *n., pl.* **spatulas** A tool with a broad, flat, flexible blade used to mix, spread, or lift material, such as food.

spe·cial (spĕsh´ əl) *adj.* Different from what is common or usual.

spe·cial·ist (spĕsh´ ə lĭst) *n., pl.* **specialists** A person whose work is restricted to a particular activity or to a particular branch of study, such as a doctor who specializes in a particular branch of medicine.

spec·ta·cle (spĕk´ tə kəl) *n., pl.* **spectacles** An unusual or impressive public show, as of fireworks. ➤ **Word History:** from the Latin word *spectāculum,* from *specere,* "to look."

spec·tac·u·lar (spĕk tăk´ yə lər) *adj.* Of the nature of a spectacle; impressive or sensational. ➤ **Word History:** from the Latin word *spectāculum,* from *specere,* "to look."

spec·ta·tor (spĕk´ tā´ tər) *n., pl.* **spectators** A person who watches an event but does not take part in it; viewer. ➤ **Word History:** from the Latin word *spectāculum,* from *specere,* "to look."

spec·trum (spĕk´ trəm) *n., pl.* **spectra** or **spectrums 1.** The bands of color that are seen when light is broken up, as by a prism. You can see the colors of the spectrum in a rainbow. **2.** A broad range of related qualities, ideas, or activites.

spi·der (spī´ dər) *n., pl.* **spiders** An animal with eight legs and two body parts that usually spins a web to catch insects.

spin·ach (spĭn´ ĭch) *n.* A plant grown for its dark green leaves. Spinach is eaten as a vegetable.

spider: a tarantula

Pronunciation Key

ă	pat	ŏ	pot	ûr	fur
ā	pay	ō	go	*th*	**the**
âr	care	ô	paw	th	**thin**
ä	father	ôr	for	hw	**wh**oop
är	farm	oi	oil	zh	usual
ě	pet	ŏŏ	book	ə	ago, item,
ē	be	ōō	boot		pencil,
ĭ	pit	yōō	cute		atom,
ī	ice	ou	out		circus
îr	near	ŭ	cut	ər	butter

sponge (spŭnj) *n., pl.* **sponges** A soft, porous material used for bathing and cleaning.

spo·rad·ic (spə răd´ ĭk) *adj.* Occurring at irregular intervals; having no pattern or order. —*adv.* **sporadically.**

spot·light (spŏt´ līt´) *n., pl.* **spotlights** A strong beam of light that illuminates a small area, often used to draw attention to an actor on a stage.

sprawl (sprôl) *v.* **sprawled, sprawling** To sit or lie with the body and limbs spread out widely.

squall (skwôl) *n., pl.* **squalls** A brief, sudden, and violent windstorm, often accompanied by rain or snow.

square (skwâr) *n., pl.* **squares** A rectangle having four equal sides.

squee·gee (skwē´ jē) *n., pl.* **squeegees** A tool having a rubber blade that is drawn across a surface to remove water from it, as in washing windows.

squint (skwĭnt) *v.* **squinted, squinting** To look with the eyes partly closed.

squirm (skwûrm) *v.* **squirmed, squirming** To twist about; wiggle.

stair·way (stâr´ wā´) *n., pl.* **stairways** A staircase.

stale (stāl) *adj.* **staler, stalest** Not fresh.

sta·tis·tics (stə tĭs´ tĭks) *pl. n.* A collection or set of numerical data.

stead·y (stĕd´ ē) *adj.* **steadier, steadiest** Unwavering, as in purpose; steadfast. —*adv.* **steadily** *It rained steadily all day.*

steal (stēl) *v.* **stole, stolen, stealing 1.** To take without right or permission. **2.** In baseball, to gain (another base) without the ball being batted, by running to the base during the delivery of the pitch.
♦ *These sound alike* **steal, steel.**

stealth (stĕlth) *n.* The act of moving or proceeding in a quiet, secretive way so as to avoid notice.

steel (stēl) *n.* Any of various hard, strong alloys of iron and carbon, often with other metals added to give certain desired properties, widely used as a structural material.
♦ *These sound alike* **steel, steal.**

steep (stēp) *adj.* **steeper, steepest** Rising or falling abruptly; sharply sloped: *a steep hill.*

stel·lar (stĕl´ər) *adj.* Of, relating to, or consisting of stars.

step·child (stĕp´ chīld´) *n., pl.* **stepchildren** A child of one's wife or husband by an earlier marriage or relationship.

stew (stōō) *n., pl.* **stews** A dish cooked by boiling slowly that is often a mixture of meat and vegetables.

stin·gy (stĭn´ jē) *adj.* **stingier, stingiest** Not willing to give or share.

stom·ach·ache (stŭm´ ək āk´) *n., pl.* **stomachaches** Pain in the stomach or abdomen.

stor·age (stôr´ ĭj) *n.* The act of storing or the state of being stored.

strange (strānj) *adj.* **stranger, strangest** Previously unknown; unfamiliar.

strat·e·gy (străt´ ə jē) *n., pl.* **strategies** A clever system or plan of action.

stray (strā) *adj.* Lost.

strength (strĕngkth) *n.* The state, quality, or property of being strong.

strike (strīk) *v.* **struck, striking** To hit with or as if with the hand. —*n., pl.* **strikes** In bowling, the knocking down of all ten pins with one roll of the ball.

strip (strĭp) *v.* **stripped, stripping** To remove the covering from.

stroll (strōl) *v.* **strolled, strolling** To walk or wander around in a slow, relaxed way.

strug·gle (strŭg´ əl) *v.* **struggled, struggling** To make a great effort; strive.

summit

stud·y (stŭd´ ē) *v.* **studied, studying** To examine closely and carefully.

stum·ble (stŭm´ bəl) *v.* **stumbled, stumbling 1.** To trip and almost fall. **2.** To come upon accidentally.

stun (stŭn) *v.* **stunned, stunning** To shock or confuse.

stur·dy (stûr´ dē) *adj.* **sturdier, sturdiest** Substantially made or built; stout.

styl·ish (stī´ lĭsh) *adj.* Conforming to the current style; fashionable.

sub·due (səb dōō´) *v.* **subdued, subduing** To quiet or bring under control.

sub·ject (sŭb´ jĭkt) *n., pl.* **subjects** Something thought about or discussed; topic.

sub·stance (sŭb´ stəns) *n., pl.* **substances** A material of a particular kind or composition.

suc·ceed (sək sēd´) *v.* **succeeded, succeeding** To carry out something desired or attempted.

suf·fer (sŭf´ ər) *v.* **suffered, suffering** To feel pain, hurt, or distress.

sug·gest (səg jĕst´) *or* (sə jĕst´) *v.* **suggested, suggesting** To offer for consideration or action.

sum (sŭm) *n., pl.* **sums** A number obtained as the result of adding numbers.

sum·mit (sŭm´ ĭt) *n., pl.* **summits** The highest point or part; peak; not the base: *the summit of the mountain.*

sun·ny (sŭn´ ē) *adj.* **sunnier, sunniest** Full of sunshine.

su·per·vise (sōō´ pər vīz´) *v.* **supervised, supervising** To direct, oversee, and manage.

sup·ply (sə plī´) *n., pl.* **supplies** Materials or provisions stored and dispensed when needed.

sup·port (sə pôrt´) *v.* **supported, supporting** To keep from falling; hold in position.

sup·pose (sə pōz´) *v.* **supposed, supposing** To guess or imagine.

sup·press (sə prĕs´) *v.* **suppressed, suppressing 1.** To put an end to forcibly: *suppress a rebellion.* **2.** To keep back; restrain: *suppress a laugh.*

sur·face (sûr´ fəs) *n., pl.* **surfaces 1.** Outer layer. **2.** One side of a solid object. **3.** Outward appearance. —*v.* **surfaced, surfacing 1.** To form or cover the top of. **2.** To rise to the top layer of a liquid.

sur·geon (sûr´ jən) *n., pl.* **surgeons** A doctor who specializes in surgery.

sur·ger·y (sûr´ jə rē) *n., pl.* **surgeries** An operation that often involves the removal or replacement of a diseased organ or tissue.

sur·prise (sər prīz´) *v.* **surprised, surprising** To come upon suddenly and unexpectedly. —*n., pl.* **surprises** Something unexpected.

sur·round (sə round´) *v.* **surrounded, surrounding** To extend on all sides of.

sur·vey (sûr´ vā´) *n., pl.* **surveys** A big investigation, as a sampling of opinions: *A survey of voters showed that people want honest government.*

sur·vive (sər vīv´) *v.* **survived, surviving** To stay alive or in existence.

sus·pense (sə spĕns´) *n.* Anxious uncertainty about what will happen. —*adj.* **suspenseful** Causing suspense.

sus·pi·cious (sŭ spĭsh´ əs) *adj.* Distrustful; doubtful. —*adv.* **suspiciously** In a suspicious way.

sway (swā) *v.* **swayed, swaying** To swing or cause to swing back and forth or from side to side.

sweet (swēt) *adj.* **sweeter, sweetest 1.** Having a pleasing taste, like that of sugar. **2.** Gentle and kind.

swift (swĭft) *adj.* **swifter, swiftest** Moving or able to move very fast; quick; speedy.

sym·pho·ny (sĭm´ fə nē) *n., pl.* **symphonies 1.** A long musical composition for orchestra. **2.** A symphony orchestra, a large orchestra with string, wind, and percussion sections. ➤ **Word History:** from the Latin word *symphōnia,* from the Greek word *sumphōnos,* "harmonious sound."

Pronunciation Key

ă	pat	ŏ	pot	ûr	fur
ā	pay	ō	go	*th*	**the**
âr	care	ô	paw	th	**thin**
ä	father	ôr	for	hw	**whoop**
är	farm	oi	**oil**	zh	usual
ĕ	pet	ŏŏ	book	ə	ago, item,
ē	be	ōō	boot		pencil,
ĭ	pit	yōō	cute		atom,
ī	ice	ou	**out**		circus
îr	near	ŭ	cut	ər	butter

T

tal·ent (tăl´ ənt) *n., pl.* **talents** A marked natural ability, as for artistic accomplishment.

tal·ly (tal´ ē) *n., pl.* **tallies 1.** A reckoning or score. **2.** A vertical mark used to record a number of actions or objects.

tam·bou·rine (tăm´ bə rēn´) *n., pl.* **tambourines** A percussion instrument consisting of a small drumhead with small metal disks fitted into the rim that jingle when the instrument is struck or shaken. ➤ **Word History:** from the Old French word *tambourin,* "small drum."

tar·dy (tär´ dē) *adj.* **tardier, tardiest** Occurring, arriving, acting, or done later than expected. —*n.* **tardiness** The condition of being late.

tambourine

telescope

tax·i (tăk´ sē) *v.* **taxied, taxiing** or **taxying** To move slowly over the surface of the ground or water before takeoff or after landing: *taxi down the runway.*

team·mate (tēm´ māt´) *n., pl.* **teammates** A member of one's own team.

tel·e·com·mute (tĕl´ ĭ kə myōōt) *v.* **telecommuted, telecommuting** To work from home using a computer connected to the network of one's employer. ➤ **Word History:** *tele,* from the Greek word *tēle,* "far off," + *commute,* from the Middle English word *commuten,* "to transform," from the Latin word *commūtāre, com-* + *mūtāre,* "to change."

tel·e·gram (tĕl´ ĭ grăm´) *n., pl.* **telegrams** A message transmitted by telegraph.

tel·e·graph (tĕl´ ĭ grăf´) *n., pl.* **telegraphs** A communications system in which a message in the form of electric impulses is sent, either by wire or radio, to a receiving station. ➤ **Word History:** from the Greek words *tēle-,* "far off," and *graphein,* "to write."

tel·e·phone (tĕl´ ə fōn´) *n., pl.* **telephones** An instrument that reproduces and receives sound, especially speech. ➤ **Word History:** from the Greek words *tēlē,* "far off," and *phōnos,* "sound."

tel·e·scope (tĕl´ ĭ skōp´) *n., pl.* **telescopes** A device that uses an arrangement of lenses or mirrors in a long tube to make distant objects appear closer. ➤ **Word History:** from the Greek word *tēleskopos,* "far-seeing": *tēle,* "far off," and *skopos,* "watcher."

tel·e·vise (tĕl´ ə vīz´) *v.* **televised, televising** To broadcast by television. ➤ **Word History:** from the Greek word *tēle,* "far off," and the Latin word *vidēre,* "to see."

tel·e·vi·sion (tĕl´ ə vĭzh´ ən) *n., pl.* **televisions** A device that receives and reproduces the images and sounds sent by a television broadcast system.

tend (tĕnd) *v.* **tended, tending** To be disposed or inclined.

ten·den·cy (tĕn´ dən sē) *n., pl.* **tendencies** A characteristic likelihood: *Linen has a tendency to wrinkle.*

ten·don (tĕn´ dən) *n., pl.* **tendons** A band of tough tissue that connects a muscle to a bone.

tense (tĕns) *adj.* Nervous.

ten·sion (tĕn´ shən) *n., pl.* **tensions 1.** The act or process of being stretched tight. **2.** Mental or nervous strain.

tent (tĕnt) *n., pl.* **tents** A portable shelter, usually made of canvas stretched over poles.

ter·rain (tə rān´) *n., pl.* **terrains 1.** Area of land; region. **2.** Surface of the land.

ter·ri·ble (tĕr´ ə bəl) *adj.* **1.** Causing great fear; dreadful. **2.** Very great or extreme; severe: *a terrible storm.* **3.** Very bad: *That was a terrible movie.* —*adv.* **terribly** In a terrible way.

ter·rif·ic (tə rĭf´ ĭk) *adj.* Very good or fine: *Your song was better than good; it was terrific.* —*adv.* **terrifically** *You dance terrifically.*

ter·ri·fy (tĕr´ ə fī´) *v.* **terrified, terrifying** To fill with terror; make deeply afraid.

ter·ror (tĕr´ ər) *n., pl.* **terrors** Intense, overpowering fear.

ter·ror·ize (tĕr´ ə rīz´) *v.* **terrorized, terrorizing** To fill or overpower with terror.

tex·ture (tĕks´ chər) *n., pl.* **textures** The look or feel of a surface: *a velvety texture.*

the·a·ter (thē´ ə tər) *n., pl.* **theaters** A building where plays or movies are presented.

the·at·ri·cal (thē ăt´ rĭ kəl) *adj.* Of, relating to, or suitable for the theater.

thief (thēf) *n., pl.* **thieves** A person who steals.

threat·en (thrĕt´ n) *v.* **threatened, threatening** To be a source of danger to; menace.

through·out (thrōō out´) *prep.* In, to, through, or during every part of. —*adv.* In or through every part.

throw (thrō) *v.* **threw, thrown 1.** To propel through the air. **2.** To hurl or fling with force.

thrown (thrōn) *v.* Past participle of **throw.**

thun·der (thŭn´ dər) *n.* The deep, rumbling noise that goes with or comes after a flash of lightning. —*v.* **thundered, thundering 1.** To produce thunder or sounds like thunder. **2.** To say angrily or to roar: *"Who sat in my chair?" thundered Papa Bear.*

Thurs·day (thûrz´ dā) *or* (thûrz´ dē) *n., pl.* **Thursdays** The fifth day of the week. ➤ **Word History:** from the Old English word *thūresdag,* "Thor's day," from the Norse god Thor.

tim·ber (tĭm´ bər) *n., pl.* **timbers** Trees or wooded land considered as a source of wood.

tire (tīr) *v.* **tired, tiring** To become weary or fatigued.

ti·tle (tīt´ l) *n., pl.* **titles** An identifying name given to a book, painting, song, or other work.

to·ma·to (tə mā´ tō) *or* (tə mä´ tō) *n., pl.* **tomatoes** The fleshy, usually reddish fruit of a widely cultivated South American plant, eaten raw or cooked as a vegetable. ➤ **Word History:** from the Spanish word *tomate,* from the Nahuatl word *tomatl.*

to·night (tə nīt´) *adv.* On or during the night of this day.

top·ic (tŏp´ ĭk) *n., pl.* **topics** The subject of a speech or piece of writing.

top-se·cret (tŏp´ sē´ krĭt) *adj.* Containing or relating to information of the highest level of national security classification.

tractor

Pronunciation Key

ă	pat	ŏ	pot	ûr	fur
ā	pay	ō	go	*th*	the
âr	care	ô	paw	th	thin
ä	father	ôr	for	hw	whoop
är	farm	oi	oil	zh	usual
ĕ	pet	o͝o	book	ə	ago, item,
ē	be	o͞o	boot		pencil,
ĭ	pit	yo͞o	cute		atom,
ī	ice	ou	out		circus
îr	near	ŭ	cut	ər	butter

torch (tôrch) *n., pl.* **torches** A device that shoots out a hot flame, as for welding or cutting metals.

tor·rid (tôr´ ĭd) *adj.* Very dry and hot; scorching: *Heat from the torrid flames was felt blocks away.*

tor·til·la (tôr tē´ yə) *n., pl.* **tortillas** A round, flat Mexican bread made from cornmeal or wheat flour and water and baked on a hot surface. ➤ **Word History:** from American Spanish, a diminutive of the Spanish word *torta,* "cake."

to·tal (tōt´ l) *v.* **totaled, totaling** To add up: *My practice time this week totaled 12 hours.* —*n., pl.* **totals** A number gotten by adding; sum: *Count the money and tell me the total.*

tow·er (tou´ ər) *n., pl.* **towers** A very tall building or a tall structure that is part of a larger building.

track (trăk) *n., pl.* **tracks** A path, course, or trail made for racing, running, or hiking.

trac·tor (trăk´ tər) *n., pl.* **tractors** A vehicle that is driven by an engine and is equipped with large tires that have deep treads. A tractor is used especially for pulling farm machinery, such as a plow or thresher.

trag·e·dy (trăj´ ĭ dē) *n., pl.* **tragedies 1.** A disastrous event; a calamity. **2.** A serious play or literary work that ends with great misfortune or ruin for the main character or characters, especially as a result of some personal flaw or weakness.

train·ing (trā´ nĭng) *n.* Instruction for a sport, art, trade, or profession.

trophy

trans·port (trăns pôrt´) *v.* **transported, transporting** To carry from one place to another.
➤ **Word History:** from the Latin word *trănsportāre: trăns-,* "across," and *portāre,* "to carry."

trans·pose (trăns pōz´) *v.* **transposed, transposing** To reverse or transfer the order or place of.

trav·el (trăv´ əl) *v.* **traveled, traveling** To go from one place to another, as on a trip; journey.

treas·ure (trĕzh´ ər) *n., pl.* **treasures** **1.** Wealth, such as jewels or money, that has been collected or hidden. **2.** A very precious or valuable person or thing.

trem·ble (trĕm´ bəl) *v.* **trembled, trembling** To shake involuntarily, as from excitement, weakness, or anger.

trem·or (trĕm´ ər) *n., pl.* **tremors** A shaking or vibrating movement, especially of the earth.

trend (trĕnd) *n., pl.* **trends** Current style.

tri- A prefix that means "three": *triangle.*

tri·al (trī´ əl) *n., pl.* **trials** The studying and deciding of a case in a court of law.

tri·an·gle (trī´ ăng´ gəl) *n., pl.* **triangles** A closed plane geometric figure formed by three points not in a straight line connected by three line segments; a polygon with three sides.

tri·cer·a·tops (trī sĕr´ ə tŏps´) *n.* A large plant-eating dinosaur having three sharp horns on its head and a bony plate covering the back of the neck.

trip·let (trĭp´ lĭt) *n., pl.* **triplets** A group or set of three of one kind.

troop (troop) *n., pl.* **troops** A group of soldiers mounted on horses or riding in motor vehicles.

tro·phy (trō´ fē) *n., pl.* **trophies** A prize given or received as a symbol of victory or achievement.

trou·ble (trŭb´ əl) *v.* **troubled, troubling** Causing difficulty.

trow·el (trou´ əl) *n., pl.* **trowels** A hand tool with a flat blade for spreading or smoothing such substances as mortar and cement.

tsu·na·mi (tsoo nä´ mē) *n., pl.* **tsunamis** A very large ocean wave that is caused by an underwater earthquake or volcanic eruption and often causes extreme destruction when it strikes land: *People left the beaches for fear of the tsunami.*
➤ **Word History:** from the Japanese words *tsu,* "port," and *nami,* "wave."

tun·dra (tŭn´ drə) *n., pl.* **tundras** A cold, treeless area of arctic regions, having permanently frozen subsoil and only low-growing mosses, lichens, and stunted shrubs as plant life.

tun·nel (tŭn´ əl) *n., pl.* **tunnels** An underground or underwater passage.

tur·bu·lence (tûr´ byə ləns) *n.* The state or quality of being agitated or disturbed.

tweez·ers (twē´ zərz) *pl. n.* Small pincers used for plucking or handling small objects.

twen·ty-two (twĕn´ tē too´) *n.* The number that comes between twenty-one and twenty-three.

twice (twīs) *adv.* Two times.

twirl (twûrl) *v.* **twirled, twirling** To spin.

ty·coon (tī koon´) *n., pl.* **tycoons** A wealthy and powerful person in business or industry.
➤ **Word History:** from the Japanese word *taikun,* title of a military leader, borrowed from Chinese, meaning "great prince."

type (tīp) *n., pl.* **types** A person or thing having the characteristics of a group or class.

U

un- A prefix that means: **1.** Not: *unable, unhappy.* **2.** Lack of: *unemployment.*

un·a·ble (ŭn ā´ bəl) *adj.* Not able; lacking the power to do something.

un·earth (ŭn ûrth´) *v.* **unearthed, unearthing, unearths** To dig up.

un·e·qual (ŭn ē´ kwəl) *adj.* Not the same; not equal.

un·e·ven (ŭn ē´ vən) *adj.* Not level, smooth, or straight.

un·for·tu·nate (ŭn fôr´ chə nĭt) *adj.* Not fortunate; not lucky.

uni- A prefix that means "one, single": *unicycle.*

u·ni·corn (yōō´ nĭ kôrn´) *n., pl.* **unicorns** An imaginary animal like a horse but with a long horn in the middle of the forehead.

u·ni·fy (yōō´ nə fī´) *v.* **unified, unifying** To make or form into a whole; unite; join.

u·nique (yōō nēk´) *adj.* Being the only one of its kind.

u·nite (yōō nīt´) *v.* **united, uniting** To join together for a common purpose.

un·known (ŭn nōn´) *adj.* **1.** Not known or familiar; strange. **2.** Not identified.

un·nec·es·sar·y (ŭn nĕs´ ĭ sĕr´ ē) *adj.* Not necessary; needless.

un·sta·ble (ŭn stā´ bəl) *adj.* **1.** Not steady or solid. **2.** Likely to change.

un·ti·dy (ŭn tī´ dē) *adj.* **untidier, untidiest** Not tidy and neat; sloppy. —*n.* **untidiness** Condition or state of being untidy.

un·wise (ŭn wīz´) *adj.* Showing a lack of wisdom; foolish.

up·heav·al (ŭp hē´ vəl) *n., pl.* **upheavals** A sudden and violent disturbance.

up·roar (ŭp´ rôr´) *n.* A condition of noisy excitement and confusion; a tumult.

up·set (ŭp sĕt´) *v.* **upset, upsetting** To distress mentally or emotionally.

up-to-date (ŭp tə dāt´) *adj.* Reflecting or informed of the latest information, changes, improvements, or style.

ur·gen·cy (ûr´ jən se) *n., pl.* **urgencies** The quality or condition of being urgent.

ur·gent (ûr´ jənt) *adj.* Calling for immediate action or attention; pressing.

u·su·al (yōō´ zhōō əl) *adj.* Happening at regular intervals or all the time: *our usual meeting time.* —*adv.* **usually** *I usually jog here.*

utensils

u·ten·sil (yōō tĕn´ səl) *n., pl.* **utensils** An instrument, implement, or container, especially one used to prepare or eat food.

va·can·cy (vā´ kən sē) *n., pl.* **vacancies** An unoccupied job, position, or place, such as a motel room.

va·cant (vā´ kənt) *adj.* Not occupied or rented.

vain (vān) *adj.* **vainer, vainest** Showing undue preoccupation with one's appearance or accomplishment; conceited.

♦ *These sound alike* **vain, vane, vein.**

val·ley (văl´ ē) *n., pl.* **valleys** A long narrow region of low land between ranges of mountains or hills, often having a river or stream running along the bottom.

vane (vān) *n., pl.* **vanes** A thin piece of wood or metal that turns on a vertical pivot to show the direction of the wind.
♦ *These sound alike* **vane, vain, vein.**

va·nil·la (və nĭl´ ə) *n.* A flavoring extract made from cured seedpods of this plant or produced artificially. —*adj.* Made or flavored with vanilla. ➤ **Word History:** from the Spanish word *vainilla*, from *vaina*, "sheath" (from the shape of the seedpods).

var·i·a·ble (vâr´ ē ə bəl) *n., pl.* **variables** A mathematical quantity that can assume any of a set of two or more values, or a symbol that represents it. —*adj.* Changeable.

var·y (vâr´ ē) *v.* **varied, varying** To undergo or show change: *The temperature varied throughout the day.*

ve·hi·cle (vē´ ĭ kəl) *n., pl.* **vehicles** Something used for carrying people or goods from one place to another, especially one that moves on wheels or runners. Cars, bicycles, and airplanes are vehicles.

vein (vān) *n., pl.* **veins** Any of a branching system of blood vessels through which blood returns to the heart.
♦ *These sound alike* **vein, vain, vane.**

ven·om (vĕn´ əm) *n., pl.* **venoms** A poison that is produced by certain snakes, spiders, scorpions, and insects, and can be transmitted to a victim by a bite or sting.

ver·dict (vûr´ dĭkt) *n., pl.* **verdicts** The decision reached by a jury at the end of a trial. ➤ **Word History:** from the Middle English word *verdit: ver*, "true," and *dit*, "speech," from the Latin words *vērus* and *dictum*.

ver·mil·ion (vər mĭl´ yən) *n.* A vivid red to reddish orange: *The tree leaves turned vermilion in October.*

ver·sa·tile (vûr´ sə təl) *or* (vûr´ sə tīl´) *adj.* Capable of doing many things well: *Its neutral color made the coat quite versatile.*

ver·sion (vûr´ zhən) *n., pl.* **versions**
1. A description or account from a specific point of view. **2.** A form or variation of an earlier original type.

weather vane

vic·to·ry (vĭk´ tə rē) *n., pl.* **victories** The defeat of an opponent or enemy; success.

vid·e·o (vĭd´ ē ō´) *n., pl.* **videos 1.** The visual part of a television broadcast. **2.** A videocassette or videotape.

vid·e·o·tape (vĭd´ ē ō tāp´) *n., pl.* **videotapes** A relatively wide magnetic tape used to record visual images and associated sound for later playback or broadcasting.

view (vyo͞o) *n., pl.* **views** A scene; something to see.

vil·lain (vĭl´ ən) *n., pl.* **villains 1.** A wicked person. **2.** A main character who harms or threatens the good or heroic characters in a story or play.

vi·o·la (vē ō´ lə) *n., pl.* **violas** A stringed instrument of the violin family, slightly larger than a violin, and having a deeper tone.

vi·o·let (vī´ ə lĭt) *n., pl.* **violets 1.** A low-growing plant having small flowers that are usually bluish purple. **2.** A reddish blue color.

vi·per (vī´ pər) *n., pl.* **vipers** Any of several poisonous snakes of northern Europe and Asia having a single pair of long, hollow fangs and a thick, heavy body.

vise (vīs) *n., pl.* **vises** A clamping device, usually consisting of a pair of jaws that are opened and closed by means of a screw or lever, used in carpentry or metalworking to hold work in position.

vi·sion·ar·y (vĭzh´ ə něr´ ē) *n., pl.* **visionaries 1.** A person who has intelligent foresight. **2.** A person who has impractical ideas; a dreamer.

vis·ta (vĭs´ tə) *n., pl.* **vistas** A distant view, especially one seen through an opening, as between buildings or trees.

vi·su·al (vĭzh´ oo əl) *adj.* Done or performed by means of sight alone.

viv·id (vĭv´ ĭd) *adj.* **1.** Having intensely bright color or colors: *a vivid blue.* **2.** Presented in a clear and striking manner; heard, seen, or felt as if real: *a vivid description.*

voice mail (vois´ māl´) *n.* A computerized system for leaving and retrieving telephone messages.

vol·can·ic (vŏl kăn´ ĭk) *adj.* Of or caused by a volcano, an opening in the earth's crust through which lava and gas flow: *Basalt is a volcanic rock.*

vol·un·teer (vŏl ən tîr´) *n., pl.* **volunteers** A person who performs or offers to perform a service of one's own free will. —*adj.* Being, consisting of, or done by volunteers. —*v.* **volunteered, volunteering** To perform or offer to perform a service of one's own free will.

voy·age (voi´ ĭj) *n., pl.* **voyages** A long journey to a distant place, made on a ship, aircraft, or spacecraft.

wage (wāj) *n., pl.* **wages** A regular payment, usually on an hourly, daily, or weekly basis, made by an employer to an employee.

vista

waist (wāst) *n., pl.* **waists** The part of the human body between the ribs and the hips.
♦ *These sound alike* **waist, waste.**

wait (wāt) *v.* **waited, waiting** To do nothing or stay in a place until something expected happens.
♦ *These sound alike* **wait, weight.**

wan·der (wŏn´ dər) *v.* **wandered, wandering** To move from place to place without a special purpose or destination; roam.

want ad (wŏnt´ ăd) *n., pl.* **want ads** A short advertisement appearing in a newspaper or magazine with others of the same type.

ward·robe (wôr´ drōb´) *n., pl.* **wardrobes** Articles of clothing considered as a group, especially all the pieces of clothing belonging to one person.

ware·house (wâr´ hous´) *n., pl.* **warehouses** A large building where goods are stored.

warn (wôrn) *v.* **warned, warning** To make aware of danger; alert: *The news report warned us that the roads were icy.*
♦ *These sound alike* **warn, worn.**

waste (wāst) *n., pl.* **wastes** Worthless or useless material, such as garbage. —*adj.* Worthless or useless. —*v.* **wasted, wasting** *We wasted a stack of paper trying to make the perfect airplane.*
♦ *These sound alike* **waste, waist.**

watch·ful (wŏch´ fəl) *adj.* On the lookout; alert.

watt (wŏt) *n., pl.* **watts** A unit used to measure power, equal to one joule of work per second or about 1/746 horsepower. ➤ **Word History:** named after the Scottish engineer James Watt.

wea·ry (wîr´ ē) *adj.* **wearier, weariest**
Physically or mentally tired.

weath·er (wĕ*th*´ ər) *n.* Outside conditions
for a certain time and place. —*v.* **weathered,
weathering** To affect or change, as in color
or condition, by exposure: *Many voyages
weathered the ship's hull.*

weav·ing (wēv´ ĭng) *n.* The act of making
something by interlacing threads, or strands
or strips of a material: *Lisa loves weaving and
recently made a shawl on her loom.*

weight (wāt) *n., pl.* **weights** The measure
of how heavy something is: *The weight of the
box is 100 pounds.*
◆ *These sound alike* **weight, wait.**

well-known (wĕl´ nōn´) *adj.* Renowned;
famous.

wheel·chair (wēl´ châr´) *n., pl.* **wheelchairs**
A chair on wheels in which a person who is
sick or disabled can move about.

wheth·er (wĕ*th*´ ər) *conj.* Used to show
a choice between things.

whip (wĭp) *v.* **whipped, whipping** To beat
something, such as cream, into a foam.

whis·per (wĭs´ pər) *v.* **whispered,
whispering** To speak softly.

whis·tle (wĭs´ əl) *n., pl.* **whistles 1.** A device
that makes a high, clear sound when air is
blown through it. **2.** A sound made by or as
if by whistling. —*v.* **whistled, whistling
1.** To make a clear musical sound by forcing air
through the teeth and lips. **2.** To produce
a clear, shrill, sharp musical sound by blowing
on or through a device.
◇ *Idioms* **blow the whistle (on)** To tell
officials about a wrongdoing. **wet one's whistle**
To quench one's thirst. **whistle in the dark**
To make a show of bravery.

white·out (wīt´ out´) *n., pl.* **whiteouts**
A polar weather condition in which the light
reflected from the snow blends into the light
reflected from the clouds, making any shadows
and the horizon invisible and making it
impossible to see where one is going: *The
blizzard soon created a whiteout.*

who (hōō) *pron.* What or which person or
persons: *Who said that?*

wheelchair

whole grain (hōl´ grān´) *adj.* Made from the
entire grain.

who's (hōōz) Contraction of **who is:** *Who's
going to the movie with you?*
◆ *These sound alike* **who's, whose.**

whose (hōōz) *sing.* or *pl. pron.* The possessive
form of **who:** *Whose boots are in the hallway?*
◆ *These sound alike* **whose, who's.**

wild (wīld) *adj.* **wilder, wildest** Not grown,
cared for, or controlled by people.

wil·der·ness (wĭl´ dər nĭs) *n., pl.*
wildernesses A region in a wild, natural state
in which there are few or no people.

wild·life (wīld´ līf´) *n.* Wild plants and
animals, especially wild animals living in their
natural surroundings.

wis·dom (wĭz´ dəm) *n.* Intelligence and good
judgment in knowing what to do and being
able to tell the difference between good and
bad and right and wrong.

wise (wīz) *adj.* **wiser, wisest** Having or
showing intelligence and good judgment.

with·hold (wĭth hōld´) *v.* **withheld,
withholding** To keep back; restrain.

work·out (wûrk´ out´) *n., pl.* **workouts**
A session of exercise, as to improve fitness
or for an athletic competition.

world (wûrld) *n., pl.* **worlds** The earth:
The world is round.

wor·ship (wûr´ shĭp) *n.* Religious ceremonies
and prayers. —*v.* **worshiped, worshiping**
To honor and love.

worth (wûrth) *n.* The quality that makes someone or something expensive, valuable, useful, or important: *Your education will prove its worth.* —*adj.* Equal in value to: *This rare baseball card is worth $27.50.*

worth·less (wûrth´ lĭs) *adj.* Without worth; useless.

worth·while (wûrth´ wīl´) *adj.* Worth the time, effort, or cost involved; important.

wor·thy (wûr´ thē) *adj.* **worthier, worthiest** **1.** Having value; useful or valuable. **2.** Honest, admirable. **3.** Having enough value.

wrench (rĕnch) *n., pl.* **wrenches** Any of various tools for gripping, turning, or twisting objects such as nuts, bolts, or pipes.

x-ray (ĕks´ rā´) *n., pl.* **x-rays** A photograph taken with electromagnetic radiation.

xy·lo·phone (zī´ lə fōn´) *n., pl.* **xylophones** A percussion instrument consisting of a series of mounted wooden bars of various sizes that sound various tones, played with two small mallets.

➤ **Word History:** from the Greek words *xulon,* "wood," and *phōnē,* "sound."

Pronunciation Key

ă	pat	ŏ	pot	ûr	fur
ā	pay	ō	go	*th*	**the**
âr	care	ô	paw	th	**thin**
ä	father	ôr	for	hw	**wh**oop
är	farm	oi	**oil**	zh	usual
ĕ	pet	o͝o	book	ə	ago, item,
ē	be	o͞o	boot		pencil,
ĭ	pit	yo͞o	cute		atom,
ī	ice	ou	**out**		circus
îr	n**ear**	ŭ	cut	ər	butter

yearn (yûrn) *v.* **yearned, yearning** To have a deep desire; long; want very much.

young (yŭng) *adj.* **younger, youngest** Being at an early stage of life, growth, or development.

youth (yo͞oth) *n., pl.* **youths** **1.** The time of life between being a child and being an adult. **2.** A young person.

youth·ful (yo͞oth´ fəl) *adj.* Characterized by youth; young.

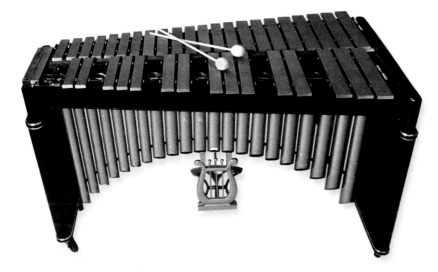

xylophone

Content Index

Numbers in **boldface** indicate pages on which a skill is introduced as well as references to the Capitalization and Punctuation Guide.

Content Index

Credits

Illustrations **4** ©HMCo/LARRY NOLTE. **37** NATHAN JARVIS. **49** ©HMCo/LARRY NOLTE. **65** ©HMCo/JOEL ITO. **67** ©HMCo/LARRY NOLTE. **91** ©HMCo/LARRY NOLTE. **97** ©HMCo/LARRY NOLTE. **140.** ©HMCo/LARRY NOLTE. **185** ©HMCo/Joe LeMonnier.

Photography **3** (ml) © Mike Dunning/DK Images. (tr) Getty Images. (tr) © Ariel Skelley/CORBIS. (br) © Digital Stock Inc. **4** (bl) Peter Bowater/Alamy. **5** (tl) © Tim Davis/CORBIS. (mr) Hemera Technologies Inc. **6** (tl) Digital Vision/Getty Images. (mr) John Wang/Getty Images. **7** (tl) JH Pete Carmichael/The Image Bank/Getty Images. **8** Richard Wahistrom/Getty Images. **9** (ml) Hemera Technologies Inc. (bl) Ingram Publishing/Alamy. **19** (bl) © Mike Dunning/DK Images. (br) © Alese & Mort Pechter/CORBIS. **20** (mr) © HMCO/StudioMontage. (mr) (mr) © Comstock IMAGES. **23** (bkgd) © Royalty-Free/CORBIS. (c) Jules Frazier/Getty Images. **25** (b) © Ariel Skelley/CORBIS. (t) Getty Images. **26** Nova Development/Art Explosion. **27** (c) © Wes Thompson/CORBIS. (mr) Hemera Technologies Inc. **29** (bkgd) Digital Vision/Getty Images. (c) Paul Cooklin/Brand X Pictures/Getty Images. **31** (bc) PICTUREQUEST. (bl) © Royalty-Free/CORBIS. **32** (br) Stock Connection Distribution/Alamy. (br) Hemera Technologies Inc. **33** Artville,LLC./Sporting Equipment. **35** (tc) Adobe System Inc./Artroom. (bkgd) P Brabant/Cole Group/Getty Images. (tc) Getty Images. **37** © RUBBERBALL. **38** © Digital Stock Inc. **39** © Robert Y. Ono/CORBIS. **41** Comstock Images. **43** © Digital Vision Ltd. **44** (tr) Steve Dunwell/Getty Images. (br) © Lucidio Studio Inc./CORBIS. **45** © HMCO/StudioMontage. **47** (bkgd) S Solum/PhotoLink/Photodisc/Getty Images. (c) Hemera Technologies Inc. **48** © HMCO/StudioMontage. **50** Peter Bowater/Alamy. **51** Hemera Technologies Inc. **55** Tom Murphy/National Geographic/Getty Images. **56** Hemera Technologies Inc. **57** (tc) Jules Frazier/Getty Images. (bc) Hemera Technologies Inc. (bc) Photodisc Collection/Getty Images. **59** Brand X Pictures/Getty Images. **61** (br) Brand X Pictures/Alamy. (bc) BananaStock/Alamy. (bl) Hemera Technologies Inc. **62** © Royalty-Free/CORBIS. **63** Hemera Technologies Inc. **65** (ml) Steve Cole/Getty Images. (mr) Lawrence Lawry/Getty Images. **68** The Bridgeman Art Library/Getty Images. **71** (bkgd) Philip Coblentz/Brand X Pictures/Getty Image. (c) Burke/Triolo Productions/Brand X Pictures/Getty Images. **73** © Tim Davis/CORBIS. **74** © Royalty-Free/CORBIS. **77** (bkgd) © W. Cody/CORBIS. (bc) PICTUREQUEST. (c) Lori Adamski Peek/Getty Images. (tc) © Royalty-Free/CORBIS. **79** (bkgd) Don Farrall/Getty Images. (bc) Nathan Bilow/Getty Images. (bl) Artville,LLC./Sporting Equipment. **80** © Araldo de Luca/CORBIS. **81** Burke/Triolo Productions/FoodPix/Getty Images. **83** (bkgd) Spencer Rowell/Getty Images. (c) C Squared Studios/Getty Images. **84** © Joseph Sohm; ChromoSohm Inc./CORBIS. **85** Brand X Pictures/Alamy. **86** POPPERFOTO/Alamy. **87** C Squared Studios/Getty Images. **91** (t) © Ariel Skelley/CORBIS. **92** Hemera Technologies Inc. **93** Hemera Technologies Inc. **95** (bkgd) © Werner Forman/CORBIS. (c) © William Manning/CORBIS. (ml) Adobe System Inc./Artroom. (ml) © VIVID DETAILS. **98** (r) Hemera Technologies Inc. (l) Barbara Penoyar/Getty Images. **99** (c) Hemera Technologies Inc. **101** (bkgd) James Randklev/Getty Images. (bl) David Ponto/Getty Images. (tl) Bruce Heinemann/Getty Images. (c) © VIVID DETAILS. **103** (t) James Darell/Getty Images. (bc) © HMCO/StudioMontage. (bl) © HMCO/StudioMontage. **104** © William Dow/CORBIS. **107** (bkgd) Michael Townsend/Getty Images. (l) Tyler Stableford/Getty Images. **109** (bc) © Bettmann/CORBIS. (bc) Hemera Technologies Inc. (bl) Amos Morgan/Getty Images. **110** Jack Hollingsworth/Getty Images. **111** (c) Digital Vision/Getty Images. (c) © Pat O'Hara/CORBIS. (c) Diana Mayfield/Lonely Planet Images/Getty Images. **113** Albert Normandin/MASTERFILE. **115** Hemera Technologies Inc. **116** Thomas Barwick/Getty Images. **120** Hemera Technologies Inc. **121** PICTUREQUEST. **122** Greg Ceo/Getty Images. **123** Digital Vision/Getty Images. **127** (bc) Akira Kaede/Getty Images. (b) © Kelly-Mooney Photography/CORBIS. **128** (br) © Andres Stapff/Reuters/Corbis. (tr) The Photolibrary Wales/Alamy. **129** © Michael Keller/CORBIS. **131** (bkgd) Stephen St John/National Geographic/Getty Images. (c) C Squared Studios/Getty Images. **133** Tony Garcia/Getty Images. **134** © Jonathan Blair/CORBIS. **135** (c) John Wang/Getty Images. (tl) © VIVID DETAILS. **137** (b) Digital Vision/Getty Images. (t) Don Farrall/Getty Images. **139** (bc) © Reuters/CORBIS. **141** (c) Artville,LLC./Sporting Equipment. **143** (t) Karl Shone/Dorling Kindersley/Getty Images. (b) Bob Krist/CORBIS. (c) © Tria Giovan/CORBIS. **145** © Dave G. Houser/CORBIS. **146** C Squared Studios/Getty Images. **147** David Ponton/Getty Images. **149** (bkgd) © VIVID DETAILS. (tc) JH Pete Carmichael/Getty Images. (c) © Michael & Patricia Fogden/CORBIS.

(bc) © Joe McDonald/CORBIS. **151** (bl) Brand X Pictures/Alamy. (bc) Gay Bumgarner/Getty Images. (bc) Hemera Technologies Inc. **153** (c) © HMCO/StudioMontage. **155** (bl) © Arte & Immagini srl/CORBIS. (c) C Squared Studios/Getty Images. (tr) Hemera Technologies Inc. (bkgd) Hemera Technologies Inc. (b) Epoxy/Getty Images. **156** © Ariel Skelley/CORBIS. **157** Hemera Technologies Inc. **158** © Dave G. Houser/CORBIS. **159** Nick Koudis/Getty Images. **163** Getty Images. **164** Andy Rouse/Getty Images. **165** (c) Hemera Technologies Inc. (tc) Hemera Technologies Inc. (bc) Hemera Technologies Inc. **167** (bkgd) © ML Sinibaldi/CORBIS. (c) © Jonathan Blair/CORBIS. **169** © Reuters/CORBIS. **170** Amos Morgan/Getty Images. **171** (c) Hemera Technologies Inc. **173** (bkgd) Jean Louis Batt/Getty Images. (c) Barbara Penoyar/Getty Images. **175** © Bettmann/CORBIS. **176** C Squared Studios/Getty Images. **177** © D. Boone/CORBIS. **179** Christie Brooke/Getty Images. **181** (bc) © Jose Luis Pelaez, Inc./CORBIS. (b) Hemera Technologies Inc. **182** Ty Allison/Getty Images. **183** © Gabe Palmer/CORBIS. **185** (bkgd) Kevin Kelley/Getty Images. (mr) Richard Wahistrom/Getty Images. **187** Holos/Getty Images. **188** Wendy Ashton/Getty Images. **189** Siede Preis/Getty Images. **191** © Images.com/CORBIS. **192** Hemera Technologies Inc. **193** Hemera Technologies Inc. **195** Hemera Technologies Inc. **199** (br) © Jim Cummins/CORBIS. (bl) © Royalty-Free/CORBIS. **200** Tim Bieber/Getty Images. **201** (c) Christoph Wilhelm/Getty Images. **203** (bkgd) Digital Vision/Getty Images. (t) Hemera Technologies Inc. (c) © Bettmann/CORBIS. **205** © Wally McNamee/CORBIS. **206** © Greenhalf Photography/CORBIS. **207** Hemera Technologies Inc. **209** (bkgd) Keith Brofsky/Getty Images. (bkgd) Artville,LLC./Sporting Equipment. (ml) Comstock Images/Getty Images. (c) Jeff Maloney/Getty Images. (c) Hemera Technologies Inc. (t) Hemera Technologies Inc. **211** (br) Hemera Technologies Inc. (bc) PhotoLink/Getty Images. (bc) PhotoLink/Getty Images. (bl) PhotoLink/Getty Images. **212** (mr) © CORBIS. (mr) Hemera Technologies Inc. **215** (bkgd) Nick Koudis/Getty Images. (tc) © Leonard de Selva/CORBIS. (bc) Ryan McVay/Getty Images. **217** Peter Gridley/Getty Images. **218** Izzy Schwartz/Getty Images. **221** (bkgd) © Royalty-Free/CORBIS. (c) Adobe System Inc./Artroom. **223** (c) Nancy Brown/Getty Images. (br) Thinkstock/Getty Images. (bl) Hemera Technologies Inc. **224** Tim Pannell/MASTERFILE. **225** (c) Hemera Technologies Inc. **227** (bkgd) © Corbis Corp. Digital Stock. (c) Hemera Technologies Inc. **228** Ingram Publishing/Alamy. **229** Hemera Technologies Inc. **230** Steve Cole/Getty Images. **231** (c) Hemera Technologies Inc. **235** C Squared Studios/Getty Images. **236** C Squared Studios/Getty Images. **237** © Bettmann/CORBIS. **238** Hemera Technologies Inc. **241** © Steve Kaufman/CORBIS. **242** © David Turnley/CORBIS. **243** Hemera Technologies Inc. **244** © Michael Prince/CORBIS. **245** Hemera Technologies Inc. **246** Ron Levine/Getty Images. **247** © Royalty-Free/CORBIS. **248** Michael Kelley/Getty Images. **249** © Brooklyn Museum of Art/CORBIS. **284** Hemera Technologies Inc. **285** Hemera Technologies Inc. **286** C Squared Studios/Getty Images. **287** Hemera Technologies Inc. **288** Hemera Technologies Inc. **289** Hemera Technologies Inc. **290** C Squared Studios/Getty Images. **291** Hemera Technologies Inc. **292** Hemera Technologies Inc. **293** Hemera Technologies Inc. **294** Siede Preis/Getty Images. **295** Hemera Technologies Inc. **296** Hemera Technologies Inc. **297** Nordicphotos/Alamy. **298** Getty Images. **299** Kaz Chiba/Getty Images. **300** Hemera Technologies Inc. **301** Rich Iwasaki/Getty Images. **302** PhotoLink/Getty Images. **303** © Dynamic Graphics Group/Creatas/Alamy. **304** © CORBIS. **305** Hemera Technologies Inc. **306** Hemera Technologies Inc. **307** PhotoLink/Getty Images. **308** Hemera Technologies Inc. **309** Hemera Technologies Inc. **310** Hemera Technologies Inc. **311** C Squared Studios/Getty Images. **312** Kari Weatherly/Getty Images. **313** © Royalty-Free/CORBIS. **314** Hemera Technologies Inc. **315** Hemera Technologies Inc. **316** Hemera Technologies Inc. **317** Hemera Technologies Inc. **318** Hemera Technologies Inc. **319** Hemera Technologies Inc. **320** © Redferns Music Picture Library/Alamy. **321** C Squared Studios/Getty Images. **322** Hemera Technologies Inc. **323** PhotoLink/Getty Images. **324** © Owen Franken/CORBIS. **325** © Tom Stewart/CORBIS. **326** Hemera Technologies Inc. **327** Hemera Technologies Inc. **328** Stewart Cohen/Getty Images. **329** Hemera Technologies Inc. **330** Hemera Technologies Inc. **331** Hemera Technologies Inc. **332** Hemera Technologies Inc. **333** Hemera Technologies Inc. **334** PhotoLink/Getty Images. **335** Hemera Technologies Inc. **336** Hemera Technologies Inc. **337** Hemera Technologies Inc. **338** Hemera Technologies Inc. **339** Hemera Technologies Inc. **340** © Dynamic Graphics Group/Creatas/Alamy. **341** © John M. Roberts/CORBIS. **342** Amos Morgan/Getty Images. **343** Hemera Technologies Inc.

Handwriting Models

a b c d e f g h i
j k l m n o p q r
s t u v w x y z

A B C D E F G H I
J K L M N O P Q R
S T U V W X Y Z

Words Often Misspelled

You probably use many of the words on this list when you write. If you cannot think of the spelling of a word, you can always check this list. The words are in alphabetical order.

A
again
all right
a lot
also
always
another
anyone
anyway
around

B
beautiful
because
before
believe
brought
buy

C
cannot
can't
caught
clothes
coming
cousin

D
didn't
different
don't

E
enough
every
everybody
everyone
everything

F
family
field
finally
friend

G
getting
going
guess

H
happened
happily
haven't
heard
here

I
I'd
I'll
instead
its
it's

K
knew
know

M
might
millimeter
morning
mother's

O
o'clock
once

P
people
pretty
probably

R
really
right

S
Saturday
school
someone
sometimes
stopped
suppose
swimming

T
that's
their
there
there's
they
they're
thought
through
to
tomorrow
tonight
too
tried
two

U
until
usually

W
weird
we're
whole
would
wouldn't
write
writing

Y
your
you're